Violent Intimacies

Violent Intimacies

THE TRANS EVERYDAY & THE MAKING
OF AN URBAN WORLD

Aslı Zengin

DUKE UNIVERSITY PRESS · DURHAM AND LONDON · 2024

© 2024 DUKE UNIVERSITY PRESS

All rights reserved

Printed in the United States of America on acid-free paper ∞

Project Editor: Bird Williams

Designed by Matthew Tauch

Typeset in Garamond Premier Pro

by Westchester Publishing Services

Library of Congress Cataloging-in-Publication Data

Names: Zengin, Aslı, [date] author.

Title: Violent intimacies : the trans everyday and the making of an urban world /
Aslı Zengin.

Description: Durham : Duke University Press, 2024. | Includes bibliographical
references and index.

Identifiers: LCCN 2023032283 (print)

LCCN 2023032284 (ebook)

ISBN 9781478025627 (paperback)

ISBN 9781478020882 (hardcover)

ISBN 9781478027751 (ebook)

Subjects: LCSH: Transgender people—Violence against—Turkey. | Transgender
people—Turkey—Social conditions. | Gender identity—Turkey—Psychological aspects. |
Marginality, Social—Turkey. | BISAC: SOCIAL SCIENCE / LGBTQ Studies / Transgender
Studies | SOCIAL SCIENCE / Anthropology / Cultural & Social

Classification: LCC HQ77.965.T9 Z46 2024 (print)

LCC HQ77.965.T9 (ebook)

DDC 306.76/809561—dc23/eng/20230902

LC record available at https://lccn.loc.gov/2023032283

LC ebook record available at https://lccn.loc.gov/2023032284

Cover credit: İnci Eviner, *Magical Rose Garden*, 2022. Acrylic and
screenprint on paper. Courtesy of the artist.

To the memory of Hande Kader
(1993–2016)
and
To trans feminists in Turkey

Contents

Abbreviations

AKP	Adalet ve Kalkıma Partisi (Justice and Development Party)
CGD	Cihangir Güzelleştirme Derneği (Association for Improvement of Cihangir)
ECRI	European Commission against Racism and Intolerance
EU	European Union
GCS	gender confirmation surgery
IKGV	İnsan Kaynağını Geliştirme Vakfı (Human Resource Development Foundation)
LGBTI+	lezbiyen, gey, biseksüel, trans, interseks artı
LGBTT	lesbian, gey, bisexual, transeksüel, travesti
LISTAG	Lezbiyen, Gay, Biseksüel, Trans, İnterseks Artı Aileleri ve Yakınları Derneği (Organization for Families and Friends of Lesbian, Gay, Bisexual, Trans, Intersex Plus People)
NGO	nongovernmental organization
PKK	Partiya Karkerên Kurdistan (Kurdistan Workers' Party)
TERF	trans exclusionary radical feminism
TOKI	Toplu Konut İdaresi Başkanlığı (Mass Housing Development Administration)

Preface

This book begins with a dilemma we all share: time. This dilemma is not personal but rather structural and intrinsic to social scientific methods and, in the particular case of this book, to ethnography itself. Ethnography, more or less, claims to keep its finger on the pulse of the present, the contemporary. But there is always a gap between ethnographic research and the time of its fruition into a book. Ethnographic time is not writing time, and neither ethnographic nor writing time is publishing time. Ethnographic accounts of the present inescapably betray their initially intended temporal framework. Instead of accounts of the present, they become archives of the contemporary.

The protagonists of this book, trans people in Turkey, are no exception to this ethnographic dilemma. Much has changed in Turkey between the time of my main fieldwork in 2010 and the writing of this preface in 2022. Therefore, this ethnography of trans lives in Turkey actually offers a contemporary history of transness in the country. The experiences, struggles, and stories from more than a decade ago still weigh heavily on the present and emergent conditions of trans lives. Yet this historical proximity can sometimes feel like distance when one considers the events and processes that have radically shifted the geo- and sociopolitical context of Turkey over the same period of time. It would be challenging to offer a comprehensive portrayal of all this change in its multiple and differential scales. Instead, I will highlight a few of these key events and processes: the launching of Twitter in 2011 and the gradual growth of other digital platforms; the Gezi protests in 2013; the 2015 general elections and the proceeding war against Kurds in Kurdistan; the coup attempt in 2016; a series of purges of Fethullah Gülen's supporters, Kurdish politicians and activists, and Academics for Peace; a rapid and exponential increase in migration from the war-torn geographies of Syria, Iraq, Afghanistan, and, more recently, from Ukraine and Russia; the COVID-19 pandemic; an aggressive, interventionist and neo-imperial foreign policy in the Middle East; and an accelerating economic crisis and hyperinflation that began in 2021. The intensifying authoritarianism, national securitization, and an economic depression have had tremendous and devastating impacts on queer and trans lives, precisely because they have shaped the everyday life of everyone who lives in Turkey.

Within the specific context of queer and trans lives, this turbulent social and political environment has produced particularly harmful public discourses and acts of violence and discrimination. The year 2015 marked the inception of gradually intensifying state warfare against queer and trans lives and their demonization in the public eye through ideological and practical instruments. Since then, the state has steadily developed a more systemic and official anti-LGBTI+ agenda and framed it through a discourse of national security, family values, public morals, and social order. The state has banned political events, campaigns, and activities regarding queer and trans issues, and has targeted those of us who were part of these struggles— claiming that we are threats to public decency and social order.

Two political events in 2021 amplified the gradual targeting, securitization, and criminalization of queer and trans activists and feminists by the Turkish state: feminist, queer, and trans protests against Turkey's withdrawal from the Istanbul Convention on March 20; and the Boğaziçi University student protests that began on February 2. These two events happened around the same time, heightened the visibility and recognition of LGBTI+ issues, and also consolidated collaborations and alliances between some feminists and queer and trans activists.

The Istanbul Convention, which is formally the Convention on Preventing and Combating Violence against Women and Domestic Violence, was signed in Istanbul in 2011. Turkey was the first state to ratify the convention, in 2012, followed by thirty-three other countries. The treaty advocates for a more comprehensive and holistic understanding of gender violence. It approaches gender violence not as an individual issue but rather as a political one, as a systemic problem permeating every sphere of life. Signatory states of the Istanbul Convention are legally bound to punish perpetrators, as well as to prevent violence and protect victims. The convention also stresses the protection of victims from violence based on their sexual orientation and gender identification, deploying the concepts of "gender as a social construct" and "sexual orientation." It is this specific emphasis that the Turkish government and its allies exploited to organize a smear campaign against the treaty, demonizing it for its inclusion of queer and trans people. Opponents of the convention argued that the treaty encouraged people to "become LGBTI+" and encouraged women to divorce, both of which were politically promulgated as contradicting the so-called Turkish family structure and its values. For instance, the state Directorate of Communications officially stated, "The Istanbul Convention, originally intended to promote women's rights, was hijacked by a group of people attempting to normalize homosexuality—which is incompatible with Türkiye's social and family values."[1] Several state officers, including the minister of the interior, Süleyman Soylu, started labeling LGBTI+ people as "perverts" and "threats to our children" through their official social media accounts and public speeches. And this anti-LGBTI+ position was not unique to Turkey. The growing right-wing authoritarianisms across the globe in countries such as the United States, Brazil, and India effectively used anti-LGBTI+ agendas to consolidate their power and international alliances with each other. In the meantime, the Middle Eastern countries of Egypt, Lebanon, and Qatar gradually invested in the growth of a more systemized antiqueer stance that led to a series of bans and crackdowns on queer activities, places, and signage. A lethal consequence of this panic was the suicide of a prominent Egyptian communist and queer activist, Sarah Hijazi, who was arrested and tortured by the Egyptian government for raising a rainbow flag at the 2017 Cairo concert of the Lebanese rock band Mashrou' Leila, whose lead singer was openly queer. Later, Sarah Hijazi was granted asylum in Canada, where she took her own life. Her death shook not only the broader queer Arab world with great sorrow and grief but also queer people in Turkey, leading to her mourning on several online platforms.

This systemic growth in anti-LGBTI+ government politics in the Middle East was accompanied by the rise of right-wing governments in eastern Europe and northern Asia, specifically those of Poland, Hungary, Romania, Bulgaria, and Russia. Within this context of the transcontinental coalescence of an anti-LGBTI+ policies and sentiments, Turkey increased its violent pressure on queer and trans lives and denounced the Istanbul Convention in 2021. In response to Turkey's withdrawal, senior government members announced that they would tackle domestic violence through judicial reform. They would write an Ankara Convention that would claim its power from "Turkish traditions and customs."

In response to the withdrawal, feminist, queer, and trans movements organized around the slogan "The Istanbul Convention saves lives." They took to the streets and social media to insist that women's lives and gender violence matter. The withdrawal meant the weakening of legal measures to prevent violence and femicides, thus encouraging perpetrators. At the time of the withdrawal, femicides and hate crimes in Turkey were in fact on the rise. In the context of the COVID-19 restrictive measures in Turkey, the risk of domestic violence against women, queers, trans people, and children increased. There was indeed a growing need for more, and not fewer, tools to prevent and eradicate gender violence in all its forms. However, state officials have ignored this need and have instead endorsed public circulation of hatred for women, queers, and trans people on social media and beyond.

The student protests at Boğaziçi University, my alma mater, constituted the second important political event that contributed to an anti-LGBTI+ environment in Turkey. Boğaziçi is a prominent public institution recognized for its liberal democratic campus life. It has historically been an institutional home for critical and creative thinking and innovative research in Turkey and abroad. It is one of the rare remaining public spaces for encounters among students who come from all walks of life regardless of class, ethnic, religious, sexual, and gender differences. Especially for first-generation university graduates like me, who moved to Istanbul from more conservative urban and rural environments in Turkey, Boğaziçi was a radically transformative and life-changing place.

Boğaziçi's democratic campus culture and critical education have long been targeted by the Adalet ve Kalkıma Partisi (AKP; Justice and Development Party) government and Recep Tayyip Erdoğan's presidency. Until the coup attempt in 2016, university rectors, who occupy roles similar to university presidents in the United States, used to be democratically elected by faculty members, and then the president would be legally bound by the election results when deciding on the appointment. After the coup attempt, statutory decrees changed this procedure. The electoral process has been removed, and today rectors are directly appointed by the Turkish president. Furthermore, the Boğaziçi rector had always been someone from that university community. But as of 2020, rectors and deans from outside Boğaziçi have been imposed on the university by the Turkish president and, in the case of deans, by the rector who is also appointed by the Turkish president. These top-down decisions have disrupted the democratic culture on campus and have galvanized both faculty members and students, who have been protesting for almost two years. On the first day of the protest, a queer woman student climbed up on the main gate and waved a rainbow flag against a sea of police officers blocking the entrance to the campus. In response, the university was placed under siege by the state's security forces. Student protests were harshly repressed by police violence and threats of torture while in custody. Kurdish queer and trans students were particularly targeted for arrests and physical attacks. Protesters were detained for simply carrying or waving a rainbow flag. The rainbow flag gained a semicriminal status during these protests.

Even though neither being queer nor being trans is illegal in Turkey, the state has turned to and mobilized extralegal instruments to demonize LGBTI+ activists and certain feminist groups and to separate their political struggles from each other as well as from other oppositional groups. The state security and legal forces have intensified their capacities to criminalize LGBTI+ people, single them out as the criminal or "terrorist" type, and hence divide the coalitions of dissidents. The rainbow flag became a de-facto semi-illegal flag during these protests. Currently, the police search for rainbow flags in protesters' backpacks and purses at every entry point to a political demonstration. Protesters have been detained for simply carrying or waving a rainbow flag. At student hearings, judges started asking with impunity whether the defendant was a LGBTI+ person. During the Istanbul Pride March of June 2022, 373 protesters were detained. While in police custody, the protestors were handcuffed behind their backs and forced to stay in detention vehicles for several hours in that position—many considered this an experience of torture. The police also attacked lawyers when they showed up to defend those demonstrators being held in custody. Five lawyers worked into the early morning to legally support 373 people, making sure to be present at their hearings on a voluntary basis. The lawyers themselves were abandoned by the Istanbul bar in spite of their calls for more legal support from fellow lawyers.

This state-backed institutional warfare was further augmented with the countrywide coordination of several civil society groups under the banner of "the Great Family Gathering" in 2022. On September 18, as many as 150 nongovernmental organizations coordinated a march in Fatih, a central conservative neighborhood in Istanbul, to stand against, as they noted, "the increasing LGBTI+ propaganda and imposition in Turkey." Fundamentalist religious groups stood side by side with ultrasecularist and nationalist ones, collectively calling on the state to ban all LGBTI+ groups and activities, including queer and trans content on Netflix and other digital platforms; to penalize people who publicly advocated for LGBTI+ issues; and to force LGBTI+ people from Turkey to migrate abroad. The state, through its broadcasting regulator, the Radyo ve Televizyon Üst Kurulu (the Radio and Television Supreme Council), officially approved the rally's call for screening on popular TV channels. The petition campaign, "Protect your family and generation from perversity," received thousands of signatures. Other cities followed Istanbul in orchestrating their own marches and petition campaigns. These rallies gradually defined LGBTI+ people as a national security problem and sought the categorization of LGBTI+ organizations as "terrorist organizations," thus demanding that the state take precautions to protect Turkish social and family values. The labels "terrorist" and "terrorism," as a figure and a site, respectively, have continued to expand at an unprecedented pace to include feminists, queers, and trans people in addition to the usual suspects, such as Kurds, Academics for Peace, left-wing organizers, and supporters of Fethullah Gülen, the latter of whom indeed began as strong allies of the AKP government and the invisible actors of the state.

To circle back to the opening dilemma of this preface, writing an ethnographic account of the everyday conditions of trans lives in this sociopolitical context is even more challenging if one is a migrant scholar in the United States writing about home, Turkey. It is more difficult to navigate the temporal and spatial boundaries of ethnography when one's research field is not a site that one enters and exits but rather part of one's individual, social, and political makeup, that is, one's home and life. When and how research ends, or whether it ever ends, becomes a personal reckoning if one is also invested in the socially and politically transformative capacities of critical knowledge production and its sustenance over long periods of time. If one is in a continuous cycle of being in and out of the time-space of home, then how does one freeze the time-space of home into research, into a book?

At the time of this book's publication, multiple variations of "LGBTI+" are constantly and frequently vocalized as a target of state discourse on TV channels and are a key concern in the state's political agenda. As much as it is horrifying and concerning, this ascending obsession with LGBTI+ at both the state and societal levels also shows how feminist, queer, and trans movements in Turkey have become key actors in state politics, powerfully shaping the political environment and discourse. The bridges and alliances among feminist, queer, and trans movements have only grown more solid and vital. Since my own participation in these struggles, a new feminist, queer, and trans generation has grown, fearlessly pushing back on increasing authoritarianism, while also gradually assuming and becoming central node of political agency in the country. The pages that follow offer you earlier chapters of this ongoing, beautiful story, a story that has multiple futures.

Acknowledgments

This book owes its fruition to a great number of people and places. It cuts across three countries and two continents on both sides of the Atlantic. It is an impossible task to give due recognition to each person who has been part of this arduous yet rewarding journey, but I will try my best. First and foremost, my biggest gratitude is to trans and queer activists and feminists in Turkey. I owe a solemn debt to all my *lubunya* friends, kin, collaborators, and comrades who made this book possible by welcoming me into their lives with immense generosity and care. I am grateful for the trust they granted in sharing with me their lives, stories, joys, and sorrows. They have touched and shaped my life and me as a person in ways that I cannot find words to describe. I can only hope that this book lives up to their trust, love, and political rage by contributing to building better queer/trans feminist worlds together in Turkey and beyond.

Writing this book required a set of skills and tools to see the world differently and to understand it critically. I consider myself extremely lucky to have attained most of them during my undergraduate and master's years at Boğaziçi University in Istanbul, where I made incredible friendships in courses, student clubs, collectives, political campaigns, and extracurricular creative activities. The academic environment at Boğaziçi has deeply shaped my passion for intellectual life and critical knowledge production and its transformative capacities. I would like to express my sincere gratitude to my mentors, Nazan Üstündağ, Nükhet Sirman, Şemsa Özar, Ayfer Bartu Candan, Meltem Ahıska, Belgin Tekçe, and Zafer Yenal, for their formative role in my critical and analytic thinking. The vibrant campus life at Boğaziçi offered me and many others the gift of intellectual curiosity, creative and imaginative living, and passion for social and political transformation. Without this environment I would not be the thinker I am today.

The first phase of this book grew out of a stimulating academic environment at the University of Toronto. Mentors and colleagues were tremendously helpful and motivating while I was writing up my research. I would like to express my heartfelt gratitude to Holly Wardlow, Naisargi Dave, and Andrea Muehlebach for their consistent support, motivation, and guidance. Many thanks to Michael Lambek, Janice Boddy, and Don Kulick for providing me with critical feedback. Several other faculty members at UToronto made my doctoral studies rewarding with their enthusiasm and encouragement. Special thanks to Amira Mittermaier, Valentina Napolitano, Donna Young, Krista Maxwell, Girish Daswani, and Christopher Krupa.

My time at Toronto introduced me to wonderful friends from across the world. Without their support and love it would have been extremely difficult to survive not only the doctoral program but also the long, harsh winters in the city. Our long nights of conversation, music, dance, games, and booze, made my life as a migrant academic possible in many ways. My warmest thanks to friends who knew how not to let life be taken over by academia but rather shared and enriched it to the fullest whenever they could. I deeply appreciate you in my life, Seçil Dağtaş, Vivian Solana, Daniella Jofre, Timothy Mwangeka Makori, Janne Dingemans, Özlem Aslan, Ümit Aydoğmuş, Deepa Rajkumar, Melanie Richter-Montpetit, Columba Gonzalez Duarte, Nora Tataryan, Alejandra Gonzalez, Begüm Uzun, Andrew Paruch, Burak Köse, Tuğçe Ellialtı, Ayşegül Koç, Nima Maleki, Shihoko Nakagawa, Jacob Nerenberg, Saafi Warsame, Nayrouz Abu-Hatoum, Salma Atassi, Coco Guzman, Zoya, Behzad Sarmadi, Glen Chua, Dylan Gordon, Nishant Uphadhyay, and Preethy Sivakumar. I would also like to extend my warm thanks to my friends from the anthropology department, Anna Kruglova, Rastko Cvekic, Kate Rice, Sharon Kelly, Laura Sikstorm, Chantelle Falconer, Hollis Moore, Sardar Saadi, and Nermeen Mouftah, and others in the Dissertation Writing Group, for making my graduate experience memorable and collegial. Last but not least, friends and comrades I met through our local public employee union (CUPE 3902), No One Is Illegal, and Queers against Israeli Apartheid have taught me a lot about cultivating and maintaining strong relations between the worlds of activism and academia. Thanks to all of them.

I have gained significant critical insights through my conversations with established scholars in the field of anthropology at panels, conferences, and workshops. Many thanks to Henrietta Moore, Elizabeth Povinelli, Tom Boellstorff, Ellen Lewin, David Valentine, Yael Navaro, Mary Weismantel, and Evelyn Blackwood. I am grateful for all their feedback and keen engagements with my research in the earlier phase of this book. This book benefited immensely from the financial support that I received through grants, fellowships, and awards over the course of my career. I am grateful for financial assistance from the University of Toronto, the Lorna Marshall Doctoral Fellowship in Social and Cultural Anthropology, the

Ontario Graduate Scholarship, the Melissa J. Knauer Award for Feminist Research, the Fellowship in Ethnographic Writing at the Center for Ethnography at the University of Toronto–Scarborough, and the Association for Feminist Anthropology Dissertation Award.

My thanks to colleagues at the University of California, Berkeley; the University of Cambridge; Columbia University; Harvard University; Swarthmore College; Brown University; Washington University in St. Louis; the University of British Columbia; the College of William and Mary; Boston University; Amherst College; the University of Minnesota; Bilgi University; SOAS University of London; Utrecht University; the University of Tennessee; Rutgers University; Concordia University; Sabancı University; and Koç University for inviting me to share my work and providing me with insightful feedback. These invitations were made possible by Gül Özyeğin, Minoo Moallem, Osman Balkan, Sima Shakhsari, Sahar Sadjadi, Nadje Al-Ali, Sophie Chamas, Nisrine Chaer, Zahra Ali, Maya Mikdashi, Tamar Shirinian, Yağmur Nuhrat, Fırat Kurt, Dina Al Kassim, Roberta Micallef, Denise Gill, Burak Delier, and Zeyno Pekünlü.

My academic journey took me to many institutions until I settled down in a tenure-track position in the Department of Women's, Gender, and Sexuality Studies at Rutgers University. Postdoctoral life has taught me serious lessons about the precarity of the neoliberal academic job market in North America. I spent my first year as a PhD adjuncting at two different institutions in two different towns in Ontario while holding a research fellowship in sexuality studies at the Center for Feminist Research at York University, which I thank for providing me with the opportunity to share my research. My first postdoctoral fellowship started my migration to the United States, where I worked as an Allen-Berenson fellow in the Department of Women's, Gender, and Sexuality Studies at Brandeis University. I am grateful for the great intellectual support and motivation that I received from several colleagues at Brandeis. Many thanks to Susan Lanser, Wendy Cadge, Sarah Lamb, Anita Hill, Aliyyah Abdur-Rahman, Anita Hannig, ChaeRan Yoo Freeze, Elizabeth Ferry, Ellen Schattschneider, Roanne Kantor, and Hikmet Kocamaner. After Brandeis, I relocated to Harvard Divinity School as a research and teaching fellow in the Women's Studies in Religion Program. Our program director, Ann D. Braude; my brilliant colleagues, Kimberly Blockett, Ferial Khalifa, Laura Prieto, and Avital Davidovich-Eshed; and our program administrator, Tracy Wall, made my academic experience highly rewarding. It was also exceptionally delightful to connect with other faculty members at Harvard and benefit from our conversations. My warmest gratitude to Afsaneh Najmabadi, Leila Ahmed, Cemal Kafadar, George Paul Mieu, Robin Bernstein, Mark Jordan, Mayra Rivera, Durba Mitra, and Ahmed Ragab.

Both Brandeis and Harvard introduced me to the wider bustling and inspiring academic environment in the Boston area. I was extremely lucky to meet people who made my life intellectually and socially fulfilling. My heartfelt thanks to my household in Somerville: Mai Taha, Bettina Stoetzer, Yajun Mo, and Vivian Solana; and to beautiful friends: Zeynep İnanç, Bengi Baran, Can Akkaya, Gaye Özpınar, Emrah Altındiş, Hikmet Kocamaner, Volkan Gündüz, Kaan Apaydın, Caterina Scaramelli, Rupa Pillai, Tom Abowd, Armanç Yıldız, Eric Biesterfeld, Alma Nizam, Hussam Jefee-Bahloul, Pep Serra, and Alvaro Ebuelto. They made Boston a third home for me by filling my life with their care, fun, joy, and support.

After Harvard, I moved to Providence for the Louise Lamphere Visiting Assistant Professorship in the Department of Anthropology and the Pembroke Center at Brown University. The rigorous and collegial academic environment at Brown introduced wonderful people to my life: Nadje Al-Ali, Georgina Manok, Alex Winder, Rawan Arar, Aliya Sabharwal, Jose Itzigshon, Meltem Toksöz, Emre Yalçın, Brian Landor, Elizabeth Lord, Dario Valles Sepulveda, Robert Chlala, Fulya Pınar, Anıl Aşkın, and Rui Gomes Coelho. I deeply treasure our conversations, dinner parties, dance nights, hiking trips, and COVID-time picnics. I am also grateful to Lina Fruzetti, Rebecca Carter, Paja Faudree, Shahzad Bashir, Bishara Doumani, Daniel Jordan Smith, Jessaca Leinaweaver, Parker VanValkenburgh, Yannis Hamilakis, and Barbara Oberkoetter for making Brown a welcoming institutional home for me.

This book's editorial journey at Duke first started with Sandra Korn and continued with Courtney Berger. I consider myself extremely lucky to have had the opportunity to work with these two phenomenal editors whose guidance was the best I could ever ask for. Some sections in this book were previously published in peer-reviewed academic journals: *Anthropologica*, *Journal for Middle East Women's Studies*, and *Cultural Anthropology*. While revisiting these discussions, I revised them significantly.

Several colleagues and friends read parts of this book and provided remarkable insights. Many thanks to Seçil Dağtaş, Elif Babül, Christopher Dole, Dana Luciano, Ayşe Parla, Sinan Göknur, Seçil Yılmaz, Aslı Iğsız, Elif Sarı, Begum Adalet, Beren Azizi, Özge Gözke, Hayal Akarsu, and Claudia Castenada. The work-in-progress workshop organized by my colleague Brittney Cooper at Rutgers provided me with a great opportunity to share a chapter draft with my colleagues in the department. I would like to express my special thanks to Brittney Cooper, Ethel Brooks, Maya Mikdashi, Kyla Schuller, Louisa Schein, Carlos Decena, and Evelyn Autry for their constructive engagement with my research. Maya Mikdashi, Evren Savcı, Sima Shakhsari, and Gökçe Günel read different versions of the full manuscript. Their close and careful reading and insightful feedback improved this book immensely.

The support, care, and love I receive from across the ocean has been exceptional since I moved to North America. Each time I visit Turkey, I am welcomed with unconditional love and care by my kin. My most profound thanks to Senem Erdoğan, Öznur Şahin, and Seçil Dağtaş for being my lifelong sisters, bringing so much beauty and wisdom into my life, and never leaving me alone. My wholehearted gratitude to another circle of amazing friends for sharing moments of trouble and happiness over decades: Oyman Başaran, Hazal Halavut, Nora Tataryan, Özlem Aslan, Ceren Yartan, Zeynep Atay, Cemre Baytok, Ali Paşaoğlu, Elif Çelik, Seçil Yılmaz, Sertaç Sehlikoğlu, and Mustafa Avcı. It was heartbreaking to lose Zeliş, Ali Arıkan, and Boysan Yakar, but their spirits have never left me and have animated the pages of this book. I feel blessed to have many other friends and colleagues who have contributed to the creativity, collectivity, solidarity, joy, and laughter in my life. Many thanks to Imge Oranlı, Gülkan Noir, Ari Büyük, Demet Demir, Ebru Kırancı Binder, Ece, Şevval Kılıç, Deniz, Eylem Çağdaş, İlksen Gürsoy, Kerem, Ecem, Matu, Nurgül Özz, Sema Semih, Bawer Çakır, Suna Kafadar, Begüm Başdaş, Özge Gözke, Kanno Akkaya, Alp Biricik, Yener Bayramoğlu, Emrah Yıldız, Banu Bargu, Amahl Bishara, Marlene Schafers, Nukhet Varlık, Alize Arıcan, Fırat Fırat, Berfu Seker, İlker Çakmak, Feride Eralp, Özgür Sevgi Göral, Derya Aydın, Leman Sevda Darıcıoğlu, Başak Can, Ergin Bulut, Nadya Mikdashi, Ziad Mikdashi, and my little bestie Zayn.

My family made my academic life possible by providing their decades-long support. I am grateful to my parents. My brothers, Atakan and Ibrahim, have always emotionally supported me with my research and my life decisions. I am privileged to have their love, tenderness, esteem, and care, and have the utmost gratitude for their presence in my life.

And the final thank you is for Maya Mikdashi, whose invaluable support, caring critique, and unconditional love have been a great treasure while inhabiting arduous times and places together. Words are not enough to express my appreciation for her presence in this life and for her brilliance, light, and laughter that she continues to throw into this world every single day.

Introduction

Violence & Intimacy

IT WAS A BRIGHT SUNNY DAY IN Istanbul in May 2010. At around noon, I arrived at the mosque for the funeral of Sibel, a fifty-five-year-old woman. A big crowd of trans women was gathered in the narrow street surrounding the mosque. Some trans women came to the funeral wearing headscarves, while others were bareheaded.[1] Sibel, a close friend to many trans women in Istanbul LGBTT, a trans-majority LGBTI+ organization, had suffered a cerebral hemorrhage a few days prior while she was soliciting sex work at night.[2] After her emergency hospitalization, people from Istanbul LGBTT started visiting and caring for her in turns. Sibel's friends informed her blood family about what had happened to her, though they had abandoned her. She lost consciousness after the hemorrhage, and she remained in the hospital. A few days after being admitted, Sibel died.

After her death Sibel's trans friends claimed the rights to her deceased body and its burial. This process was not easy; it involved long negotiations with Sibel's blood family members over certain terrains of intimacy, that is, over care and belonging. This situation was not unique to Sibel. For trans people I worked with in Istanbul, kinship ties were a domain of incessant negotiation and contestation because abandonment by the blood family was a common experience. They had to cope with familial rejection of gender recognition, the refusal of financial or emotional support, and, at times, the denial of funeral rituals and practices after death. At such times, trans friends often took the initiative, reclaimed the body, and organized the funeral. In doing so, they replaced the family and announced themselves as the "real" family. The entrance of these friendships into the domain of family through particular structured practices was an intimate survival strategy in the face of everyday social marginalization and abandonment. Sibel's funeral evinced some of these intimate survival strategies.

The domain of family and kinship is part of a broader social world that produces forms of abandonment, exclusion, and marginalization for trans lives. Sibel's friends also had to negotiate with state authorities and religious figures whose collective decisions were strongly shaped by cisheteronormative legal regulations, institutional practices, and religious interpretations of social and familial life in Turkey. Sibel had identified and lived her life as a woman. However, in the eyes of the Turkish state, she was a man: she held the blue state-issued ID that until 2017 identified male citizens, whereas a pink one identified female citizens.[3] Had Sibel completed her official gender transition, an arduous medicolegal process that takes approximately two years, she could have held a pink ID card that officially recognized her as female at the moment of her death. She had only partially completed the state-designated trans surgical procedures and hence died in a bodily configuration that transgressed the strict binary institutional categories of sex/gender.

Sibel's funeral ceremony and burial ritual evoked a crisis of illegibility about her body, causing a variety of social actors to debate and negotiate her gender/sexual difference. Her sex/gender-transgressive body became a source of multiple interpretations and inscriptions of categories of sex/gender, kinship, religion, and citizenship. Religious authorities, particularly imams, emphasized Sibel's "real" sex and gender, as did Sibel's blood family members and the state's medicolegal actors from the Mezarlıklar ve Cenaze Hizmetleri Şube Müdürlüğü (the Department of Cemeteries and Funeral Services). Sibel's friends from the LGBTI+ activist community, who were also part of these negotiations, challenged some of those claims and advocated for Sibel to be mourned as female/woman and as their kin. They contested a violent framework of cisheteronormativity through their intimate attachments to Sibel and her deceased body.

This book is about these creative and constructive tensions between violent efforts to define and disambiguate sex/gender transgression, on the one hand, and trans people's incessant negotiations with these efforts in the trans everyday, on the other. As much as trans people are shaped by the cisheteronormative powers of the state, the family, and religion, they also act on these powers to transform them. *Violent Intimacies* argues that everyday troubles with sex/gender transgression in personal, social, and institutional life shape trans lives and deaths as well as state power, family and kinship, regimes of sexuality and gender, urban geography, and feminist and LGBTI+ activism in Turkey.

Cisness is not about the perfect harmony or untroubled relationship that an individual is assumed to have between their sexed/gendered self and their assigned sex at birth or while in utero. As trans studies scholars potently demonstrate, this assumed harmony is in fact a fantasy, an idealization that makes cisness an uninhabitable normative category.[4] Yet, at the same time, cisness powerfully operates as an institutional regulatory tool to treat or mistreat people. As Jules Gill-Peterson shows, cisness can be an effective tool for the state to strengthen its political domination over social life. The state can weaponize cisness against its trans citizens and their families to restrict their participation in public and political life.[5] Joining these critical trans approaches to cisness, this book refers to cisheteronormativity as a political ideology that systematizes violence, exclusion, and discrimination in social and institutional life.

In the trans everyday, cisheteronormative violence works as a currency in social and institutional life, causing gradual exhaustion and leading to everyday stigmatization, injury, and even the slow or premature death of trans people. Institutions such as schools, hospitals, courts, the military, and government offices saturate trans lives with biopolitical and necropolitical techniques through which state power diffuses, expands, and legitimizes cisheteronormative violence in quotidian, intricate, and intimate ways.[6] Relations of cisheteronormative violence shape trans lives, taking the forms of "terror as usual" or "a multitude of small wars and invisible genocides conducted in the normative social spaces."[7] This violence, however, is not only about sex, gender, and sexuality; rather, it is a social currency produced in a relational economy of neoliberal governmentality, regimes of surveillance and securitization, authoritarian nationalist religiosity, and ethnic and racial discrimination. Other marginalized groups, such as Kurds, non-Muslims, workers, Romas, and refugees, also pay significant prices in this political economy. For instance, the police deploy securitization techniques on LGBTI+ people and sex workers that were originally developed and deployed against racialized groups like Kurds, or vice versa. Similarly, state-initiated or -approved urban transformation projects may target not only sex workers and trans people but also the underclass, Romas, Kurds, migrants, or refugees. Violence is intersectional and an institutional resource for the state to intimately govern, manage, and securitize the marginalized based on forms of control and punishment of social difference. Urban displacement, social discrimination and exclusion, sexual and gender regimes, blood family and kinship, medicolegal regulation, police surveillance, and religious interpretations are threaded together in the production of differential values over life and death for different social groups. This threading intimately shapes the everyday experience of sex/gender embodiment for both trans people and other marginalized people. In fact, cisheteronormative violence forms a connecting tissue between these processes and actors and establishes intimate alliances between them.

This book is an immersion into these differential yet relational domains of (un)making trans worlds in Turkey. Beginning in 2010, I started to collaborate with trans people as a *natrans* (nontrans) queer feminist anthropologist for my doctoral research, a collaboration that has gained multiple definitions and meanings over time.[8] Long before this, as an undergraduate college student, I had become intellectually and politically involved in building bridges and forming coalitions across queer, trans, and feminist theories and struggles. This endeavor has always been *about* and *beyond* research purposes, begetting its own intimate fruits in the form of friendships, comradeships, and more across sites of queer/trans feminist struggle. Our work together intersected with a variety of political sites in the urban queer, trans, and feminist world of Istanbul, ranging from conferences to meetings, and from demonstrations against femicides, urban transformation, and police violence to campaigns for sexual and gender rights. Alongside our political work, we shared our lives in homes, cafés, restaurants, bars, and parks and streets and attended dance parties, socials, and *meyhane* nights, as well as funerals.[9] This everyday involvement provided a comprehensive understanding of the both world-shattering and world-making conditions of the trans everyday.

Violent Intimacies approaches transness not only as a category of identification but also, and most importantly, as a condensed site of a relational economy of violence in and through which social difference is produced and managed. Transness, at the same time, is a site of intimacies in the plural. With this approach I join other scholars of trans studies who critique the concepts of sex, gender, and sexuality as the only vector to understand trans issues and instead shed light on a wider scope of analysis of hierarchies of life, existence, social organization, and ways of knowing. I echo Susan Stryker and Aren Aizura's salient identification of the analytic and political need for the circulation of "transgender" and need for multiple modes of analysis rather than its signification as a static identity category or specific way of being in the world. Trans studies significantly contributes to "the proliferation and articulation of new modes of embodied subjectivity, new cultural practices, and new ways of understanding the world, rather than becoming an enclosure for their containment."[10] In the introduction to *Transgender History*, Stryker defines *transgender* in its broadest possible sense by approaching it as "the movement across a socially imposed boundary away from an unchosen starting place, rather than any particular destination or mode of transition."[11] This definition not only provides a compass that navigates us through various meanings, workings, and movements of gender but also allows for an understanding of multiple meanings of transness that are present, under construction, emergent, or potential. In this formulation of transgender, once the movement starts, there is not necessarily a fixed, stable, or determined point of arrival. However, this definition, at the same time, presumes a place of origin, a socially imposed location of gender, from where the person departs. Recent scholarship in critical trans studies helps us contest this underlying assumption that there was a clear origin or place of departure in transness.[12] It has generated understandings of transness as a formative site for relations of race and racialization, diaspora and migration, surveillance and securitization, political economy and labor, disability, and indigeneity.[13] Building on this critical scholarship, *Violent Intimacies* offers new perspectives for studies of state power, securitization and surveillance, urban geography, family and kinship, and, more broadly, intimacy.

The trans everyday in Turkey is a site of potentiality and world-making at the thresholds of dominant sociocultural life, a terrain that is both violent and intimate, extraordinary and ordinary, oppressive and productive. This location of transness is also a transnational site of theory that aims to transgress the ongoing hegemony of North American–centric and Eurocentric accounts in trans studies. Contrary to implicit or explicit scholarly assumptions, locations outside Euro–North American contexts are not solely the places where theories are tested for their applicability or failure. Howard Chiang succinctly criticizes "the ethnic supplementary" position that non-Americanist and non-Europeanist scholarship is expected to occupy as a fixer to intellectual content created by Americanists and Europeanists in trans studies. He notes, "To this day, Americanists and Europeanists are still considered the proprietor of novel theoretical insights concerning transgender proper."[14] In agreement with these statements, I underscore that the "non-West," including Turkey, involves multiple and diverse geographies of theoretical production to understand the world beyond local, national, and regional boundaries. This book is one such theoretical endeavor.

I show how transness in Turkey theoretically makes us rethink the notions of violence and intimacy and the relationship between them. I claim that in the entangled world of the trans everyday, one currency is violence, and the other is intimacy. This world, moreover, includes family members, landlords, neighbors, police officers, medical personnel, legal experts, religious actors, clients, lovers, partners, activists, and strangers. Trans people's bodies, their personal relationships, and trans spaces of inhabitation and socialization are, in very violent ways, made sexually and morally legible and less ambiguous by these social actors. For this reason, this book offers a novel concept, *violent intimacies*, as a means with which to understand the concurrent work of violence and intimacy which, I argue, exposes the connective tissue of a cisheteronormative social order that is intertwined with neoliberal governmentality, biopolitical and necropolitical order, and authoritarian management of social difference. Incorporating intersectional aspects of the trans everyday in a single framework, each chapter illustrates a specific site of violent intimacy from which violent manifestations of intimacy or intimate manifestations of violence emerge: the street, the police, the medical institution, the legal domain, and the family and kinship, as well as trans femicides and funerals.

The violent conditions of trans lives in Turkey are, at the same time, the conditions of trans empowerment, resistance, resilience, and struggle in intimate ways. The everyday life of trans people involves not only victimization, objectification, and suffering but also the formation of affinities, solidarities, proximities, sentiments, and care in, through, and/or in reaction to relations of violence and regimes of power. Like at Sibel's funeral, trans people adopt and care for their friends and reclaim their friends' funerals and meet their friends' monetary needs in the face of familial abandonment and disowning. They turn violence into the creative substance of family and kin work. They redefine their political organizations and community spaces by turning them into their homes. They actively participate in the transformation of urban geography. They invent tactics to cope with state violence, and they pressure the police to formulate new extralegal tactics of securitization. They create themselves as political actors in organizing and mobilizing around hate crimes, police violence, state control over the gender confirmation process, violence against women, and gender-based discrimination in general. The trans everyday also unfolds through dance parties, performances, brunches, picnics, dinners, and *meyhane* nights where intimacies manifest and mediate between people as love, care, joy, and laughter, as well as tears. These sites of intimacy create incandescent beauty through which trans and queer people cultivate belonging, form coalitions, and imagine as well as act on affective and collective forms of social transformation. An immersion into these everyday practices, sites, and struggles helps us approach violence and intimacy as constitutive of, conducive to, and immanent to each other and as the source of both oppression and resistance.

Theorizing *Violent Intimacies*

This book does not take the domain of intimacy for granted. Rather, it closely dissects intimacy in its multiple layers and analyzes how violence constitutes it through the lenses of sex/gender transgression. In an endeavor to theorize the formative relationship between violence and intimacy, I engage with anthropological theories of violence that examine it as productive and formative, molding people's understanding of themselves and what they fight for.[15] Violence is part of people's everyday existence, a human condition, and it is "not something external to society and culture that 'happens' to people."[16] Anthropologist Veena Das is one of the most influential scholars who has written extensively on the social life of violence and its relation to the intimate domains of everyday life. Das theorizes violence as entrenched in everyday life as a site of the ordinary. "The [violent] event," she notes, "attaches itself with its tentacles into everyday life and folds itself into the recesses of the ordinary."[17] According to Das, there is a mutual absorption between the violent and the ordinary, and the lives of particular communities and persons are embedded in this violence (or the memory of such events), turning the everyday itself into the eventful.[18] Das is interested in those intimate moments/sites of the everyday to trace how the event folds into ongoing relationships through speech, sexuality, and domesticity.

I owe Das a great deal for my discussion of the ordinary of everyday trans lives in Turkey as embedded in violence and eventfulness. However, there is an underlying presumption in Das's definition of intimacy, which prioritizes cisheteropatriarchal formulations of domestic, kinship, neighbor, and communal relations. My work intervenes in studies of both violence and intimacy by not only showing how violence *attaches* itself to the intimate domains of everyday life beyond cisheteropatriarchy but also demonstrating what intimacy *is* within relations of violence, what intimacy becomes *through* violence, and how violence *generates, forms,* and *begets* plural intimacies in a wider framework. In that sense, I also distinguish *violent intimacies* from the common notion of *intimate violence*, which some readers might conflate with the central concept of this book. While scholars frequently associate intimate violence with multiple meanings of domestic or partner violence, violent intimacies centers on the formation, organization, and circulation of intimacy through violence and hence encourages readers to rethink the very notion of intimacy itself.

In spite of its common usage and circulation, *intimacy* eludes an easy definition. Popular understandings of intimacy render it synonymous with the body, the household, domesticity, or sexuality. Indeed, *intimacy* captures these meanings but cannot be reduced to them.[19] Human geographers Natalie Oswin and Eric Olund define it as "a protean concept, a heterogenous ensemble," and stress its capacity to afford closeness and belonging even when unwanted.[20] Intimacy is plural, fluid, flexible, and contingent, and hence it is complex, capacious, and difficult to contain. Yet its ambivalent and eccentric qualities allow for an analytically and theoretically rich conceptual framework to trace circuits, exchanges, flows, and entanglements between the worlds of the individual and the social.

Intimacy is integral to the formation of what is called "the human," the self, subjectivity, as well as communities, publics, collectives, and socialities.[21] It is a site of constant query, "the sensory, the affective, and domestic space," or a domain that "builds borders, creates distances, marks off knowledge and shared forms of it."[22] Intimacy challenges the accustomed boundaries between private and public, personal and political, familial and state, and global and local and reveals their porous and interwoven constitution. In my own interpretation of the term, I find *affective and physical proximity* the most concise definition that facilitates an examination of an ensemble of relations among power, space, bodies, and affect.

This book addresses intimacy as embodied proximities formed and mediated through social relations, affective ties, and senses, including family, kinship, friendship, cohabitation, reproduction, sexual and gender relations, care, love, joy, hate, disgust, jealousy, touch, gaze, and death. Attention to embodied proximities enables me to scrutinize intimacy in its close and tangled relation to power and violence. What interests me in this relationship between intimacy and violence is not the sphere of individual subjectification.[23] Rather, along similar lines as other scholars of intimacy, I am more interested in the social and political qualities of this association.[24]

Intimacy can take creative and imaginative forms in the production of the ordinary. As critical theorist Saidiya Hartman demonstrates, intimacy can be the site of a radical position in life, a fugitive possibility from the regimes of the proper, a refusal of assimilation and erasure, and a reservoir for hopes and dreams of survival and change.[25] In the ordinariness of life, intimacy can constitute "a revolution in minor key."[26] This book traces these forms of intimacy in trans people's laborious, creative, and imaginative endeavors in building a place for their lives in this world. One example is *gullüm*, a unique way of socializing and conversing among both queer and trans people. *Gullüm* indicates a social gathering, a gossipy conversation, a social occasion of drinking alcohol and chain-smoking, dancing, or simply engaging in shared humor. It is a creative and resilient collective attempt at inserting laughter, fun, joviality, and euphoria into the violent world of everyday trans and queer lives. It is a source of self-empowerment as well as collective fulfillment. So much beauty is generated in these moments of *gullüm*, through shared laughing, gossiping, joking, dancing, chatting, drinking, smoking, playing music, singing, flirting, kissing, making out, and/or getting laid. It is the joy of queer and trans life that is affectively and collectively produced, a life that embraces crying and laughter at once. Both as a verbal repertoire (especially in terms of conversational skills and a source of fun) and as a bodily repertoire (in the form of dance parties, brunches, political meetings, and demonstrations), *gullüm* provides trans people with an affective temporal shelter and shield from the exhaustion of everyday violence and discrimination. Hence, it perfectly exemplifies the theorization of violent intimacies, and this book offers multiple moments of *gullüm* throughout its pages.

Intimacy with violence and death is a significant currency of everyday trans existence in Turkey, a situation that makes violent intimacies also sites of the political. Violent intimacies can become sources of resistance, alternative modes of living, world-making socialities, and transformative practices of affective labor. A shared sense of both past and present experience with everyday violence weaves together trans friendships and communal relations. Learning further from trans understandings and experiences of the world shows us the working of intimacy in desiring, dreaming, and designing "new forms of life beyond the bounds of law and suffocations of patriarchy and [cis]heteronormativity."[27]

The theory of violent intimacies establishes the coconstitutive relationship between violence and intimacy that is manifest in the everyday lives of not just trans people but all those who inhabit ethnic, racial, religious, sectarian and economic margins. This book takes trans lives as one ethnographic, and heavily understudied, site from which to understand the mutually generative relationship between violence and intimacy. For trans lives, the theoretical concept of violent intimacies brings together stories of victimization and survival, abandonment and adoption, marginalization and resistance, and death and life that might otherwise appear dissimilar. The particularities of trans lives show how relations of violence constitute a social field of creative living within which trans people shape and invent forms of intimacy that allow them to inhabit the world. These particularities will no doubt be different in the case of other marginalized groups, whose living will take on its own creative forms. But they will share with trans lives the powerful uses and effects of violence coupled with intimacy.

Violent Intimacies of Space

One crucial component of violent intimacies is space. Intimacy marks spaces and bodies as much as it is marked by them. Here I take inspiration from critical theorists Lauren Berlant and Michael Warner's discussion of sex and sexuality as something "mediated by [the] public," and anthropologist Sertaç Sehlikoğlu's related conceptualization of intimacy as part of this public mediation.[28] Dominant forms of intimacy, as in cisheteronormative, procreational, familial, or kin-based relations, reaffirm and preserve their coherency through cultural narratives, discourses, symbols, and practices that mediate these forms of intimacy in public. Intimacy is a site, medium, and product of sensory experiences: "sound, smell, taste; the ways bodies and objects meet and touch . . . zones of contact and the formations they generate."[29] The organization and distribution of spatial arrangements, along with bodily differentiation, stability, movement, and habitation, are processes that can also give rise to the formation of plural intimacies, including violent ones. Bodily encounters, interactions, and exchanges mark spaces with social boundaries that are sexual, gendered, ethnic, racial, and classed. Sensory engagements through touch, gaze, smell, and sound produce intimate spatialities of embodiment. Proximity, as well as distance, in both physical and emotional terms, shapes social geographies of life and "spatialities of intimacy."[30]

For example, streets have always been integral to the formation of a vibrant social and intimate life in Turkey. People spend long hours chatting, walking, standing, and playing games in the streets. In some parts of Istanbul, one can even talk about a blurred line between public and private, as one may find women, senior people, and youth treating streets as an extension of their homes, meeting with their neighbors and friends. Random street corners can easily turn into popular hangout spots. Not only coffeeshop and restaurant owners but also any shopkeeper may extend their workspace into the street by putting tables and chairs on the sidewalks without facing obstacles. Street vendors of various kinds pop up everywhere. Beyoğlu, my main field site, exemplifies this vibrant and intimate urban life. As you will read in the following chapters, the streets of Beyoğlu function as an essential infrastructure for everyday socialities and everyday intimacies.

Yet the same intimacies of the street can turn violent to strangers, outsiders, or transgressive social actors like trans people, sex workers, racialized others, or homeless people. Spatial mediation and bodily encounters, philosopher Sara Ahmed argues, also foreground the formation of communal intimacies, such as the national, ethnic, and, I would add, cisheteronormative "we."[31] Ahmed stresses how the determination of who is considered "we" is affectively shaped across bodies and signs, marking individual and collective bodies with the very effect of the surfaces and boundaries.[32] By way of example, Ahmed argues that the specific emotions of hate and fear circulate among people and stick to some bodies more than others, thus creating zones of intimacy among those who become proximate with each other in their alikeness, while establishing relations of distance with the others, deemed as dangerous or as strangers. The mediation and formation of these intimacies always has a violent spatial component through which certain bodies are made "out of place" or "made into strangers on the shape and skin of everyday life."[33] In that sense, violence, or, more precisely, the threat of violence posed by the unfamiliar, transgressive life or body, creates and conditions certain intimacies based on similarity and familiarity.

In Istanbul, for instance, cisheteronormativity, as a form of communal and spatial intimacy, incessantly marks trans people's bodies as unfamiliar, out of place, and transgressive. Trans people are displaced from the visual and material field of public life in violent ways that include the use of spatial techniques of surveillance and securitization, extralegal police violence, urban transformation projects, and the flow of neoliberal capital into their neighborhoods. Sex/gender transgression and transness are instrumentalized and utilized in the violent organization and production of urban geography. Yet trans people also shape the urban landscape through their intimate work of emplacement in forms of inhabitation, cohabitation, resistance, and survival. Urban geography indeed is a field of incessant struggles that is mutually shaped by trans lives and forces of cisheteronormativity, neoliberal governmentality, and securitization techniques. I analyze this geography at length in chapters 1 and 2 to illustrate the violent production of spatial intimacies, or *violent intimacies of space*.

Trans people are not the first to engage in the struggles that emerge in Istanbul's urban geography. The city has always been a contested terrain of not only violence but also protest. Beyoğlu, a neighborhood that has historically been popular as a place of entertainment, culture, and commerce, has a special significance in this political urban geography. Over decades, it has been a crucial site for voices of political protest, including feminist and queer/trans issues, labor rights, the Kurdish struggle for freedom and equality, commemorations of the Armenian genocide, the rights of refugees and migrants, and oppositions to projects of gentrification. Trans and LGBTI+ Pride Marches were always organized in Beyoğlu until their prohibition in 2015.[34] These marches were a regional event that attracted LGBTI+ people from the wider Middle Eastern region for almost a decade. During the Gezi protests in 2013, thousands of people attended these marches, where one could also see a growing number of placards and banners written in Arabic and Persian alongside Turkish, Kurdish, and Armenian. The parades saturating Beyoğlu's streets with songs, dances, and slogans are still vivid in my memory: people slowly moving between tall buildings, hanging from their balconies, smiling, waving their hands, joining their voices in slogans, or simply watching the assembly with bewilderment and curiosity, the sea of people gradually becoming louder and louder. At the top of our voices, we were filling the neighborhood with slogans of love: "Aşk aşk hürriyet, uzak olsun nefret" (May love and freedom prevail, not hate); "Ayşe Fatma'yı, Ahmet Mehmet'i; birbirlerini sevebilmeli" (Ayşe should be able to love Fatma; Ahmet should be able to love Mehmet); and "Nerdesin aşkım? Burdayım aşkım! Ay ay ay!" (Where are you, my love? I am here, my love. Ay ay ay!). Words and tunes of love occupied the streets, creating an intimate and affective soundscape in Istanbul.

Without a doubt, the street has political significance for feminist, queer, and trans struggles beyond Pride Marches. These movements mobilize in the streets to raise political awareness around allegedly private and personal issues such as domestic and familial violence, sexual harassment, rape, child brides, and trans and *natrans* femicides, as well as love, desire, sex, and body positivity. The spatiality of the street and the temporality of the night, in other words, have always been constitutive of feminist politics, particularly since the 1980s and, for LGBTI+ movements, since the 1990s. The street is an essential "infrastructural condition" and "good" for bodies to assemble, and for political organizing.[35] It supports bodily action and provides the conditions for bodily political expression. As Judith Butler notes, when the street is foreclosed, that has a direct effect on bodily capacities.[36]

Prior to 2015, the streets of Beyoğlu maintained their status as places of assembly for dissent. This situation started changing drastically in the post-Gezi period, which intensified further with the declaration of a state of emergency in July 2016. Not only queers and trans people but also other dissenting groups—feminists, secularists, leftists, Kurds, minor conservative parties, non-Muslims, peace activists—are struggling to find a space to challenge the neoconservative authoritarianism in the country. The state has used punitive and prohibitive measures against any political organizing for democratic participation, social and political rights, inequality, and the socioeconomic and environmental costs of neoliberal capitalism. In short, Beyoğlu's streets and many other streets have become increasingly vulnerable spaces. And yet trans lives have always been vulnerable in the streets (chapters 1 and 2), and the intimate yet violent exercise of state power, especially as embodied by the police, is central to this dynamic. The state and its organization of power is another, crucial pillar of violent intimacies in the trans everyday.

The Color of Intimate Citizenship: Pink and Blue IDs and the State

One of the goals of this book is to show how the state in Turkey gains intimate content and produces its trans citizens as intimate subjects through its biopolitical and necropolitical government suppression of sex/gender transgression. The book contributes to anthropological studies of the state that treat it as a form, "the presence and content of which is not taken for granted but is the very object of inquiry."[37] This approach problematizes understandings of the state as a uniform, autonomous, fixed, bounded entity, institution, or thing, replacing them, as Begoña Aretxaga stresses, with subjective dynamics that are key to understanding the state in its relation to people and movements.[38] The lived experiences of such dynamics establish the phenomenological ground between the state administration and its "proxies," paving the way for the state to come into being in particular forms of presence.[39] My discussions draw on trans people's intimate—subjective, embodied—experiences with state power.[40]

Modern states have always been intimate with their citizens. Scholars have drawn widely on the involvement of the state in the so-called private sphere of its subjects, from affective and sentimental ties of domesticity to the zones of desire, sex, and sexuality, which it imbues with political content.[41] Areas such as marriage, sexuality, and reproduction, to name a few, tend to be critical sites of state regulation and the focus of persistent state projects. As historian Nancy Cott underscores, "No modern nation ignores the intimate domain, because the population is composed and reproduced there."[42] With the implementation of biopolitical practices and governmental techniques, the so-called private sphere emerges as a locus of constantly evolving forms of state power that determine what kinds of intimacies (sexual, domestic, familial)—and who—will be deemed legitimate.[43] Socialization is a process in which the workings of state power operate through the establishment of intimate (including sexual) links that reach into the inner lives and bodies of its citizens. Paying attention to these intimacies exposes a story of the affective, visceral, corporeal workings of everyday state power and a particular shape the state takes.

The categories of sex and gender are integral to the formation and intimate workings of Turkish state power as the state seeks to govern and regulate not only bodies and sexuality but also its subjects' intimate conducts and desires. The state has little room for ambiguous or ambivalent gender and sex. It actively produces and deploys governing projects that constantly strive to disambiguate ambiguously sexed and gendered bodies and recruit them as heteronormatively gendered national subjects. These projects lead to the formation of violent intimacies between state actors and trans people across a wide range of institutional settings, including the medicolegal world of sex/gender confirmation, the security and police departments controlling the public presence of sex workers, the judicial world of hate crimes targeting trans women, and the bureaucracies of death, cemetery, and inheritance services.

Everyday encounters and interactions in these institutions set the stage for constructing what Aretxaga calls "terrifying forms of intimacies" between the state and trans people's bodies that are integral to modern disciplinary practices and rational technologies of control.[44] This is particularly evident when it comes to the sex/gender confirmation process, in which the state plays the role of vagina inspector and becomes preoccupied with penile penetration as a tool for eliminating, and hence regulating, sex/gender transgression. The institutional fixation with penetration, I argue, paves the way for a violent politics of touch and tactility. Developing a conceptual nexus of corporeality and the sensorium, I analyze *the politics of tactility and touch* shaped in the knot of violence, intimacy, and sex/gender transgression. I suggest that the sensory apparatus, specifically various forms of violent touch by institutional actors on people's bodies, helps us to understand the organization and exercise of intimate state power. This focus informs us about sex/gender-transgressive people's subjective, embodied experience with the state and its power, and the unique combinations of intimacy and violence through which the state takes a masculinist, cisheteronormative, patriarchal, and penetrating form. I conceptualize these forms of touch and corporeal proximities as *the violent intimacies of the state.*

The state had no medicolegal regulation surrounding transgender identity or gender confirmation surgery (GCS) in Turkey until 1988, when Bülent Ersoy, a famous trans woman singer, won her seven-year legal struggle to change her sex in her official record from male to female, thus gaining the right to a pink ID card (chapter 3). The legal code, introduced with her case, remained unaltered until the change in government in 2002, with the inception of the rule of the Adalet ve Kalkınma Partisi (AKP; the Justice and Development Party), a neoliberal conservative political party that entered the political scene in 2001 and held the parliamentary majority until 2018. When they came to power, the AKP changed several aspects of the legal system, including modifications to the Civil Code. With these changes, the gender confirmation process was put under rigorous medicolegal control and institutional supervision.

During my research, changing their government-issued ID cards from blue to pink, or vice versa, was a significant concern for trans people. To have GCS and change their ID cards today, trans people are required to undergo a psychiatric evaluation lasting one and a half to two years, various medical tests, and until very recently, sterilization (see chapter 3). One's age, marital status, and reproductive status also constitute significant legal barriers to receiving a new ID card: a person must be unmarried, be older than eighteen, and have no children. This system involves the constant evaluation of trans people's gender role performance and bodily configuration by various institutional actors (i.e., therapists, doctors, forensic medicine people, juridical authorities) according to the dominant categories of sex and gender in Turkey. The gender confirmation process, including the issuance of new IDs, is based on bodily reconfiguration and requires trans people to reconstruct their sex-assigned bodily parts in accordance with their gender, thus rendering obligatory a particular production of bodily materiality. In other words, before issuing a new ID, the state insists that trans people prove their "true" gender identity and modify their bodies accordingly. This medicolegal path to a pink or blue ID is not unique to Turkey but rather a transnational product of European scientific approaches to sex/gender nonconformity and transness. Scientific modalities, largely produced in English, German, and Swedish medicolegal environments, have shaped the institutional discussions and practices regarding trans bodies and their sex/gender in Turkey, an issue that I discuss in detail in chapters 3 and 4.

The spatialized state project of sex/gender disambiguation extends beyond the medicolegal world of gender confirmation. It also includes the displacement of trans women from their houses and neighborhoods (chapter 1), the criminalization and securitization of trans presence in public (chapter 2), the distribution of criminal justice at court cases over targeted trans femicides (chapter 5), and the organization of trans people's funerals and intimate claims over their lives, relationships, and bodies (chapter 6). The achievement of sexual and gender legibility via the cisheteroreproductive couple and family life is at the center of the entangled world between trans people and state actors (i.e., police officers, doctors, forensic scientists, and juridical actors). In fact, the dominant Turkish family structure and morality function as the cornerstone of a broader dominant intimate order that shapes state discourses and policies as well as everyday sociocultural life.

The Intimate Order of the Turkish Family and Cisheteronormativity

Like many other family models around the world, the hegemonic model of cisheteroreproductive blood family in Turkey, with all its emotional, material, and symbolic work, draws borders between lives, bodies, and desires in terms of inclusion and exclusion, belonging and nonbelonging.[45] Most blood families expect the internalization of these norms and values by their members, especially their children. Lives outside the cisheteroreproductive family structure are socially recognized as lesser and hence receive fewer shares of social capital, such as respectability, status, and power, as well as state resources, such as legal and financial protection. "The Turkish family structure" (*Türk aile yapısı*) is a common reference point in every social site, from popular media to the news, from political speeches to ads. Extended family members (such as grandparents, aunts, uncles, etc.) are also considered part of this structure through the consolidation of blood ties. Children, parents, and extended family members have debts toward each other, and together, as citizens, they owe debts to the state through their social reproduction.

Far from being new, family-oriented intimate state projects date back to the Ottoman modernization reforms of the nineteenth century. Historians of the late Ottoman Empire have extensively documented the imperial state's introduction of new forms of intimate control over women's bodies as part of its emerging population policies on public health, reproduction, and progeny.[46] When the Turkish Republic was established after the collapse of the empire in 1923, the focus on nation making was equated to the construction of the new civic man/woman and the making of the modern family and its well-being.[47] Acting, feeling, and identifying as "modern" has been strongly linked to a nationally shared domestic intimacy established by how people married each other and how they lived their domestic space, among other practices.[48] The calculation and valuation of modern national membership at the affective level, or the sentimental formation of the new collective national Turkish "we," has been tied to the construction of the emotional content of citizenship, or national identity, through specific institutional pedagogies and discourses—a relationship that also has been a topic of research beyond Turkey.[49] That is, the public redefinition of the ideal modern Turkish national subject has been established through protocols for how people are to live their domestic and private lives.[50] In particular, Turkish citizenship has emerged as an intimate modernization project that is grounded in a more private (personal, familial, and sexual) morality. A patriotic and patriarchal model dominates the relations of the "public sphere" through the promotion of a strong connection between the intimate domains of the quotidian and the survival of the nation. Citizens are expected to love their nation in the same way they do their families and are led to believe that their family lives directly affect the future of the nation.

As historians of sexuality in the Middle East widely document, same-sex desire and sexual acts, particularly between men, were prevalent and not considered deviant until the modernization process in Arab, Ottoman, and Persian contexts.[51] Beginning in the nineteenth-century, the social institutionalization of heterosexuality transformed intimacy to become the marker of modern citizenship. Adaptation to (European standards of) modernity was equated with a strictly heteronormative monogamous model of sexuality and desire.[52] Heterosexualization, as a project of modernization, required that straight love and sexual desire be instituted as the dominant and most efficient intimate currency of social and private life. The historical shift from same-sex to opposite-sex, from homoeroticism to heteroeroticism, from polygamous to monogamous marriage in socially accepted forms of sexual intimacy has grounded the present-day normative structure of desire, sex, gender, and intimacy in Turkey and beyond.[53]

Throughout the republican era, a series of institutional practices and regulations secured the blood family as a site for the reproduction of gender and sexual inequality. These institutional conventions inscribed intimacy mainly as a family asset bound by blood, and granted blood family members and the spouse legal rights over the body of a citizen after the citizen's own individual rights (inheritance or funeral rights, for example—see chapter 6).[54] The desire for a cisheteroreproductive nuclear family is cultivated carefully from an early age, socializing boys and girls into specific masculine and feminine roles. The production of these gender roles and the gender hierarchy further shapes the processes, desires, discourses, and practices of family making and family life.

For instance, most Turkish families and state institutions organize themselves around a regime of gender and sexuality that idealizes hegemonic masculinity as cisheterosexual, able-bodied, authoritarian, conservative, culturally Sunni Muslim, middle- to upper-class, Turkish (as an ethnic self-identification; not Kurdish, Armenian, or Jewish, for instance), and light-skinned (rather than dark). Popular culture (mainstream movies, TV shows, novels, ads, etc.) provides ample material to examine these dominant sexual, gender, racial, and classed patterns.[55] Their representative currency largely revolves around discouraging Turkish boys/men from overtly displaying emotions that are considered stereotypically "feminine," and hence weak, including pity, fear, sadness, and compassion. In popular soap operas and movies, boys/men usually express emotions considered to be representative of strength, such as aggression and outrage. Protectiveness and possessiveness, which can take financial, cultural, national, and sexual forms, are also significant aspects of idealized masculinity. A constant play of vigilance and willingness to claim and protect, as well as sacrifice for family, kin, community, and flag and nation, is essential.

As scholars of masculinity in Turkey suggest, a boy's/man's performance in the following sites shapes how his masculinity is perceived in private and public environments: the circumcision ceremony, education, soccer culture, military service, employment, marriage, and reproduction.[56] The military is one of the most prominent domains for the production of gender in Turkey, particularly hegemonic masculinity. Excluding women and the feminine, the Turkish military enables cisheterosexual, able-bodied male citizens to represent the nation-state through fraternal links and a sense of superiority over women. The completion of compulsory military service solidifies hegemonic masculinity insofar as a man becomes a proper candidate for marriage only after having received his discharge certificate from the army.[57]

My aim here is not to depict ahistorical, homogeneous, and uncontested notions of gender in Turkey but rather to establish the historically specific socioculturally and institutionally idealized masculine and feminine norms and patterns that are at work in everyday life. The presentation of a general framework here is meant to provide a comprehensive sociocultural background against which it becomes possible to grasp what it means to be a trans or a gender-nonconforming person who has to tackle and negotiate normative gender roles in everyday life. The prevailing binaries of sexuality and gender in Turkey exert powerful forces in people's lives, whether they are trans or *natrans*.

These forces might differ in their effects on trans women, trans men, and trans nonbinary folks, since they are differently positioned in intersectional hierarchies of sexuality and the sex/gender binary. For example, obligatory military service figures differently in the lives of gays, trans men, male-assigned trans women with blue IDs, and gender-nonconforming people with blue IDs. Trans men, even after they receive their blue IDs, are considered disabled and thereby exempted from military service. Others can avoid the draft in three ways: by evasion, by declaring conscientious objection to military violence, or by receiving a "rotten report" (*çürük raporu*) or "pink discharge paper" (*pembe tezkere*).[58] The first two options are difficult because they are illegal and put people at risk of imprisonment. The third option, receiving a "rotten report," is tied to the applicant's medical condition, which can include severe health problems ranging from neurological to psychological illnesses, and from vision loss to internal diseases. These health problems are evaluated according to the Health Regulations for Turkish Armed Forces, which include "homosexuality" under the category of "psycho-sexual disorders" (Article 17).[59] The regulations' definition of homosexuality includes some gay practices and excludes others. As sociologist Oyman Başaran aptly argues, the militarized medical discourse defines homosexuality in relation to specific gender values, roles, and norms that are socially and culturally considered "feminine" in Turkey, producing "homosexuality" as an effeminate institutional category.[60] It is not the engagement in same-sex sexual intercourse but the gender role that one holds in this contact that demarcates one's sexual orientation. In this sense, the cultural distinction between the masculine, "active" penetrator and the feminine, "passive" recipient allows men to enter same-sex relations without challenging their straight sense of self.[61] Men who participate in vaginal or anal penetration may still pass as straight, while the recipient partners of these sexual interactions are dominantly marked as feminine.[62] While feminine gay men, male-assigned trans women, and gender-nonconforming people with blue IDs receive a "rotten report" relatively more easily in that they are collectively categorized as "homosexual," gay men who deviate from the military's imagination of homosexuals as effeminate are subject to a much more meticulous and difficult process.

As noted previously, once *natrans* men accomplish their duty as soldiers, they are socially encouraged to be the patriarchal heads of their own families (*aile reisi*). Outside the private space of their homes, these men are invited to identify with the state and are granted control over women's bodies and sexuality, often through the deployment of "morals" (*ahlak*) or "honor" (*namus/şeref/ırz*) discourses. The notion of honor is contentious. It has been internationally exhausted as an analytic trope to mark Middle Eastern and Mediterranean geographies as inherently backward, violent, and timeless landscapes.[63] Within Turkey it has also been weaponized against Kurds through the discourse of "crimes of tradition," later revised as "crimes of honor."[64] Turkish people and state institutions have deployed criminal "honor killings" as a racializing discourse to imagine themselves as modern subjects who favor greater gender equality between men and women than Kurds, who are stereotyped as victimizing their women through "honor killings," an issue that I discuss extensively in chapter 5. A critical body of feminist work undermines this othering, as it historicizes the continuous preoccupation with honor in modern Turkey and demonstrates how cultures of honor have also been appropriated, maintained, and cemented in modern institutions of the state, ranging from medical to juridical settings.[65]

Anthropologist Ayşe Parla compellingly argues that there is a need for careful and thick descriptive work that avoids defining honor as a generalized and timeless cultural notion but instead recognizes its historically specific cultural power in everyday practice and institutional discourse.[66] I agree with her important insights to the extent that the sociocultural valuation of honor continues to inflict sexual violence on women, queers, and trans people. Yet I also think that the discourse of "honor" was much more common in popular and political discourses up to the 2010s and has more recently shifted to a discourse of "morals" or "decency" (both words are translations of *ahlak*), which reflects the importance of paying attention to historically shifting and specific dominant discourses of sexual morality.

As cisheteropatriarchal concepts, "honor," "morals," and "decency" organize power relations not only between men and women but also among men, establishing strong links with female sexuality and social hierarchy.[67] In Turkey dominant gender regimes encourage men to compete with each other in terms of their capacity to possess and protect the female body and sexuality. The famous Yeşilçam studio movie period of the 1960s and 1970s, the booming industry of Turkish soap operas locally since the 1990s, and, more recently, the internationally influential industry of Turkish television series are saturated with performances of men's sexual morality displayed through the sexuality and embodiment of female family members (e.g., wife, fiancée, sister, mother) or girlfriends.[68] These melodramas, as both reflections and producers of everyday gender relations on the ground, represent masculinity in terms of entitlement to possess and discipline female sexuality and women's bodies.

Women in Turkey have wide access to education and the world of employment. However, discourses of chastity, domesticity, reproductivity, and moral purity continue to value and prioritize women as wives and mothers. Tying women's social recognition to their cisheteroreproductive capacities and the institution of the family marginalizes other practices of life that women may inhabit and enjoy. Although large urban environments provide people with alternative forms of intimacy and opportunities for nonmarital sex, the general conservative texture of social morality mostly disapproves of and actively prohibits intimate and sexual relations outside the boundaries of marriage. That is, family functions as the condition of women's social recognition, and marital intimacy as the totality of their (recognized) sexual experience.[69] Women are pressured not to display any sign of active sexuality in public and are expected to control their sexual drives in social life. Acts that might defy such normative expectations would approximate them to being a "slut" or "prostitute" in the public eye, disturbing "common morals" or "public decency." Men normatively see themselves as entitled to perform specific dominant masculine roles to regulate female sexuality and femininity in public and private life.

That said, I should underline the varied relationship among public female sexuality, sex/gender nonconformity, and the spatial organization of life in Turkey. There are wide variations, for example, between urban and rural environments, between touristic sea towns and interior regions, and between smaller and megaurban settings. Even in megaurban centers like Istanbul, class, religion, neighborhood, and other forms of social difference varyingly shape how women and sex/gender-transgressive people (are expected/permitted to) display their sexuality, gender, and bodies in public. For instance, my first book on sex work, *İktidarın Mahremiyeti (Intimacy of Power)*, showed that while visible and active forms of female sexuality and sex/gender transgression might be readily penalized in a more lower-class or conservative neighborhoods of Istanbul, the same practices might be welcomed in fancy or elite neighborhoods.[70] This spatial fragmentation also manifests itself in the publicity of trans lives in urban landscapes, a theme that I expand on in the next chapter.

In this social geography of sexual morality, active and "illegitimate" female sexuality and same-sex relations among men can damage men's reputations, which also extends, most significantly, to family reputations. Ahmet Yıldız's murder in 2008, for instance, was the first publicly known gay "honor killing" in Turkey.[71] A twenty-six-year-old Kurdish gay man and university student, Ahmet was shot dead on the street in front of his apartment in Istanbul. The murder case remains unsolved, but his runaway father is the primary suspect. As this incident, which involves a gay man, indicates, what constitutes sexual immorality is not the female per se but *illegitimate* or *transgressive feminized sexuality*. As noted previously, the stereotypical public view of gay men in Turkey associates them with femininity and being "soft" (*yumuşak*), which is to say they are not manly enough. Ahmet's openly queer life feminized him in his family's eyes, breaching the norms of hegemonic masculinity and thus staining his family's reputation and bringing the punishment of death. Hearings on Ahmet's case mobilized LGBTI+ activists in Istanbul to demand equal human rights and hate crime legislation in the broader struggle for sexual and gender justice. In a masculinist and cisheteronormative society, both queer murders and trans/*natrans* femicides make the availability of killing a shared gendered experience.[72]

The majority of these killings, as in Ahmet's murder, are intimately tied to sociocultural devaluation of the feminine in general. For over a decade, I have participated in and organized several protests against these killings as a member of feminist and LGBTI+ groups. In all of these protests, the rallying cries were the same: hate, death, violence, misogyny, exclusion, masculinity, patriarchy, men, the state. Chapter 5 focuses on the court cases related to these femicides and the political life around them.

The specific sociocultural meanings of cisheteronormative sexuality and gender roles and hierarchy in Turkey are formed through strong intimate ties and alliances among the cisheteroreproductive familial order, the dominant regime of gender and sexuality, and the social and legal organization of state power. These ties and alliances constantly reaffirm and endorse cisheteronormative structures of everyday life that plague and exhaust those who fall outside them.

The current AKP government has only intensified this historically rooted dominant intimate order by investing further in the circulation and cultivation of desires for a national future that is oriented around the cisheteroreproductive family. Since the AKP took power in 2002, everyday life in Turkey has been changing relentlessly through a raft of government measures and locally enforced directives embracing even more conservative norms and values. The state has introduced further legal amendments that strengthen the institution of the blood family and family values and regulate women's sexuality by effectively attaching them to the demands of family, men, and the state. Consider these examples: in 2004 the government attempted (and failed) to modify the Turkish Penal Code by criminalizing adultery (*zina*); in 2008 then prime minister Recep Tayyip Erdoğan initiated a pronatalist discourse, encouraging married couples to have at least three children; in 2017 he increased that number to five; in 2010, shortly after the government issued a circular on equal opportunities for men and women, Erdoğan explicitly stated that he did not believe in gender equality; the Ministry of State for Women and Family Issues, founded in 1991, was renamed as the Ministry of Family and Social Services erasing women's status as specific subjects of state concern. Intermediary mechanisms and local state actors (including bureaus attached to the Presidency of Religious Affairs) were used to convince couples to remain married if they were contemplating divorce, in order to protect family life.[73]

The state's hegemonic discourse on family life and gender roles, corresponding with the promotion of religion to younger generations in schools, brought new interventions into the organization of everyday life. There has been an escalation of state involvement in popular concerns related to how people drink, kiss, and entertain themselves; what kinds of homes they can have; and with whom they live, among others. The government has introduced new regulations on abortion and women's reproductive rights, restricted the sale and consumption of alcohol, introduced exorbitant taxes on alcohol and tobacco consumption, promoted women as the primary caregivers of families, prohibited single-person apartments in some construction plans, introduced more Sunni Islam religion courses into the elementary and high school curricula, forcibly removed two passengers who were kissing each other on public transport, investigated student apartments where females and males resided together, and banned political protests and demonstrations, including, since 2015, the LGBTI+ Pride March.[74] These state actions under an authoritarian administration have contracted both private and public spaces for dissenting groups, including trans people. Lives beyond the limits of the blood family and kinship structure are deemed less valuable and undeserving of state protection or distribution of resources. Official discourse privileges the family, denying recognition to those who do not represent themselves in familial terms. Trans people's claims and struggle over their intimate relations with their friends and their bodies are contested, negotiated, and shaped at the intersection of those legal regulations, institutional practices, and norms that inscribe the cisheteroreproductive nuclear family as the hegemonic model of intimacy in Turkey (chapter 6). Transness and sex/gender transgression, in fact, is one site among others (e.g., sex work, straight or queer single womanhood, gay manhood, nonmonogamy, single motherhood) where intimate ties and alliances between the state and the family are consolidated.

Needless to say, people in Turkey are not passive recipients of gendered and cisheteronormative frameworks of intimacy and embodiment. In fact, feminist groups in Turkey have been organizing against the hegemony of marriage, marital sex, and sexual violence since the 1980s. Beginning in 2012, feminist, queer, and trans groups and people have increasingly collaborated against the organization of social and everyday life within the strict confines of the family and the sex/gender binary.[75] My research and my political work over the years have shown me how participation in feminist, queer, and trans struggles and the finding of common vulnerable ground spawns new intimacies and affections for many. These political groups reject the social and institutional insistence on recognizing women as part of the family rather than as individuals and have organized to promote alternative forms of living arrangements, relatedness, love, sexual life, or networks of solidarity beyond the cisheteroreproductive nuclear family model. Several trans people who were injured by police violence or abandoned by their families found shelter, care, love, and survival in these communities. The intimate and affective ties that have emerged and grown among the community have translated into networks of care, political organizing, and struggle against police violence, familial abandonment, and social exclusion. The pleasurable, the joyful, and the humorous also played a significant part in the trans everyday through, for instance, *güllüm* moments. Communal energies, affect, and labor derived from relations of intimacy facilitated a radical environment of self-care.

Hence, *Violent Intimacies* is also a story about the world-making agency, capacity, and conditions of the trans everyday. The following pages demonstrate collectively produced moments of fugitivity, temporary worlds of suspension and transcendence, spaces for restoration and recovery, strategies of survival, and the embrace of laughter and tears in an otherwise cruel and violent world. Before diving into these stories of the trans everyday, it is crucial to provide a short history of trans activism, as political organizing constitutes one pillar of these world-making efforts.

LGBTI+ and Trans Activism: A Brief Transnational History

This book approaches transness in Turkey as transnational, a context that is constantly interacting with global medical discourses on transness, Western LGBTI+ terminology, political and legal discourses on hate crimes and human rights, and multifaceted understandings of sex and gender from scattered locations in the Global South.[76] The global mobility of people, capital, information, and identities, as well as its hierarchies and asymmetries, significantly shapes the trans everyday in Istanbul. Similar to other sites in the broader Southwest Asian region, local understandings of gender, sex, and sexuality in Turkey are far from untouched by transnational flows of northern (understood also as Western, global, modern) scientific, medical, and political discourses and practices.[77] These discourses and practices travel across local contexts, informing particular understandings of trans identification. As anthropologists Evelyn Blackwood and Saskia Wieringa argue, cultural location and global connectedness are in a dynamic and complicated relationship, such that gendered and sexual subjectivities are neither simply local nor wholly determined by northern discourses and practices.[78] Queer and trans lives, such as those I consider in this book, necessarily "reproduce and reconstitute the specific discourses, knowledges, and ways of understanding the world of their particular locations," which are both local and global.[79]

It is crucial to approach this transnational framework as a more scattered than coherent environment, with multiple spatialities and temporalities that connect across different postcolonial or occupied contexts in the Global South. For instance, the recent displacement of people en masse has given the transnational geopolitical situation even more prominence in Turkey. Wars, invasions, authoritarianism, and economic precarity in Iraq, Syria, Yemen, Afghanistan, Pakistan, Somalia, and Sudan; government oppression in Egypt; sanctions against Iran; and colonial projects targeting Kurds and Palestinians have made Turkey a crossroads for refugees and migrants. Multinational refugees stay in Turkey temporarily while seeking resettlement in Canada, the United States, or European countries, as Turkey provides refugee status and long-term settlement for Europeans only.[80] This situation has significantly impacted the lives of LGBTI+ refugees, who are subject to transnational and national legal regulation of sexuality, gender, mobility and borders, and racial discrimination in the liminal space and time in Turkey and beyond.[81] Therefore, it is important to recognize Istanbul, especially, as a multilayered and scattered transnational location that hosts queers and trans people from elsewhere in Southwest Asia and North Africa.

These cross-cultural and long-distance encounters can also create zones of what Anna Tsing calls "friction," that is, "the awkward, unequal, unstable, and creative qualities of interconnection across difference."[82] With regard to local nonconforming sexualities and genders, such frictions can occur in myriad settings, ranging from the nation-state's reproductive policies to civil law, and from family life to the general heteronormative culture prevailing in everyday social life. One should approach these processes also as part of larger transnational stories that intersect with multiple competing projects within the national context varying, for example, from neoliberal frameworks to attempts to join the European Union (EU). Some of these competing projects take place also within the "developing/emerging nation" context with agendas of state modernization and the expansion of NGOs and the spread of human rights discourse, and more.

The human rights/NGO synergy with LGBTI+ movements and organizations has been crucial, and in relation to them, the facilitating role of EU accession should not be underestimated. However, from the perspective of contemporary dynamics, the most influential and fundamental of all these trends is probably the shift to neoliberalism. With the opening of Turkey to relatively unrestricted trade and financing through the economic model of private enterprise and free markets in the early 1980s, Turkey in general, and Istanbul in particular, became a popular destination for the in- and outflow of global capital, labor, discourses, images, lifestyles, and identities.[83] It is no surprise that these global flows have influenced and shaped the lives of trans people as profoundly as those of *natrans* people. What follows is a brief history of LGBTI+ and trans activism that has emerged from this transnational location of Istanbul.

The emergence of broader organizational efforts around LGBTI+ rights in Turkey dates back to the early 1990s with the foundation of Lambdaistanbul (1993), the first LGBTI+ organization of Turkey, later followed by Kaos GL (1994) in Ankara. While 1996 proved to be a key year in terms of organizational visibility, it was not until the mid-2000s that these organizations formally established themselves as associations.

In Istanbul LGBTI+ people used to organize regular gatherings in various places, including clubs and cafés.[84] When preparing for its first organized public activity in 1996, Lambdaistanbul invited local, national, and international figures, including intellectuals, artists, and representatives of LGBTI+ organizations from abroad, to participate in a series of events. The governorship of Istanbul prohibited the events the day before they started. Following the cancellation, the European Parliament Subcommittee on Human Rights decided to add "homosexuals" to its reports on Turkey.[85]

Meanwhile, the first gay and lesbian radio program on Açık Radyo (Open Radio) began streaming regularly on Sundays between midnight and one in the morning; it lasted for a year and a half. This occurred during the organization of the United Nations Habitat II Conference, preparations for which included increasing police violence and pressure against trans people living in apartments close to the conference venue (chapter 1). At the Habitat conference venue, Lambdaistanbul organized a table together with the İnsan Kaynağını Geliştirme Vakfı (IKGV; Human Resource Development Foundation) a pioneering NGO established in 1988 that researches and develops intervention programs around marginalized sexuality, HIV/AIDS, sex work, and sex trafficking in the context of urban migration.[86] One of my field sites, Kadın Kapısı (Women's Gate), was a center initiated by the IKGV (see appendix on methodology).

Due to Lambdaistanbul and the IKGV's table at Habitat, the LGBTI+ organization gained visibility in the local media. They used this to release a press statement drawing attention to the police violence being used in the ongoing displacement of trans women; then, organizing under the Lambdaistanbul banner, they mobilized various local and international actors—individuals and institutions—to visit trans women's neighborhoods and protest against the police violence and the violation of the women's rights.

In July 1996 the first Pride event took place at a dance club. In the years that followed, Pride expanded to include talks, panels, and movie screenings, gaining its current status as an annual event. Two years later, in 1998, the first nationwide LGBTI+ gathering took place, attended by Lambdaistanbul, Kaos GL, Sappho'nun Kızları (Sappho's Girls/Daughters), Bursa Spartaküs (Bursa Spartacus), and Almanya Türk Gay (Germany Turkish Gay); these meetings continued at six-month intervals until 2004.[87] Besides organizing these meetings, the groups listed took a lead role in organizing social events such as dinners, picnics, movie screenings, and parties to bring LGBTI+ people together and create a space for bonding and conversation.

These activities continued into the 2000s at an increasing pace and with growing attendance. The rainbow flag made its first wide public appearance in Ankara on May 1, 2001, at the initiative of Kaos GL. The following May 1, LGBTI+ people marched through Istanbul under the banner of the "No to War Platform" (Savaşa Hayır Platformu) against the impending US war in Iraq and the Turkish involvement in it.[88] With its strong ties to the transnational political arena, this demonstration established LGBTI+ visibility. The protestors chanted "Homofobini sorgula" (Question your homophobia), "Zorunlu heteroseksüellik insanlık suçudur" (Forced heterosexuality is a crime against humanity), and "Eşcinsel hakkı, insan hakkıdır" (Homosexual rights are human rights), which all had clear connections to international discourses on human rights. Toward the end of the same year, Lambdaistanbul participated in another mass demonstration against the war in Iraq, this time with its own banner reading "Lambdaistanbul EŞCINSEL Sivil Toplum Girişimi" (Lambdaistanbul HOMOSEXUAL Civil Society Initiative). Until 2006, Lambdaistanbul did a lot of organizing work at universities, at conferences, and in the streets, which made it possible for the organization to develop more permanent relations, communication, and collaborative work with other political organizations, particularly with feminist and nongovernmental organizations working on human rights issues.

From the early 1990s through 2008, Lambdaistanbul was also a political home for trans people. Until the late 2000s, trans women anchored the trans activist scene, whereas trans men emerged as political actors later, in the early 2010s. At first, some trans women perceived trans men as unfamiliar. I remember hearing some trans women reacting to the slogans including the word *trans man* at the LGBTI+ Pride in Istanbul in 2010, trying to make sense of the term.

Trans men gained more visibility and recognition within the LGBTI+ movement in Istanbul with the 2007 establishment of the Voltrans Initiative by three trans men. One of the founders was Ali(gül) Arıkan, a longtime activist in the feminist and LGBTI+ movement prior to Voltrans. Before his passing in 2013 as a result of ovarian cancer, he dedicated his last years to fighting against transphobia and struggling for the betterment of trans men's lives. Ali also started a blog in 2009 to talk about his trans experience and the problems of trans people in general and in Turkey in particular.[89] His blog received wide readership and became popular as a source of advice and guidance, especially for young trans men. Regarding the initial confusion about or nonrecognition of trans men as an identity in the LGBTI+ movement, in 2009 he commented as follows:

> When one says "trans," the first person that comes to mind is usually a transsexual [*transseksüel*] woman. There might be two reasons for this: first, our perception; second, society's perception. Society disregards, looks down on, and so torments trans women because they are women, and also they have "given up on their manhood." Mainstream media portray them as "monsters." For me, trans women are the pioneering actors of the LGBT struggle. This issue of "visibility" is similar to the case of gay men, who are the first people to come to mind when one mentions "homosexuals" [*eşcinsel*, lit. same-sexual]. So, lesbians and bisexuals become invisible. Yet transsexual and transgender men are at the bottom of the list when visibility is at stake. There might be many reasons for that, including the values attributed to "manhood," people's preferences to not organize, thus remaining invisible, or the dominant misperception that *erkek fatmalar* (tomboys) are relatively well-respected members of society, so trans men will have less trouble.[90]

Meanwhile, trans women, who had previously organized under Lambdaistanbul, decided to create a trans-majority space and, in 2007, founded a center, initially as a civil initiative, which they named Istanbul LGBTT. This was the second trans-majority organization in Turkey after the foundation of Pembe Hayat in Ankara in 2006.[91] Although used mostly by trans women, Istanbul LGBTT was open to everyone from LGBTI+ circles. During my fieldwork trans women would talk about the long-lasting transphobia within the LGBTI+ movement at various levels, ranging from the biased distribution of jobs in LGBTI+ associations to the prioritization of problems on the political agenda. Hence, they had found it necessary to create a predominantly trans space. Esra, Sedef, Sevda, Ceyda, and Meryem, trans activists for more than two decades in the early 2010s and the protagonists of many stories in this book, formed the core group of the organization. Esra and Sedef were the main founders of Istanbul LGBTT;

before Istanbul LGBTT, they had worked in several political organizations, including leftist political parties and Lambdaistanbul. Separating from Lambdaistanbul was a story of escalating tensions that had long existed between trans and *natrans* people in the urban queer/trans world of Istanbul. Neither Lambdaistanbul nor Istanbul LGBTT hold permanent spaces anymore since 2016 and 2019, respectively, but they continue to organize occasional events as groups.

Philological Troubles: Use of Terms, Categories, Identities

Categories are archives. How we produce and define categories, what kinds of categories we choose over others, how we use or refuse them, or why we disidentify with them has a social and political history. Transness in Turkey is a site within which the category of transgender has emerged transnationally and undergone shifts in meanings over time. As anthropologist Gayle Rubin notes, "Categories invariably leak," they are limited, and "they can never contain all the relevant 'existing things.'"[92] They are historical, volatile, temporary, and inadequate containers in a sea of complexities and excesses of life. The contemporary trans scholarship presents invaluable efforts to turn this excess into a powerful element in the definition of transgender. To again draw on Susan Stryker's definition, *transgender* refers to "a wide variety of phenomena that call attention to the fact that 'gender' as it is lived, embodied, experienced, performed, and encountered, is more complex and varied than can be accounted for by the currently dominant binary sex/gender ideology of Eurocentric modernity."[93]

As much as they are excessive and volatile, categories are also crucial to the organization of our lives, our desires, our identities, and our senses of self. They have a dialectical power intrinsic to their construction, organization, and circulation: they function as regulatory instruments or even as weapons in the hands of normalizing institutions that impose a certain normative template on the complexities and ambiguities of life, thus perpetuating large-scale harm to those who do not fit or who cannot be contained. They serve for the production of norms that produce security for some populations and vulnerability for others.[94] They objectify us to establish truths and realities about our lives and bodies. At the same time, however, we objectify, instrumentalize, or use them to claim subjecthood, personhood, and belonging. We use them to make meaning about life and to establish and mobilize political claims. We use them to resist hierarchies of truth and reality and to transform logics of state power and unequal conditions of life.

Against this backdrop of categorical work, queer and trans activists in Turkey draw from the transnational proliferation of diverse categories for labeling distinctive understandings of sexed/gendered beings and sexual behavior, identity, and/or rights. Some of the local terminology of the LGBTI+ movement in Turkey "dubs" Western categories of sexual identity, mimicking them, yet animating them in a distinct fashion.[95] Turkified versions of LGBTI+ terminology form a sense of belonging in a global LGBTI+ community and allow for strategic access to transnational rights discourses. At the same time, they gain a life of their own by producing difference, which situates them in a "grid of similitude and difference."[96] How people work with them and the kinds of content they give to these discourses are of great significance. As anthropologist Tom Boellstorff underscores, "The similarity in terminology might mean similarity in identity, or it might not. It is an empirical question and thus depends on (1) careful listening that comes from actual research, and (2) how we determine what counts as 'similarity.'"[97] The LGBTI+ activists constantly negotiate the specification of sexual/gender identities and the rapidly changing discourse on gender and sexuality in their everyday lives. They mediate, modify, and shape the categories borrowed from the West along with the local queer terms, especially *gacı*, *dönme*, *lubunya*, *eşcinsel*, and *ibne*. Fundamentally, with respect to the issue of transnational categorization, the cultural, social, and political practices in Istanbul's trans and queer world show that people approach sexual and gender identity "as something [they] build and protect, rather than as a static category to which they either do or do not belong."[98] Simple translation becomes particularly fraught, therefore, and I avoid it here.[99]

The word *dönme*, similarly to *queer*, was widely reappropriated by trans people and integrated into colloquial parlance during my fieldwork. Originally, *dönme* meant "convert" and was historically used to denote people who changed religion, especially crypto-Jews under the Ottoman Empire who became Muslims in the seventeenth century.[100] The current use of the term among trans people has no religious implications (at least none that are obvious or conscious) and merely signifies conversion from one sex to another. In the local lexicon, however, I found *gacı* and *lubunya* to be more commonly used than *dönme*.[101] Both *gacı* and *lubunya* have more comprehensive meanings than *dönme* to the extent that they refer to the feminine gender. In other words, whether one has undergone any degree of GCS or not does not affect one's identification as *gacı* or *lubunya*. Indeed, trans people might also address some gay men as *gacı* or *lubunya*, depending on the men's level of feminine gender role performance. To a certain extent, the local categories of *gacı* and *lubunya* embrace trans people, gay men with feminine gender, and those who occupy a liminal position between the two.

Between the time of my main fieldwork and the time of completing this book, there have been notable social transformations in the world of queer and trans people in Turkey. The chapters that follow extensively discuss these transformations with a specific focus on the trans everyday, but here I want to focus on the specific category of *lubunya*, as it has gained more popular currency and been embraced by the wider trans and queer community since 2019. On one level, this shift reflects a powerful example of transness as an excessive site that cannot be represented, signified, or contained by a single category or by the international categories of LGBTI+. On another level, there is a much more interesting story to tell about the porosity of categorical borders. *Lubunya* now also embraces *natrans* lesbians, queer women, trans men, and nonbinary *natrans*/trans people alongside trans women, gay men with feminine gender, and those who occupy a liminal position between the two. The recent expansion of *lubunya* to include a wider group of LGBTI+ people, I argue, has something to do with the formation of new alliances among feminist, queer, and trans groups around transfeminism, alliances that emerged in reaction to the local forms and discourses of TERF (trans exclusionary radical feminism).

Starting especially with the International Women's Day March in 2011, the feminist scene in Istanbul has been marked by tensions between some *natrans* feminist women and a group of activists, including trans, queer, and other *natrans* women. While for some *natrans* feminists, trans politics has meant just another form of identity politics and is thus not engaged in a struggle to liberate women, trans activists often saw *natrans* feminists as gender essentialists and gatekeepers of the category of "woman."[102] In 2012 the *Amargi Feminist Journal* organized a series of roundtables to provide a platform for dialogue among feminist, queer, and trans politics. These exchanges, later published as a book, are characterized by questions now familiar to those of us at the intersection of feminism and trans activism:[103] What is feminism? Whose feminism counts as feminism? Which demands herald a more feminist agenda? Who is a woman? What's the difference between having "feminine experience" and "compulsory feminine experience"? Transfeminism emerged as an urgent and central topic in these conversations.

Some of the *natrans* feminists have transformed through these conversations and revised their approach to feminism in general. Consequently, the 2012 Women's Night March included trans, queer, and some *natrans* feminist activists carrying their own placards that read "Transfeminists are here!"

In 2018 another crucial trans-related topic caused rifts and tensions among trans/*natrans* feminists and LGBTI+ people, inflaming the political scene once again. This time the issue revolved around the use of puberty blockers and hormone replacement therapy among trans children and youth, and its vilification by some *natrans* feminists. Conversations around hormone therapy triggered long-standing biases against trans women, which found expression in transmisogynistic phrases like *trans women's male privilege*. The entire exchange turned into months-long intense fights between trans/queer feminists and TERFs (who preferred to identify as "gender critical feminists"), that frequently flared up and continue to do so.[104] Because the disputes spilled over onto social media, they reached out to a wider audience, leading to growing support for trans and queer people among academics, journalists, human rights lawyers, NGO workers, and some political parties in addition to feminists and LGBTI+ people from across the country. Hence, the recent reclaiming of *lubunya*, I argue, is a product of this stimulating environment. The language we use to create categories and terms for our lives is a terrain of living; it evolves, responds, reacts, and reconfigures assemblages and alliances.

By bringing these local terms to the reader's attention, my intention is not, as already criticized by some scholars, to recover the "authentic" sexual and gender vocabulary or to safeguard the "traditional" terminology from the global discourses on sexual identity and thus to replicate a "self-romanticizing" gaze.[105] Although I distinguish in my usage between the "foreign" and "native" depending on my immediate focus in the text, I do not seek to maintain a sharp, rigid, or in any way purist division. Rather, my intention is to highlight the coexistence of both the local and the global terms for sexed and gendered practices, identities, and bodies and to draw attention to their relations and deployments in everyday language. And it should be noted that the local and the global are multivariant and not oriented only to Europe or North America.

Here I would make the point that the "borrowed" terms, such as *trans* or *transgender*, have more institutional and political value; they have a more formal register and are thus more commonly used as written forms. The local thus becomes colloquial. For example, when trans people visit a doctor or lawyer, they do not use the terms *gacı* or *lubunya*. Not only would they defer to the medical setting and the professional world of doctors and other health workers, but it would not make much sense to claim medical or legal services from the state with these terms, since no assistance is available on the basis of what they name. In these examples, language and space map onto each other in interesting ways and connect to intimacy, in that colloquial terms are reserved for friends and chosen family members, while more formal ones function as a marker of institutional relations or otherness/violence.

My primary selection of terminology has been shaped by these types of considerations. In reporting linguistic interactions and exchanges, I am attentive to people's choice of words in talking about themselves and their lives, identifications, disidentifications, and bodies, as well as those of other trans and queer people. When local terms were used in our conversations and interactions, I convey the original, without modification. I have also deployed the local words *gacı* and *lubunya* when I describe or talk about more informal and intimate settings, interactions, and encounters. I use *trans* as an umbrella term to refer to people who transitioned between genders or were transitioning through (varying degrees of) gender confirmation processes, who disidentified with any existing category of gender, and/or who, at the time, identified themselves as *transseksüel*, *trans*, *transgender*, or *travesti* but still considered themselves within the general category of trans.

Turkish is a gender-neutral language. There is only one pronoun for third-person reference, with suffixes added for the plural and other noun cases. No matter how much I try to do justice to the original meaning of words and their embedded cultural values and significations, there is an inescapable layer of incommensurability between the Turkish and English languages in this regard. In this book I sometimes deploy *they/them/their* to resolve this problem of translation. I am not concerned with making a strongly ideological point here, however, and prefer to casually accept the gender dichotomy of standard English, with, for example, feminine forms along with *trans woman* when referring to someone self-identifying as *gacı* and *lubunya*.

Mapping the Book

Chapter 1 is a story of trans geography in the urban landscape of Istanbul. Situating the sexual and sex/gender-transgressive character of Beyoğlu within a broader social context of racial, religious, economic, sexual, and gendered spatialized otherness, I delineate the historical and contemporary significance of space and place making to trans lives and queer possibilities. Trans people's everyday violent experiences of spatial discrimination, marginalization, and displacement by a range of institutional (e.g., the police) and noninstitutional (e.g., capital owners, landlords, neighbors, etc.) actors shape and remake urban geography through the lenses of sex/gender transgression. Their everyday struggles over the urban landscape are not only about constant displacement and forced mobility but also about spatial intimacies in forms of inhabitation, cohabitation, and emplacement.

Building on spatial forms of violent intimacies, chapter 2 examines the changing relationship among law, order, and trans people between the 1960s and the 2010s. This period experienced significant transformations in the deployment of the police force to criminalize and punish trans people in both public and private spaces. I elaborate on the forms of violent intimacies constituted between trans people and police officers, who embody state power through legal and extralegal means of surveillance and securitization.

Violent intimacies between the state and trans people's bodies become more apparent in sites of medicolegal regulation and control of "transsexuality" and gender confirmation, the topic of chapters 3 and 4. To change the color of their government-issued IDs, trans people must follow stringent institutional steps and search for ways to prove their "true" sex/gender for medical and legal authorities. This evaluation process opens trans people's bodies to various practices of violence, including specific forms of touch between the medicolegal actors and the trans body. I detail the entire gender confirmation process becomes as a site from which to scrutinize how the Turkish state, through its medicolegal techniques and actors, gets violently intimate with trans people's bodies.

Chapter 5 continues with the inscription of trans lives, bodies, and queer desires into the domain of law through femicides. Bringing together trans and *natrans* femicides, I look at the political life that is organized around sex/gender-transgressive and transgender deaths. My specific focus is on trials for trans femicides—which contribute to the mobilization of legal claims on "hate crimes," a category of crime that has not yet passed into the Turkish criminal law—and on the elimination of "unjust provocation" as a mitigating factor in the culprit's sentencing. These court cases constitute a crucial site to explore the intimate yet conflicted relationship between law and justice within the context of LGBTI+ politics.

Chapter 6 sheds light on the resilient, imaginative, and creative labor of trans people by telling their intimate stories of friendship and family and kin making. I demonstrate how trans people recast everyday conditions of violence, familial abandonment, and death, transforming them instead into relations and currencies of intimacy. They deploy the family as a form of intimacy strategically reworked through queer alignments and ties. Through an intertwined network of care, labor, love, joy, and affect, trans women consistently invest in their friendships, contest the primacy given to blood families, and survive a violent urban geography.

Finally, the coda reflects on the changing forms and meanings of violent intimacies in trans lives in the ongoing sociopolitical transformations in Turkey, particularly since the Gezi protests in 2013 and the coup-attempt in 2016.

Chapter One

Displacement as Emplacement

IT WAS HER HAIR COLOR that first drew my attention. Yeliz Anne (*anne* is Turkish for "mother") entered the room with her tiny frame and dyed platinum blonde hair with long gray roots. Platinum blonde is a hair color popularly associated with wanton and lascivious femininity in Turkey, and it is unusual to see women using it, especially past middle age. The Turkish film industry has widely used this hair color to signify stereotypical prostitute figures, especially during the classical Yeşilçam studio movie period. When Yeliz Anne started speaking, I heard a deep, strong, and rusty voice, most probably the result of longtime heavy smoking and drinking. As I got to know her, I discovered it was hard for her to stay in the same place longer than half an hour. She was extremely active, constantly moving around Beyoğlu, from one spot to another, but all our conversations took place at Istanbul LGBTT. Her accounts of Beyoğlu and particularly of Abanoz Street were precious and crucial data. She was one of the elderly trans women from whom I collected historical information about trans lives in Beyoğlu. Trans women, as well as the LGBTI+ community at large, respected her as the most senior trans woman in Istanbul—hence the epithet *anne*, which they used to address her (see chapter 6). Yeliz Anne was born in Adana, a southern city in Turkey, in 1943. I met her when she visited Istanbul LGBTT one day while I was there.

In 1961, at the age of eighteen, Yeliz Anne had run away from Adana to come to Istanbul because of the pressure and exclusion she faced from her family due to her nonconforming gender appearance and behavior. Decades later, she described to me how she had spent her adolescent years back in her hometown feeling like a girl and watching the women working in the brothel next to her family's house. She heard about Beyoğlu, specifically Abanoz Street, for the first time from one of those sex workers with whom she had become friends. She recounted her sex-worker friend's words: "Go to Beyoğlu in Istanbul! And when you go there, you should find Abanoz Street. People like you hang out in those streets!" At that time, "people like you" did not refer only to trans women but also to effeminate gay men (i.e., those displaying gender roles and norms normatively associated with femininity). There was no particular conceptual separation of different gender and queer identities, such as gay, transvestite, transsexual, and transgender. They were all lumped together and referred to mostly as *lubunya* or sometimes as *eşcinsel* and *ibne* (see the introduction).[1] Occasionally, trans women would be separated as a different group, addressed as *kadın kılığındaki erkek* (men in female attire), a category deployed by the police at times to criminalize trans women (chapter 4). The *gacılar*, including Yeliz Anne, reflected the then blurred lines between feminine gay men and trans women in their colloquial language by mostly using the word *lubunya*.[2]

For *lubunyalar*, Beyoğlu has always had a special meaning because of its relationship with sex/gender-transgressive practices and subcultures in the history of Istanbul. Its spatial landscape is a rare archive of sex/gender-transgressive everyday life. The majority of the trans women I knew had lived and/or worked for varying lengths of time in specific neighborhoods in and around the district of Beyoğlu. Trans people's relationship with Istanbul has been marked by a history of constant displacement, particularly in the Beyoğlu area. In particular, the police force occupied a unique role in using trans people's sex/gender-transgressive lives and sexual practices as an excuse to implement wider projects to transform and organize the urban space into zones that attract neoliberal capital as well as comply with dominant, cisheteronormative sexual and gender values and their associated morality. The spatial production of sexual and gendered otherness has shaped the past and present conditions of trans lives, paving the way for a violent destruction as well as for the production of urban space.

Despite this relentless banishment, trans people have created material and imaginative practices of place making. Their compulsory and ongoing mobility within particular districts of Istanbul has resulted in tales of trans geography, in a localized history of searching for and fashioning a space of their own. As anthropologist Holly Wardlow states, mobility can be an important component of marginalized sexual identities and of the construction of autonomy and forms of agency.[3] Similarly, there is a powerful connection between trans displacement and trans mobility, which also forms a "ground of sociality, a new way of inhabiting the world," in terms of establishing a spatial belonging.[4] I address this process as *displacement as emplacement*.

Transgender issues are always spatial issues. Critical studies of social geography owe a great deal to Henri Lefebvre's assertion that spaces and subjects mutually constitute and shape each other, that social relations and the locations of everyday life are tightly coupled, constantly producing and structuring each other.[5] The production of urban space always also means the production of social relations.[6] Human actions and movements make and shape spaces and places, just as these spaces and places simultaneously mold humans as particular subjects and inform specific actions, interactions, and identities.[7] Sexualities and genders are part of this dynamic, and our geospatial relationships are structured by certain assumptions, norms, and values with regard to gender and sexuality.

My aim in this chapter is to show how everyday struggles over space and place are at the heart of sex/gender-transgressive lives, producing "subaltern or alternative geographic patterns" for trans people alongside or beyond dominant geographies in the city.[8] Here I refer to Katherine McKittrick's understanding of geography "as space, place, and location in their physical materiality and imaginative configurations."[9] Trans people actively construct this subaltern geography on an everyday basis through their movements, attachments, and imaginations.

This trans geography, however, is not a separate, isolated one but rather a patchwork of safe places such as certain streets, shared homes, rooms, hotels, centers, hair salons, coffeeshops, bars, and clubs. Trans people develop creative strategies and intimate networks through this patchwork that makes it possible for them to survive as well as to thrive. In the following pages, I offer stories of not only displacement but also emplacement, an arduous yet significant labor of place making in a hostile and unequal environment. A focus on the making of Beyoğlu as a sex/gender-transgressive geography offers a different way of knowing and crafting a social world in an urban environment. And this geography, like any other geography, I argue, is both violent and intimate. A study of its production and organization allows us to understand the coconstitutive relationship between violence and intimacy through the spatialized registers of sex, gender, and sexuality, that is, the geography of violent intimacies, or spatial intimacies.

First, I walk you through the Beyoğlu area in 2010 and examine its social and cultural history. Then I detail its historical and contemporary significance for sex/gender-transgressive lives and possibilities. The last section returns to Yeliz Anne's and other trans women's oral histories and focuses on their individual recollections and collective narratives of continuous displacement and emplacement in the Beyoğlu area beginning in the 1960s. The role of nonconforming genders and sexualities in the politico-economic transformation and uneven distribution of urban space in Istanbul remains unfortunately understudied. Depicting trans women's past and present perceptions, movements, attachments, and intimate experiments in the everyday urban fabric of Istanbul contributes toward animating that field of urban geography.

Walking in Beyoğlu

A typical walk during my research in April 2010: I left my apartment in the city-center neighborhood of Beşiktaş, took a bus to Taksim Square, and walked to Istanbul LGBTT in Beyoğlu. The crowded, chaotic, and noisy soundscape of the city was amplified in Taksim Square and only intensified once I walked toward and through Beyoğlu (see figure 1.1). Street vendors selling *simit*, chestnuts, or rice with chickpeas hawked their wares; kids approached people to sell bottles of water or tissues or to ask for money; some elderly women sat in their casual outfits, trying to sell flowers to people passing by; passengers huried to catch their buses or looked exhausted from standing and waiting for their bus; some people stood on the sidewalks, puffing on their cigarettes, chitchatted with others while gazing at the scene; cars were usually stuck in the traffic surrounding Taksim Square, blowing horns; people jaywalked and ignored traffic lights; suited-up businesspeople walked with their black leather bags.[10] Rushed steps, loud voices, car noise, and the smell of tobacco assailed me from all sides.

Right behind me was the internationally recognized Gezi Park, backing onto Taksim Square. Back then, in 2010, the French-designed park was still relatively unknown and invisible, even to the vast majority of Istanbul's citizens, let alone to the rest of the world. In May 2013, when Gezi faced the threat of demolition to make way for a retro Ottoman shopping center and mosque complex as part of the urban transformation of the area, it

1.1 Istiklal Street, Beyoğlu, May 7, 2010. Courtesy of Wikipedia Commons, http://upload.wikimedia.org/wikipedia/commons/b/ba/Istiklal_busy_afternoon.jpg.

shot to fame as the central node in one of the largest expressions of popular resistance in the history of Turkey emerging as a counterpublic on both national and international levels.[11]

The park area originated in an Armenian graveyard, the Surp Agop Cemetery, which was established during the Ottoman Empire in the sixteenth century. In the late 1930s, the Turkish state seized the cemetery, destroyed the church, and transformed the area into a park as part of its nation-building projects.[12] Until the Gezi uprising, the park and its surroundings were overlooked by many. It was seen as a lower- or underclass site, a place where the families of building superintendents resided in the basement apartments of the neighborhood. Gezi was also a clandestine queer park.[13] The majority of its visitors included gay men looking for casual sex in the park's many blind spots, young rent boys under eighteen years old, and trans women selling inexpensive sexual services, as well as recent trans and queer migrants to Istanbul seeking connections with other trans and queer people in the city.[14] Especially late at night, unlicensed trans sex workers would emerge to publicly solicit on the main road alongside Gezi that linked Taksim Square to Harbiye, Dolapdere, and Kurtuluş, districts that had become popular among trans women over the and two decades before 2013 as places to live do and do sex work. Hence, when the protests started, the LGBTI+ presence was very visible, as the demolition of the park posed a significant threat to the lives of queer and trans people and sex workers. The prioritization of capital flow, public morality, and urban renewal aesthetics has long shaped queer and trans people's relation with the space of the city. The possible destruction and transformation of Gezi epitomized yet another chapter in this history. Thus, LGBTI+ people made the threat to trans and queer livelihoods a significant site of struggle for the Gezi movement and played a key role in occupying and "commoning" Gezi Park, challenging neoliberal and heteronormative geographies of urban life.[15] The character of the park changed tremendously following the Gezi protests, and these clandestine queer practices have largely disappeared and reappeared elsewhere.

Leaving Gezi Park behind, I crossed Taksim Square to Istiklal Street, which marked the start of Beyoğlu and served as its central reference point. The downtown crowds became even more intense as I stepped into this famous pedestrian thoroughfare; a streetcar ran from the top, at Taksim Square, down to the Galata, Pera, and Asmalımescit neighborhoods. This long cobbled street and the intricate weave of alleys and side roads running off and alongside Istiklal were the pulsating, bustling hub of contemporary popular and cultural life in Istanbul. Istiklal has always been a commercial street, but in the early 2000s, the commercialization of the street and its environs increased to an unprecedented level, with the transformation of its historical buildings into neoclassical fronts for shopping malls and hotels running parallel to the rising property prices, urban renewal projects, and gentrification, both generalized and planned, which began to displace marginalized and lower-income residents. Gezi's planned demolition was, in fact, a part of these recent phenomena.

Among its many artistic, touristic, entertainment, and other cultural functions, Beyoğlu had also been the center for political activities until the mid-2010s, housing the main centers of numerous political parties, associations, and human rights NGOs. It was not surprising to stumble on a political demonstration, march, press campaign, or table to gather petitions while walking down Istiklal. Most of these political events took place at the midpoint of the street, at an intersection of streets and intense human traffic that opened out into a small square in front of the French-language Galatasaray High School. However, since 2015 the Istanbul governorship has banned all political activity in Beyoğlu. Yet Saturday Mothers/People, who have been mobilizing since 1995, continue to gather in Beyoğlu every Saturday at noon to demand truth and justice about the enforced disappearances of their relatives in the 1990s. Similarly, feminists and LGBTI+

1.1 Map of Beyoğlu, showing Istiklal Street and local districts; historically, the Beyoğlu area covers all these districts as far north as Tarlabaşı/Gezi and parts of Dolapdere, excluding Kurtuluş and Pangaltı. Courtesy of Google Maps screenshot, November 2012.

feminists and LGBTI+ groups did not give up on reclaiming Beyoğlu, as they insisted on organizing both the International Women's March and the Pride March there up until 2022 in spite of clashes with the police.

Regardless of the changes in its architectural and social structure over the decades, one never saw Istiklal Street quiet or empty, either late at night or early in the morning. Life continued nonstop here, just with changing figures at different times of the day and changing intensities. When one turned off the main street and entered the crisscrossing alleys and backstreets, dilapidated structures met the eye. Even though they looked as if they received no maintenance, many of them were historical buildings, beside which improvised constructions rose over the years to create an architectural collage. Once housing residential buildings as well as shops and stores, these streets were now packed with cafés and restaurants, bars and clubs, offices and centers for political and other associations, sweatshops, and cheap hotels used for sex work. Even though low in number, there were still apartment buildings and rented rooms that attracted sex workers, trans women, LGBTI+ and also non-LGBTI+ people, and other outcasts. For trans women, sex workers or not, the area represented a focal habitat and survival zone due to its relatively welcoming and less violent social body. Sex workers also found the Beyoğlu area spatially convenient, since they could have a home there near their workspace.

In the vicinity of these streets, there were also higher-end neighborhoods, areas that were gentrified in the mid-1990s or were in the process of being gentrified. Cihangir, for example, used to house trans women until their violent ejection by the police in the mid-1990s as part of the gentrification of the area. Since 2004 a similar process has been at work in the Tarlabaşı neighborhood, on the opposite side of Istiklal (see map 1.1). Until recently, this was home to various marginalized populations, especially Roma people, displaced Kurds from Turkey's southeastern Kurdistan region, West African migrants, trans women, and sex workers.[16]

In short, Beyoğlu has long been a major district for the racially, ethnically, and sexually marginalized, alongside and partly defining its character as a sexual, recreational, and cultural center. When I talk about Beyoğlu as my fieldwork site, I mean a patchwork of neighborhoods, together with the practices and encounters there between different marginalized, as well as dominant, groups insofar as they touched on trans lives, contextualized their interactions and encounters, and shaped their subjectivities, motions, and mobility in the city.

History of Beyoğlu and Its Sex/Gender-Transgressive Subcultures

Beyoğlu is located on the European side of old Istanbul, which itself is divided by a major waterway, the Golden Horn, into two zones that are socially, culturally, and economically distinct. Encompassing the famous districts of Eminönü, Eyüp, Süleymaniye, and Sultanahmet, the opposite side of the strait has historically been known as the heart of the sultanate and the traditional center of the Ottoman Empire, with its distinguishing

Ottoman architecture (including Topkapı Palace). Beyoğlu, in contrast, has represented a more Westernized, or "European," part of the old city, with its distinctive style of architecture, recreational activities, and residential history having grown out of links to the Italian trading cities.

Previously known as Pera (Greek, "across") until the founding of the Turkish Republic, when the Turkish state expunged non-Turkish names as part of its nationalization process, some people still call central Beyoğlu by its old name.[17] Developing up the hill from the dockside activities at the Bosporus and Golden Horn, the area has a residential history linked to the establishment of Venetian, French, British, and Danish diplomatic embassies opened in the sixteenth and seventeenth centuries.[18] The Europeans who took up residence there were called Levantens under the Ottoman Empire, while other now-minoritized communities, such as Rums (local people of Greek origin), Armenians, and Jews also moved in.

Located next to Pera, Galata was the neighborhood where non-Muslim people were concentrated in large numbers. This area had been the center of foreign trade since the Byzantine period, and it was mainly through the non-Muslim groups that it maintained its merchant character during the Ottoman Empire. Thus, Galata, together with Pera, also stood for a non-Muslim religious center, with synagogues and churches in the region, and had been associated with non-Muslim lifestyles for centuries. Pera was always identified as a higher-class area than Galata, a difference that has even been a subject in novels that talk about nightlife, prostitution, and the culture of recreation in these two neighborhoods at the end of the nineteenth and the start of the twentieth centuries.[19] As Beyoğlu, it gradually grew into an attraction point for a "cosmopolitan" lifestyle, with a fashionable set combining with its multiethnic residents; the opening of recreational activity places, such as bars, clubs, restaurants, and theaters for the well-to-do; the construction of art deco hotels and European-designed apartment buildings; and the establishment of schools offering French, English, Italian, and German education. A multilingual environment thus developed, as described in Giovanni Scognamillo's 1990 *Bir Levantenin Beyoğlu Anıları* (A Levanten's memories of Beyoğlu).

A Levanten film critic and author with an Italian background, Scognamillo published widely about Istanbul and Beyoğlu. In *Bir Levantenin Beyoğlu Anıları*, he states that the two previous generations of his family did not have to learn Turkish until their adulthood, when they started to do business, and he describes Beyoğlu as the "safe zone" (*kurtarılmış bölge*) for non-Muslim communities.[20] Indeed, Beyoğlu of the nineteenth century seems to have resembled a typical European city; nothing about it was particularly "Turkish," as stated by the French author J. H. A. Ubicini.[21] Levantens and the other non-Muslim residents of the area, who were socially, economically, and culturally distinct from the rest of Istanbul society, are described as composing the first bourgeois social group of Ottoman society.[22]

At the same time, Beyoğlu became a hub for brothels, low-class cabarets, *meyhaneler*, and hashish cafés. As opposed to the glamorous and flashy bourgeois life on the main street, the backstreets and alleyways were claimed by the underclass and working class, those excluded by high culture and shunned by the bourgeoisie. Murderers, thieves, beggars, and prostitutes were the main social actors of this backstage, with trash, mud, epidemics, and dilapidated houses their props. Galata, in particular, had gained a reputation as the red-light district of Istanbul from Byzantine times.[23] In these neighborhood brothels, one could not find Muslim prostitutes. In fact, under Ottoman rule, the state allowed prostitution as long as it was limited to red-light districts and non-Muslim areas; Muslim prostitutes were not officially permitted to work in these public brothels, as they were allowed to provide sexual services only for Muslim men in their own houses and private brothels.[24] Hence, the sex economy in Beyoğlu was mainly in the hands of Armenians, Greeks (Rums), and Jews.

Historical research on prostitution in the nineteenth-century Ottoman Empire emphasizes the Crimean War (1853–56) and the Russo-Turkish War of 1877–78 as producing an escalation in prostitution, particularly in Istanbul, as the war conditions left thousands dispossessed and caused an unprecedented rise in the number of refugees from the Balkans and the Caucasus, along with migrants from rural areas to Istanbul.[25] In the harsh economic conditions of the time, many women looked to survive by creating financial opportunities in the sex economy, particularly those who had lost their husbands, fathers, and brothers to the war. This increase caused sexually transmitted diseases to spread across the city, resulting in the Ottoman state's implementation of new measures in 1878 to regulate and tax brothels.[26] Under these measures, the opening of brothels was subject to strict rules, and Muslim women were prohibited from working as licensed prostitutes.

Later, during World War I, the number of prostitutes and prostitution houses increased on a massive scale, among both the non-Muslim and Muslim populations, due to the war economy, widespread poverty, and migration.[27] There is some agreement also that the increase in prostitution in Beyoğlu at that time resulted from the considerable involvement of White

Russians in the sex trade.[28] Toward the end of World War I, Istanbul was a popular destination for White Russians who migrated from Russia following the October Revolution in 1917. The White Russian presence and influence in Beyoğlu's everyday life was strongly felt, specifically between 1920 and 1924, a period that also overlaps with the 1918–23 British, French, and Italian occupation of Istanbul. During this short period, apparently, Taksim, Tarlabaşı, Galata, and Pera were swarming with entertainment places and restaurants opened by White Russians, and the Istanbul nights were enlivened by special dance and song shows, cabarets on the main roads, pavilions in the side streets, and restaurant tables placed outside on the pavement, as patrons could no longer fit into the packed restaurants.[29]

With the defeat of the occupying countries and the establishment of the republic, official policies and reforms sought the homogenization of the nation based on a Sunni Muslim Turkish identity, leading to a significant decline in Turkey's non-Muslim populations. The 1927 census— taken in the aftermath of the "population exchange," in which Muslims in Greece and Greeks in Turkey were forcibly relocated and resettled in the first "population exchange" organized by international law (the Greeks of Istanbul were exempted)—showed minorities as composing 2.5 percent of the national population.[30] Since then, the non-Muslim minority population has dropped drastically, from over 350,000 to 80,000–90,000 nationally, even as the population of Turkey as a whole has increased sixfold.[31] The decline resulted from several nationalist initiatives, including the "Citizen, speak Turkish!" (Vatandaş Türkçe konuş!) campaign from 1928, which placed pressure on non-Turkish-speaking communities to speak Turkish in public; the imposition of a punitive capital tax (*Varlık Vergisi*) on wealthy non-Muslim groups in 1942; and the Istanbul Pogrom of September 6–7, 1955, which targeted mostly the Greeks.[32]

As a consequence, Beyoğlu became considerably more "Turkified." Its particular form of cosmopolitanism vanished as it was turned into "a national synthesis" in the 1930s through the 1950s.[33] Thereafter, from the 1960s onward, socioeconomically driven interregional and urban migration accelerated. Istanbul became the country's most common migrant destination, offering a relatively high level of infrastructure; services and facilities; and cultural, educational, and, especially, employment opportunities. Hence, internal migrants combined with Turkish locals in gradually replacing Beyoğlu's predominantly non-Muslim profile. This demographic shift brought tastes that were stereotyped as provincial to the neighborhood. Now people could hear *arabesk* music rising from music stores instead of classical European and more contemporary American tunes, or they could eat traditional "Turkish" food, including various kinds of kebabs and *lahmacun*.[34] The change in Beyoğlu's cultural, social, and economic profile led the Turkish intelligentsia to perceive it as "becoming rotten," degenerate, and deprived of its "true nature," which, allegedly, had represented the heart of modern high-culture elegance—in short, everything identified as Western.[35]

At the same time, different parts of Beyoğlu were regarded as already ghettoized and transformed into dens for sex work, the informal economy, and the drug business, with Tarlabaşı, in particular, attracting attention over these issues. Thus, the 1960s witnessed constant police raids of bars, pavilions, and hotels to "cleanse" Beyoğlu of prostitution and establish public morality.[36] The shutdown of two major licensed red-light districts, along the Büyük Ziba and Abanoz Streets, in 1954 and 1964, respectively, forced sex work onto the streets.[37] Abanoz was also the street, as noted in Yeliz Anne's story earlier, where *lubunyalar* started to concentrate later in the 1960s.[38]

Beyoğlu and Abanoz in the 1960s and 1970s

After her first move to Istanbul in 1961, Yeliz Anne moved back and forth between Istanbul, Adana, and Bursa until the late 1960s. In these years, she explained, visible *lubunyalar* were few in number, and even they were mostly closeted. Whether queer or trans, their lives were imprisoned in a narrow, constricted environment, and they were scared to go out in public except in specific streets. Otherwise, they would face violence—verbal harassment and physical attacks—both by police officers and by random people in the streets. Even though the brothels in Abanoz were shut down in 1964, there were still a few houses (illegally) offering sex. From around 1973 on, these houses grew in number. An oral history project by an LGBTI+ organization in Izmir, Siyah Pembe Üçgen Derneği (Black Pink Triangle Organization), which brings together nine trans women's testimonies and stories from the 1980 coup d'état period, reveals that prior to the closure of the entire street in 1978, Abanoz Street was in its heyday, embracing not only local trans women but also foreign trans women from countries such as France, Italy, Greece, Yugoslavia, and the USSR who came to work in Istanbul.[39] However, Yeliz Anne stated that the number of openly trans women in Istanbul at that time was small, not exceeding ten or twelve people. They tried to survive as a group, living and working in Abanoz Street and the local area.

In 1978, sex work in Abanoz was stamped out by the police force, and trans women had to leave the area. Melis, a trans woman in her early fifties, experienced the last days of Abanoz before being displaced from the area with other *lubunyalar*. As one of the prominent members of Istanbul LGBTT as well as an active participant in LGBTI+-related protests, Melis had a unique ability to speak nonstop and at top speed, sometimes repeating herself and not finishing sentences. I remember her being scolded by other *gacılar* at Istanbul LGBTT for talking too much. She had long, straight, black hair with some clusters bleached close to her forehead, adding a platinum blonde contrast. She wore revealing clothes, presenting her slender body in tight jeans, skirts, and blouses. She loved to be filmed during protests and to pose for the cameras in her heavy makeup and eye-catching outfits. Unlike most of the Istanbul LGBTT *gacılar*, she enjoyed spending time at the hairdresser's and paid a lot of attention to her physical appearance. In fact, she first met *lubunyalar* in Istanbul through a hairdresser in Beyoğlu. Some of the hairdresser salons in Beyoğlu were popular hangout spots for *lubunyalar*.

When she first came to Istanbul at the age of fifteen, Melis was homeless for months, and she engaged in sexual transactions with middle-aged men. Like Yeliz Anne, she had also heard about Beyoğlu, and she started to spend time there. One day, she saw a *lubunya*, or in her words, "a man in a female outfit," on the street and followed her to the hairdresser's. Entering, Melis saw many *lubunyalar*, all together in one room. Getting excited, Melis approached them and explained that she, too, wanted to become one of them. This was her story of finding other *lubunyalar* like herself, after which she started unregistered sex work in the Abanoz brothels. At the time of my fieldwork, she was still an unregistered sex worker. Melis said that the brothel where she worked was raided several times back in the 1970s, but the managers could always hide her. After a few years, however, the raids became more frequent and targeted all the houses in Abanoz:

> They started to raid all the houses. We escaped to the roofs. Some of us escaped to other buildings. All of us hid somewhere. Meanwhile, they shut all the houses down. It was in Abanoz Street. It is one block away from Bayram Street. I wanted to move to Izmir [a western city on the Aegean] at that time, but then I heard it was the same over there too. They took me into custody during one of those raids. They cut my hair.

They were also planning to return me to my family, but they could not do that since I was over eighteen. They released me after a while. Once you were caught, you would be automatically sent to Cancan [Sexually Transmitted Diseases Hospital].[40] We would stay four to five days. At last, one of the police chiefs said to the hospital staff, "What are we gonna do with these ones? They come back anyway. You should keep them at Cancan for a minimum of twenty days."

Lubunyalar were ultimately violently forced out of Abanoz by the police. After their expulsion from this street, some of the trans women searched for a new place and started to work in Dolapdere, a shabby neighborhood to the north of Tarlabaşı that was full of derelict buildings (see map 1.1). In those days, all these neighborhoods lacked proper infrastructure, giving Dolapdere the appearance and feel of some kind of distinct zone. Meanwhile, Turkey was headed toward the coup of 1980, with rising tension and fights between right-wing and left-wing groups. Streets in the city were divided into zones, each associated with a particular political camp, thus limiting people's mobility depending on their affiliation or sympathies. Bombings, shootings, political raids, and attacks were part of everyday life.

September 12: Being *Lubunya* under Military Rule

Despite the vast literature on the coup d'état of September 12, 1980, and the subsequent three-year military government, there was no research on the queer and trans experience and testimony of this period until Siyah Pembe Üçgen's 2012 work *80'lerde Lubunya Olmak* (Being lubunya in the 1980s). Even though *lubunyalar* were severely victimized under the military regime, their stories, alongside the history of other sexual and gendered forms of violence in that period, have been significantly obscured by the lack of intellectual and political attention until very recently.[41]

Under the military government, sex workers and *lubunyalar* in Dolapdere and Tarlabaşı were displaced. They joined their coworkers in the brothels of Bayram Street, now one of just two streets with brothels left in Beyoğlu. In some of my interviews with *gacılar,* September 12 was recounted as as a catastrophic day that changed their lives. There was a before and an after September 12 in terms of the social and economic conditions for *lubunya* lives, as Sedef explained:

Prior to September 12, there was a huge *lubunya* population. At each club, at each bar, there was a *lubunya* taking the stage. Many of them were feminine gays. They were making significant sums of money. No matter if one lacked the talent for singing, it was enough to entertain people simply by going onstage to do belly dancing in female clothing. With the coup government of Kenan Evren [leader of the military coup and later president], all these spaces were banned from providing *lubunyalar* with a stage to perform. So those who used to make a living in the entertainment sector had to switch to the sex-work economy, since there were no other jobs available to them. This sectorial transition brought more violence and pressure.

Under the military regime, not only *lubunyalar* but also other groups were treated violently. Everyday life in Turkey was in crisis, with a wide set of rights and freedoms suspended. The military government shut down political parties and terminated the activities of associations and organizations except for the Red Crescent, the Child Protection Institution, and the Turkish Air Association. The sale and circulation of books, movies, magazines, newspapers, and songs with political content were banned. Thousands were stripped of their citizenship and sentenced to death or life imprisonment. Hundreds died under torture or just disappeared into the hidden cells of police stations, prisons, and military offices. Yeliz Anne recounted several stories of her friends who were beaten, murdered, raped, and/or disappeared by the military.

In 1981 the minister of the interior Selahattin Çetiner released an order on radio stations banning all "male artists in female outfits" from performing in bars, cafés, clubs, and pavilions. The order was followed by a dramatic increase in police raids on these places. *Lubunyalar*, who were predominantly working as performers, drag queens, or sex workers in nightclubs, music halls, and bars, could no longer make a living. Some of them continued to work in bars and clubs secretively, under the constant threat of being caught and arrested. In addition to the prohibition on nightlife performances, the daily midnight curfew interrupted the flow of money earned from sex work. Hence, trans women had to adapt to working and soliciting in the street before midnight, while simultaneously trying to hide from military officers and policemen. Predictably, the number of clients was far fewer than it had been when one could work through the night and early morning.

One night under the military regime, as Belgin Çelik testified in Siyah Pembe Üçgen's oral history project, the police collected all trans people and gay men from their houses, bars, cafés, and clubs, as well as from the street, and brought them to the old police station in Sansaryan Inn in Sirkeci (across the Golden Horn from Beyoğlu).[42] Police officers forced *lubunyalar* to board a train to deport them en masse from Istanbul to Eskişehir, a city in the middle of Turkey.[43] Ahlak Polisi (the Vice Squad) stood next to them on the train and beat them with batons, aiming at specific body parts as they were packed onto the train. Various aspects of this deportation story were repeated during my conversations with the older trans women. Melis was one of them: "They exiled me. They sent me to Eskişehir. We ended up in a small village in Eskişehir. They brought us cheap plastic shoes. We were barefoot. All our feet were pricked! They used to lump us all on trains and send us that way. They didn't want us to return to Istanbul. But we came back! Then I found myself being exiled to Izmir. Then to another place. . . . They would just drop us off at places in the middle of nowhere. They would leave us there."

Melis survived this deportation and found a way back to Istanbul. Others managed to escape from the train on their way to Eskişehir. Not everyone was so fortunate, however, and some did not return and disappeared entirely. As the account of the exile train reveals, the state violence against trans women was extremely brutal. Chapter 2 visits these stories in detail; for the moment, I want to prioritize the spatial dimensions of this violence with a particular focus on the forced transportation as an attempt to erase *lubunya* presence from public life in Istanbul, and on the trans women's response with practices of emplacement. Despite the severity of the state violence, most *lubunyalar* found ways to return and reestablish themselves where they felt they belonged. Although a few *lubunyalar* died (were killed) in this process and others disappeared, the state did not succeed in banishing them all—and the community as a whole—from Istanbul's urban space. Drawing on and developing a resilience born of their forced mobility, *lubunyalar* returned to Istanbul and in so doing transformed their displacement into a form of (re)emplacement.

Displacement as emplacement took place not only across Istanbul and other cities but also within Istanbul, particularly in different neighborhoods of Beyoğlu. The intensity of everyday violence made safety and survival a vital concern for trans women. *Lubunyalar* were constantly changing apartments within Beyoğlu due to discrimination by landlords and neighbors and the financial pressure of increasing rents. Most of them stayed in Tarlabaşı, either by staying in cheap hotel rooms with a few other trans women or by renting a dilapidated apartment with others. Some of the luckier ones with means were able to find houses on Ülker Street in Cihangir, on the east side of Istiklal Street, a street that gradually became a place—a home—for trans people in the following few years. Before moving on to the story of this street, let's revisit the residential *lubunya* history in Tarlabaşı.

Tarlabaşı: The Place of the Marginalized

After the deportation of its non-Muslim residents, Tarlabaşı was commonly regarded as a place ghettoized by the marginalized people of the city.[44] Moreover, a major part of Tarlabaşı was destroyed for an urban renewal project during the tenure of Mayor Bedrettin Dalan in 1984–89. This urban project was enacted within the context of a series of political and economic changes that were introduced in the aftermath of the September 12, 1980, coup. With the reduction of the import substitution model and the shift to a more liberalized macroeconomic approach under prime minister (later president) Turgut Özal, Turkey entered the new neoliberal era of globalization.[45] As part of this process, Istanbul became the locus of transnational flows of capital, commodities, and images as well as of capital accumulation.[46] Since the mid-1980s, the urban landscape rapidly transformed with the rise of five-star hotels and office towers, the construction of gated communities, the marketing of Istanbul as a tourist destination, and the removal of small businesses from the central districts.[47]

Reflecting this rapid urban transformation, the destruction of Tarlabaşı was part of a broader project that linked the newly developing business areas to the main airport via the city center.[48] Mayor Dalan had hundreds of historic buildings demolished to make way for the new Tarlabaşı Boulevard, establishing a boundary between Beyoğlu and Tarlabaşı that separated them (see map 1.1). This division led to Tarlabaşı's further marginalization and ghettoization, as it became of a neighborhood for those groups living the most precarious lives, the underclass of bottom-income and marginalized groups, including sex workers, trans people, and queers, along with undocumented immigrants, Roma people and displaced Kurds, the addicted, and the physically and mentally disabled and ill. Some of the trans people renting houses in the new Tarlabaşı slowly started to move to Cihangir. Sedef was one of those trans women who lived in Tarlabaşı for a while before moving to Cihangir, explaining the reasons for her move as follows: "There were better houses in Cihangir, and we were able to find more clients. Tarlabaşı was a place where mostly vermin and junkies lived.

Not everybody would go into that neighborhood to buy sex. In a way, moving to Cihangir represented a jump between different [social] strata for *lubunyalar*. I moved to Cihangir in 1987 and started to live with a friend. This place gradually filled with several trans women in the same year."

The move to Cihangir beginning in the late 1980s started a new era in trans women's lives. Cihangir, particularly the Ülker quarter, became the site of the making and unmaking of a home for trans women. The glory days of the community unfolded, as did fierce fights and a notorious "battle" between trans women and the police in the 1990s. Some trans people refer to the events in this street as Turkey's "Stonewall," a story that I detail in the following pages.[49] Despite their eventual defeat and displacement by the police, *gacılar* showed notable resistance against police violence in the mid-1990s. The communal experience of state violence in Ülker Street still plays a significant role in shaping *lubunya* subjectivities, lives, and present-day relations among different generations of trans people.

Ülker Street: *Lubunistan*

Today considered a home for the bohemian bourgeoisie (artists, intellectuals, etc.) of Istanbul, Beyoğlu's Cihangir district during the 1990s embraced the marginalized people of the city. With the municipality's spatial reconfiguration of Beyoğlu in the 1980s, trans women were displaced from Abanoz and Tarlabaşı, from where, along with Dolapdere, they started to move to Cihangir. They inhabited several streets in Cihangir and claimed it as a home, as a relatively secure place to exist. Trans people were not the sole residents of the neighborhood; intellectuals, artists, university students, and single people who were deemed or identified as "progressive" and had no issues with living with *lubunyalar* and sex workers in the same streets also dwelled there. Among my trans friends, former residents of Cihangir described these streets back then as the "safe zone" and "Trans Empire," dubbing the area "Lubunistan" and "Ibneistan."

Sedef is one of the oldest residents of Ülker Street. She resisted leaving the street even when nearly all of the *lubunyalar* were later displaced (again by the police). Since the early 1980s, she has been a dedicated communist and trans feminist activist. Sedef is also a popular spokesperson on issues of police violence and state discrimination against trans women and sex workers. At a teahouse in Beyoğlu, Sedef told me about the Ülker Street days. She recounted how in the early 1980s trans women began to move to Cihangir, a neighborhood with better housing conditions than Tarlabaşı. At that time, housing in Cihangir was still affordable but more expensive than in Tarlabaşı. Only those trans women who could make enough money from sex work were able to move. In 1985 Pürtelaş, Başkurt, Ülker and Kazancı Yokuşu Streets in Cihangir were attracting quite a few trans inhabitants. By mid-1986, in Sedef's words, trans women "began to *seize* the neighborhood" (emphasis added).

When they first moved to the neighborhood, trans sex workers used to go to the main roads to find clients, but slowly they started working from home, calling to prospective clients from their windows. The neighborhood became a popular sex-work zone with the transformation of its four or five streets into "nearly an open brothel," as Sedef emphasized. As sociologist Deniz Kandiyoti also notes, the Ülker Street *gacılar* would make plenty of money from the lucrative sex economy back in the 1990s; their clients would line up at the street entrances with their cars to buy sex until the early hours of the morning.[50]

Cihangir brought a spatial stability to trans women's lives after years of having been constantly pushed from one place to another and working on the street subsequent to their return to the city after the coup period. The *gacılar* who were residents of the area during that period talked to me about it nostalgically, describing the peace cultivated between them and the *natrans* dwellers of those streets. Police officers initially countenanced the sex economy in this neighborhood because they would take their cut from the *gacılar*'s income. Some of the *gacılar* sigh about those days, memorializing them as "the halcyon days of their community." Their physical concentration and proximity to one another in a single urban area had empowered them, and they had begun to see Cihangir as their community's home. Within a decade, though, this was gone.

The shift to a neoliberal economic model initiated an unprecedented epoch of privatization, leading to flows of international capital into the emerging market that was Turkey, and especially its metropolitan center. Identified as a future global megacity, Istanbul began to undergo rapid urban transformation with an accelerating pace of development. By the late 1980s, some of the downtown neighborhoods with historical value had become primary targets for this transformation. Cihangir was among the old neighborhoods that were the target of the first wave of gentrification in Istanbul in the early 1990s.[51] Its localized majority *lubunya* population were seen as undesirable for, and obstacles to, Beyoğlu's new design. Hence, a decade-long gentrification process started that eventually transformed Cihangir into an upmarket place to live in.

Toward the late 1980s, Sedef explained, a gradual change occurred in *natrans* residents' attitudes toward trans women. The residents began to complain about the *lubunya* presence and sex work in the neighborhood. Yet Ceyda, who also resided in Cihangir at that time, claimed that the change in the neighbors' attitude could not be explained simply by an increasing sense of disturbance from the *lubunya* presence. She emphasized the systematic attempt by the police to pressure the neighbors to take a hostile stance toward trans women. From her perspective, by no means all of the neighbors wanted them to move out of the neighborhood; they were, in fact, getting along well. Their nontrans neighbors used to visit them in their homes. She even stated that *gacılar* had developed such intimacy with the residents of Cihangir that nearly all of them had a lover from the neighborhood: "But the police and the local government also pressured the residents. The grocery store owner where we used to get our groceries for years started to refuse to sell us their products due to police pressure. Such police pressure also caused a hairdresser, another grocery store, and a water station [supplying drinking water] to shut down their stores and move out of the neighborhood. The police visited real estate agents to warn them not to rent any apartments to us. Even the ones that were willing to support us could not do anything because of the police."

When the police started to raid *lubunya* houses, Sedef took an active role in organizing trans women and resisting the state violence. To my questions about police violence and what *lubunyalar* went through in Cihangir, she responded with a detailed account of the displacement in two stages: first, the trans women's displacement within Cihangir and subsequent "incarceration" in just one street, Ülker Street; and, second, their eventual displacement from Ülker Street: "In Cihangir we expanded beyond soliciting from our windows and stood at the street entrances to pick up clients. This situation lasted until 1989, when the chief police officer, Doğan Karakaplan, initiated mass raids on our houses. Those raids had the air of raids that usually took place in the houses of illegal political organizations. Two hundred to three hundred policemen would surround and blockade the entire neighborhood with their rifles and other sorts of guns. Then they started to smash our doors by force."

The police justified these raids as protecting public sexual morality. In fact, as Sedef explained, it was a cover-up for a more complicated story involving a brothel owner, Matild Manukyan, who collaborated with the police. Manukyan, an Armenian woman born in Istanbul in 1914, had inherited a brothel in Galata, Beyoğlu from her father. Over time, she expanded her sex business, signing further lease agreements with the state to increase the number of her brothels to fourteen. In the 1990s she became a well-known public figure due to being the top taxpayer in the country for five consecutive years. It was no coincidence that her breaking tax records overlapped with the augmented pressure and violence against trans women in Cihangir because, as Sedef explained, the demand for trans women's sexual services worked against Manukyan's business. The trans women's neighborhood was packed until the early mornings, and Manukyan was losing many clients. Thus, as Sedef and her friends later discovered, Manukyan bribed the police chief, Doğan Karakaplan, with the gift of a Mercedes car. When Sedef pointed out that the Mercedes was an import with a huge sales tax, she made sure that I knew its color as well: "It was the latest version, a gray one!" As her story went on, Sedef revealed an even more complicated dynamic behind their displacement from Cihangir:

> In the 1990s the majority of the trans women were displaced and evacuated from their houses in Cihangir. There was only one street left: Ülker Street. Some of the girls moved to this street, while others started to gather on the E5 [highway].[52] With the move to the E5, there was a massive increase in the number of trans deaths. . . . We were more experienced in Ülker Street. I insisted on not running away but resisting because we had nowhere else to go. Of course most ran away! They had told us that Hortum would be in power for the short term.[53] It was the time of the Habitat meeting [the United Nations' meeting on the question of human settlements]. The first attacks started on May 21 and 22. Whoever heard the name Hortum Süleyman [Süleyman the Hose] fled the neighborhood. He stayed as the Beyoğlu police chief until 1997. He is the one who struck the final blow against trans women in Cihangir.
>
> . . . There was this woman, Güngör. She had bought a charity building at a low rate. Initially, she was on good terms with us; she was keen to rent out her apartments to us. But she had two apartments on each floor, a front and a rear one. The latter were not well lit, and she asked for three times their actual rent value. Once, we wanted to rent the front apartments, but she stipulated that we had to rent them both. Upon our refusal, she resorted to the authorities, including ministers and mayors, to report, "This neighborhood has turned out to be a brothel, but we families are living here!" They mobilized the neighborhood, started

to keep guards in the streets, and attacked people who wanted to visit us. People from the neighborhood did all this! The police supported them. . . . We also had trouble with the mafia, and we tried to resist.

In 1992 there was a mafia group one street down from where we lived. They used to extort fees from *lubunyalar*. They attempted to do the same thing in Ülker Street. The chief of this bandit gang was my client, and he was in love with me. All the gang members gathered together in the street. For the residents of the street, it was so much better! At that time, we were fewer in number. Maybe thirty-five. These bandits intercepted, beat, and robbed our clients on their way to our homes. Some of the girls started to fight with them, but the police supported those bandits. Even some of the girls, who were the lovers of policemen, were on their [the bandits] side. This situation caused many trans women to flee the neighborhood for a while. We were down to five people from thirty-five. Five of us insisted on staying, and we made lots of plans. But we sorted them out! [She chuckles.]

Neighbors, police officers, landowners, bandits, brothel owners, lovers, clients . . . Sedef's story vividly demonstrates the multiplicity of social actors involved and the diversity of economic and social interests and processes that went into marking and targeting trans women for displacement from Cihangir. The majority of the trans community was displaced by the systematic police raids and violence in the "cleanup" operation prior to the 1996 United Nations Conference on Human Settlements (Habitat II) in Istanbul. In expelling trans women from their houses, the goal was to "cleanse" the entire Cihangir district from unwanted sexual practices and people with nonconforming gender and sexual identities. From the police perspective, this goal was achieved because shortly after this displacement the neighborhood saw a significant change in its residents' profile: bohemian upper-middle-class people invested in real estate in Cihangir and renovated the houses.

The displacement was also facilitated by the collaboration of other social actors. The Cihangir Güzelleştirme Derneği (CGD; Association for Improvement of Cihangir), an organization founded in 1995 by architects, other professionals, and the old residents of the neighborhood, played a prominent role in making the district desirable for a particular segment of the public by promoting the renovation of buildings and rehabilitation of the streets. The CGD organized itself around providing a safer and cleaner physical and social environment in Cihangir, and the neighborhood gained a positive reputation among the public.⁵⁴ However, the drive to make Cihangir a desirable residential area for the elite transformed trans women into a targeted population that needed to be ousted from the district. Thus, while recounting the Ülker Street era, *gacılar* remember not only the police officers but also the CGD members who called on the police and worked closely with them to expel the remaining trans community from Cihangir.

During the notorious struggle between trans women and the police forces, many trans women were arrested and subjected to violence and torture. According to my interviewees and other sources, the early 1990s were the harshest years, with police pressure taking extremely violent forms and trans people being severely persecuted.⁵⁵ This event is referred to as a lost battle between state forces and the trans women community. An often-told story recounts that Hortum Süleyman, then head of the Beyoğlu Police Department, allegedly claimed, "The citadel has fallen!" referring to the eviction of trans women from their houses.

That said, the last five trans women succeeded in staying in their homes, including Sedef. For Sedef, the struggle with the police signified a personal triumph over place but a collective defeat for trans women. She emphasized the need to draw lessons from this defeat and held some members of the trans community responsible for the lost battle: "Our trans friends also made a lot of mistakes. They invited men from the neighborhood [to be clients]. They broke bottles on people's heads. They screamed, yelled at people. In other words, they exaggerated their freedom rather than appreciating it. Then they ran away after two police raids. They should have taken responsibility for what they did. But they didn't. The empire that we seized, our ghetto, disappeared. Five to six streets belonged to us. In the end, there was only Ülker Street left—only a small part of it. Eventually we lost that as well."

When it came to fighting against gender, sexual, or economic inequalities, Sedef always displayed a more militant stance than the majority of the *gacılar*. She would frequently complain that the LGBTI+ community at large lacked political awareness and motivation to change their lives and the unequal system in general. She demanded that other trans women become as politically engaged as she was, and tried to convince and rally the people around her toward her communist-LGBTI+ political agenda. As I came to know her better over time, I could see what might have upset her about the struggle in Ülker Street. Not every trans woman would have taken the Ülker Street struggle as politically motivated and as seriously as did Sedef, and many must have stopped wanting to risk their lives in the face of police violence. That some trans women preferred to leave, or had to leave, left Sedef with a sense of betrayal.

When I asked her about the meaning of Ülker Street for her, she explained that the trans community had experienced Cihangir as a place that embraced *lubunya* existence, referring to a spatial intimacy. After Ülker Street, *lubunya* have never again attained such spatial connectedness as a community. The place that had once operated as a "safe zone," providing a source of empowerment and representing a sense of community, instead became a source of vulnerability, fear, and anxiety for those who survived the police violence and stayed in the neighborhood. The sense of safety had largely derived from the number of *lubunyalar* living and working in close physical proximity with one another; the spatial togetherness conditioned the formation of a sense of community, which simultaneously produced a sense of place for the community. In other words, the Ülker Street experience showed the workings of space as a medium to cultivate a sense of community and an alternative world; it showed trans women's use of spatially bound practices to make a place of their own in this world. Sedef's complaint indicated that trans women lacked the freedom to choose where to live that others enjoyed. Hence, a sense of "placelessness" was prevalent, or they saw Beyoğlu as an intimate space, as the only place of belonging and homemaking, which was key for Sedef and many other trans women while defining their relationship to Istanbul in general.

Years later, Ülker Street remains a central spatial, political, and communal reference in trans people's lives. There are friendships that grew stronger from this experience and others that fell apart. Ülker Street has come to symbolize how morality, sexuality, sex/gender, capital, violence, and intimacy are interwoven for the simultaneous production of a transgender place and a sense of community in urban geography. Environmental studies scholar Gordon Brent Ingram defines community as, in large part, "a reflection of the level of repression and unequal distribution in resources and access to them."[56] *Lubunyalar* created an enclave and emplaced themselves in Cihangir as a historical outcome of a chain of displacements and the unequal distribution of space in Beyoğlu and Istanbul (indeed Turkey) generally. This was trans world-making. Their intricate and tangled relationship with the city space became a condition for the tight and intimate networks they developed, for their group formation and empowerment. *Lubunyalar* were able to politically mobilize around their claims to Ülker Street, even to the extent of gaining the strength to resist the security forces of the state.

Some scholars of geography stress that the claiming of urban spaces and appropriation of them as visible, distinct neighborhoods requires not only residential concentration and the development of a network of voluntary and service organizations but also the material control of residential and business property.[57] Recall Sedef's use of the word *seize*. In the case of Ülker Street, however, although some of the trans women owned properties as residents, it was unable to provide them with spatial security. Spatial security was strictly tied to the intertwinement of property with the majority social norm, with "properly" sexed and gendered, moral bodies. For this reason, while trans women owned some of the Ülker Street properties, they would still have remained vulnerable to the imposition of the will of the dominant.

Although *lubunyalar* remember their time in Cihangir before police violence as the golden age of their collective history, they also draw lessons from what they could and could not achieve as a trans community during that period. For example, Sevda, who lived with Sedef in Cihangir for years, summarized the pros and cons of the spatial concentration of the community as follows:

> We used to call that area "Lubunistan" or "Ibneistan." I saw those streets as a ghetto. Cihangir was the first LGBT ghetto to me. Maybe the first real one! It was perfect in terms of the communal dynamic. Yet it was a step back with respect to our integration into society because all our friends were trans people. Our role models were all trans as well. Our community was antisocial and introverted. This way, we became more exposed to hate crimes. Hortum arrived, broke down our doors, invaded, and burned them down. Despite everything, now we have acquired some places in Kurtuluş and Pangaltı [districts neighboring Beyoğlu; see map 1.1].

Sevda's account reveals another dimension to the relationship among sexuality, sex/gender transgression, place, and community, a dimension that contradicts the frequently repeated story of Ülker Street as the good old "safe zone." The literature on queer space suggests that designated safe spaces for queer people might also become targeted spaces for queer bashing.[58] Sevda's words tell a similar story in emphasizing how Ülker Street as a trans enclave shaped their experience of violence by rendering them spatially vulnerable to persecution by multiple groups. The very conditions of spatial empowerment simultaneously functioned as the source of their vulnerability and weakness, making Ülker Street a destination for social actors who wanted to attack and displace trans women. Hence, in some situations, the dynamics of safety and vulnerability may operate in a dialectical relationship, shaping the production of places as well as the subjects who inhabit those places.

With the displacement of trans people from Ülker Street, the bohemian elite has gradually formed the new profile of Cihangir. Small art galleries, cafes, and restaurants have sprung up, and rents have gone up. Trans women have been dispersed across several neighborhoods, diminishing their spatial strength as a community concentrated in particular streets. When it comes to trans women's residential practices, present-day spatial relations take more flexible, mobile, fluid, and individualized forms. This results in a sense of placelessness as a community, but this placelessness should not be understood as "place's opposite" but rather "as an embodied experience or practice that *is* or *does* anything."[59] Placelessness is not just a negative, an absence, or a lack; it also stands for something positive, related to plasticity and, shorn of the restrictions of place, unlimited possibility. Thus, it is true that compared to the years in Ülker Street, the strong sense of trans community has dissolved, leading the majority of trans people either to live by themselves or to share an apartment with one, two, or more roommates. But it is also important to be attentive to what trans people have done with their placelessness and to how they have mobilized themselves to create new spatial possibilities, expanding their trans geography to different sites and spots.

One example of this new mobilization is their making of the spaces of "communality without community," that is, the "constellation of strategic sites for sexual minorities, with various associated behaviours, forms of contacts, and alliances across the landscape."[60] Displacement from Cihangir might have deeply shattered the spatial conditions of a strong community, but it has also spawned conditions for spatial intimacies, practices of emplacement in the form of scattered sites of communality across the Beyoğlu area. *Lubunyalar* have developed communal spaces by collectively making and inhabiting places for survival, politics, and social gatherings loosely connected across but not specifically contained in a wider urban environment. Istanbul LGBTT, for example, is one example of such spatial dynamics. In concluding this chapter, I will further elaborate on Istanbul LGBTT's spatial significance and meaning for trans people, but first I provide a more comprehensive portrayal of the reasons behind trans people's current dispersed, mobile, and fluid spatial conditions.

The Situation in the Early 2010s

The gentrification and urban renewal projects in Istanbul began in the 1990s with a few districts, including Cihangir, and reached a previously unseen scale and speed with the implementation of new urban transformation projects during the 2000s. The renovation of existing buildings via these projects combined with the construction of gated communities for professionals and the well-to-do. New housing projects for the new middle class built on state-owned (or requisitioned) land by the Toplu Konut İdaresi Başkanlığı (TOKI; Mass Housing Administration) and new shopping malls have become the defining markers of the new neoliberal era.[61] The massive state actor TOKI was first founded in 1984 to address the housing problems of low-income groups by promoting the construction of housing cooperatives with cheap loans; it also distributed pretitle deeds to the *gecekondu* (squatter housing) owners, who were promised title deeds upon upgrading their dwellings.[62] This promise led many *gecekondu* owners to construct low-quality apartment blocks to rent out for profit. As more *gecekondu* owners invested in the rental economy, tensions resulted between state agents and *gecekondu* owners, resulting in changes to the TOKI policies. Then the *gecekondu* owners were targeted as the "invaders" of the city who needed to be displaced.[63]

Concurrently, the decade-long integration into the global world economy brought new approaches to economic development by prioritizing city investments in the tourism sector and promoting historical heritage. Hence, the poor urban dwellers residing in the inner-city historical districts of Istanbul became the next target population for displacement in the bid to renew and develop the urban landscape—and TOKI became an efficient agent in realizing such goals. With the establishment of the AKP government following the 2002 general election, TOKI began, in fact, to operate as a privatization agency with the appearance of a public enterprise. Enacting new laws and amending existing ones, the AKP government paved the way for the burgeoning of TOKI contractors/subcontractors and pressured the organization to increase its construction capacity to the maximum over short periods of time (using, e.g., strict time-limit penalty codes).

The capital of TOKI comprises public places and other real estate properties. Since 2002 it has administered the appropriation of these properties from other state agencies and their sale, transforming a majority of them into higher-end housing and shopping malls, especially in Istanbul.[64] The present era thus represents the transformation of the inner city into a main source of capital accumulation, whereas the urban development projects of the mid-1980s were merely oriented toward expanding the city limits by transforming squatter settlements.[65] With this new era, capital has begun to transform areas that are proximate to historical zones and business centers in the name of urban renewal projects.[66] Some of these areas were inner-city squatting zones inhabited by socially, economically, and culturally disadvantaged and/or marginalized groups, as was the case with Cihangir, and the properties started to change hands rapidly, displacing the former residents of the area.[67]

Spreading to all the historical neighborhoods of the city, this urban trend began to appear to politicians, government officers, and policy makers as a magic bullet: "It helps to avoid earthquakes, reduces crime, decreases segregation, removes stigma, decreases poor living conditions and even combats terrorism!"[68] Geographer Neil Smith analyzes the present situation as a particular kind of uneven development, one within which gentrification vis-à-vis suburbanization stands as "internal differentiation of already developed spaces."[69] Istanbul in general and Galata and Tarlabaşı in particular lie at the heart of this uneven development through their recent transformation into, and thus spatial production of, neighborhoods in high demand among young consumers and the elite social groups of the city and international tourists.

However, as we have seen from the aforementioned stories of displacement, the processes of spatial production, transformation and development are also stories of class, ethnicity, sexuality, sex, and gender. For example, the impoverished Kurdish and Roma inhabitants of Beyoğlu are two groups targeted by policies of displacement, spatial exclusion, and marginalization, programs that not only result from but also, in fact, impel and direct these urban transformation projects. Some groups can no longer afford to live in their former neighborhoods; others become targets due to their illicit behaviors and/or nonconforming gender identities and sexual practices.

Trans women's residence in Beyoğlu has hugely decreased, as much from the police pressure and violence since the 2000s as from the skyrocketing rents accompanying the capitalization of the area through urban transformation projects. Consequently, trans women have been pushed into looking for places to live at the edges of the Beyoğlu area, in Kurtuluş, Dolapdere, and Pangaltı, to name a few.[70] Ironically, perhaps, now that the location of the marginal has been taken for the dominant, the marginal are displaced to its margins. However, trans women still spend most of their time in Beyoğlu, for various reasons.

First, trans women who are also sex workers have their established networks and places to find clients in Beyoğlu; second, with its relatively tolerant sexual culture, Beyoğlu embraces different bodies, sexualities, and genders that face severe discrimination and exclusion in other parts of the city; third, Istanbul LGBTT was in Beyoğlu until 2019; and, fourth, the area still feels like a "real" home for some *lubunyalar*, as they have articulated. The presence of this place has been essential to the reproduction of a sense of trans communality, since it was one of the few permanent places where trans people could meet and spend time together without fear of the consequences or other pressure from the outside world. And notwithstanding the series of displacements in their history, trans people succeeded in establishing a form of emplacement by founding Istanbul LGBTT and creating an intimate space of proximity with and for one another. The lost physical proximity from the Ülker Street times was partially re-created and to a certain extent compensated for by the institution of a new space enabling trans people to gather together in the "safe zone" of Istanbul LGBTT. This was not the intense and ghettoized, bounded space of residence/work that developed in Ülker Street but rather a networking space defined by a core place that residence/work gravitated around and interacted with.

Istanbul LGBTT was located in a tiny room on the top floor of an old, dilapidated building on a side street parallel to Istiklal, the popular and crowded main street of Beyoğlu. At the time, the side street was packed with small restaurants and bars mostly frequented by university students, corner stores, coffee houses, cheap hotels, and billiard spots. There was no sign of Istanbul LGBTT unless someone lifted their head and saw a rainbow flag waving out of a window of the gray five-story building. The building looked crammed between the others on the street. The smell of paint thinner in its dark and damp entrance was overwhelming, would hit one in the face. The odor came from the cobbler on the second floor.

On the first floor, there was a tea maker who served the store owners and workers in the neighborhood. He had an eight-year-old daughter, Ceylan, who worked for him. Once in a while, when we ran out of tea at the center, *gacılar* would order tea from this tea maker, and he would usually send his daughter to bring tea for us. I remember being impressed by the tea maker's lack of prejudice with regard to having his daughter interact with trans women, as usually people would behave otherwise, trying to "protect" their children from such interactions. The *gacılar* were very affectionate to Ceylan, a rather shy and sweet girl. Back in 2013, the organization had started a project, Trans*Evi (Trans*Home), an alternative retirement home for elderly trans women with little means that would provide them with safety and shelter.[71] The apartment was a rental unit located in Beyoğlu and could accommodate only five to six people. It survived with European funds and individual donations from 2013 to 2019. In its last few years, Trans*Evi sheltered mainly trans refugees from North African and Middle Eastern regions. Due to financial hardship and threats of eviction, it was difficult to relocate, and eventually the project ended a few months after the closing of Istanbul LGBTT in 2019.

Until recently, trans women sex workers still held one small trans-majority residential location in Beyoğlu, two buildings on one small side road, Bayram Street. Parallel to the now-demolished Abanoz Street, Bayram Street was one of the city's oldest brothel streets. The two brothels accommodated approximately twenty trans women, who both lived and worked there. In 2020 the Beyoğlu police station used the COVID-19 pandemic measures as an excuse to raid these houses and take eighteen trans women into custody. The police banned public access to Bayram Street by taping off its entry and exit and announced that they would seal these houses soon, eventually shutting them down.[72] This left many trans women homeless upon their release from jail. They had to seek shelter through their personal relations.

Other than this microarea, trans women have not been concentrated in one specific part in Beyoğlu since the mid-2010s. Despite no longer residing in the district center, however, they constantly navigated the Beyoğlu streets, thus reaffirming their spatial attachment with Beyoğlu through their very mobility. Meanwhile, they tried to avoid the everyday violence, as exemplified here by Nalan:

> I was walking in Tarlabaşı, talking on my cell phone. I heard someone calling me, "Psst! Psst!" but I didn't dare to look. Lots of people verbally assault us that way. So I thought it was one of them.... I kept walking . . . but in a sec, two policemen showed up standing next to me!! . . . I saw them holding batons over my head and getting ready to hit me. And then they started threatening me: "Don't walk here! Go to the side alley and walk there." I couldn't even utter a word and rushed into one of the backstreets. I am glad that I didn't say a single word to them. Otherwise I could've easily found myself in the hospital.

This suggests a final note on the limits and possibilities of sex/gender-transgressive publicity. Trans women sex workers were told by the police to work in the side alleys to find their clients rather than on main streets. As long as they remained invisible, the police might not bother them. However, interviews with trans women showed contrasting results after police warnings. There were incidents when the police caught trans women soliciting in side alleys and fined them for blocking the traffic on a main street. This ticketing practice restricted and shaped trans women's and sex workers' mobility in the urban environment during the 2010s. Trans women faced the constant risk of being ticketed by police when they went out, and those with lower incomes especially avoided certain areas of the city, including Beyoğlu. This way of using space punished the public presence of trans women, trapping many of them in the immediate area around their residences. In the next chapter, I focus on this mechanism of monetary punishment to explore forms of extralegal violence and surveillance practices targeting sex/gender transgression.

Chapter Two

Extralegality, Surveillance, & Police Violence

MELIS STORMED INTO ISTANBUL LGBTT cursing and shouting at a volume one would not expect from her slender body. We stopped chatting and turned our attention to what she was saying: the police had a new strategy; they were penalizing trans women just for being outdoors. Melis was fuming after being issued yet another ticket, pushing her total that year into the double digits. "I was just standing in the street, not even soliciting!" she angrily protested.

The other *gacılar* in the room joined her in cursing the police and complaining about how the police had gone out of control lately. They were fining trans women at every corner on Istiklal Street regardless of whether the women were involved in an illicit sexual exchange. *Gacılar* had been receiving tickets from the police while they were walking, shopping, running errands, taking a cab—in other words, when going out in public and participating in everyday, mundane activities. Each ticket was a fine of sixty-nine Turkish liras, and trans women gradually accumulated debt that sometimes reached thousands of liras.[1]

This ticket system began in 2009, representing a shift away from brute force in the exercise of state power against trans people. In fact, this shift corresponded to a period when the AKP came to power and claimed to be transitioning to a new era of democracy and transparency through a policy of "zero tolerance" toward torture beginning in 2003. During the 1980s and 1990s, state violence in Turkey had shown its extreme face to leftist and marginalized sections of society, including trans people, as demonstrated in the previous chapter. The violence inflicted on trans people had included long-term custody and torture, kidnapping, expulsion from certain neighborhoods, and transportation to other cities, as well as public humiliation in the form of forced haircuts on the street.[2] While the arrival of the 2000s saw an end to this specific kind of cruelty, trans women witnessed new forms of attack, such as police fines or judicial harassment.

Thus, the AKP government largely replaced excessive use of police force with other strategies of state oppression and abuse of trans people's civil rights. The standardization of the police force and the increase in its technical capacity through EU-sponsored projects altered the way the state exercised hegemonic control.[3] The state monopoly on violence is applied to the same ends but in a way that is legally enshrined by quantitively multiplying its repertoire of security and penal resources. The emphasis on professionalization and efficiency has increased with the introduction of new technologies and strategies in the police force. As sociologist Zeynep Gönen argues, the restructuring of the police is in fact "both a shift and continuity in the Turkish state's authoritarian regulatory arrangements since the 1980s."[4] The police, as a central element in the sustenance of state sovereignty, still continued to function according to an authoritarian logic that did not necessarily manifest itself in overtly violent forms until the Gezi protests in 2013 but rather disguised itself in the discourse of law and order. In post-Gezi Turkey, the police have resumed using physical violence and torture alongside new technologies and strategies of securitization.

The police have a complicated relationship with the law. The incomplete and contradictory character of the law allows for an extralegal space within which police officers might blend the legal with the illegal, blurring the assumed boundaries between the two.[5] This chapter examines this space of extralegality by centering trans women's narratives of their past and present experiences of violence with the Beyoğlu police over the past forty years. I deploy the concept of extralegality to discuss the sexual and gendered repertoire of security and the penal resources of the police, which, most of the time, occupy an ambiguous zone between the legal and the illegal, or represent "the intersections of the il/legal."[6] An examination of the changing relations (forms of conduct and contact) between the police and trans people—the disciplinary, regulatory, and punitive practices of the police regarding trans women's lives, bodies, and sexual practices—helps us understand how sex/gender transgression, particularly transness, has constantly been a key extralegal site for the state to produce, enact, shape, and reinvent its regime of security through varying configurations of violence. Specifically, I examine how the state in the form of the police establishes distinct forms of transitions and collaborations between sovereign and governmental forms of violence to control and regulate nonconforming sexualities and genders, and how this process features the extralegal character of the police, which can become intimate from time to time. The decades-long surveillance of transness, and hence the securitization of cisheteronormative public life, shows how the police reproduce and reinvent extralegality as constitutive of its formation. Extralegality is manifested both overtly and covertly as torture, blacklists, criminalization, and practices of targeting that turn trans people into hypervisible figures of public life.

Hypervisibility is closely related to the formation and deployment of the category of transgender in specific ways. For instance, in the context of US security regimes, gender studies scholar Toby Beauchamp illustrates the partial production of the categories and figures of sex/gender transgression through the everyday surveillance and security practices of the police.[7] Yet, as much as surveillance produces, regulates, and contests the category of transgender, this category is also a material and symbolic lived reality for trans people.[8] They contest these categories as much as they dispute the extralegal practices of police surveillance and securitization.[9] Trans people may be victimized by police violence at times, but they are not passive victims, and they act on the conditions of their marginalization.

Violence should not be reduced to some essential core concept or fixed definition and seen only as destructive.[10] Just as it deconstructs, violence also reconstructs social relations, group subjectivities, individual lives, and specific survival practices. Hence, the following pages show how police violence, in the forms of torture, surveillance, stop-and-search tactics, ticketing, and so on, also elicits material practices, spatial tactics, and narrative strategies through which trans women deploy their creativity and imagination to survive and thrive. By constantly and productively negotiating the process of surveillance and securitization, trans women oblige the police to introduce new legal and extralegal strategies to control and regulate, and hence, these trans women shape the police itself. In fact, violence, as a social and cultural relation, conditions and transforms the praxis of law and the domain of extralegality into a process that is mutually shaped and coformed by trans people and the police. Not only police officers but also trans people contest the fuzzy boundary between legal and illegal through their responses to surveillance and security technologies. A focus on trans women's oral history accounts and narratives of police violence demonstrate how life is shaped by changing forms of violence, surveillance, and securitization. At the same time, these oral histories are a creative, resilient, and imaginative endeavor that constructs communal intimacies through the work of collective memory and political agency.

Securitization and the Police in Turkey

The present national security state in Turkey owes its consolidation to the coup on September 12, 1980. The Turkish police, which has played a key role in securitization since the 1970s, gained a more authoritarian and militarized character with the expansion of its capacities during the military rule of 1980–83.[11] The police used both legal and extralegal techniques not only to suppress political dissent and activity but also to terrorize everyday life. Among these techniques, *işkence* (torture) was the most widespread one that marked that era with extreme state violence and brutality.

The term *işkence* is loaded and has a long history in Turkey. Research on torture in contemporary Turkey demonstrates that the police have been the primary perpetrators, while police departments, police stations, and prisons constitute the central places of torture. A repertoire of violent acts may constitute torture, most commonly beating, killing, pressuring, shocking, undressing, raping with batons or sexual organs, sexually harassing, injuring physically, cutting the skin or organs, Palestinian hanging, and bastinadoing.[12]

Historically, the two main target groups, regularly and frequently announced as "terrorists" and thus considered to be deserving of torture, have been leftists and Kurds—those who have fought for and/or supported the independence of a Kurdish state since the 1980s, either by taking up arms or by providing the guerrillas with some sort of logistical support (funds, food, shelter, etc.), or else by writing about and promoting the idea of liberation for Kurds. The acceleration of the war between the Turkish state and the Partiya Karkarên Kurdistan (PKK; Kurdistan Workers' Party) in the 1990s greatly restructured the police, increasing its power and technological capacity. Especially in the Kurdish region, where the state declared a state of emergency (Olağanüstü Hâl) between 1987 and 2002, as Gönen argues, "[the police force] was equipped with new powers, material resources and ideological and political support."[13] Portraying the Kurdish guerrilla resistance as a national security problem, the state further militarized the police in its "war on terror," increasing its regulatory force in social life via legal and extralegal violence, including enforced disappearances, torture, and abuse.[14]

Thus, far from being exceptional, extralegal force and violence are fundamental to the institution of the police.[15] In "Critique of Violence," critical theorist Walter Benjamin famously theorizes the dual character of the police as both a lawmaking and a law-preserving institution.[16] The police occupy a quasi-autonomous and flexible status in relation to law. They intervene frequently in situations where public security is allegedly at stake and where a legal ambiguity or issue in need of clarification is present, thus acting as de facto lawmakers. The police can legitimate the use of extralegal violence as a means to its ends. Or the police can legitimate illegal ends through the legal character of the means. For example, the disappearance or torture of people in police custody or the receipt of bribes can be considered as the employment of illegality in the service of legality. This shuttling between the legal and the illegal is also at hand when police officers in Istanbul arbitrarily stop and search trans women and sex workers on the street or remove them from public places if they are perceived as posing a "threat" to public order. Depending on various social factors (i.e., race, class status, sexual and gender identity, etc.), the alleged "threat" can be defined quite flexibly, endowing police officers with a range of possible actions. In short, the police can simply interpret, manipulate, and act beyond the law each time they enforce the law. The duality of lawmaking and law preserving might manifest itself differently under legal reforms and gain novel appearances, which is the story of the police in Turkey since the 2000s.

In the early 2000s, the institution of the police started facing various challenges to its violent operations as a result of Turkey's attempts to join the EU. The EU required major transformations in the national security regime in accordance with human rights, accountability, transparency, and democratization. When the AKP government came to power in 2002, their antitorture discourse was represented by the slogan "zero tolerance for torture" (*işkenceye sıfır tolerans*). In her work, anthropologist Elif Babül shows how the General Directory of Security initiated the AKP's agenda of police reform in an attempt to professionalize the police force as security experts who were respectable, predictable, and efficient agents in a rational bureaucratic machinery.[17] However, rather than eliminating violence, these reforms led to "the standardization of the police force" by introducing appropriate technologies and tools that promoted a "proportional" use of force.[18] This in turn has resulted in the professionalization of police violence and has refashioned the police as "force experts," a novel formulation that, as anthropologist Hayal Akarsu argues, has "in fact enabled police in Turkey to redefine and ultimately reclaim [instead of deny or hide, as they mostly did in the 1990s] the violence they are professionalized in."[19] In other words, the language of torture has been replaced by the use of force.

This does not mean that torture, abuse, and extralegal violence have disappeared from the police repertoire. Instead, these have gained a novel linguistic and technical currency through the reframing of torture as disproportionate use of force, which is still illegal and bound by law. But, as Akarsu highlights, "unlike torture, disproportionate force is open to contestation, technical calculation, and deliberation, if the officer knows well how to proportion their force according to the resistance they face."[20] This is, in fact, how the police force has justified its accelerated use of violence in the face of any form of active resistance since the Gezi protests, while increasingly reimplementing the 1990s strategies of torture and violence at the same time, especially since 2015 (see preface).

But what is the role of sex/gender transgression in shaping this period of intensified securitization and changing forms of police violence? What do the particularities of trans lives reveal about the organization of police violence and its relation to law, securitization, moral order, and the hegemonic regime of gender and sexuality? Most studies on the police and its transformation in Turkey do not address sexual and sex/gender transgression with the exception of Evren Savcı's recently published book *Queer in Translation*. Savcı shows how trans sex workers have always constituted a key target group for increased securitization in Turkey through the logic of terror, which rendered its subjects as criminal and monstrous. The mainstream news media coverage of the 1990s extended the notion of terror to trans sex workers and portrayed them predominantly as monstrous, dangerous, criminal, and irrationally violent figures of *travesti terörü* (transvestite terror).[21] During this period Ülker Street was under constant police attack and surveillance, and *lubunyalar* demonstrated a remarkable resistance against the forced displacement from their neighborhoods and homes. To illustrate the violent intimacies between the police and trans people, I now turn to trans women's experiences and narrations from this period.

Extralegal Repertoire of the Police in the 1980s

The core group of trans women I spent my fieldwork with had fought against the *lubunya* displacement from Ülker Street. They had lived through raids, deportations, beatings, and abasement in police custody. Almost every single day, when we sat around the table in the small room of Istanbul LGBTT for hours, drinking tea, chatting and smoking, narratives of violence from the 1990s were a popular topic of conversation. Referring to these violent practices as *polis işkencesi* (police torture), *lubunyalar* over and over again recounted days filled with extreme police violence. During the most intense period of state violence in the 1980s and 1990s, *gacılar* were certainly exposed to many of the aforementioned practices of police brutality and torture. Especially in the 1980s, the police deployed witch hunts as a widespread violent tactic, raiding homes, workplaces, shopping areas, and streets to forcefully take trans women into custody. Trans women were harassed, undressed, beaten, and sexually abused while in custody. Photographing them, shaving their heads, and taking their fingerprints and blood samples were other forms of bodily violation that took place in police stations. After their time in custody, the police forced some of them onto trains and exiled them to Eskişehir, a provincial town in Turkey.

Same-sex sexuality and transness are not illegal according to the Turkish Penal Code of 1926. However, the state has periodically amended the Polis Vazife ve Selahiyet Kanunu (Law on Police Duties and Power) of 1934 and strategically instrumentalized it to punish sexual and gender transgression. For instance, in June 1985, the state modified Article 11 to expand the police power against "persons whose behavior is against morality and public customs."[22] Even though the clause does not mention anything about same-sex sexuality, the then minister of the interior, Yıldırım Akbulut, noted in a parliamentary debate, "The new law ... empowers us to arrest people suspected of homosexuality for a term of twenty-four hours. ... We have to be tough against persons who have such perverted thoughts and tendencies. The number of such persons increases daily. They became [*sic*] the cancer of society. ... We therefore shall introduce measures against these people everywhere, but especially in the big cities."[23]

Amid the increasing police violence against gays and trans people, three salient events marked the 1980s. First, in 1986 then prime minister Turgut Özal, who would later play a major role in the legal endorsement of ID changes for trans people (see chapter 3), applied for full membership in the EU, which some people later considered beneficial for the LGBTI+

struggle. Second, that same year Arslan Yüzgün, an economist, published *Türkiye'de Eşcinsellik* (Homosexuality in Turkey), a book based exclusively on interviews and surveys with *lubunyalar* and suggested that there were one million *eşcinseller* (homosexuals) solely in Istanbul and two million across Turkey. The book was categorized as harmful to youth and sold in sealed plastic bags, the packaging style used for pornographic magazines. Yüzgün later published *Mavi Hüviyetli Kadınlar* (Women with blue ID cards), a book of short stories inspired by the everyday troubles of trans women in Turkey. Yüzgün also joined several international meetings on LGBTI+ issues abroad and acted as a spokesperson for gays' and trans women's problems in Turkey. His main goal was to politicize these issues. While the mainstream media denounced Yüzgün and his work, some alternative journals, such as *Nokta* (Period) and *Yeni Gündem* (New Agenda), presented gayness as an existential issue or a lifestyle, contributing to the emergence of a popular public discourse on *eşcinsellik* (homosexuality).

Third, in 1987 *lubunyalar* took the first steps to formally politicize their problems and played a significant part in establishing the Radikal Demokrat Yeşil Parti (Turkish Green Radical Democratic Party), which brought together feminists, gays and trans women, antimilitarists, environmentalists, and atheists under the leadership of Ibrahim Eren in Istanbul. On April 29, 1987, with the support of the party, a group of *lubunya* started a hunger strike to protest the incessant police brutality and torture. The next day, the group decided to move their protest to a public place and occupied the steps in Gezi Park (see figure 2.1). However, the police dispersed them by resorting to violence. The hunger strike then continued for a few weeks in houses, yet it remained marginal and received little support from a larger group of gays and trans people (see figure 2.2). It eventually ended without solid achievements.[24]

The Intimate Sovereign in the House: The Reign of Hortum Süleyman

Violence against trans people reached its peak during the tenure of Hortum Süleyman (Süleyman the Hose) as the head of the Beyoğlu Police Department (1992–97).[25] Hortum Süleyman's real name was Süleyman Ulusoy. Trans women described him as one of the most horrifying police figures because of his unique techniques for torturing detained people. His "hose" epithet derived from his use of hoses to punish and beat trans

Eşcinseller dağıtıldı

POLİS baskısını protesto etmek amacıyla önceki gün açlık grevine başlayan eşcinseller, Taksim Meydanı'nda polisin müdahalesi üzerine eylemlerine son verdiler. Özellikle akşam saatlerinde yol kenarlarında beklerken, polisçe karakollara götürülen eşcinseller, "Baskıdan bıktık" diyerek, açlık grevini başlatmışlardı. Açlık grevlerini sürdürmek üzere dün sabah da Taksim Parkı'nın merdivenlerine ellerinde gül ve karanfillerle oturan eşcinseller, "Polisin kötü davranışlarından vazgeçmesi için ölene kadar aç kalmaya razıyız" dediler. Eylemlerini zafer işaretleri yaparak sürdüren eşcinseller, çevredekilerin de büyük ilgisini topladılar. Ancak, daha sonra Taksim Parkı'na gelen polisler, eşcinsellere eylemlerinin yasadışı olduğunu söyleyerek, dağılmaları için uyarıda bulundu. Polisin kendilerine karşı çıkılması halinde grevcileri zorla dağıtacağını belirtmesi üzerine de eşcinseller, Taksim'den ayrıldılar. Eşcinseller, açlık grevini evlerinde sürdürebileceklerini söylediler.

2.1   Gay and trans hunger strikers on the steps of Gezi Park. The headline translates as "Homosexuals Are Dispersed." *Milliyet*, May 1, 1987. Courtesy of the *Milliyet* newspaper archive.

women. Once in his custody, a trans woman was liable to be showered in cold water and then beaten with a hose. One story describes his office as housing a collection of hoses in different colors and sizes, and when people were taken into custody, he would ask them which one they would like to be beaten with. The "battle" for Cihangir and the *lubunya* displacement from Ülker Street took place during his tenure.

In the early 1990s, prior to his appointment at the Beyoğlu Police Station, Süleyman had been in charge of the Kurdish region. During this period, state violence against the Kurds reached an extreme, with hundreds of unidentified murders and enforced disappearances. Thus, when Hortum Süleyman came to the Beyoğlu Police Station, he already had a reputation for advanced techniques of violence and torture against the Kurds. Some of the *lubunyalar* recall him as the cruelest and most violent police figure:

2.2 Gays and trans people on hunger strike together. The headline translates as
"Protest by Homosexuals." *Milliyet*, May 5, 1987. Courtesy of the *Milliyet* newspaper
archive.

Three of us were driving at night. Suddenly, we heard the police car
calling out our license plate and telling us to pull over. After the ID
check, we were put in the police car without being given any information. They took us to the police station and made us wait in the hall-
way. We were hoping we wouldn't meet or be questioned by that awful
person. But not long after, we heard his voice roaring with frustration,
and then we saw his huge belly and sputtering mouth. He was standing
with his famous toy [the hose] before us: Hortum Süleyman! He was
shouting as much as talking: "You faggots, who's had it cut off?" One
of us had had the surgery. They put her in the women's holding cell,
and calling us "men," they transferred us to the men's cell. After two
days, they released us. Of course there was a "farewell party." We were
thirty or thirty-five trans women, lined up like a welcoming committee.
Hortum Süleyman appeared right in front of us again with his toy in
his hands. After he made sure that everybody had had their share of his
"treat," the farewell party was over. Normally, parties end with people
having foot pain [after long hours of dancing], but our parties always
ended with us having headaches and painful hips.

Lubunyalar told me plenty of stories about Hortum Süleyman and his
violent reign. He appeared as an extremely familiar, intimate figure of mon-

strosity and cruelty in trans women's narratives of violence in the 1990s. Despite the years that had gone by, *lubunyalar* could still provide vivid portrayals of him, referring to his "huge belly," "evil face," "buggy eyes," "reproving voice," and "always sullen and jittery face." The continual violent contact with Süleyman left its traces embedded in *lubunya* memories and words and established among trans women an intimacy of violence that was still palpable, even after decades. Frequent narration of these stories also mediated a sense of communal intimacy through a shared experience of a violent past. With the suspension of law in the dark corners of the police stations, *lubunyalar* faced many years of the naked brutality of Süleyman. Calling on the police's institutionalized state power but deploying extralegal means, Süleyman's police used torture in custody as a violent tool to reorder, tame, and reform the state's gendered and sexual others.

Remember Begoña Aretxaga's argument on the formation of "terrifying forms of intimacy" under state rule. She draws attention to "the intensification of bodies and intimacies that result from [the state's] technologies of management."[26] It is possible to translate Aretxaga's assertion into the intimacy established between the police and trans women in the form of an intensely felt proximity constructed and manifested by physical violence. This intimacy was conditioned not only by the torture and physical violence trans women endured during their detention but also by the porosity between what is private and what is public, especially in the case of police raids on their houses. The home, ostensibly private and intimate, lost such status when it came to the raids on trans women sex workers.

The state's sovereign power did not function only in police offices. Trans people's lives outside the police station were overwhelmed by Süleyman's and his crew's efforts to establish their sovereignty over trans women's houses and bodies. The police smashed doors, broke security chains, and destroyed telephone landlines during the raids; some *lubunyalar* recounted that the walls in their houses were destroyed. In one of our conversations, Ceyda revealed further vivid details about the extralegal practices of the police:

> They knocked on our doors. According to the law, they had to show us a search warrant to search our houses. We know the legal codes, we're not dumb! We used to open the door, and they would say, "Let's go to the police station. Somebody filed a complaint about you." And we never caused trouble when they took us to the station. But they used to

take us in without a single piece of evidence. They beat us with hoses, they poured water on us. There were hoses in different colors, blue, red, yellow. Those hoses also had cables inside. They would wet them and beat us with them.

A trans woman friend of Sedef, Zeren, did something extraordinary during one of her many spells of detention and torture by the police. In the past, especially in the years following the September 12 coup, trans women were commonly remanded into custody for a week to ten days. Rebelling against her incarceration, Zeren cut off her penis and threw it in Süleyman's face from behind the bars. According to Sedef, Zeren could not take it anymore. She was crazy enough to do such a thing. Like those of some of the *lubunyalar* in the room, my face changed with shock and repulsion on hearing this story. Others who already knew the story started laughing and bragging about Zeren, as Sedef continued to provide more details about how the holding cell was awash in blood. Zeren was immediately hospitalized, therefore managing to leave her cell. This story of violence revealed another dimension of this "terrifying intimacy" between persecutor and persecuted self-harm.

After recovering from visualizing this story, I asked for a more detailed account of how Zeren had managed to sneak a sharp object into her cell. Like Süleyman's notorious collection of hoses, this story may be apocryphal, as I did not receive a convincing account of the sharp object from any of the *lubunyalar*. Regardless of its veracity, however, such stories do some powerful symbolic work of resisting the ways state violence operated in relation to the sexed/gendered body. In this case, Zeren transformed her body into a resource that allowed her to exit her cell. Bringing together the most "public" and "private," or the most exposed and hidden body parts— the face and the sexual organs, respectively—this story is rich in meaning.

Cutting off her penis and fragmenting her body surface, Zeren broke with the official gender norm of her sexed body as constituted by the dominant regimes of truth and signification. By throwing her penis at Süleyman's face, she transformed her body into the condition and possibility of transgression that stained and parodied the face of the police in its administration of the gendered and sexual regime. Even if Zeren's story was an invention, the circulation of this rumor among *lubunyalar* still functioned to discursively render the police defaced and desecrated. In fact, it functioned thus *especially* as rumor. As anthropologist Allen Feldman indicates, rumor mediates what can happen within given formations of disarray and therein produces a countersociety.[27] The result is a "social production of collective experience in the absence of wide-scale social credibility."[28] Zeren's story was perfectly comprehensible—and perhaps more believable—as the projection of a desired act against the police.

Zeren's story was a kind of "counterspectacle," resisting the violence of sovereign power. The police made a spectacle of discipline and punishment, and the subject made a counterspectacle of her own body, disfiguring and brutalizing it by severing the penis, of course, but also displaying the power to do so. Thus, on one level she humiliated the sovereign in its own castle and thus, temporarily at least, claimed the state's space by spraying blood, but at the same time, she also made an individual claim to sovereignty over her own body and thus reclaimed it from the capture of the state's sovereign power, literally as well as figuratively. A self-deployed violence directed at her own body became the condition of her resistance to the state and its sexual/gendered logic and hence the condition of reestablishing both her individual value in a state-defined space of no value—an unregulated jail—and also her individual sovereignty of and over her body.

Last, as much as it was dreadful, Zeren's story also conveyed a sense of humor because *lubunyalar* would regularly narrate it as part of *güllüm* moments, and this recurrent narration would mock the police terror yet, at the same time, transmit its horrors. Through humor and rumor, *lubunyalar* would achieve a sense of resistance, subversion, and suspension by laughing at what violated, injured, and damaged them. The structures of power would be reversed momentarily. This reversal allowed for a fleeting time of fugitivity through the medium of mockery, jokes, and laughter.

The Hospital: An Extralegal Police Station

Extralegality in trans women's everyday life might also correspond to an alliance between different state actors. After being released from the police station, trans women were often transferred directly to the hospital Cancan for a medical examination. Remember that *Cancan* is a colloquial name for the Istanbul Dermal and Venereal Diseases Hospital, which provided medical services until 2009 (see chapter 1). Although it was a public hospital, the doctors in Cancan treated only registered and unregistered sex workers, and non-sex-worker women either avoided visiting this hospital or were not allowed to enter past the official gatekeepers without special permission from the governor's office. The Turkish code on prostitution obliges registered sex workers to visit this hospital twice a week; otherwise, the police have the right to bring them to the hospital by force. The situation of unregistered sex workers is a bit different: usually the police bring them to the hospital after raids on their houses and workspaces.[29]

During Hortum Süleyman's tenure, this hospital collaborated with the police and carried out extralegal practices per Süleyman's instructions. Usually, the police would arrange hospital transfers right before the weekend. This meant that *lubunyalar* had to wait until Monday for their examination and thus would have to remain in the hospital from Friday to Monday. The doctors would use small scars or pimples as an excuse to detain them in the hospital longer than necessary. Recounting one of the times when she was transported to the hospital by the police, Melis verified this with a similar anecdote:

> The chief police officer at the time turned to the hospital staff and said, "They should sleep on top of each other in the hospital. They can sleep in rooms or the hospital garden, I don't give a shit! You shouldn't let them out of the hospital for fifteen to twenty days. Once they go out, they should be ill. If they are not diseased and they are healthy, you should give them an injection, you should make them faint. You should make them ill!"
>
> They gave me one of those injections that they give to mad people. They would make me go crazy. One day, I reacted, "I don't have syphilis!" ... They made scars on my hands. ... I was completely fine. The doctor didn't want to let me go: "You should stay, you shouldn't go! The chief doesn't want you out!" When I finally managed to get out, the same police officer brought me back again. We were tortured every single minute. ... All our houses, our clubs were being raided. We had to go out on the highways [to look for clients]. We ended up working anywhere. I worked on the highways for five or six years. I got into an accident. A car crashed into me. While I was trying to escape from the police, a car ran me over. ... I've spent my life running away. This world, this life has been overwhelmed with police violence. Always the police ...

The collaboration between the police and medical actors demonstrates how extralegal violence systematically disperses, as well as quarantines, trans bodies and lives through the mediation of governmental techniques. In the case of injections given to trans women's bodies, the application of biopower was individuated: human biology became the domain for a literal injection of control and discipline. With the collaboration of security forces and medical authorities, the police violence took extreme sovereign forms by first imprisoning and then occupying (entering) trans women's bodies. I tried to gather more information on the institutional practice of injection, but Melis could not provide me with further details, changing the subject with, again, "Because of all this, I spent my whole life running away."

Standardization and Professionalization: The Era of Hüseyin Çapkın

During the 2000s, and particularly during Celalettin Cerrah's tenure as the head of the Istanbul police (2003–9), trans women experienced a significant reduction in the terrorizing police violence and harassment. The raids on houses continued, but less frequently than before, and beatings also became less common. Gizem, a woman of thirty-nine, recounted of the Celalettin Cerrah period: "Cerrah's times were looser in terms of police control. The police would raid and then go. There were specific days. . . . For example, once a month or every two months, the police would make visits to certain areas for inspection. On those days, we would not go out to solicit. Now we work under the threat of internment every day! Before we used to be taken into custody maybe every three weeks or every two months, whatever, but now you're being jailed every day!"

The increased "efficiency" in police surveillance and control of transgressive sexualities and genders started with the appointment of Hüseyin Çapkın as the head of the Istanbul police in 2009. His tenure instituted a new reign of police discipline and control, and new attempts to displace and disappear trans people from public life. However, the strategies introduced to achieve these objectives were profoundly different and brought new negotiations with law and novel computations of legal and extralegal practice. Physical violence, torture, and terror were no longer the principal tools of state power. Instead, Çapkın promoted the use of law as a punitive strategy of securitization by tracking, profiling, and fining trans women; charging them with crimes; and taking them into custody within the limits of the law, for shorter intervals yet far more frequently.

Some of my interlocutors denied that the police's techniques had changed that much. For example, Ceyda refused to see torture as something that belonged to the past. Rather, she spoke of its present-day, diffused forms in the trans everyday and drew attention to how legal authorities and practices utilized torture in a newly governed fashion:

Torture has always been around! It only changes form and color now and then. Sometimes it goes up, sometimes down. It takes different forms like physical violence, curses, and insults. And sometimes during the police raids, they register us as "pimps," or as illegal brothel owners, even though we bring our clients to those houses as sex workers, not as pimps or owners of the house. If the prosecutor has some problem or other, then he orders to keep us imprisoned until the first court appearance comes up. They don't bother to prove the alleged crime. Their order is enough to jail us! This is also violence. . . . After the first court appearance, you can prove yourself a sex worker and not a pimp with your friends' testimonies, but you still stay in jail until your release. That's the problem! I have friends who stayed in prison from three to forty days. They got released after the first court appearance, but the cases went on for a year or two.

In our conversations, Hortum Süleyman and Hüseyin Çapkın appeared as two major figures in the shared consciousness of the trans everyday, alike in their extraordinary efforts to dominate and, when necessary, displace and erase trans people from social life. Their different approaches nevertheless deployed mostly correlating practices and strategies; juxtaposing the two thus reveals how the Beyoğlu police force incorporated evolving technologies of violence to surveil, govern, and discipline. Despite the alteration in its forms, police violence always operated according to a consistently cisheteronormative and patriarchal logic that utilized a range of both legal and extralegal means involving commitment to and employment of objectifying oppression and the consistent and widespread abuse of human rights in order to track, profile, supervise, control, and regulate sexual behavior and sex/gender transgression.

Comparisons between present and past experiences of police violence were a popular topic of conversation in our meetings, though *lubunya* references to the past and specific experiences with the police depended on their age. Notwithstanding their different views on the matter, when it came to certain aspects of the police's attitude, every single trans woman agreed that there had been a pivotal change in the police use of power against trans women. Even though present-day police violence is less physically intimate and painful and less psychologically terrorizing and brutalizing, *lubunyalar* still complained bitterly about it, referring to the unchanged punitive logic it relied on and reproduced.

During our conversations I was struck by the insightful analysis behind casual comments about the shift in police violence. Gamze's words exemplify this with her emphasis on the development of novel forms of violence, such as the "ideological," linked especially with the AKP government: "From the late 1990s to 2002, the situation was not that bad! There was violence from time to time. Yet with the AKP government—this is very crucial to note—an intellectual reaction against LGBTT people started. You know, when Hortum Süleyman beat trans people with hoses, his acts were perhaps more shaped by patriarchy at large, perhaps his hidden sexual feelings, or maybe his personal homophobic hatred. But the current actors do ideological violence. This is really important! We have a thesis. For the first time, the government counters us with an antithesis."

Gamze's "thesis vs. antithesis" statement speaks to the public production and circulation of official discourses about "homosexuality" by AKP government actors in response to LGBTI+ campaigns about hate crimes and human rights. I turn to this point later on, but first I want to discuss her focus on ideological violence, a significant theme that provides a productive trope identifying what has changed since the AKP government came to power in 2002. The regulations, practices, and discourses of the present 2022 AKP government can be interpreted through an ideological lense as a mode of expressing the newly introduced techniques of power during its term.

As anthropologist Eric Wolf suggestes, ideologies are "programs for the deployment of power" and "suggest unified schemes or configurations developed to underwrite or manifest power."[30] They are systemic and are infused into the lives of their subjects at many levels. Philosopher Louis Althusser's influential essay, "Ideology and Ideological State Apparatuses," shows the extent of this infusion by highlighting the ideological apparatuses of the state and their role in subject formation.[31] The ideological state apparatus (educational, religious, legal, military, and political institutions; the family; the media; etc.) works by interpellating, or "hailing," individuals as socialized subjects, transforming them into subjects of ideology through repeated discourses and ritualized practices. Philosopher Slavoj Žižek refers to this process as the internalization of "the symbolic machine of ideology."[32] Within this, a change of government may become crucial, insofar as it involves an alteration in the collective mindset of those who hold these ideological state apparatuses and, hence, the material and discursive resources of the state. The ideological experience is malleable.

In countries with heavily politicized bureaucracies (civil service sectors) and a relatively strong centralization of civil power in the executive, like Turkey, each change in political administration tends to bring with it the introduction and establishment of the governing party's cadre in public offices. The appointment of a range of new figures to key public positions—such as the heads of police, schools, and universities as well as governorships—is usually the first step once electoral power changes. Naturally, such a system of patronage works even more effectively when the elected party succeeds in forming a single-party, majority government and, moreover, when it achieves this over successive terms in office, which was exactly what the AKP did.

With the power in Parliament to pass legislation at will and to further determine public policy through its administrative appointments, the AKP introduced a raft of material, discursive, and symbolic transformations in various domains of institutional practice that directly impact daily life, including the judiciary, security forces, and education and healthcare. These changes claimed to be replacing the long-standing oppressive and discriminatory state structure with a more democratic and transparent one. In fact, they endorsed the organization of institutional and noninstitutional life alike according to a socially conservative ideology shaped by the values of Islam. The republic's history of social engineering, from forced population movements to nationalist citizen production, was continued in accordance with these new ideological norms and values.

As part of this ideological rectification, the government sought to restructure the Turkish state into an actual "state of law," the context in which the "zero tolerance for torture" discourse was introduced.[33] This disguised how violence was incorporated into the everyday lives of social actors, especially via the legal system. Since the basic approach to the hegemonic gender normativity did not change, its instrumentalization through state agencies such as the police remained fundamentally unaffected. Hence, Gamze's phrases "intellectual reaction" and "ideological violence" referred, on one level, to the change in the official discourse and exercise of violence: the replacement of simple, brutalizing, and sometimes barbaric forms of physical violence by the police with more technical, calculated, and subtle forms. Yet the manifestation of ideological violence operated at other levels also.

In 2009–10, Selma Aliye Kavaf, then head of the Ministry of Women and Family (now the Ministry of Family and Social Services), released several statements about LGBTI+ people, denouncing "homosexuality" as a sickness. A discursive space developed as certain columnists, known to be strong supporters of the government (see chapter 5), followed suit and opined similarly. It was possible to interpret this discursive space as a product of several social, cultural, and religious factors; the most significant, however, was the decade-long heightened visibility of LGBTI+ activism in Turkey.[34] Gamze's emphasis on the dialectical relationship between the current government and LGBTI+ people, that is, in her words, the "thesis" and "antithesis," should be understood within this discursive context.

The government was faced with the obligation to develop an official discourse on transgressive sexualities and genders, an "antithesis," in response to the LGBTI+ "thesis"—their political claims to human rights and equality. In other words, the government unintentionally helped LGBTI+ people force the state to develop a language on queer issues according to the state's own ideological demands. Thus, the discourse of legality and practice of law, not overt forms of physical violence, had begun to characterize the relationship between state institutions and actors, on one hand, and the LGBTI+ community, on the other, until the Gezi protests. A synthesis had emerged in which the LGBTI+ community enjoyed significant agency.

Nevertheless, law and the legal system—seemingly independently—were manipulated toward different ends, paving the way for the exercise of subtler forms of governmental violence. In the hands of the police, the law was instrumentalized to render individuals as subjects of ideology. In the police's call of "Hey, you there!" trans people recognized themselves instantly as the addressee. In this routine drama of everyday state oppression, it is also crucial to stress the police's selective and differential economy of stopping and searching. As Sara Ahmed argues, "Some bodies more than others are 'stopped' as the subject of the policeman's address.... The 'hey you' ... [is addressed to] the body that cannot be recruited, to the body that is 'out of place' in this place. In other words, the 'unrecruitable' body must still be 'recruited' into this place, in part through the very repetition of the action of 'being stopped' as a mode of address."[35]

In the next section, I focus on this stop-and-search strategy of the police, namely, the bonus system, to analyze how the police deploy extralegal means to produce categories of sexual/gender transgression and exercise violence as a technology of gender and sexuality production, "recruiting" trans women's "unrecruitable" bodies into the system. Through this process the police amplify public visibility for trans women and turn them into hypervisible figures in the punitive sexual and gender economy of street patrols. As several scholars have remarked, hypervisibility has a certain logic that causes more material, institutional, and symbolic violence: while predominantly solidifying mainstream (and harmful) representations of transness and hence leading to heightened surveillance, at the same time, "the logic of hypervisibility" paradoxically renders trans women invisible or unrepresentable as social beings.[36] Trans people become "not recognizable as complex, legitimate, participatory subjects or citizens."[37] But in the section to follow, I also demonstrate how trans people cope with this hypervisibility and develop resilient mechanisms in the face of police surveillance, compelling the police to invent new, subtler forms of violence (and thus further detailing Gamze's point about the dialectical thesis-antithesis relationship). In other words, they are not only subject to the police's extralegal means but also play an essential role in shaping and challenging the extralegal economy of surveillance and securitization.

The Bonus System

Toward the end of 2011, a police document was leaked on social media and went viral. This document was divided into three columns: "the name of the crime," "points," and "in case of arrest." It laid out eighteen different categories of crime, assigning each of them a specific number of "points" (see figure 2.3). These were the bonus points that a police officer would receive if they captured the associated criminal type (with further bonuses available for multiple arrests on the same day).

At the top of the list were "Molotov cocktail and terror-related incidents," which brought the maximum of 1,500 points to the police officer, 500 points more than for the next categories, a broad spectrum of standard categories, namely, homicide, kidnapping, mugging, and various types of theft (including house and car). After this slightly strange (and politicized) start—equating car theft with murder, which was itself rated as less serious than throwing a Molotov cocktail—the list continued in more predictable fashion with items related to holding a gun, drugs, and assault. Lower on the list, between obstructing a police officer and substance addiction, there appeared two new categories of criminals, *travesti* (transvestite) and *bilinen bayan* (the known lady).[38] They were worth 10–20 points for the ticketing officer.

The head of the Beyoğlu police, Hüseyin Çapkın, initiated this bonus system in 2009 to provide police officers with a new means of recompense, in the form of pay, leave, and promotions. Officers collected points based on their performance, as measured by the type and number of "criminals" caught.[39] Clearly, this mechanism was grounded in increasing police efficiency by distributing performance-based rewards. For example, accumulating a thousand points per week was sufficient to receive a vacation or financial bonus.

Regardless of exactly how this bonus system operated, it was clearly intended to be motivational, aiming especially at preventing certain types of crimes and promoting the arrests of certain types of criminals—or preventing particular sex business activities and sex/gender-transgressive possibilities. During my fieldwork I became aware of this bonus system as almost every one of my trans women friends was ticketed. The tickets themselves, as written documents, authenticated the police's recently developed punitive practice, yet there was no public information about its grounding categories, other than the leaked document. This document at least solved the mystery of the upsurge in arrests and revealed the logic behind the recent practices of police violence. Now let's focus on the importance of documents themselves.

The social life of documents warrants the attention of critical research. For example, it is important to investigate the kinds of social and political relationships that are made possible by and mediated through the production and circulation of documents. Documents, as anthropologist Tobias Kelly urges us, should be not be viewed "as abstract entities, but must be understood in the wider institutional and political context in which they are produced, verified, and take effect."[40] This is clearly also the case for official documents; the relationship between the state and documents is also noteworthy.

Anthropological scholarship on bureaucracy has developed a particular interest in studying documents as the state's material culture.[41] As anthropologist Yael Navaro points out, documents are one of "the primary paraphernalia of modern states and legal systems," and ethnographic research on documents provides analytic insights into the logic of administrative control and shows the kinds of subjects, objects, and socialities that documents construct.[42] An analysis of state policies and laws focusing on documentary practices also allows us to examine the institutionalization of sexuality, "state-sexuality" or "the state-sexuality nexus."[43] From this perspective on documentary practices, the documents produced invite discussion of the specifics of contemporary relations between the police and trans people.

In my conversations with trans women, they noted that they were worth 20 bonus points, while glue sniffers (*tinerciler*) and drug dealers brought in only 5 and 10 points, respectively. That was how they explained the then

ÖNLEYİCİ HİZMETLER BÜRO AMİRLİKLERİ PUAN CETVELİ

S.N.	SUÇ ADI		PUANI	TUTUKLANIRSA
1	MOLOTOF-TERÖR OLAYLARI		1.500	
2	CİNAYET		1.000	
3	GASP		1.000	1250
4	KAPKAÇ		1.000	1250
5	HIRSIZLIK	Evden	1.000	1250
		İş Yerinden	1.000	1250
		Oto	1.000	1250
		Otodan	1.000	1250
		Resmi Kurum	1.000	1250
		Çalıntı Motor	200	
		Tescilsiz Motor	30	
		Yankesicilik	50	
		Dolandırıcılık	50	
		Açıktan Hırsızlık	30	
6	SİLAH	Ruhsatsız	250	
		Ruhsatlı/Bulundurma	50	
		Kurusıkıdan Bozma	50	
		Kurusıkı	10	
		Av Tüfeği	50	
7	NARKOTİK(Faili Elde)		100	
	NARKOTİK(Faili Elde Olmayan)		10	
8	YARALAMA	Yaralama Faili	50	
9	ARANAN ŞAHIS	Parmak İzi Tespitli Aranan	250	500
		Aranan Şahıs	20	100
10	SAHTE KİMLİK		250	500
11	MEMURA MUKAVEMET(Hedef Kitle)		20	
12	TRAVESTİ		10 - 20	
13	BİLİNEN BAYAN		10 - 20	
14	MADDE BAĞIMLISI		10	
15	TERK OTO		5	
16	İZRAR		5	
17	KABAHATLER KANUNU		2	
18	KARAYOLLARI ÜZERİNDE SATICILIK YAPAN(Mendil Satan, Cam Silen Vb. Şahıslar)		15	

NOT:	1- Yukarıdaki puanlar failler ekipler tarafından alındığında verilecektir.
	2- 1 günde birden fazla aranan şahıs tutanağı olan ekiplere; Birinci aranan şahıs tutanağı=20 İkinci aranan şahıs tutanağı=30 Üçüncü aranan şahıs tutanağı=40 puan gibi 10 puan artırılarak verilecektir.
	3- 1 günde birden fazla NARKOTİK şahıs tutanağı olan ekiplere; Birinci NARKOTİK tutanağı=100 İkinci NARKOTİK tutanağı=150 Üçüncü NARKOTİK tutanağı=200 puan gibi 50 puan artırılarak verilecektir.
	4- Buluntu Narkotik dışında Ticarilerden alınan her icraate 2 katı puan verilecektir.

2.3 Police categories of crime and bonus points, circulated via social media, 2011.

recent increase in police stopping trans women in Istanbul and issuing tickets. On the other hand, *lubunyalar* were not even aware of the listing of *travesti* and *bilinen bayan*, which the police had apparently constructed as punishable identity categories. Certainly none had ever received a ticket that cited them for falling into either of these categories. But the categories patently authorized police officers to stop and investigate trans people along with sex workers at any time. What came across as an arbitrary practice for trans women was in fact an outcome of the standardization, and hence, the professionalization, of police violence. Both *travesti* and *bilinen bayan* were in fact absent in written law and were instead invented by the police as part of the recent reforms implemented in surveillance and security practices in urban life.

When it came to fines imposed on trans people, the police used two different laws: the Traffic Law and the Misdemeanor Law. The Traffic Law was used to sanction trans people when they were believed to be, or could be construed as, blocking traffic while bargaining with potential clients on the street; the Misdemeanor Law prohibited trans people from soliciting in public places, referred to violating public decency and thus "breaching the peace." The Misdemeanor Law went into effect at the end of March 2005 and outlines administrative sanctions for a range of publicly displayed misdemeanors, including disorderly conduct, begging, gambling, insobriety, uproar, causing a disturbance, occupation of public spaces, consumption of tobacco products, failure to present an ID card when asked, pollution of the environment, putting up of posters, and carrying a gun. Trans women were typically fined under Article 37, "disturbing others in the streets by selling goods or services." However, trans women who did not work in the sex trade were also booked for violating this article.

In one incident, for example, the police fined a trans woman under the Misdemeanor Law on the grounds that she was a "man walking in a female outfit" (kadın kılığında dolaşan erkek), which was also construed as contravening public decency. "Public decency" here refers to the hegemonic normative displays of gender roles and sexed bodies, particularly those of manhood and male sexual identity.

The police have not always followed a steady trajectory when applying the law; rather, the patterns and punishment categories have changed since the initial implementation of the bonus system. In this developing history, not only the police but also trans women shaped the praxis of law and extralegality, as Gizem reveals:

First, they used to fine trans women for being exhibitionists. Trans women were charged with exhibitionism, but nobody was actually sentenced because of that. They all beat the rap. Then they started to make me out as a pimp on the ticket, even though I was selling myself; I was working the street as *sermaye* (capital).[44] They would jail me, and I'd spend a month in prison. Now they've started ticketing us using the Traffic Laws. They thought they would be able to stop us this way. Girls started to carry tiny cams fitted into their key holders to record police malpractice, because they didn't block traffic or cause any problem for traffic safety. Now the police started not giving the girls their ticket receipts, which girls can make their payments through or use in court. And, in return, the girls started to call Gayrettepe 155 and say, "Sir, they didn't give me my receipt, I want my receipt." So now they give us the receipt whenever we ask.[45]

Each time the police came up with a new strategy to punish trans women, the women responded with countertactics and forced the police to search for new extralegal tools with which to exclude and marginalize trans women. Critical theorist Michel de Certeau argues that everyday life is full of a multitude of "tactics" that are developed in the face of "strategies," that is, disciplinary technologies or forced relationships set by institutions and power structures.[46] Even though people are "caught in the nets of 'discipline,'" they are caught in them with their "dispersed, tactical, and makeshift creativity."[47] Groups or individuals constantly manipulate relations and events that are set by strategies. From this perspective, the main goal of the police is to produce strategies that reproduce a normative public life from which certain people and lives are ejected, absented, or rendered invisible. In the case of trans women, the police tried to execute this plan by not giving them a copy of the ticket. Legally, one of the two ticket copies should be handed to the person fined, and the other is sent to the court. Nevertheless, many police officers avoided giving a copy to trans women. This way, the police precluded trans women from taking up the issue in court. Without a copy of the document, they could not dispute their penalty.

Since legal requirements are purposely not openly accessible, some trans women thought that they were exempted from the fine because they did not have a copy of the ticket. When they received their summons to appear in court, they were shocked to learn about their financial punishment. And because they lacked the copy, they were unable to make any claim against their recorded "crime." Moreover, when the fines for these tickets exceeded a certain value, the police could sue the trans women, thus ensuring that the state retrieved the unpaid fine. By keeping the second copy, the police facilitated the process of recording and following up on unpaid fines.

This was the latest plan that the police were deploying to further their main strategy during the period I was engaged in my main fieldwork. Trans people were anticipating that many trans women would be pressed to pay huge fines, which would eventually lead to their imprisonment when they could not.[48] However, each violent experience of and interaction with the police on the part of trans women was itself translated into a newly improved tactic. What impelled such tactical moves, however, was a much more immediate imperative: they were simply coping mechanisms to deal with the everydayness of extralegal violence. Istanbul LGBTT and the center for sex workers Kadın Kapısı (Women's Gate) started to educate their visitors and friends on legal issues and taught them to insist on getting their copy of the receipt whenever they were caught and forced by the police to sign a document on the street. During my fieldwork Kadın Kapısı started to work with a part-time lawyer, who would visit the center once a week to provide legal assistance and respond to sex workers' questions regarding the implementation of prostitution codes as well as police regarding violence in general. This legal assistance helped empower trans women before the law and dispute some of the fines in court.

Sevda was one of the main people who worked hard for this legal empowerment. She assessed the situation in an interview in 2010:

> There is not as much physical violence in police stations as in the past, but the present police take advantage of some gaps in the law. They ticket *gacılar*. We, as Kadın Kapısı, wrote numerous petitions. Due to these petitions, some of the charges against girls have been dropped. But now the police have started to not give a written notice to *gacılar* concerning their fines. They stop *gacılar* in the street, ask them for their IDs, and pretend that they are checking *gacılar*'s general record on the spot. In fact, they issue tickets, but they don't give the receipt. *Lubunyalar* are not even aware of being ticketed! Once these tickets reach a certain number, girls are put into prison since they didn't pay their fines. Many of our friends have been jailed this way. They are only nineteen to twenty years old, and they have criminal records. Their only misconduct—though it is not legally defined as such—is prostitution. . . . Doing sex work in itself is not a crime as long as one does it

by oneself. . . . One is found guilty for either establishing an organized prostitution network or having the status of a pimp and providing space for prostitution.

The gradual increase in fines to the state was not the sole problem. There were more substantial issues and motivations at stake behind the operation of this bonus system. First, as the police allegedly tried to prevent sex work on the street, they indirectly motivated trans women to do more sex work since most of them had no way other than prostitution to make money to pay their fines. In a way, we can talk about a paradoxically circular system: the more the police fined trans women (attempting to make them invisible or just punish them for not being invisible), the more trans women searched for ways to increase their share in sex work to stay free from debt to the state (thus became increasingly visible). This paradox once again speaks to "the logic of hypervisibility" that marks trans women as intensely visible as objects of police force and public gaze, while rendering them intensely invisible as ordinary subjects in everyday life.

Second, and more significantly, this legal regulation placed trans women in a difficult situation where they could no longer move freely in public. Their lives unfolded in a circular relationship among hypervisibility, criminalization, and subsequent punishment. Not only could they not easily do sex work on the street, but many of them were also afraid even to shop or walk in the neighborhood because of the punishment mechanisms that could be applied at any moment, without warning or reason.

Trans women told me about different instances when they were caught and fined by the police while taking a cab or shopping. During my time with the *gacılar*, I also heard rumors that police officers dug into trans women's purses to search for condoms. If a trans woman happened to be carrying more than one condom, she could be automatically suspected of sex work and get a ticket. Fines targeted their public presence regardless of whether or not they were sex workers, let alone actively on the job.

As discussed in chapter 1, what is at stake is the place of trans people in public. They had been pushed from the main streets to the side streets, and from the center (of Beyoğlu) to the periphery, both of which have historically been fluid but fixed spatial configurations. Now they were being physically, financially, and emotionally hounded out of the social sphere altogether as a matter of extralegal police force. Hence, there is a complicated and intricate tension between trans hypervisibility and invisibility, between an unwanted inclusion in the public (as abject figures) and an exclusion from the possibilities of full civic life. Visibility does not always bring empowerment or a respectful recognition to its subjects, and it can, on the contrary, remove the very possibilities of an ordinary life.[49] Trans visibility, while a claim in and to public life, at the same time invites unwanted attention, material violence, and more policing. Sevda gives a powerful account of the perils of such visibility:

> Natrans women have a chance to hide their identity as sex workers even when they are in striking clothes. When they say, "I am not working, I am not a sex worker," they can camouflage themselves successfully. But the police know that trans women have no economic choice but to do sex work. A trans woman can always be ticketed as an unlicensed sex worker, anytime. I know girls who got tickets from the police when they left their houses to buy some milk for breakfast in the early morning. Trans individuals have no way to be invisible. That is why, whenever they are visible in public life, they are seen as an easy target and ticketed by the police.

Police units tended to see all trans women in public as unlicensed sex workers or as legitimate targets for detention and verbal and physical assault. Merely having a sex/gender-transgressive appearance became a justification for police violence. Sedef made remarks similar to Sevda's when she compared being a trans woman to being an unlicensed *natrans* sex worker in the eyes of the police: "Natrans women get ticketed only when they solicit illegally in the street. They don't get tickets anywhere else. But trans women get tickets just because they are trans women, not because they are illegally prostituting in the street. They cannot hide what they are. I start to panic and use side alleys to hide from the police even when I am walking home. I haven't been working as a sex worker for years now, but still, in the street, I constantly watch out so as not to get caught by the police."

The motivation behind the extralegal punitive practice became clear when the document with its categories of *travesti* and *bilinen bayan* was leaked. Trans people saw the textual proof of what they had long suspected: just being a trans person (particularly a trans woman) was sufficient for police punishment. The police were straying far beyond their specific role of maintaining public security, thus creating a space for their own punitive (and remunerative) action and manipulation of existing law; in fact, they had gone further and taken it upon themselves to enact new crimes and new criminal categories.

The leaking of the details of the bonus system led to a reaction from some politicians. One member of Parliament, Melda Onur, from the main opposition party, the Cumhuriyet Halk Partisi (CHP; Republican People's Party) submitted a written question to the minister of the interior. Onur first requested verification of the existence of such a chart and the bonus system, apparently enforced by a six-hundred-strong special force established with the installment of Hüseyin Çapkın as head of the Istanbul police in 2010. Then, among other things, Onur requested an explanation of the categories of *travesti* and *bilinen bayan*, noting that "under the Law of the Turkish Republic and International Agreements being a transvestite/transsexual is not a crime." An official response was received, albeit several months later, written not by the minister of the interior but by the governor of Istanbul.[50]

The governor's reply broadly acknowledged the existence of the bonus system and stated that the points corresponded with types of crime and their concentration in individual districts. The ubiquity of certain crimes in particular neighborhoods led those crimes and criminals to be assigned the maximum number of points for the police officers in those areas. Every four months, the staff with the highest performance would be promoted to positions that demanded more active missions (although no clue was provided as to what an "active mission" might be), while officers with a lower performance would be redistributed to other positions deemed to be a better fit for their skills. In response to the category of *travesti*, the governor stated that trans people would face no investigation because of their "cinsel tercih" (sexual preference) but that a legal process would be instigated against people causing problems for traffic safety without regard to the person's trans identity or sexual preference.

The late response acknowledged and presented a rationale for the points system, but it provided no explanation for the creation of the *travesti* category, nor did it explain it with an accurate definition of sexual orientation, to which reference was made, thus essentially treating this as interchangeable with gender identity, which was not mentioned. When it came to the issue of the *travesti* category, the governor neither denied nor accepted it as an official crime/criminal type. He thus ascribed a ghostly status to police violence against trans women: the category of *travesti was not recognized in law* but could nonetheless be *deployed as the law* via its enforcement by the police.

By contrast, the governor's reply did offer a definition of *bilinen bayan* as a woman who jeopardizes traffic safety by indecently exposing her body on the street. The interpretation of "indecency"—what amount of exposure or which body part constitutes indecency—and the relative responsibility of a driver distracted by such indecency were unaddressed, thus leaving the definition still unclear (practically, to be determined in the absence of official guidelines by police action and sanctioned by court judgments). In fact, if the issue is soliciting on the street, the misdemeanor is not of primary importance; but if the issue is traffic safety, it is the soliciting in general that is relevant rather than the "indecency" in particular. As I argued elsewhere, exposed female body parts are rendered dangerous not because of traffic safety but as explicit displays of female sexuality in public.[51]

This particular category of *bilinen bayan* embeds a logic that marks active female sexuality and the unrestrained and improperly dressed female body as threatening to the general organization of public life. Public displays of femininity have been strictly tied to the historical process of nation-state making and its modernization projects (see the introduction), and it is impossible to think of this particular operation of the Misdemeanor Law as detached from this historical context. The same logic goes for the category of *travesti* in its functioning to regulate the bodily production of a public. As constructed by the police, both categories, *travesti* and *bilinen bayan*—materially realized in the form of the bonus system chart and their forcible production through tickets—were deployed to diminish and limit trans *and natrans* women sex workers' lives and bodily expressions. In turn, this shaped the moral, sexual, and gendered production of urban geography.

To address the fundamental issue of governance here, it is helpful to return to Benjamin's analysis of the police as the dual holder of lawmaking and law-preserving functions. The bonus system demonstrates the police's role as a lawmaker. They invented categories of *travesti* and *bilinen bayan*, when no such category was present in the existing legal framework, and then punished social actors according to these categories. The categories criminalized trans people and sex workers by declaring them misfits and deviants who pose a threat to the existing cisheteronormative order. At the same time, the institution of the police functioned as a law preserver, because the newly created categories served to preserve and continue the sexual and gender organization of the present social order, which is also inscribed in the existing legal order through a separate set of legal codes and norms (including civil law and the prostitution code). Stopping and ticketing was an effective, rational, and profitable extralegal strategy that pressed violently on the bodies of trans people, hence including them in public life as abject while excluding them from the possibilities of full civic life.

Yet trans people were not only "victims." They were actors in this extralegal economy of surveillance, securitization, and criminalization. They acted on the conditions of extralegal police violence and produced tactics that constantly challenged the police in their implementation of extralegal strategies. The production of tactics was a collective work of creativity and imagination and rapidly became communal knowledge, shared as part of everyday conversations and interactions. Shared accounts of police violence were repositories of "poisonous knowledge" whose circulation socialized trans people into historical consciousness about a violently intimate past with the police, raised awareness of the insidious and shifting character of police violence over decades, equipped trans people with necessary information on coping and resistance mechanisms, and, last but not least, mediated a sense of communal intimacy grounded in shared experiences of past and present violence.[52] Trans women's poisonous knowledge of the police was a form of violent intimacy that emerged out of the trans everyday through conversations and exchanges with each other.

Police violence shaped the conditions of trans women's lives. In its various but distinctly governmental (sometimes intimate) forms and modes, this violence affected their sense of selves and their bodies at all levels, from the most public domains to the most private. The relationship between the state and trans lives extended into other institutional spheres, including medicine and jurisprudence (as already indicated). The following chapters bring into focus how these institutional actors and practices are part of a nexus of law, intimacy, and violence. Together they form the state's power to regulate and control gender and sexual difference and transgression. The next chapter draws also on trans men's experiences with the juridical and medical domains in Turkey to delineate transsexuality's history as a medicolegal category as well as its contemporary deployment.

Chapter Three

Psychiatric Demarcations of Sex/Gender

IT WAS THE EIGHTEENTH ANNUAL PRIDE WEEK in Istanbul in 2010. I was sitting in a packed room, waiting for a panel to start. Titled "Transgender Body, Transition Process" and organized and hosted by Lambdaistanbul, it brought together two psychiatrists and one trans man. The audience were especially excited by the prospect of a conversation with these medical authorities, because trans people often struggle with the intricate medicolegal process governing GCS in Turkey, where the process includes a variety of surgical operations, such as genital surgery, breast enhancement or mastectomy, facial feminization or masculinization surgery, chondrolaryngoplasty (tracheal shaving), and voice surgery.[1] Trans people might fully or selectively benefit from these surgical resources depending on their embodied sense of gender. A psychiatric report is one part of the complicated and painstaking process that makes GCS legal and permissible for an individual. It comes after approximately two years of psychotherapy, and is compulsory for GCS, which was the only way for trans people to have their ID cards changed to blue or pink according to their reassigned sex. Even though the current ID cards are no longer colored, sex/gender are still reported categories, and hence, it is still important for many trans people to have their ID cards changed.

The psychiatrists on the panel had run some of these psychotherapy sessions and produced medical reports authorizing GCS. Among the panel's audience were people who had received medical reports from them. But as the panel and its subsequent Q&A session proceeded, I could observe a general disturbance among the audience, especially during the discussions around psychotherapy sessions, the rules about hormone intake, and the legal procedures concerning the gender confirmation process. A gap between trans people's understandings of their sex and gender transition and the doctors' approach to sex was evident, and widening, reflecting a larger problem that also informed the psychotherapy sessions. The questions of what sex, sexuality, and gender mean, and how gender confirmation should take place, had different answers depending on who was speaking: the psychiatrists or the trans people.

The proof and production of one's "true" sex/gender also involve other medical and legal actors. Medical certification functions as a prerequisite for producing legal scripts of one's sexual identity that are commensurate with one's sexual and gender identity. During the Q&A session, trans activists among the audience harshly criticized the medicolegal measures of the gender confirmation process for their strict reliance on particular notions of bodily time, gender identity, and the sexed body, as well as for how these notions led to rigorous criteria for evaluating trans people and their proof of their "true" sex. They also challenged these medicolegal frameworks for carrying specific temporal and bodily assumptions about gender transition, about being a woman or a man, and for punishing people unable to comply with such rules.

As noted previously, the production of "transsexuality" as a medicolegal category dates back to 1988 in Turkey. In 2002 the regulation of gender transition was amended; it now requires psychiatric observation during the transition period, putting trans people under strict institutional supervision and evaluating them in terms of their performance of gender roles. My point in this chapter concerns the proof of *transsexual nature*, a term used in the legal codes on transsexuality. Medical processes in general, and psychiatry in particular, are promoted as means to achieve this proof. To explore this, I have organized this chapter into two sections. First, it examines the scientific history of the contemporary regulation of sex/gender nonconformity and transness and situates these medicolegal models within a transnational framework of sexological and psychiatric knowledge production and circulation in Turkey. Focusing on the time since the mid-1970s, I show how scientific modalities that were produced in European (particularly British, German, and Swedish) medicolegal environments have shaped the scientific discussions and practices regarding trans people's bodies and sex/gender in Turkey. This scientific environment has functioned and still functions as "a central cultural site where meanings about gender and sexuality are being worked out."[2] Close attention to medical debates before and after the passage of legal regulations on "transsexuality" demonstrates how science has shaped an understanding of "true" sex and its evidential status in Turkey within a transnational flow of knowledge, practices, and bodies.

Second, placing the normalizing practice of psychotherapy at its center, this chapter illustrates the medical steps trans people must take to collect evidence of their "true" sex, and it shows how psychiatrists evaluated these steps. This psychiatric interaction constitutes an institutional environment for violent intimacies within which the most intimate aspects of a person (that is, their bodies, inner senses of the self, erotic and sexual desires, etc.) are dissected and assessed under the guidance of the norm, which from time to time functions as an institutionalized form of violence. Trans people revealed themselves as more than passive recipients or subjects of such medicolegal discourses and practices. They actively negotiated, interpreted, produced, and desired various configurations of sex, gender, and sexuality within a multiplicity of options, ranging from relatively normative configurations to new and radical imaginings. Sometimes what psychotherapists wanted for/of them overlapped with trans people's desires for, or imaginations of, the "properly" sexed/gendered body but was propelled by different aims and purposes. Hence, throughout, I also discuss those imaginings and configurations through a special focus on negotiations between doctors and trans people over conflicting meanings of bodily time, sex, gender, and sexuality. The psychiatric space of sex/gender confirmation allows for examining trans multiplicities and ruptures that emerge from institutional efforts to tame bodily time into a psychiatric timeline.

The Medical Context in the 1980s

Until 2017, the pink or blue color of the ID made gender the most immediately and obviously visible aspect of the card, signaling that the cisgender binary was foundational to the organization of the state. The information on the ID card included the person's name, birthplace and date, marital status, religion, and identification number as well as their parents' names.[3] Representing a citizenship agreement between the state and individuals, the ID card endowed people with civic, social, and political rights. Access to education, health care, marriage, and inheritance required having an ID card. The pink and blue IDs were a substantial political concern for trans people in their fight for their sex to be recognized by the state.

Until 1988, it was extremely difficult for trans people to change the color of their IDs because GCS was illegal except for intersex people. However, a small number of doctors would still discreetly practice GCS, specifically bottom and top surgery. One of these doctors, Ali Nihat Mındıkoğlu, became popular in 1981 because of a court case that concerned GCS and that preoccupied the public for a few years. Mındıkoğlu was a famous plastic surgeon at the Cerrahpaşa Medical School. He had completed a residency in plastic surgery in England after his medical training in Turkey. On his return to Turkey, he had performed numerous GCSs in multiple hospitals and private clinics in Istanbul, including the private Çapa Clinic, the Bulgarian Hospital, the French Hospital, and Ömür Clinic.[4]

Mındıkoğlu's medical experiences took shape at the convergence of media sensationalism and legal restrictions, capturing the risks that physicians took during this period when performing GCS. On October 25, 1981, *Günlerin Getirdiği* (Brought by the Days), a very popular sensational reality show produced by Uğur Dündar, initiated a long-lasting social and legal debate on GCS. The October 25 episode of the show was the first one released under the junta government. Previously, the show had been interrupted for a year by the 1980 coup. Dündar, then a highly influential journalist and anchor in the mainstream Turkish media, hosted "men who became women" (*kadın olan erkekler*) or "feminized men" (*kadınlaşan erkekler*) and aired sensationalist accounts of surgical experiences and "sex-change" operations. The show received widespread attention in mainstream newspapers, which encouraged parents to watch these stories with their children in order to teach them a lesson.[5] Dündar had produced this episode in collaboration with the Vice Unit of the Istanbul Police Department. The program also hosted "men of science" (*bilim adamları*) from legal and medical fields to share their expert opinions with the public. Mındıkoğlu was one of these medical experts. During the program, however, he was accused of practicing surgery without the prerequisite medical conditions, leading to unfavorable legal consequences. The allegations included surgery on minors under the age of eighteen. After the program, the prosecution office in Istanbul brought charges against him along with eleven trans women on whom he had performed surgery. According to Article 471 in the Turkish Penal Code at that time, these surgeries constituted a crime as they intervened in the patient's bodily integrity. The actual crime was not the reassignment of sex/gender but rather the performing of an operation that would deprive women and men of their reproductive capacities. It did not matter whether the patient had consented to the surgery.[6] Indeed, whether consensual or nonconsensual, sterilization constituted a crime. Based on this legal regulation, the court ordered the collection of evidence that would verify the fertility status of the defendant trans women prior to their GCS. Had they been fertile before GCS, the women could be imprisoned for six months to two years. Mındıkoğlu could receive up to twenty-two years in prison for operating on eleven trans women. [7] In response, a scientific committee was formed at Haydarpaşa Numune Hospital to examine the fertility status of these trans women before Mındıkoğlu's surgical procedures. Eventually the committee report proved all of the trans women to have been infertile before the surgeries, and all charges were dropped by March 18, 1987.

Dündar's reality show and the mainstream media coverage of the court case proliferated a popular scientific discourse on the medicolegal status of transgender surgery. Lawyers, doctors, artists, and laypeople gradually became more vocal, sharing a variety of opinions through a range of media channels. For example, the physician in chief at the French Hospital joined the conversation, claiming that he was the first doctor in Turkey to perform this operation, back in 1972, on a child who was diagnosed as "transseksüelist" as a result of a comprehensive medical committee report released at Şişli Children's Hospital.[8] He underlined that he denied GCS to people who lacked a similar medical report. Another chief physician, at the Bulgarian Hospital, noted that Mındıkoğlu performed such operations in their hospital in 1975, 1977, 1980, and 1981, but these were all attempts to fix unformed genital organs.[9] In fact, prior to 1988, there were several legal cases in which trans women appealed to the lower courts to change their sex on official records after they had had GCS either in Turkey or abroad. Despite the legal approval of those pleas by the lower courts, the Supreme Court rejected them all.[10] Consequently, "transsexuality" remained absent from Turkish law until 1988, when Bülent Ersoy, a famous trans woman singer, finally won her seven-year long legal struggle to change her ID card to female. The next section is on the scientific legislation of transsexuality through the lenses of Ersoy's story.

Striving for Legal Recognition: Bülent Ersoy's Story

Bülent Ersoy is a controversial celebrity among the larger LGBTI+ groups, as she has distanced herself from any political claims about trans people in Turkey. After her legal victory, she developed strong relations with government authorities, including prime ministers and presidents of Turkey. In

June 2016, when the month of Ramadan coincided with the Trans Pride March, the police harshly attacked LGBTI+ people in the street. On the same day, hours later, President Recep Tayyip Erdoğan and his wife invited Bülent Ersoy and a few other artists for iftar to break their fast. They dined together in a fancy Istanbul restaurant, posing together for the cameras with smiling faces, which attracted backlash from the LGBTI+ groups. The same person who had ordered the ban on the Pride March and the beating of protesters, was breaking his fast with a celebrity trans woman. In response, many LGBTI+ activists condemned Ersoy for her collaboration with Erdoğan and declared her to be a betrayer. Yet others interpreted these close interactions with state authorities as a survival tactic in an antitrans world. Regardless of her politics, Ersoy's remarkable struggle in the 1980s formed the legal foundations of transness in Turkey, and thus had transformed trans people's lives.

Ersoy entered the music scene in 1971 with a body assigned male at birth and quickly became famous. Nine years later, in 1980, she publicly identified as a woman with a desire for men. Owing to her countrywide celebrity, she attracted a high level of attention from mainstream Turkish media. The public was glued to the mainstream media's recurrent news about her body, behaviors, sexuality, and desires. By January 1981, under the prohibitions and restrictions introduced by the September 12, 1980, military government, the governor of Istanbul, Nevzat Ayaz, had banned *eşcinseller* (homosexuals) from performing on stage (see chapter 1). The category of *eşcinsel*, as in other countries and societies in the region, was rather ambiguous and inclusive, masking the distinctions between gay and transgender as we understand them today. As historian Afsaneh Najmabadi discusses in the Iranian context around the same time, "gayness" denoted a wide spectrum of nonconforming sexual and gendered desires, presentations, and performances that structured everyday practices of life.[11] In spite of Ersoy's public disidentification with homosexuality and insistence on her sex/gender identification as a straight woman, she was banned from performing on stage, as were many other sex/gender-nonconforming artists.

This ban included a few other trans women who already had pink IDs. For example, Serbülent Sultan, another famous performer and singer of the era, had actually received a pink ID in 1971 after she had GCS. Sultan was born in 1952 with an intersex body and had lived as a man until the age of nineteen. After completing her military service, she started to publicly identify as a woman and joined the underground musical scene, performing in various cities. When the ban took effect, she was considered homosexual, "a man in female outfits," and hence denied a space in the musical scene, despite her pink ID. To escape the military government's violent measures, she, like many others, fled the country and joined a transnational circuit of *lubunya* living in Germany and England.

Bülent Ersoy was also part of this circuit. After she and others were banned from performing, she fled to England for nine months. During her stay abroad, she performed onstage in several cities across Europe. She also had GCS at Charing Cross Hospital in London, a city that trans people regarded as the best place for GCS at the time due to its reputedly pioneering and well-educated plastic surgeons. Mındıkoğlu, after all, had spent his residency in London. During her nine months of self-imposed exile, Turkish national newspapers and magazines were obsessed with Ersoy, regularly reporting on her life and concerts abroad and consistently addressing her as *Bayan* Ersoy (Lady Ersoy), a gender identifier that was not often used for other women celebrities in news media (see figures 3.1–3.6). In her absence, the feature film *Şöhretin Sonu* (The end of fame) screened in Turkish cinemas for weeks. The movie starred Ersoy as herself and depicted the discrimination she experienced as a trans woman (see figure 3.7). When Ersoy returned to the country, the mainstream media met her arrival with great enthusiasm. She was presented as a woman and as a miracle of science. Public attention reached its peak, and everybody responded to the media's tempting call to judge, approve or disapprove, and comment on her body and female identity. One interview with a random woman on the streets of Istanbul includes perhaps one of the most interesting comments of this era: "My only hope is that she better take good advantage of womanhood rather than abuse it"—meaning she should behave like a modest, proper, and chaste woman and live up to the dominant feminine roles rather than display active female sexuality and improper feminine behaviors (see the introduction).[12]

However, although she had had GCS to accord with her sex/gender identity and no longer represented a source of "confusion" or an "enigma," Ersoy was still not allowed to perform as a singer. The mayor of Istanbul considered all trans people in Istanbul to be gay and banned their public performances. For the mayor, they were merely "gay men dressed up in female outfits," thus posing a notable threat to public order and moral life (see chapters 1 and 2). When Ersoy's lawyer objected to the prohibition given that she no longer had "a male body," this objection was denied on the basis that Ersoy was still a former *eşcinsel* who only became woman later on in "his" life. Having "fixed" her body was not enough; she had to have been born female.

Notwithstanding her GCS, the state would not yet recognize her as a female subject. In official records, she was still presented as a male subject without any official note or record of her female body or gender identity. Yet there were conflicting official decisions pertaining to her sex/gender identity. She was imprisoned for nineteen days in Kuşadası for physically attacking a journalist who harassed her. She was placed in the women's section in spite of her blue ID. The state, with all its institutions and practices, was in fact more fragmented and less uniform than it would be generally assumed by its subjects when it came to her sex/gender.[13]

Despite her continuous struggle to change her legal sex status to female, it took seven years for the state to recognize her as a woman and issue her a pink ID, which represented the ultimate indication of the state's recognition of her sex, as well as her body. In that sense, Bülent Ersoy is a key figure in trans people's history in Turkey, since she is the first trans woman who was not born with an intersex body yet who still could force the state to officially approve her sex as female. For seven years, she fought her case in courts and her case was constantly dismissed—four times, in fact—by the Supreme Court.[14] Since there was no legal precedent pertaining to trans people, these cases, in the end, went to the Supreme Court, and the authorities rejected Ersoy's case based on existing regulations that did not recognize any individual right to choose one's sex unless they were intersex. According to their judgment, the legal codes of the time provided no room for an "arbitrary" sex change, or for demands to change one's sex in official records following GCS.

Nonetheless, Ersoy did not give up and continued to pursue her case. She applied to the court for a fifth time to start a new case. Thereafter, she made statements indicating the level of pressure she felt to prove herself as a woman: "I am leading a corporally and spiritually proportional life. I am now a complete woman with everything. For four years, I have been going on with my life in an orderly and ladylike manner" (referring to the proper displays of dominant femininity—see the introduction).[15]

In the midst of her struggle, she even wrote to the prime minister to ask for legal recognition as a woman as well as for the abolishment of prohibitions on trans women's public performances. A few years after this letter, the repeal of interdictions in 1988 allowed "men in female outfits" to perform at clubs and entertainment places. The same year was also a landmark in trans women's lives as the court decided to grant Ersoy state-recognized status as

Resmen kadın olacağı günü heyecanla bekleyen Bülent Ersoy Londra'da değişik kadın giysileri denedi. Çeşitli renklerde Hint sarileri satın alan sanatçı daha kadın olmadan değme dişilere taş çıkartı ve erkeklerin hayranlığını kazandı.

Bülent Ersoy'un kadın olmasına iki gün kaldı

(Yazısı 13. Sayfada)

3.1
Bülent Ersoy posing in Indian sari dress and attracting attention from men in London. The headline translates as "Two Days Left until Bülent Ersoy Becomes a Woman." *Hürriyet*, April 12, 1981. Courtesy of the *Hürriyet* newspaper archive.

3.2
First picture taken after Bülent Ersoy's surgery. The headline translates as "Lady Bülent Ersoy Is Content with Her Life." *Hürriyet*, April 17, 1981. Courtesy of the *Hürriyet* newspaper archive.

AMELİYATTAN SONRA ÇEKTİRDİĞİ İLK RESİM

Londra'nın Charring Cross Hastanesi'nde salı günü geçirdiği ameliyattan sonra uzun süre baygın yatan Bülent Ersoy dün sıhhatine kavuştu ve ameliyat sonrasında ilk kez resim çektirdi. Yeşil sabahlığı içinde etrafına sürekli tebessümler yağduran Bülent Ersoy, odasında kendisiyle görüşen basın mensuplarına ne kadar mutlu olduğunu anlattı.

Bayan Bülent Ersoy hayatından memnun

● Salı günü geçirdiği ameliyatla kadın olan Ersoy dün ilk kez resim çektirdi ve etrafına gülücükler dağıttı.

● Doktorlar Ersoy'un sağlık durumunun çok iyi olduğunu serumların bile çıkarıldığını söylediler. (Yazısı 15. Sayfada)

3.3
Bülent Ersoy sits next to one of her nurses on her hospital bed and makes the victory sign. The headlines translate as "She Attained Her Desire after 29 Years. She Changed Her Sex after 3.5-Hour-Long Surgery . . . and Lady Bülent Ersoy." *Hürriyet*, April 15, 1981. Courtesy of the *Hürriyet* newspaper archive.

3.4
"Lady Bülent Ersoy Popped a Champagne to Toast Regaining Her Ability to Walk after Surgery." *Hürriyet*, April 21, 1981. Photo by Ali Ülgenalp. Courtesy of the *Hürriyet* newspaper archive.

Tüm hayatı tehlikesini göze alarak ameliyatla kadın olan Bülent Ersoy, dün kalmakta olduğu Londra'nın ünlü Charring Cross Hastanesi'nden taburcu oldu. Ameliyatını yapan doktoru Peter Philip tarafından son bir kontrolden geçirildikten sonra "Kadınlık raporu"nu alan Bayan Bülent Ersoy, güç günler geçirdiği hastaneden ayrılmadan önce Kur'an'ı öptü.

Bülent Ersoy kadınlık raporunu da aldı!...
(Yazısı 13. Sayfada)

3.5
Bülent Ersoy kisses the Qur'an before her discharge from Charing Cross Hospital. *Hürriyet*, April 24, 1981. Courtesy of the *Hürriyet* newspaper archive.

3.6
Bülent Ersoy's first postsurgery concert took place at the Festhalle in Frankfurt, Germany, as part of the "Sound of the Homeland" concert series organized by Turkish and Kurdish migrant laborers and their families in Germany. Other famous singers, such as İbrahim Tatlıses, Zerrin Özer, Erol Evgin, and Tülay Özer, were part of the concert. After Frankfurt they also gave concerts in Cologne, Munich, Berlin, and Rotterdam. The headlines translate as ". . . and Lady Ersoy Went on Stage." *Hürriyet*, May 25, 1981. Courtesy of the *Hürriyet* newspaper archive.

Londra'nın Charring Cross Hastanesi'nde başarılı bir ameliyatla rüyalarını gerçekleştiren Bülent Ersoy, dün ilk kez kadın olarak Frankfurt'ta sahneye çıktı. Frankfurt'ta dünkü konserine saçına bir gül iliştirilmiş olarak çıkan Bayan Bülent Ersoy, hayranlarının sevgi gösterilerine cevap verebilmek için uk uk konserini kesmek zorunda kaldı.

...Ve Bayan Ersoy sahneye çıktı

3.7   Advertisement for *Şöhretin Sonu* (1981) printed in the newspaper. The head-line translates as "The Erler Film Türker İnanoğlu [the company name] Presents the Spectacular Event of 1981. The Most Popular, the Most Sensational Artist of Recent Years: Bülent Ersoy. The End of Fame. 'Disgrace.'" The film was directed by Orhan Aksoy. *Hürriyet*, April 5, 1981. Courtesy of the *Hürriyet* newspaper archive.

female and thus, the pink ID. Her legal victory came under the one-party government of the Anavatan Partisi (the Motherland Party), which won the elections in 1983 following three years of military rule and introduced a neoliberal economic program in Turkey. Some authors argue that this neoliberal regime took advantage of Ersoy's case to promote itself as a new era of individual rights, freedom, and tolerance.[16]

As the *Milliyet* (Nationality) newspaper reported, the legal authorities resorted to a forensic report to reach their final verdict, and they were convinced by the forensic scientific testimony: "Bülent Ersoy has been leading a mature, peaceful, womanly life for seven years, and her situation is observed to be permanent and continuous."[17] The same newspaper published the court's decision: "The plaintiff is observed to be a complete woman with all the features of her appearance, manners, gestures, and voice." With this decision, Ersoy was recognized as a woman before the law and permitted to the right to a pink ID.[18]

The production and circulation of these official documents and signatures related to Bülent Ersoy's sexual identity is one example of "the incarnation of the state in written form" or its existence as "a spectral presence materialized in documents."[19] Through its "writing technology," its final signature, the state marked Ersoy's body as a female one and inscribed her into the domain of law.[20] This verdict led to the legal introduction of the first scientific regulations regarding transsexuality, regulations that were attached as a new article to the twenty-ninth clause of the Civil Code of 1926. The new article stated, "In cases where there has been a change of sex after birth documented by a report from a committee of medical experts, the necessary amendments are made to the birth certificate."[21] This made it possible for trans people to apply for a new ID after GCS. Subsequent to surgery, if a trans person could obtain a health report documenting the operation and its results, they could provide that report to the court and easily obtain a new pink or blue ID.

Cinsiyet Kargaşası (Sex/Gender Chaos)

A number of prominent law specialists have criticized the 1988 legal regulation for exceeding its intended results and creating contradictions in practice. The legal codes were compared to European countries' (especially Swedish and German) legal regulations on transsexuality. One noteworthy criticism was that this article created room for cinsiyet kargaşası (sex/gender chaos) by allowing anyone to be reassigned to a different sex.[22] As opposed to the Swedish and German codes on transsexuality, which required the petitioner to be unmarried and infertile in order to undergo GCS, the Turkish regulation, and by implication the state, did not mention marriage or reproductivity.[23] Problems resulted: for instance, when people changed their official sex, their marriage would automatically be annulled, as same-sex marriage was (and still is) illegal in Turkey. Moreover, according to Aydın Zevkliler, a law professor and well-known commentator on the issue, if a person was married and/or had children, this was itself proof of a person's nontranssexual identity, because that person had "succeeded" in forming an intimate relationship with the "opposite"-sex partner and reproduced using their sexual organs. This meant there was no fundamental problem with the viability of their sexual organs at birth. Furthermore, Zevkliler argued, gender confirmation would damage children's mental health as well as the family structure itself, which the state had vowed to protect via numerous laws.

These legal debates urged the state to iron out legal contradictions and ensure its politics of intimacy by protecting family life. They provided justifications for limiting sex changes to those diagnosed as "hermaphrodites," having both male- and female-assigned sexual organs simultaneously, and those whose anatomy contradicted their inner sense of sex such that they adopted the feelings, instincts, and behaviors of the opposite sex.[24] Zevkliler interpreted sex change as an anatomical necessity for the former group and as a "psikolojik, psikiyatrik, psikanalitik sendrom" (psychological, psychiatric, psychoanalytic syndrome) for the latter.[25] Alongside psychiatric evaluations, he also promoted the introduction of other medical experts, such as gynecologists, urologists, endocrinologists, and general surgeons, into the domain of transsexuality as professionals who could approve one's transsexual status.

Despite these discussions the article on transsexuality remained unaltered, and the GCS process was not strictly governed until a change of government in 2002. When the AKP came to power with a neoliberal-conservative one-party government, it brought several amendments to the legal system, including modifications to civil law (see the introduction). The earlier critiques of the sex transition law led to the proliferation of institutions charged with governing state-assigned sex/gender identity under the AKP government. Changes to the Clause 40 in the Civil Code put the gender confirmation process under rigorous medicolegal control and supervision, similar to the German and Swedish process.[26] The results of the aforementioned legal debates were integrated into a strictly regulated gender confirmation process:

A person who wants to change her or his sex has to apply to the court personally and ask for permission for a sex reassignment. For this permission to be given, the applicant must have completed the age of 18 and must be unmarried. Besides he or she must prove with an official health board report issued by an education and research hospital that he/she is of transsexual nature, that the gender confirmation is compulsory for her or his mental health and that he or she is permanently deprived of the capacity of reproduction.

If it is confirmed by an official health board report that a gender confirmation operation was effected based on the permission given and in accordance with the purpose and medical methods, the court will decide for the necessary changes to be made in the civil status register.[27]

Prior to 2002, trans people did not need an official report to have GCS, but now a comprehensive medical report became necessary, with particular attention to psychiatry and psychology. This report must prove that "sex change" is necessary for the person's mental health; with this report in hand, the individual appears in court to request permission to have the surgery. When the person appears in court, they should be unmarried, have no children, and be sterile.[28] After surgery the individual is required to receive a report stating that they have a "proper" penis or vagina, an issue that I elaborate on in the next chapter. With this report, the individual returns to court to complete the gender confirmation procedures and be issued their new ID. According to the former regulations, the court had no authority to decide on one's reassigned sex but rather functioned as a legal mechanism to confirm it; that has also changed.[29]

Gathering medical evidence of a person's transsexual identity and, in the end, medical guarantees of the "true" sex represented by pink or blue IDs is an arena in which the Turkish state actively—and most times forcibly—endeavors to reincorporate the trans body into the order of normality and to "materialize" sex "within the productive constraints of highly gendered regulatory schemas."[30] In this respect, we can talk about "the political uses of psychiatry" to affirm the proper production of the sexed/gendered citizen subject.[31] We know from Michel Foucault that the category of sex has had a normative function from the very beginning; in other words, it is regulatory.[32] In this respect, Judith Butler asserts, "'sex' not only functions as a norm, but is part of a regulatory practice that produces the bodies it governs, that is, whose regulatory force is made clear as a kind of productive power, the power to produce—demarcate, circulate, differentiate—the bodies it controls."[33] Given the vexed history of psychiatry and sex/gender nonconformity, here it is salient to underline the role of psychiatry in normalization and control. Psychiatry occupies a chief role in imposing state-sponsored sex/gender norms.

I now turn to detailing this process, illustrating the medical steps taken by trans people to provide evidence of their "true" sex and the ways the state's medical authorities, particularly psychiatrists, examine these steps during the transition. As will become clear, the medical certification functions as a prerequisite in legal scripts of one's sex/gender identity. Because medical authorities rely on particular understandings of gender in doing their work, they also influence the gender identity, and at times the sexual desire and practices, of the trans people they authorize.

Setting the Trans Body for the Medical Stage

The Turkish state insists—before, during, and after GCS—that trans people modify their bodies and explore ways to prove their "true" gender identity. This process involves many legal steps such as the provision of a *heyet raporu* (comprehensive health report), which authorizes trans people to have GCS. People can, of course, have these surgeries without an official permit; however, those operations are regarded as illegal. Yet there were doctors who took advantage of this legal procedure and saw these operations as a lucrative business. Some of these operations harmed trans women and their health, and caused so much suffering later in their lives.

These illegal operations did not give trans people any right to change their official records or get a new ID card because they were not supported by a *heyet raporu*. The *heyet raporu* could only be provided by a *heyet*, a board of doctors similar to the oversight boards in North American teaching and research hospitals. The *heyet* was composed of specialists from multiple departments, including internal diseases, general surgery, neurology, psychiatry, ophthalmology, ear-nose-throat, gynecology, and plastic surgery, as well as the head of the board. In Turkey a *heyet raporu* can also be required on other occasions. For instance, employers might request recent hires to submit a *heyet raporu* to provide evidence of good health. Students also have to provide their principals with a *heyet raporu* when they need to take a long leave of absence. Depending on the situation, the hospital creates a board and selects representatives of different departments depending on each individual case.

In the case of trans people, psychiatric, urological, gynecological, genetic, endocrinological, and plastic surgery evaluations are required. All these departments serve the scientific evaluation of one's sex and gender. Medical genetics, for instance, checks trans people's chromosomal combination to see whether they are intersex or not. Endocrinology, in turn, runs three different tests, namely, liver and kidney function tests, a complete blood test, and a thyroid-stimulating hormone test, both before and after hormone treatment. Medical tests help doctors observe fluctuations in trans people's hormone levels. Based on the test results, an endocrinologist decides on the required level of hormone intake. Once each of these medical actors is scientifically convinced of the need for GCS, they gather their individual reports to prepare a final *heyet raporu*, which includes the signature of each of the above-mentioned specialists. However, the psychiatric examination represents the chief phase since, of all the necessary medical steps, it involves the most detailed investigation of whether a subject is trans or not.

The inception of this psychiatric examination dates back to 1987, when Şahika Yüksel, now a renowned psychiatrist specializing in clinical work with trans people, established the first special unit at the Psychiatry Department of the Istanbul School of Medicine dedicated to the evaluation of "gender identity problems."[34] Later, mostly inspired by the World Professional Association for Transgender Health's Standards of Care, she introduced some psychiatric methods into her clinical work with trans people. One example was group psychotherapy, a product of a particular interpretation and application of the association's Standards of Care.[35] Over the course of ten years, this psychotherapy method spread to other psychiatry departments in public teaching and research hospitals in Turkey.[36]

These standards were in some ways more customary than legal. For instance, two years of psychotherapy was not set as obligatory in the law; nor was it mandated as part of the psychiatric report needed for GCS. But psychiatrists still refrained from providing that report before the completion of approximately two years of psychotherapy. Even when the psychiatrist was convinced of a trans person's sex/gender identity, the issuance of the medical report could still be arbitrarily postponed depending on the subject's financial situation. Unless one had the financial means to undergo surgery, the person might not be granted a medical report for a long time.

Finances also played into other aspects of the psychiatric component of the *heyet raporu*. For instance, trans people could receive a psychiatric report from a private psychiatry clinic, although they still had to consult with public teaching and research hospitals for other tests and for the final *heyet raporu*.[37] They might do this because they might prefer individual psychotherapy. While private psychiatry clinics organized their psychotherapy into similar temporal intervals, they offered individual rather than group psychotherapy. Receiving individual therapy at a private clinic allowed the person more time to talk about their problems in a one-on-

one setting. But while group therapies at teaching and research hospitals were financially covered by public insurance, individual psychotherapy services at private clinics were excluded from insurance coverage. For this reason, trans people's class background, as well as family support, played a significant role in determining their psychotherapy experience.[38] Whereas those with wealth had the option of private psychotherapy, those without wealth and family support had to undergo group psychotherapy provided by public hospitals.

My access to ongoing psychotherapy sessions was prevented by both pragmatic and ethical concerns. Not all trans people followed the state's obligatory medicolegal route to have their sex confirmed. Back in 2009–10, the psychotherapy process was a more substantial issue for a younger generation of trans people than for older ones, as the latter had changed their IDs prior to the 2002 legal regulations. There were also others who avoided or who were debating whether to undergo such a stringent medicolegal process. Hence, psychiatric knowledge and expertise could easily become a topic in everyday conversation outside the clinic.[39] Alongside everyday conversations among younger generations of trans people, my knowledge of these psychotherapy sessions is mostly based on firsthand accounts by three psychiatrists who were facilitating psychotherapy sessions and by five trans people who either had completed or were trying to complete the psychotherapy process. They all worked at and visited the same hospital and thus were part of the same psychotherapy group.

The therapy groups were composed of thirty to forty people, and they met for two hours once a month. Even though the average completion time was two years, it varied slightly from person to person depending on their needs and response to therapy. Before someone joined the group, the psychiatrist assessed the person individually, which also gave them an idea of the therapy time needed. My doctor interlocutors noted that they continued to keep track of the person's condition even after the person was accepted into the group. However, the frequency of one-on-one sessions could change, again depending on one's psychological state during the transition process. For example, if doctors observed confusion or hesitation about having GCS, then the group psychotherapy took longer, as one of the doctors told me during our interview.

Part of the psychotherapy consisted of directions about hormone intake. Usually people were asked to provide their endocrinological, gynecological, and urological examination results at the end of their first year. As long as the outcome was fine, they could start with regular intake of hormones. Another function of the therapy group was to deliver adequate technical information about GCS, as well as about the subsequent transition period. Visits by a plastic surgeon and former therapy participants helped current members of the psychotherapy group gain more information on details, disadvantages and advantages of the surgery, and developing technologies in plastic surgery. According to the doctors, listening to former group members' pre- and postoperation experiences gave people hope.

On the surface, the psychiatric support appeared to be positive and to help trans people a great deal with their bodily transition. Nevertheless, doctors' and trans people's accounts regarding psychotherapy sessions were at odds with each other. Whereas psychiatrists depicted psychotherapy sessions as merely supportive mechanisms, trans people offered accounts of the varying level of violence they claimed that these therapies did by obliging them to stage an intimate performance of a sexed/gendered self for the institutional gaze. First, I review the doctors' descriptions and then portray how trans people experienced these psychotherapies. I had three doctor interviewees, and all them were *natrans* women who trained with Şahika Yüksel.

Psychiatric Materialization of Sex

One of the major benefits of psychotherapy, as stated by psychiatrist Gaye Bilgin, was to prepare trans individuals for their transition, including the emotional, psychological, and social changes they were expected to face in their post-op lives. According to her, trans people sometimes had high expectations of GCS that were far from realistic. For example, some trans people strongly believed that the surgery would radically change their lives by resolving every problem they had to cope with regarding their gender identity. Or they thought that their "female or male past" would no longer exist after GCS.[40] Thus, the first goal of therapy, according to the psychiatrists, was to temper these expectations and to ensure psychological well-being by easing other anxieties and tensions.

Each psychotherapy session would begin with individual accounts of the previous month and of its members' positive and negative experiences. Doctors would highly value these accounts because they brought together trans people in different stages of transition. They shared their experiences and problems acknowledging their own gender identity, managing relationships with their families, and coping with dominant gender roles in society. Some experiences were shared by many. For example, according to another of the psychiatrists I interviewed, Duygu Sözer, the two most frequent sources of distress were "coming out" to parents and negotiating religious concerns surrounding operations and sexual life. More experienced members of the group would help other less experienced trans people with their doubts by allaying their concerns. Psychiatrists also saw these sessions as valuable ways to ease the loneliness of people who saw their transsexuality as an exclusively individual problem and thus experienced isolation and alienation from their social environment. In short, from Sözer's perspective, psychotherapy sessions provided a supportive environment and source of empowerment for trans people.

At the same time, psychotherapy participants' willingness or tendency to talk about their experience varied from person to person. For instance, Bilgin discussed a female-assigned trans man who came from a religiously conservative Muslim background and hence needed to wear a headscarf to meet religious rules pertaining to the female body. His transition to manhood was regarded as far more complicated than many others because his public gender role alteration included taking off his headscarf. However, pressure from his religious community was so drastic that he did not dare take it off, let alone come out to his family. On top of that, he was married and pregnant at the time. As Bilgin emphasized, his experience could have been immensely informative for other participants if he had chosen to speak in the group. Yet, despite his two years of participation in the group, he resisted saying a single word, detailing his life story only during private sessions. Bilgin gave this example to stress the differences in each individual's capacity to engage with group psychotherapy and benefit from it.

One reason for doctors' insistence on a two-year psychotherapy period was to counter some trans people's rush to have GCS. Doctors claimed that although the psychotherapy seemed long, trans people who "graduated" (the word they used for completing the calculated psychotherapy time) from therapy usually provided positive feedback, saying they had benefited greatly from it. These graduates sometimes even continued to participate in the group, sharing their pre- and postsurgery experiences.

Psychiatrists also invoked a specific need for "role models" to emulate, which they claimed many trans people wanted to have during their transition. These role models provided trans people with examples/guidelines for how to "pass" as a man or woman. One instance of this "modeling" could be observed in terms of dress codes. When trans people came to psychotherapy, many of them did not feel obliged to dress according to the code they were expected to follow in everyday life (that is, that of the gender they were transitioning from) and felt freer to dress according to their perceived sex. In this respect, the group psychotherapy space also functioned, as doctors pointed out, as a stage: a place where everyone could observe each other, identify mismatches to the appropriate gendered dress code, and settle their style accordingly.

For instance, Rengin Aysan recounted how some trans women who at the very beginning of their psychotherapy were "gaudy looking" gradually wore more reasonable and casual attire as their treatment extended into its second year. When I asked her how to interpret this "gaudiness," she framed it as an effort by trans women to compensate for feelings of inferiority, of having "fallen behind" in womanhood. In this model, trans women would try to "catch up" with a womanhood that they believed they could already have attained if they had been allowed to live as women all along. In her view, these "lost" years of not being a woman profoundly shaped trans women's exaggerated performances of various gender roles. She thus saw the long duration of psychotherapy as necessary to make trans women understand that their sex/gender had nothing to do with high-heeled shoes or heavy makeup. Growing such awareness, she said, would also increase self-confidence. Thus, psychotherapy was also used to discipline participants into societal gender norms.

Another positive outcome of psychotherapy described by doctors was improved skills of self-expression for trans people. One common exercise was role-playing, which focused on interactions between trans people and their parents. Therapists highly valued this method since, they believed, it would develop the ability and courage trans people needed to communicate with their parents, which would make a huge difference when they first came out to them. When I asked doctors if they did anything to help trans people with their family situations, they mentioned organizing two psychotherapy sessions for trans people's families every year. All family members, aside from the trans people themselves, could join these sessions. The main purpose was to bring family members together to dismantle prejudices and create a space for sharing experiences with each other. Medical research in Turkey also stated that families lacked sufficient information about transness; when a family discovered that a child was a trans person, most families preferred to conceal this at all costs rather than speak about it openly.[41] In this environment it would be helpful for families to see how other families experienced similar challenges. Attendees at these meetings were usually curious and willing to work on their biases against transness. Strongly biased family members rarely appeared at these meetings.

Bilgin also talked about having witnessed a level of "homophobia" among group members. For example, she described trans people who felt thankful for not being gay or who evaluated their womanhood and manhood in relation to their desire for the opposite sex. It was interesting to hear this because, as you will read in the following section, many trans people complained that doctors could not make a clear distinction between gender identity and sexual orientation, explaining the former in terms of the latter. This conflation of gender identity and sexual orientation was also one of the most significant tensions between participants and their doctors.

In her work on transgender lives in Iran, Najmabadi points out a similar tendency to define gender identity in terms of one's sexual orientation.[42] In Iran same-sex practices are religiously and legally prohibited, but sex change is a religiously sanctioned, state-subsidized legal practice. To start the GCS process, a gender-nonconforming person is required to undergo psychotherapy for four to six months. Najmabadi argues that the ban on same-sex practices and desires adds to the pressure on gays and lesbians, who might consider participating in GCS and psychotherapy to "transsexualize" themselves in the eyes of the state and receive religio-legal approval for their same-sex desire, allowing them to practice it under the guise of heteronormativity. That is why psychotherapy is colloquially referred to as "filtering" in Iran, as it is used by the state, together with hormonal and chromosomal tests, to recognize and separate "true transsexuals" from the others.[43] According to the Iranian state authorities, transgender people's same-sex desires and practices are in fact straight because they were born in the wrong body and sex. Therefore, their pre-GCS same-sex desires and practices are diagnosed as symptoms of transsexuality, not homosexuality. Further, there is no religio-legal recognition of transsexual lesbians or gays (that is, trans women desiring women, or trans men desiring men), because desire and sexual practice should always be straight. Same-sex desires and practices are perceived as markers of moral deviancy, and hence gays and lesbians are identified and filtered out through psychotherapy.[44]

Najmabadi's work is helpful for discussing how allegedly universal medicolegal models of sex/gender transition are modified and shaped locally. While the state uses psychotherapy and GCS as a heteronormative corrective measure, queer people in Iran can manipulate it to more creative ends, creatively using their sex/gender to live their sexuality. In a similar vein, trans people in Turkey negotiate, rework, and contest the existing medicolegal models of transsexuality to establish their own diverse meanings and definitions of, and relations between, gender nonconformity, sex, and sexuality.

Bodies That Speak the Time and the "Truth" of Sex

"If you are a crazy person, then you cannot be a transsexual," İlker joked, referring to the Rorschach and IQ tests that were the very first step in the institutionalized medical path to GCS. The Rorschach test analyzes people's perceptions of inkblots to evaluate their personality characteristics and emotional functioning. Psychologists used Rorschach tests, together with the IQ test, to judge trans people's mental health—specifically, any level of schizophrenia or tendency toward depression. An observation of either of these led psychologists to declare trans people ineligible for GCS, preventing their participation in group psychotherapy, the second step in meeting medical regulations.

Those who continued to group psychotherapy first met the chief psychiatrist and her two assistants, who were responsible for the entire group. The assistants would take notes, convey trans people's concerns to the psychiatrist, and prepare the authorization of the medical report on the completion of psychotherapy. The main psychiatrist would survey both her assistants and the group, and make the final decision, but rarely join the psychotherapy sessions. When she attended, she would usually listen, observe, and intervene only if she found it necessary. İlker, a trans man who graduated from one of her psychotherapy groups, expressed his and his peers' annoyance with her "lawlike attitude," evoking Foucault's description of a doctor as "at the same time a doctor-judge."[45] This "lawlike attitude" made trans people feel vulnerable at times because they felt that the main psychiatrist's medical decision functioned in fact as a verdict on the credibility of their self-identified sex/gender. Without her word, they would not be able to access legal recognition of their sex/gender.

For trans people who managed to prove their mental health and became part of the psychotherapy group, the primary concern would become the size of the group, amounting to some forty people. There was a wait list, as an existing client had to "graduate" (or otherwise leave) before a "junior" one could enter. Further, the two-hour length of each session meant each member had only approximately ten minutes to express themselves. What one could say in these ten minutes was limited not only by time but also by the institutionally structured way of speaking about their problems, which most of the time were very intimate. Trans people reported that psychiatrists imposed specific speech prompts on participants during psychotherapy, rendering them silent or unheard if they attempted to deviate. For example, the most popular prompt was reported to be approximately: "Tell us something positive or negative that you experienced in relation to your sex this past month." The reply had to be given in ten minutes, and people were silenced when they went over time and wanted to elaborate in more detail about, for instance, the connections between their intimate senses of their body or sex and the many spheres of everyday life. Enclosing the group dynamic with such a temporally and verbally rigid structure left trans people facing the risk of being frozen out of the group if they crossed the boundaries of what was speakable. They were expected to conform to this institutional template.

Consider a detailed example of this verbal regulation, which came along with a depiction of other problematic issues essential to the psychotherapy. İlker was a twenty-seven-year-old trans man and a LGBTI+ activist, well equipped to discuss gender and sexual issues. He had already graduated from psychotherapy when I met him. When I interviewed him, he had had top surgery but still was looking for a trustworthy place to have bottom surgery. He frowned while talking about his psychotherapy experience and the compulsory legal regulations surrounding surgery:

İLKER: You must wrap your entire appearance up into socially compromised norms of gender so that you can socially reintegrate into the society. All this process of psychotherapy is for saying, "Due to psychotherapy she or he obtained this proper look! This is our achievement!" In psychotherapy, consultants always want to hear about themselves: "Are you content with the psychotherapy? Has it been helpful for you? How have you been feeling about psychotherapy?" These questions are constantly seeking evidence of what they are doing to reintegrate people into society, for self-vindication. They brag about restoring us to society as desired females and males. For example, I have a trans gay friend. If he consults with them, he would never be able to get a report from them.

ASLI: So, do you mean you must be a straight person to be able to go there?

İLKER: Well, yes! At best you can be a bisexual but never a gay. What they inspect is whether you use your genitalia you were born with or not. You know, they're gonna give you an authorization for GCS. So, if you are still using your sexual organ, then it should stay; you cannot cut it off, you cannot dump it, because it means you are at peace with your organ. In any case, you should be troubled with your body. You should be unable to use your genitals you were born with. . . . If I declare I am a man, then I am a man! That's it!! What is the difference between the saggy boobs I had before and the current ones? Only fat came out of them. What has changed? Nothing has changed for me!

Extremely discontent with the therapists' approach to sex/gender and sexuality, İlker claimed that the entire purpose of the psychotherapy sessions was to produce sexed and gendered trans subjects fitting the cisheteronormative standards of Turkish society. To satisfy this aim, medical authorities attempted to treat sex in relation to the heterosexual usability of genitalia and/or one's degree of emotional attachment to those organs. For instance, if a preoperative trans man still received pleasure from his vagina, then he was not considered transsexual by medical authorities.

While there were trans people who used similar heteronormative assumptions to understand their sex, others, like İlker, radically contested such understandings. They drew clear boundaries between their sexuality and sex/gender, complicating not only the relationship between the two but also the assumed stable link between the body and sex/gender. These contestations were important because they demonstrated how trans people in Turkey experienced and negotiated medicolegal scripts and practices of sex and transsexuality, configuring and imagining sex and gender in multiple ways.

Contesting the relationship between the body and sex/gender also had a temporal dimension. Trans people's understanding of their bodily time and the disciplinary time of psychotherapy showed discrepancies. As critical theorist Elizabeth Freeman succinctly puts it, "The body politics and power relations are made possible by manipulating time."[46] As discussed, one's "truth" of transsexuality was strictly tied to a disciplinary institutional time and the requirement of two years of "treatment" by medical authorities. Within the temporal framework of psychotherapy, one's past and present gender role performances and self-accounts of sex/gender had to comply with each other, presenting narrative coherence and persistence, submitting to a linear temporal logic. This temporal logic can be considered violent as it denies multiple and singular temporalities of the self and instead imposes a uniform and linear one. The psychotherapy timeline would function to make trans people achieve bodily legibility and internalize specific values and norms of gender. However, work on queer temporality insists on the analytic salience of temporal heterogeneity and "the present's irreducible multiplicity"—not necessarily only for trans people but for everyone.[47] In contrast to the stubborn medical timeline, which subjects sexual/gender and bodily transition to a linear temporal discipline, some trans people's sense of sex/gender and the body displayed a more flexible, multilayered, and interrupted understanding of temporality. Adem's story was one portrayal of this phenomenon.

Adem, a thirty-one-year-old trans man, worked as a nurse in the emergency department of a hospital. He also described psychotherapy as an oppressive use of power designed to mold individuals within a stringent medical configuration. Adem said that, unlike many people who had female-assigned bodies at birth, he had never experienced a regular menstruation cycle, causing him stress and countless health problems. After grappling with these problems for twenty years, he was diagnosed with polycystic ovarian syndrome, which led to intensive hormone treatment, including especially high doses of estrogen. However, ten years of treatment did not produce any concrete results. He kept feeling that his body was not female but male. He told his gynecologist that neither the functioning of his body nor his feelings about it had changed. He experienced increasing pain and was taking painkillers nonstop. He no longer wanted to keep living in pain and decided to have ovarian removal surgery, following his doctor's advice.

When Adem made the decision, he was in a GCS psychotherapy group. To be able to legally perform this operation, his gynecologist asked him to receive official permission from the group therapist and also forwarded a written note about his situation to the psychiatrist. The psychiatrist got angry with Adem for pursuing the operation, because ovarian removal surgery would be a late stage in the gender confirmation process and hence should not have been authorized until psychotherapy was completed. But Adem's gynecologist had been convinced to give permission after recognizing this surgery not as part of the gender confirmation process but as the response to a health problem. Adem's ovaries were removed at the end of his fourth month in psychotherapy.

While he was on leave due to the ovarian removal surgery, Adem also decided to undergo a top surgery. When the therapist found out about his breast removal, she was furious. They argued about how Adem had to comply with the stringent rules of psychotherapy. According to these rules, the period of psychotherapy was organized into different phases: participants were expected to start hormone intake within the first six months to one year; then they were required to wait until the completion of their psychotherapy to be legally authorized for GCS, whether top or bottom surgery. Adem said that this argument was the first time he had heard about these rules. He was given no information about the group timeline at any point during psychotherapy.

Some days after his argument with his therapist, Adem called the hospital to arrange the following month's meeting, only to find out that he was no longer part of the group. The hospital staff advised him to start looking for some other place to get his medical report. He was essentially excluded from the group for not obeying the rules of psychotherapy time, which determined when and how to intervene in configuring his body into a "male" one. He had interrupted its linearity by following his own personal, bodily felt time. As a significant element in constituting the "truth" of his sex, the normative interval of psychiatric time denied the alternative temporalities of his body and sex/gender. However, I should also add that it would be incorrect to define Adem's personal, bodily time as completely *his* time, because the temporality of his body and sex/gender was also partly a "medical" decision, which made this alternative temporality still institutional to a certain extent. My point here is to draw attention to temporal ruptures and multiplicities in the institutional construction of bodily time.

Proof of "true" sex in this medical stage was also strongly mediated by the prescription of hormones. The time I spent with senior trans women presented me with some background information about trans people's hormone intake. Prior to 2002, when there was no medical regulation, people could go to a pharmacy and easily buy hormones without knowing their side effects. They did not need prescriptions. In the absence of sufficient medical instruction, trans people advised one another in mapping out the medical route of sexual/gender transition. Hormones represented one of the most crucial steps in this process, and many trans women started regular and heavy hormone injections as early as possible. Today hormone intake is more seriously regulated, especially through the timeline of psychotherapy. Moreover, trans people have a stronger awareness of the medical side effects than they did thirty years ago. However, this regulation does little to consider trans people's personal expectations, demands, desires, and feelings regarding their bodies, compared to the importance attributed to the state's designation of gender roles and "appropriate" body features.

According to therapists, a waiting time of six months to one year was vital because, they claimed, trans people might demonstrate risky levels of hormone intake to hastily compensate for the difference between their body and the body they aspired to have. However, some trans people thought that taking hormones based on their own time frame helped them establish a more balanced and calm personality, as they gradually approached their body ideal or their imagined body of the self-identified sex.[48] In either case, hormone intake was tied to strict regulations that caused major disturbances among trans people, raising questions about rights to possession of and control over one's own body.[49] Adem's words elucidate an issue also shared by other trans people:

> When I asked the assistant about when to start with my hormone treatment, she said it would vary, from six months to nine months from the first day of the psychotherapy. Why would I wait that long? I am neither starting a new life nor trying to adapt to one that I have never been familiar with. I have been like this since my childhood. In their minds there is this logic: this person has been living as a female since he was born, and then he decided to change his sex from female to male. So, we need to help him with his transition process from womanhood to manhood. However, this logic does not apply to me; I have been feeling and living as a man since my childhood! I explained this sentiment during therapy to no avail.

While trans people like Adem insisted on a more flexible schedule for hormone intake, therapists denied the felt temporality of their clients' bodies (a temporality that was, at the same time, socially shaped) and instead forced them to integrate into a particular institutional temporal norm. This temporal norm also operated to construct and advance normativity in their desired sex/gender identity. The time and surface of the body were entwined with certain institutional norms and expectations, denying the self-interpretation of temporal and bodily accounts. There were also others, like İlker, who opposed the enforcement of hormone treatment as part of the psychotherapy period, or who opposed the enforcement of a properly sexed body in general. This issue came up several times in our conversations. İlker repeatedly showed his irritation at obligatory hormone intake, telling me how therapists would not issue a medical report for GCS unless trans people complied with the necessary hormone prescriptions.

Another significant complaint about the "truth" of their sex/gender articulated by trans people involved consultants' tendency to see their bodies in aggregate rather than as individual ones. Because trans people would foreground every individual's uniqueness and singularity, they felt immensely perturbed when psychiatrists lumped them all together as, for instance, a uniform group of people. Preferring to stress the distinctness of life stories and experiences, they felt that they were forced—sometimes subtly, sometimes not—down a prescribed path of sex/gender identity during psychotherapy. This enforced "sameness" could be considered an effect of formulating transsexuality as a medicolegal category, produced and shaped within the intertwinement of dominant social norms of gender, sex, desire, and eroticism. For example, Lale, a trans woman I met at Istanbul LGBTT, told me about her first visit to the group psychiatrist. When she mentioned that she was a trans lesbian, the consultant hesitated to put her on the wait list for the psychotherapy group. "She couldn't make up her mind about me," Lale said. She asked Lale to visit her a few more times in order to come to a decision. But Lale said she knew exactly why the therapist called her back: "They are teaching you how to be a woman according to social norms. Psychotherapy is so much focused on society's expectations. They seek social integration for trans individuals. Since this is the goal, they teach you social masculinity and femininity in psychotherapy. . . . She is going to carve out a heterosexual woman from me and build up proper feminine manners for me to efface any existing masculine attitude. In other words, my femininity must be precise!"

In Lale's case, lesbian desire fell outside of "proper feminine manners," thus potentially disqualifying her for GCS. Her individual experience failed to conform to the generic "sameness" the process required. In 2010 she was still visiting the doctor for further "clarifications" about her gender identity. This example shows how medical authorities, while criticizing trans people for confusing sexual orientation and sex/gender identity, fall into the same trap and explain sex/gender in terms of desire.

In psychotherapy, consultants would also examine trans people's adjustments to homosocial environments and groups. For example, some trans men were asked how they felt in male-dominated spaces such as traditional coffeehouses and soccer games, or when they walked on the streets late at night. These questions referenced a few of the Turkish hegemonic masculine values and behaviors that I detailed in the introduction. In turn, trans women would be questioned about their feelings while they were in places or engaged in activities that were regarded as feminine, such as going to hairdressers, shopping, or doing housework. A female-assigned person could claim that he was a trans man, but it was important for therapists to see if he was bodily and behaviorally attuned to a masculine environment or group, or if he was capable of persuading others of his masculinity. According to trans people I spoke with, therapists relied on the dominant social norms of gender and sexuality in doing so and made sure that each trans individual fit into proper gender roles per social and cultural expectations.

Through psychotherapy sessions, trans people (were) constantly examined to see if they qualified to have "a body for life within the domain of cultural intelligibility."[50] The space of psychotherapy was made into a site for testing trans people's sincerity and ability to "pass." For Sandy Stone, one is considered as passing if one can live up to the dominant gender roles and make oneself accepted as a "natural" member of that gender.[51] In this regard, psychotherapy would turn trans people's bodies into "the object[s] of a technology and knowledge of rectification, readaptation, reinsertion, and correction," through the workings of a homogeneous and linear institutional temporality.[52]

While fitting into those gender roles, trans people also needed to stick to moral, as well as "moderate," boundaries and not display exaggerated performances of gender. For instance, one trans woman told me about two adolescent trans women who were kicked out of the group because they were constantly looking in the mirror and reapplying lipstick during the therapy sessions. At another time, the psychiatrist got angry with some other trans women and showed them the door for not sitting properly, showing their underwear while wearing miniskirts.

Finally, trans people's problems with their families were another salient topic in therapy. In fact, the adjustment of one's family to one's sex was the most scrutinized dimension of the group therapy. Psychiatrists would check if a participant lived with their family in peace, if the person could persuade their family to reconcile themselves to their sex/gender identity. The success of therapy and the length of time needed to get the medical report for GCS strongly hinged on the sexual and gender status achieved in the family. When family members refused to recognize their children's sex/gender transition, therapists did not recognize their refusal as part of a larger social and cultural network of cisheteronormativity that also shaped families' approach to their children. On the contrary, they would continue to burden the trans individual with tackling the problems within their family. Therapy, by framing the familial distress as an individual issue and forcing the trans individual to reconcile with the family, functioned to restore the dominant intimate order.

Even when a trans person had completed all the aforementioned steps—or, so to speak, even when the psychiatrist was convinced of a trans person's sex/gender identity—the issuance of the medical report could still be arbitrarily postponed depending on the person's financial situation. Unless a person had the means to undergo the surgery or was on good terms with their family, they would not necessarily be granted a medical report for a long time. Some people still had not received their medical report after four years.

Conclusion

The overall picture of psychotherapy's engagement with trans people in Turkey indicates that medical standards, utilized during psychotherapy sessions and in the authorization of the final medical report, involved conflicting constructions of the temporality of the trans body, of sex/gender, and of transsexuality. While medical authorities tested (and, while testing, simultaneously constructed) evidence of the body's "true" sex/gender over roughly two years, delivering a prologue to trans people's legal transformations to the other sex as the state's sexed subjects, trans people themselves came up with queerer, plural understandings of their bodily time, sex, gender, and trans identity.

In the space of psychotherapy, the need for bottom surgery was tested in accordance with the presence or development of other aspects of bodily materiality. For example, critical theorist Gayle Salamon argues that bodily features such as hairstyle, way of walking, style of dress, pitch of voice, and body shape and size are crucial elements of a body's materiality when determining one's gender, indeed even more crucial than genitals themselves.[53] In a similar vein, anthropologist Eric Plemons discusses the importance of facial feminization surgery as a crucial step in the gender confirmation process.[54] These qualities, have an impact on sex attribution. To explain this point, Salamon refers to Sigmund Freud's observation that "the first determination we make about a person we pass on the street is an instantaneous *male* or *female*? and in nearly every case we make that determination with no information at all about genital configuration."[55] Social psychologists Suzanne Kessler and Wendy McKenna take this understanding one step further by elaborating this imagined genital configuration into a "cultural genital," a genital "which is assumed to exist and which, it is believed, should be there."[56]

Part of what psychiatry did was to examine the trans person's bodily features and body language in a temporally distributed fashion, evaluating whether the trans person presented enough material and performance to produce the sense of a "cultural genital" and then deciding whether to authorize GCS. That is to say, the psychiatrists allowed trans people to have surgery according to the gender that a person successfully "passed" as, rendering a particular production of bodily materiality obligatory over a specific time interval. In this psychiatric assessment, the hegemonic norm of sex/gender and sexuality functions as institutionalized violence, infiltrating the intimate accounts, performances, and temporalities of trans embodiment.

Some trans people have a strong desire to have varying degrees of trans surgery according to their sex/gender and according to their own bodily calendars. Meanwhile, others do not necessarily want to undergo trans surgery in terms of these institutional expectations. The issue is not whether to support GCS or not. Rather, it is about how the state's regulations stubbornly insist on a temporal equation of sex/gender with genitals, producing sex/gender in a predetermined material form and foreclosing other possible surfaces and temporalities of the body.

What does this institutionalization say about the role that sex/gender transgression plays in the organization of state power? And how can we understand this organization in relation to the broader discussion of violent intimacies? I turn to this question in the next chapter by examining the role of the sensorium as a technology of sex and gender in the formation of violent intimacies of the state through medicolegal practices.

Chapter Four

Touch, Gaze, & the Heteropenetrative State

ON A COLD, RAINY WINTER DAY, I was sitting with Seval, a twenty-two-year-old trans woman sex worker, in her long, narrow, and poorly lit living room on the fifth floor of a ten-story building. She had recently undergone bottom surgery and told me about her latest visit to one of the public teaching and research hospitals in Istanbul to have her vagina checked. Seval was impatient and excited because, as she articulated, her painstaking, two-and-a-half-year medicolegal gender confirmation process was finally coming to an end. Soon she would have her pink ID. The doctor had given Seval an instrument and advised her to use it regularly, pushing it in and out of her vagina, so that her vagina could function "normally." She explained that this vaginal exercise was central to her receipt of the pink ID and that she had to endure one more medical check during which state medical authorities would scrutinize her newly reconstructed genitals. They would insert an instrument into her vagina to ensure that it was "deep enough"—only then would she be able to apply for her pink ID. I asked Seval what forensic people meant by a "deep enough" vagina. "A constructed vagina should be minimum 3.5 inches deep," Seval continued. Even though this measurement was not specified in the legal code on transsexuality, Seval said she had a friend who had been unable to receive a pink ID because she had a 1.5-inch-deep vagina, preventing her from acquiring legal recognition as a female. Hearing these details, I could not help but call it a form of rape. After a few seconds of silence, Seval cracked a bitter joke with a forced smile: "Yes, of course! The state rapes us to make sure we are female enough." Seval's story in fact highlighted the state definition of the female body as strictly fixated on a penetrable vagina. The state's medicolegal technologies intensified the sex of Seval's body through obligatory penetration, a violent touch that might also be regarded as institutional rape at times, depending on how it is felt and perceived by trans women.

This chapter shows how this institutional fixation develops specific proximities and forms of touch by the state on and in the bodies of trans women, which in turn plays a pivotal role in the institutional production of sex/gender difference and the normative regulation of sexuality, desire, and sex/gender in Turkey. I call these institutional forms of touch and proximities *violent intimacies of the state*. These violent intimacies are a central mechanism of modern disciplinary practices and rational technologies of control.

To delineate these violent intimacies, I focus on the role of the sensorium—particularly touch and the gaze. The sensorium plays a vital role in materializing the surfaces and the contours of a body's sex. The first half of the chapter focuses on the medicolegal materialization of sex through genital surgeries and demonstrates how genitals—specifically vaginas—are integral to the formation and operation of the intimate workings of Turkish state power, as state actors deploy a sensorial method to govern and regulate not only bodies and sex/gender but also subjects' intimate conduct and desires. Thanks to Michel Foucault, we now have an extensive literature that analyzes the gaze as a political tool to understand the exercise of state power vis-à-vis the supervision and observation of bodies in myriad institutional settings.[1] My previous chapter also provides ample material on this institutional gaze through the psychiatric observation and evaluation of transness. Yet touch is a less examined issue in the formation and operation of state power. An analysis of touch and tactility as political tools builds novel theoretical approaches to the exercise of intimate state power and thus the formation of violent intimacies of the state.

The second half of the chapter broadens the conceptual framework of violent intimacies by redirecting the attention from the medicolegal environment of the state to the role of the sensorium in everyday encounters with the sex/gender-transgressive body. While it is important to discuss the specific intimate content that the state gains from its haptic institutional practices regarding the trans body, trans people are both subjects and objects of a wider sensorial environment that demonstrates multiple forms and registers of violent intimacies. To understand the broader framework of violent intimacies, one should not limit the role of the sensorium to merely institutions. Instead, institutions and the broader intimate social world of touch and the gaze shapes the corporeal life of sex/gender in the trans everyday. Hence, in the second part, I focus on the sexual/gendered gaze as a structuring and materializing force in the corporeality of everyday life. My goal with this section is to blur the boundaries between the gaze and touch and to show how a body's sex matters under staring eyes. In brief, eyes can also touch bodies violently and materialize their contours and surfaces intimately. Hence, I approach the gaze also through the lenses of touch and tactility.

The Regime of Tactility and the Politics of Touch

Human geographer Paul Rodaway argues that touch is the most intimate and direct of all the senses because it is constrained by the grasp of the body and is always reciprocal: "to touch is always to be touched."[2] When we talk about touch, we should not restrict our understanding only to fingers. Haptic experience concerns the whole body or the whole skin covering the body.[3] It is also a constant sensual account of our relationship with the world. Through our haptic relationship with the world, we also make sense of it. Touch, as a form of "dwelling on the surface of the body of the other," has a tremendous world-making capacity in marking surfaces with value and meaning, establishing boundaries, and indicating borders.[4] From this point of view, it connotes something beyond merely the physical; it is a corporeal situation charged with emotional, political, social, and cultural processes.

A close analysis of touch requires differentiation between ways of touching. For example, a touch is not always about a tactile world that involves, for instance, rubbing, massaging, stroking, soothing, caressing, fondling, and patting. Rather, there is an enormously inimical side to what touch can do when it takes nonconsensual violent forms such as beating, slapping, kicking, hitting, punching, and, in some instances, penetrating.[5] Within this violent economy of touch, our skin, as collector and registrar of tactile information, may function as an organ not only of protection but also of exposure.[6] Our skins shape and produce the very conditions of our vulnerability before life. If we apprehend violation, appropriation, or exploitation as a specific mode of touch, then touching someone's skin manifests itself as a means of subjugation.

A touch, in its mutuality, can open one's body to other bodies. It is the most intimate cementing force of embodiment, which Sara Ahmed calls us to understand as a lived experience with other bodies, or "the social experience of dwelling with other bodies."[7] In this theorization one's body can no longer be regarded as a private realm; rather, it is a realm of incessant opening out to other bodies and thus a realm of vulnerability. To delineate this process better, philosopher Maurice Merleau-Ponty uses the term *flesh*, which cannot be comprehended merely in relation to the materiality of the body but is an outcome of complex relations among my body, the other's body, and the world altogether.[8] Hence, it is not the body per se but the mutuality of touching, or being both the subject and object of touch, that becomes a phenomenological account of one's lived experience.

Yet bodies are not undifferentiated; they are not a unitary category of either analysis or embodiment.[9] A power differential between different bodies is intrinsic to the formation of this cartography of embodiment. Not everybody is deemed to be capable of touching other bodies the same way. The mutuality of touch is not symmetrical. While, at the point of contact, touching coincides, touching and being touched are quite different—especially, for example, when pain results. Moreover, bodies are conditioned, as well as conditioning themselves to one another, within a set of unequal and uneven relations of power. These asymmetric relations also shape how "bodies are touched by some bodies differently from other bodies."[10] Some people may refuse to touch or be touched by others, or touch may be prevented. In fact, the social economy of touch itself is constitutive of racial, sexual, or gender difference.

To further clarify, the management and mediation of contact between different social groups and communities has long been an effective political tool wielded to implement projects of modernity, transform urban space, and organize city life.[11] One can recount these stories of modernization and gentrification also as stories of transformation in contact—and thus touch—between different social groups. For instance, the previously described forms of displacement and forced mobility that trans people experienced in Istanbul can be thought of as a haptic politics of population management that takes spatial forms through minimizing, or at times eliminating, contact between people occupying different orders in the social hierarchy. Close contact with marginalized groups—such as not only trans women but also sex workers, refugees, ethnic and racial others, and the urban homeless—represents a source of contamination in the everyday discourse of the privileged, leading to the manipulation and control of city life through the moral organization of contact (including touch) between these groups. The disenfranchised groups thus find themselves deprived of certain forms of contact with the rest of the society.

Some touches are destructive, and they communicate power, oppression, and domination. Rape, for instance, is one of them. Hence, it is crucial to draw attention once again to what Ahmed reminds us are "economies of touch" to ruminate on how each touch, depending on the distinct and complex conditionings of bodies to one another, forms and deforms bodies, lives, and communities. In a nutshell, touch has power, and it works as a means of manipulation, control, and discipline.

The question of who can enact and prevent particular forms of touching thus becomes critical. This position of tactility can be both the constituent and the product of specific forms of power, especially state power, taking governmental forms. Establishing more contact with individuals or groups (queers, minoritized women, the poor, etc.), for example, could be an emphasis in institutional practice and discourse. Reaching out to those people and making more contact with them could function as a governmental tool to render them more visible and proximate to state power.[12]

As political theorist Davina Cooper points out, "While touch can thwart or upset hierarchies, it frequently works to confirm and solidify relations of power."[13] State power might operate to regulate different forms of touch (sexual, desirous, etc.), defining normative meanings of touch and conditioning who can touch whom and when and how. One can approach regulations around matters like domestic abuse, child adoption, sex work, and pedophilia from this perspective. In these intimate and sexual domains of life, the state's regime of tactility and touch might be "protective," but it might also take coercive and violent forms.

Finally, the state might not operate its power on the structural grounds of a mutual civic touchability but ensure instead that the active role of touching is ascribed only to its own actors (as in its monopoly of violence). Ultimately, torture and execution express the sovereign forms of violent touch under state rule; routinely, this is performed by policing practices from illegal to casual brutalization; less obviously, it is institutionalized in medicolegal settings.

Penetration and Sterilization as Violent Touch

Seval's story at the beginning of this chapter reveals how the state in Turkey uses such instruments of touch and tactility to control, "straighten up," and "fix" the sex/gender-transgressive body, aided by the normalizing gaze and judgment.[14] For her new ID to be issued, Seval had to pass a final test. When we spoke, she was preparing her vagina to smoothly take in an instrument at least 3.5 inches long. Similar to Seval, trans women who underwent GCS were sent to forensics to have their genitals scrutinized in detail by medical authorities. In public hospitals they would be exposed to institutional observation and practice that was preoccupied with penile penetration as a tool to eliminate, and hence regulate, sex/gender transgression.

Here it is important to take a step back and turn the focus to *natrans* women's vaginas. Genital reconstructive surgeries are not unique to trans women; *natrans* women also undergo these operations. The physical structure of vaginas varies widely. Some *natrans* women are born with a short vagina, a partial vagina, or an absent vagina. Medical discourse categorizes these as "genital anomalies" or "abnormal/irregular vaginas." Turkish names for these are *kısa* (short), *güdük* (stubby), and *kör* (blind) vaginas. These vaginal shapes may go unnoticed until *natrans* women reach adolescence or adulthood. For example, in many instances women find out about their distinct vaginal characteristics during penetrative sex when their vaginas cannot receive sexual organs (or objects such as sex toys), and hence they suffer from physical pain. Or some *natrans* women may discover the specificity of their vaginas when they attempt to get pregnant and find themselves having a miscarriage, experiencing abdominal gestation, or giving birth prematurely. In the case of an absent vagina, the external appearance may not give any clue about its interior structure, which leads most adolescents to discover its absence on reaching puberty and not having a period. They may also develop urinary problems associated with the absence of a vagina. As a solution to these "irregularities," medical intervention is highly recommended, and reconstructive surgery is advised.

Trans women's genital reconstructive surgeries in Turkey are in fact rooted in these reconstructive surgeries on *natrans* women's vaginas.[15] Due to lack of medical training in gender confirmation techniques, medical professionals mainly resorted to the surgical logic of "genital anomalies" when they started operating on trans women's genitals. Needless to say, both trans and *natrans* women (and nonbinary people) may desire various types of vaginas: short, deep, large, tight, and so on. And they are certainly entitled to do whatever they want with their vaginas as long as it is consensual. *Natrans* women, trans men, and nonbinary people, furthermore, may gain reproductive capacity thanks to these interventions. Also, *natrans* surgical interventions are not always related to "genital anomalies." There is an entire medical industry that produces both social and economic value based on commodified vaginal aesthetic standards. Some women, for instance, may have beautification operations on their vaginas, while others may benefit from tightening procedures for their post-birth vaginas. Actually, all these operations may help both trans and *natrans* women gain more sexual satisfaction and pleasure.

My intention is not to pass judgment but rather to emphasize the problematic sexing/gendering logic behind the particular ways these medical remedies and interventions are put into practice. First, there is an underlying presumption that a vagina should have a certain size and a specific appearance and that medicine should intervene to approximate "irregular" vaginas to this ideal vagina. The source of this ideal is not clear, and it serves to reduce the diversity of vaginas to a standardized form. Second, the sexing/gendering mentality that operates through these reconstructive vagina surgeries applies differently when trans and *natrans* women are compared. *Natrans* women who were born with short or absent vaginas are not denied the sex/gender category of female/woman, nor is this category taken away from them when they are diagnosed with a "genital anomaly." There is no question or doubt about their sex/gender identification depending on their vaginal configuration, which is highly diverse in itself. But trans women are forced by state institutions to have a particular vagina with a certain depth in order to attain a new ID based on their sex/gender. Shorter or absent vaginas may not make them eligible for the institutional category of female/woman. Here something else is at stake: the imposed institutional fantasy of a female-assigned biology in the eyes of the state.

The Turkish state invents and rationalizes "technologies of sex" and "technologies of gender" through a channeling of particular cisheterosexual fantasies and gendering practices based on penile penetration.[16] Forensic authorities' insertion of an instrument into trans women's vaginas, which I addressed earlier as a particular violent touch, is in fact a product of cisheteroreproductive normative assumptions and fantasies of sex/gender. It highlights how the success of GCS is tied to patriarchal, phallocentric, and heterosexual assumptions about the female body.[17] The female body is defined by its capacity to be sexually penetrated by a penis. There is a kind of legal equivalence made between the vagina and the female body, both of which are constituted through the capacity for male heterosexual penetration.

When a trans woman's vagina achieves an institutionally designated capacity of penetrability, the state grants her a pink ID and incorporates her into its world of female citizens. At the state level, the capacity to be penetrated by a penis becomes the authoritative mark of sexual difference. In noting this, I do not deny the possibility of pleasure or joy from penetrative sex. Indeed, trans and *natrans* women might take great pleasure in penetration. They might even prefer to deepen their vaginas beyond what the state dictates as the minimum. My point here is not about their individual pleasure or fantasy worlds but rather about the state's standardization and materialization of the female body. In this context, law and medicine do more than subject trans women to genital reconstruction for the purposes of approving their female identity. Instead, they form the terrain of not only sexed/gendered subjects but the sexed/gendered and sexual state as well. It is the state (medical legal expertise) that is penetrating the orifice to see if a penis can fit and thus determining that the orifice is a vagina and the body is female. The institutional fixation on penetration as a medicolegal gender/sex corrective becomes also a site for the materialization of the state as heteronormative and penetrative, that is, what I call the heteropenetrative state."

It is important to highlight that the heteropenetrative state is not unique to Turkey but rather gains specific content in other social contexts. For instance, in her book *Sextarianism*, Maya Mikdashi makes a similar argument with regard to the state's deployment of anal and hymen exams against vulnerable groups in Lebanon. Syrian refugees and migrant workers who were targeted and arrested for engaging in "unnatural sex" and Lebanese women who sought divorce and alimony in the court system may meet in the same legal system through the requirement of anal and hymen tests respectively. These tests, while examining the physical body parts—anus and vagina—for traces of sexual activity, also check whether the subjects failed at practices of normative heterosexuality. Mikdashi conceptualizes the institutional staging of these tests as "the authorial power of the phallus," through which the state secures the gender binary and legitimate sexuality, and performs sovereign violence and itself as a bounded entity.[18]

Comparably, in Turkey, the legitimate female body and its corresponding sexual activity are secured via the institutional fixation on penetration. Furthermore, the definition and regulation of sex and gender at the state level intersect with the state's privileging of specific intimate worlds and intimacies that are based on particular notions of the heteroreproductive family. For example, to go back to the legal regulations that determine if one can apply to the state for GCS, the applicant has to be at least eighteen years old and may neither be married nor have any children. Thereby, the state renders GCS a matter of age, or adulthood. Trans children lack institutional recognition. Moreover, until 2017 the law demanded that trans people be permanently deprived of reproductive capacity prior to GCS.[19] In practice, this meant trans men could not keep their ovaries and uterus, and trans women could not keep their penis and testicles, and they needed proof of their infertility from a gynecologist at an education and research hospital. This legal requirement was removed by the Constitutional Court in Turkey in 2017 in response to a local court case in Edirne, a city in northwestern Turkey. The original petition belonged to a trans woman whose application for a pink ID was rejected in the local court. The local court of Edirne eventually ruled that mandatory sterilization was a violation of human rights and handed the issue to the Constitutional Court, which later removed it as a legal requirement for the issuance of the new ID.[20] Until this ruling, trans bodies were turned into a site of nongenealogical reproductivity, making sure the cisheteronormative family remained the site of social and national reproduction. In other words, the law delineated familial space as an arena that should be devoid of trans subjects, who threatened the dominant intimate order through their break with culturally configured alliances of sex and gender.

Marking who is encouraged to give birth and rear children in a regime of heteroreproductivity is important. Given the Turkish state's strong emphasis on the reproduction of its citizens, it is ironic that the law, while encouraging some individuals to reproduce, at the same time banned others from reproducing by requiring their sterilization. Here sterilization was another site that formed the violent intimacy of the state through violation. Trans people's prohibition from reproducing should be interpreted within legal terms that gave the state the right to diminish, amputate, and restrict trans people's biological capacities. Hence the state implemented medicolegal regulations that not only reshaped and reconfigured the surfaces of trans people's bodies but also further expanded to the interiors of their bodies, eradicating their reproductive capabilities.

Trans men are also subject to the same medicolegal requirements as trans women, with the exception that there is no minimum size requirement for a penis. The technical aspects of bottom surgery place many trans men in an arduous situation, as phalloplasty takes approximately seventeen to eighteen hours, and the state declares a trans man as disabled on the completion of the operation.[21] When I inquired about the reasons for the status as disabled, one doctor stated that the postsurgical body would become physically weaker due to the loss of skin parts that were cut and utilized to build a penis. I think, however, that the immediate medical ascription of disability to postsurgical trans male bodies has something to do with the key role the military plays in the hegemonic construction of manhood in Turkey. Unless postsurgical trans men were categorized as disabled, they would become eligible for the obligatory military service, one of the key rites of passage of manhood in Turkey, reserved for a certain group of *natrans* men with hegemonic masculinity (see the introduction). But disability would exempt trans men from the obligatory military service.

It is also salient to underscore the institutional prejudices regarding the availability of GCS in the medical world. By law, every hospital should perform GCS as long as a person has obtained the court decision permitting the operation. Nevertheless, this was not the situation most of the time, and doctors rejected trans people on the grounds that their hospital would be stigmatized for performing such surgeries. The state, which was involved in regulating every single step of gender confirmation process, withdrew its leverage when it came to implementing regulatory tools to pressure hospitals to perform the operations. In one of our conversations, İlker articulated this sense of betrayal or abandonment by the state: "The state doesn't get itself [involved] in any of the troubles we are facing. It looks as if it is intervening in everything but, in fact, doesn't do anything except cause lots of legal impediments. It does nothing about either doctors or hospitals. It never holds doctors responsible for destroying one's body. However, we [trans people] face lots of legal barriers set by the state."

Here İlker specifies two possible forms of violence: First, the state may turn into an ignorant and unprotective entity when hospitals reject or fail trans people. Second, the medical establishment itself may deny trans surgery to trans people or cause irrevocable harm to their bodies. The state's meticulous involvement in the entire GCS process is indeed not about protecting its individual trans citizens but about sustaining a broader regime of gender binary and heteroreproductive sexuality. The state, as embodied in its medicolegal actors, is heavily invested in what Gayle Salamon calls *structuralization*. Quoting Paul Schilder, Salamon notes that one's body image (or a person's perception of their own body) is not a structure but a *structuralization*: "It is a creation and a construction and not a gift. *It is not a shape . . . but the production of a shape*."[22] The state's continuous logic of structuralization is apparent in the court space where a judge investigated İlker's sex/gender during his GCS trial. İlker had chosen to trick the legal system by trying to receive permission for GCS without undergoing sterilization. He had made an agreement with his doctor, but things did not turn out as he expected:

What is important for the judge is the law. He wants to see the paper, the paper that certifies your infertility. It doesn't matter if it is really the case or not, but he wants to see it officially written. I had already reached an agreement with my doctors, and the judge was going to give the permission to have the surgery as soon as he saw the record of my infertility. But the doctors did not want to write that I was infertile. They did not want to lie. Then the judge wanted to have two witnesses to support my case. My father brought two people from my home village. First the judge asked me to go out of the courtroom. Then he spoke a little bit with the witnesses. When he called me back, he started asking questions of the witnesses. One of the questions was "Did they ever wear a skirt?"[23] This question drove me crazy!!! The witnesses said, "No, we have never seen them wearing skirts, they used to wear pants." The judge: "Did they ever go to the coffeehouse?" The witnesses: "They were always with us in the coffeehouse." The judge: "Did they use to gamble in the coffeehouse?" He was asking about the most extreme cases of being a man!!! I have never done these things in my life. I was almost going to cry because I encountered something very remote from myself, very remote from *how I feel as a man*. I was so close to saying, "Forget about the report! I don't want your report anymore!" This made me feel very sad. If the judge had ever looked at my face, he could have seen that I was crying. But he kept asking, "Which games did they use to play?" And the witnesses answered something really masculine. Those questions were so intense for me. Those things that I have never done and I would never ever want to do!! The judge: "Did they have female or male friends? Which did they prefer more?" The witnesses said, "They did not have female friends at all. They would always make friends with males." Even the man from my village later asked me, "What do the games you play have to do with your maleness??" After questioning the witnesses, the judge permitted me to have a gender confirmation operation.

All these answers spoke to the rigid and stereotypical scripts of hegemonic masculinity in Turkey and demonstrated how İlker was successful at passing as a man in everyday social life. The state judge needed multiple actors who could reaffirm and hence *structuralize* İlker's body through their words. İlker could not recognize his gendered self in these statements. He did not feel like the man who was on display in the court space. Yet, at the same time, he was touched that his father's friends, despite knowing little about him, still agreed to support him by providing the necessary accounts of stereotypical gender for the judge to return a verdict of İlker's "true" sex. İlker's acquisition of the desired bodily surface was officially tied to his adequacy and capacity to give an account of the dominant performances of gender that were considered appropriate for his sex. And other male members of society had to testify to his adequacy in the dominant life circles of manhood. The state needed the gaze of its male citizens on İlker's body and lifestyle to make the final verdict about his sex/gender.

So far I have focused on medicolegal sites within which the state instrumentalizes the gaze and touch through its forensic scientists, judges, or legal witnesses for the normalization and control of the trans body. In this environment the state treats the trans body as passive and inanimate, as an objectified entity, as a surface to be inscribed and materialized with the signatures of state actors. This *structuralization* is not solely the product of medicolegal practices but rather is entangled in an entire world of everyday encounters, interactions, discourses, practices, and spaces that produce, and are produced by, a specific sociocultural logic of sex and gender. Our bodies might be objects for others, but they are at the same a lived reality for ourselves, as subjects. In general, the body represents a subjective material reality, which mediates people's "being-in-the-world."[24] Social reality is a bodily process. How one relates (oneself) to the world in general dynamically filters and is filtered by subjective perceptions of everyday life. Everyday perception thus becomes the main concern. One's body skillfully copes within the constant flow of sensory experience to gain an optimum grip on the situation. We become conscious of the world through the medium of our bodies in the realm of the physical: "Things are the prolongation of my body and my body is the prolongation of the world, through it the world surrounds me."[25] The body itself is the very maker of subjective material reality.

Hence, while being objectified by the state's medicolegal projects, trans people themselves acted on their subjective material reality through dynamic, productive, and imaginative forms of embodiment. For sure, they were also part of the process of materialization as well as the *structuralization* of the body, along with dominant understandings of sex/gender. But they were, at the same time, the actors of transgression, disruption, transformation, and rupture through multiple attachments to and experiences of trans embodiment. From inanimate, passive, or static representations, they reclaimed a corporeality that was productive, unruly, disruptive, and animate.[26]

Starting in the next section, I elucidate these bodily subjective material realities through the intimate dialogues and encounters in the trans everyday. These accounts indicate a variety of ascriptions as well as contestations of anatomy as evidence of one's sex and gender. It is salient to listen to how trans people negotiate the institutional transformation of their bodily materiality through the surgical process. For sure, attachments to trans surgery were multiple and diverse.

Vagina Dialogues

During our long afternoons in Istanbul LGBTT, we had lots of conversation about the gender confirmation process. While sitting around the table, chain smoking for hours, usually Sedef would start recounting one of the many horrible GCS stories from the beginning of the 1980s. Back then, having GCS and getting a new pink ID were strictly forbidden, resulting in a high number of informal GCSs. One person became very famous for these operations; he was nicknamed Timuçin the Butcher after having destroyed many trans women's genitals. In 2010 Sedef shared details of this history:

> A friend of ours attempted to cut her penis off by herself. . . . You know, it was not that easy to find a doctor to perform the operation in those days. . . . It is still not easy, but more or less you can find a way today. . . . This friend tried to cut her penis off but didn't succeed. . . . After a few days, her wound got really bad. She needed to see a doctor, but, you know, she wasn't able to visit just anyone. So, she went to this one, Timuçin the Butcher. He was already famous among us for performing the operation. . . . She went, and he laid her on his table and started doing the operation. . . . In fact, girls would not even call his place a doctor's office but a slaughterhouse.

Sedef then repeatedly mentioned the devastating and depressing effects of these operations on trans women's senses of their embodiment. These emotional and physical injuries also had to do with girls' economic status. Financial means played a crucial role in building up a desired female body, similar to any aesthetic surgery in a beauty economy.[27] However, in some cases this vaginal contract failed, and the dominant scripts of biology could no longer stand as a ground for one's sex/gender identification.

Instead, several trans women breached such doctrinal sexual/gender difference as biology and reinvented their own. For instance, some trans women would regard *natrans* women's reproductive capacity as a drawback rather than a norm and thus discursively dismantle hierarchies of cisness through moments of *gullüm*.

One day at Istanbul LGBTT, I was suffering from menstrual cramps, looking pale and sick. Esra asked me what was wrong, and I told her I had my period, hence the pain. On hearing this exchange, Ceyda, with her usual humor, said, "For goodness' sake! Thank God I don't menstruate. What would I have to do with bleeding, cramping, and getting depressed?! Also, I don't wanna get pregnant and be tormented by the cries and demands of babies. As long as my cunt eats up cocks, I don't need anything else!" And we all burst into laughter.

Another absorbing topic of conversation was the hymen and its construction during bottom surgery. The hymen and virginity carry a significant social value in materializing female-assigned bodies and their sexual contacts. With a strong symbolic value in connection to a woman's sexual morality, the hymen plays varying roles in defining, controlling, and concealing the female body from the heterosexual male gaze across social worlds including the Mediterranean, the Middle East, and beyond. In simple and quite general terms, while there is a wide social and patriarchal consensus in favor of men having sexual intercourse prior to marriage, women are expected to remain virgins, sexually untouched, and to keep their bodies "pure" for their husbands' access.[28] That said, it is crucial to underscore the key role that social class plays in young women's negotiations over their sexual agency in Turkey. Sociologist Gül Özyeğin's conceptualization of the "virginal façade" speaks to these negotiations and demonstrates how young elite *natrans* women in Istanbul reveal different sexual selves to their families and their friend circles by managing familial expectations for sexual modesty and the preservation of virginity and personal expectations for liberal sexuality.[29] Hence, they may retain their "technical virginity" by engaging in sexual relations except for penile-vaginal sexual intercourse.[30] If they have penetrative sexual contact, there is also the medical option of hymenoplasty, which has recently attracted scholarly attention from *natrans* perspectives in the Middle East, but trans interpretations of the hymen and its surgical construction are still ignored as a research topic.[31] *Lubunyalar* embraced this hymen discourse by narrating the loss of female virginity as part of their gender confirmation process. But they mostly ridiculed female virginity through hilarious stories that turned its symbolic power upside down. For example, one day Sedef started a conversation on virginity and hymens. She told her own story of losing her virginity to a young grocery store clerk from the same neighborhood. She used to work as a sex worker, and he was her client. After her bottom surgery, she chose him to "deflower" her. She burst into loud laughter on concluding the story. The ludicrous collocation of being a sex worker and a virgin at the same time precipitated laughter. Everybody in the room joined the conversation and told their stories one after another. Mockery and laughter were always a powerful linguistic terrain to disrupt hegemonic scripts of sexed/gendered biology and redefine or reinvent them anew. We all stressed and reiterated virginity as a symbolic source for patriarchal understandings of the female body/sexuality, yet, at the same time, undermined and deconstructed it through humorous stories of sexual bodily autonomy. It was a great moment of *güllüm*.

Vagina stories are not exclusive to trans and *natrans* women. Trans men or nonbinary people also have vagina stories, contesting the dichotomized materiality of the body as a condition for the definition of sex/gender. For instance, take İlker's following conversation with a middle-aged *natrans* man. İlker was incredibly skilled in playing the oud, a common instrument in Middle Eastern and North African music. He used to offer one-on-one tutorials, and one of his students was a middle-aged male solicitor. İlker told me about his constant discomfort and annoyance during the tutorials because his student would treat him like a woman, not a man. The solicitor would ask him irritating questions by slightly expressing his straight desire for women and sometimes even hit on İlker. One day İlker decided to confront him; he recounted their interaction as follows:

> One day we had lunch together, and I told him that I was a transsexual. He was so shocked that he could hardly swallow the morsel in his mouth. Then I continued, "You treat me like this and that. I am extremely bothered by your attitude. I feel like a man myself, but you treat me like a woman." There was a moment of silence, which was interrupted by his questions: "Well, for example, I am a man, and I like women. Do you like women?" I said, "Positive!" He again tried to challenge me: "Are you sure that you are a man? Maybe it is something psychological. Maybe it is a matter of time; you might be feeling like a man temporarily, then you will feel like a woman again." He kept asking questions. I guess he thought there was a problem with me, and he

could solve it. He repeated again, "Perhaps it is a psychological problem. You can see a doctor!" Then I replied, "Not mine, but perhaps your situation poses a psychological problem. You better see a doctor!" He said, "No way! My maleness cannot be a psychological state. I have organs!" I said, "So I think it is even worse! Perhaps since you've seen your penis in front of you, you might have thought that you are a man. I urge you to go and see a doc! Despite my vagina, if I still feel like a man myself, then my manhood is indisputable. But yours is dubious." After this conversation he never wanted to see me again" [laughs].[32]

This whole conversation was about the hegemonic insistence on staging the bodily surface as a site of evidence to reveal the "truth" of a body's sex. The solicitor's words reflected not only social and cultural accumulations of normalized sex/gender configurations but also the ways heterosexual desire, far from being external, was inherent to the production and reproduction of such combinations. However, in this dialogue, desire still represented a secondary source of evidence. When the solicitor detected İlker's absent desire for men, he then appealed to biological verification as the ultimate ground for establishing the "truth." In response, İlker remarkably undermined anatomy as a self-referential indicator of a body's sex and accentuated its complexity beyond a pure physical category.[33] In this way, he shows a way of "seeing [genital] difference differently."[34] İlker's words resonate with what feminist biologist Anne Fausto-Sterling reminds us over and over again: "A body's sex is simply too complex. There is no either/or. Rather, there are shades of difference. . . . The more we look for a simple physical basis for 'sex,' the more it becomes clear that 'sex' is not a pure physical category."[35]

Through the preceding stories, the corporeal is set not only as an official stage for materialization of sex by the state's medicolegal discourses and practices but also as an unofficial stage through everyday sensorial and haptic relations as well as through conversations. This domain of the trans (as well as the *natrans*) everyday, moreover, encompasses more than verbal and practical indications of a body's sex. It is also saturated with affects, senses, perceptions, and emotions that materialize and structure our bodies. In the final section, I return to the role of the sensorial in the materialization of sex/gender, this time in the everyday corporeality of social life in the streets. The boundaries between touch and the gaze are blurred, as the latter, I argue, gains the characteristics of the former, feeling invasive, and at times, almost haptic.

The Touching Gaze

Bodies are constantly touched not only by the gendered or the sexual gaze but also by the racial gaze, the ethnic gaze, and the classed gaze. The tactile violence of the gaze has indeed been at the center of critical race and colonial studies. Frantz Fanon, with his piercing analysis of internalized psychology under colonial conditions, pioneered the phenomenological work on racialization and racism as a structuring mechanism for the self and the other. In *Black Skins, White Masks*, Fanon provides a poignant description of the Black body in relation to the white gaze:

> I had to meet the white man's eyes. An unfamiliar weight burdened me. In the white world the man of color encounters difficulties in the development of his bodily schema. . . . Consciousness of the body is solely a negating activity. It is a third person consciousness. The body is surrounded by an atmosphere of certain uncertainty. . . . A slow composition of my *self* as a body in the middle of a spatial and temporal world—such seems to be the schema. . . . [I]t is, rather, a definitive structuring of the self and of the world—definitive because it creates a real dialectic between my body and the world. . . . I was battered down by tom-toms, cannibalism, intellectual deficiency, fetishism, racial defects, slave-ships. . . . I took myself far off from my own presence. . . . What else could it be for me but an amputation, an excision, a hemorrhage that spattered my whole body with black blood?[36]

Here the white gaze is a structuring force. It can weigh on, amputate, cut, or "break up the black man's body," or, in George Yancy's words, it changes, deforms, and makes the Black body into an ontological problem.[37] An everyday navigation of life becomes a constellation of affective registers that leave their traces on the surfaces of bodies, on the skin, or simply shape them. A moment of this bodily encounter is saturated with an array of feelings that comprise ambivalence, unease, terror, fear, hate, disgust, anger, and so on. Through a mediation of these feelings, the white gaze violently touches the Black body.

My purpose here is not to equate the Black experience of violence with the trans one, or racism with transmisogyny (though, for many, they also intersect) but rather to find a language to delineate the uneven material and affective undercurrents of a sensorial exchange between normative and marginalized bodies, which are also not fixed in themselves. The geographic location I am writing and theorizing from has also historically been marked, staged, fantasized, circulated, and consumed through a particular economy of the gaze, namely, the oriental one. Critical studies of orientalism extensively discuss the centrality of the gaze in regimes of knowledge production and power pertaining to the creation of "the East" and "the Eastern other" within colonial and imperial economies of passion, desire, fantasy, and exoticism.[38] The wider geography of the Ottoman Empire (which includes the territories of present-day Turkey and their shared capital, Istanbul) was a popular landscape in this orientalist economy of the gaze, which continues to shape global perceptions of the Middle East and its multiple and diverse people into a monolithic representation mainly characterized by primitivity, an uncivilized way of life, simplicity, barbarism, and perpetual chaos and violence. In this orientalist framework, the gaze is mainly white, Western, male, and straight, and it incessantly reproduces a distorted reality of the East through standardization, objectification, and cultural stereotyping. Edward Said's *Orientalism* delineates how this process of dehumanization has created the ideal other for Europe by fixating it outside history, in an eternal image of irrationality and excess violence and sexuality. This uneven representative framework, whose racial, sexual, and erotic legacy continues to this day, has been fundamentally invested in a particular regime of vision, a "scopic desire," or the orientalist gaze.[39] Hence, putting critical studies of race into conversation with studies of orientalism, I aim to develop a more nuanced framework of violent intimacies that emerge out of sensorial and affective exchanges, especially out of the gaze and its tactile capacities.

The gaze—or stare—is an important aspect of cultural and social life in Turkey. *Nazar* (gaze), for instance, is associated with the evil eye that brings harm to those people touched by its gaze (*nazar değmek*). As Sertaç Sehlikoğlu notes, in the sensational registers of everyday life, the gaze may feel tactile rather than visual through its violating and even penetrating capacity.[40] As a woman, I have neither become used to it nor entirely normalized it. Its diminishing and restricting power can reach the level of sexual assault, focusing on particular body parts and attacking one's sense of one's own body. People also direct strong looks generally in judgment of other people's physical appearance, bodily features, and outfits. Indeed, everyday life can become quite violently intimate through the mediation of the sexual and gendering gaze.[41]

For instance, on one of the very first days I met Sedef, Ceyda, and Esra in 2009, we prepared to go home after a long afternoon at Istanbul LGBTT, and they asked me to walk with them until Taksim Square, where I was to take the bus home. It was a Friday evening, which meant people from all over the city would be arriving for the night's entertainment. Ceyda and I walked together, with Esra and Sedef following behind. Then Ceyda took my arm. I was surprised to find myself being drawn into this physical contact so quickly. As we walked along the street, arms held tight, I began to ask some questions, addressing her as Duygu, the name with which she had introduced herself when we first met. She made a face and said, "Don't call me Duygu anymore; my real name is Ceyda! Duygu is my sex-worker name."

Drawn into this intimacy and walking with Sedef, Ceyda, and Esra sensitized me to the heaviness of the gaze and the questioning looks to which our bodies were subjected. It was a relatively familiar experience of exposure to such intense scrutiny from all different directions on the street. Growing up in Turkey as a *natrans* woman had familiarized me with a particular style of harassing heterosexual male gaze, which always made me feel highly conscious of my body in public. But this was more intense. The looks were sexual as much as judgmental, causing a powerful sense of bodily self-consciousness as I walked, a feeling of limitation and confinement made by being stared at. Here, though, I should note and recognize the performance of consensual eye contact or the exchange of gazes as a currency of desire in flirting cultures and cruising economies. Nevertheless, the gaze we were exposed to was nothing like flirtatiousness but rather nonconsensual and penetrating. It felt powerfully violent.

When I stared back at them, they would not shy away but kept staring even more stubbornly. In this unsettling exchange of looks, the words of another trans friend resonated in my mind: "You feel at ease nowhere! You feel comfortable at home, but you become bashful outside. As if you are a beast passing near them. You see how they move their shoulders, mouths, and heads to signal each other to mark you. This attitude destroys a person psychologically. Yet they don't understand that we are living under the same sky and breathing the same air. They don't know that we're human too."

The intensity of the gaze began to annoy me, but Ceyda just smiled and told me to ignore it. She had had to develop a thick skin herself to endure such looks, that is, to cope with this violent intimacy between her skin and the beholder's eye on an everyday basis. Her ignorance was a protective sensorial shield to comfort her body in public and claim her corporeal space in the streets. Everyday eye contact can be/feel so violent that we can no longer speak about clear boundaries between the gaze and the touch.

Even the phrase *eye contact* (also in Turkish, *göz teması*) linguistically refers to a certain capacity of touch that rests in the eye: *The eye can touch.* These optical encounters can operate as a performance of domination, subordination, dismemberment, and dislocation.

More broadly, cultural and social codes shape the ways people look at each other. These codes, in turn, may function as a disciplinary and/or punitive sensorial tool that organizes social life, gender roles, and sexuality in particular. Unless one fits into the norm, one feels the strong presence of these piercing looks as one navigates public spaces in either urban or rural settings. The gaze can be a form of investigation directed at a stranger entering a communal space. Or, inversely, young women can be trained to shy away from looking men in the eyes as it might be interpreted as consenting to sexual intimacy. Associated gender conventions tend to socialize women and girls into not looking authoritarian male figures in the eye, such as the father, the husband, male state officials, or older men in general. These modes and meanings of looking require us to stress the organization of everyday cultural and social life in Turkey and its strong phenomenological character, which functions on various power differentials based on sex/gender, age, religion, class, and ethnicity. Yet marginalized groups also look at the dominant in the eye to challenge the distribution of power.[42]

Conclusion

The bodily materialization of sex/gender can take myriad ways and forms, one of which was the topic of this chapter, that is, the use of the sensorium in the form of touch and the gaze. Be it the penetrative touch in the state forensic offices or the penetrative look outside on the streets, the sensorium and its uneven distribution among social groups shape the contours of our bodies, and the surfaces of our skin, materializing our sense of embodiment.

Penetrative medicolegal practices exerted on trans women suggest that the state in Turkey can become quite intimate with the bodies of its citizens by incorporating sexual practices derived from particular heterosexual desires and fantasies that ascribe the institutional actors the position of the penetrator. Deploying instruments of touch, the state plays a central role in the production and regulation of sexual difference, a normative domain of sexuality and gender, and "properly" sexed bodies. The touching characteristics of the medicolegal practices allow the state to establish violent intimacies with trans people's bodies as well as gain a specific content, that is, an active penetrative, masculinist, and heteronormative body.

Indeed, state institutions are not the sole actors in attempts to objectify the sexed/gender body. Everyday life in the streets unfolds in a sensorial regime of the gaze that constantly marks and structuralizes bodies with gendered/sexed expectations. At times, the sexual/gendered gaze can also become violently intimate by gaining an ability to touch the bodies under staring and judgmental eyes. Being gazed at can feel like being touched.

The body is not fixed, passive, and stable but rather fluid, active, and unstable. It always exceeds the limits or boundaries that are determined to restrict it to the sites of particular inscriptions and representations. In that sense, the vagina stories in this chapter demonstrate a generous account of bodily capacities that are subjective, affective, and material. A closer look at them draws attention to how trans people sense and live their bodies and bodily selves. Some trans people might desire to incorporate the norms of the sexed/gendered body, and some might prefer to break them down and invest in nonconformity. It is of great importance to remember Judith Butler's words: "I may feel that without some recognizability I cannot live. But I may also feel that the terms by which I am recognized make life unlivable."[43] The problem occurs when one form of materialization becomes the norm, forecloses other possible forms, and provides the only available means of recognition in the dominant sexual and gendered order.

Bodily experience and the body, with its tremendous capacities, will always exceed the objectifications (including trans and *natrans* people's own self-objectifications) that define it as a writable, observable, and controllable object. It can breach, trespass, break down, or dismantle reductionist frameworks and restraining orders of institutions and social life. In fact, the next chapter problematizes a similar issue by focusing on the writing of the trans body into the domain of law through femicides, illustrating queer and trans activist attempts to legalize "hate crimes," and discussing the unjust repercussions of legal verdicts.

Chapter Five

Justice, Criminal Law, & Trans Femicides

IN 2016 HANDE KADER, a twenty-three-year-old trans woman sex worker, was found dead in Zekeriyaköy, a wealthy suburb in the northern outskirts of Istanbul. She had been gang-raped, tortured, mutilated, and burned. Hande was also a well-known trans activist. The year before, she had been at the forefront of clashes with the police when they used rubber bullets, water cannons, and batons to suppress the Pride March in Istanbul for the first time since its initiation. Hande's murder caused an outcry among sex workers, queer and trans activists, and feminists, leading to a series of protests and campaigns to raise voice and awareness about the targeted killings of trans women in Turkey. The LGBTI+ Student Club at Boğaziçi University created a fellowship in her name to financially support one trans student per year. Yet later this initiative was discontinued by the office of the university president.

Hande was one of the ninety-one trans women who we know were viciously murdered by *natrans* men between 2002 and 2019 in Turkey.[1] These men were typically either the trans women's lovers or their clients. After each trans femicide, LGBTI+ activists and feminists held protests and campaigns and vocalized their struggles and legal demands for justice from the state. It is crucial to highlight once again that neither same-sex sexuality nor transness is legally criminalized in Turkey, but the Turkish criminal justice system has a number of legal tools that make it challenging for queer and trans activists to seek justice for these murders. Even when the perpetrators are charged in court, Turkish criminal law manifests a culture of impunity and has failed to develop effective sanctions against perpetrators, often reducing the culprit's sentence on the grounds of "unjust provocation" (*haksız tahrik*). During some other trans women's murder trials, the victim's suggestion of or request for same-sex intercourse was one of the most recurrent defenses that appeared in the perpetrators' confessions. Many alleged that they had met the victim via the internet and hence had no idea she was a trans woman, in their words, a "male" since the victim still had a penis. They claimed that they felt humiliated and killed her. Courts considered this a mitigating factor in their judgment, and the perpetrators received a lesser punishment on the grounds of unjust provocation.

In response to the frequent use of unjust provocation as a defense in trans murder trials, queer and trans activists started to deploy and mobilize the discourse of "hate crimes" to reframe the culprit's criminal act. They aimed to erase homophobia as a mitigating factor from the criminal law and to redistribute justice to sexual and gender minorities. Through their campaigns and demonstrations, queer and trans activists also held the state responsible for targeted killings of trans women, since the state's security forces and judicial institutions showed little interest in finding or punishing the criminals, further solidifying their impunity.

In an attempt to examine the urban LGBTI+ political life and discourse that emerge from the relations between the legal categories of unjust provocation and hate crimes, this chapter centers the case of İrem, a trans woman sex worker who was murdered by a client in 2010. The LGBTI+ politics was grounded in a set of claims to rightful living and gender and sexual justice that recognize trans lives as lives that matter and that should be respected. While one pillar of this political struggle was repealing the unjust provocation defense at trans murder trials, the other pillar was advocating for hate crime legislation, a legal struggle that worked within a broader transnational lexicon and framework of human rights. This discussion allows me to draw attention to the tense and intimate relationship between law and justice within the context of LGBTI+ politics in the urban setting of Istanbul. I also explore the Turkish criminal law and the ways it is implemented as a significant source of injustice in the lives of LGBTI+ people, especially trans women sex workers. A salient focus is on how the calculations of justice in the form of the law foreclose specific desires, sexualities, and bodies, thus simultaneously producing and shaping unjust lives. A closer look at trans femicides shows how law plays a role in cultivating a culture of impunity that leads to the continued killings of trans women by implicitly announcing that trans women have criminal bodies rather than developing effective sanctions against the perpetrators. But as I have stressed several times, trans people were not passively determined by this law but rather contested its violent design and organized campaigns and demonstrations to claim their rights, lives, and relations. In that sense, LGBTI+ political organizing against trans killings was another story of violent intimacies, as the process of organizing itself generated bonds, affinities, solidarities, attachments, and affects.

"Unjust" Sexual Acts

In September 2010 İrem was found dead in her house, stabbed forty-four times and cleaved from throat to abdomen. Her murderer was a twenty-two-year-old man whom İrem had met online. When the police arrested the culprit, he tried to reduce his penalty by using the logic of unjust provocation. During the investigation by the police and his trial, he admitted:

> We had been seeing each other for a while. When the incident happened, I was paying one of my visits to their place.[2] I drank a bottle of beer. I had sexual intercourse with them [*Kendisiyle cinsel ilişkiye girdim*]. Then they asked to have sex with me [*Sonra o benimle ilişkiye girmek istedi*]. I didn't accept. We argued. When they cursed me, I went insane. I got hold of a knife and stabbed them twice. I don't remember the rest. . . . Not to leave any trace behind me, I took the laptop, cell phone, and some jewelry, and I ran away.[3]

In his defense the culprit makes an interesting point with his use of unjust provocation. He says, "I had sexual intercourse with them," which could mean that the culprit took either the "active" (penetrator) and/or the "passive" (recipient) role in sexual intercourse. However, the way the next sentence, "Then they asked to have sex with me," is phrased in Turkish makes it clear that the culprit first took an "active" role in the sexual intercourse but then was asked to take the "passive" role. His gendered self as a straight man seems not to have been threatened until this moment of the putative sexual proposal. However, when he was asked to be penetrated, the form of sexual intercourse became destructive to his straight self, thus insulting his manhood. In the eyes of the culprit, the nature of sexual intercourse and the roles of "active" and "passive" defined masculinity and femininity, as well as heteronormativity more generally, an issue that I discussed in the introduction.[4] The culprit was seeking a reduction in his punishment based on this particular definition of same-sex sexuality. A feeling of threat or insult to one's straight masculine self would be legally regarded as unjust provocation. One can also argue that the state brings closure to the sexual and gender anxieties of straight men through unjust provocation.

İrem's lawyer requested her GCS report from the hospital. According to this report, İrem had had testicular removal surgery as part of her gender confirmation process, losing reproductive capacity. Until the arrival of the report, her body was appraised as male, and her alleged proposal to take the active role in sexual intercourse with the culprit was listed as proof of insult, sexual assault, and molestation. However, once the evidence of her bodily surface made its way to the court, the judge reinterpreted the sexual relationship as a non-same-sex one, since she did not have testicles.[5]

However, İrem was also not regarded as a female before the law. The removal of her reproductive capacities meant no legal category of sex would apply to her. There could not be any same-sex intercourse. The judge rejected the demand of the defendant's attorney to take unjust provocation into consideration. In contrast to the defendant's use of unjust provocation related to a sex act, the court decision relied on the materiality of the body and its meanings. They passed judgment on the body, not the act, or whatever acts particular bodies can and cannot do. The defendant's use of "unjust provocation" as a mitigating facto was not taken into account. As a result, he was sentenced to twenty-eight years in prison for committing murder.

Some LGBTI+ activists considered this the first time trans people had received some justice in the legal system. The sentence of twenty-eight years of imprisonment signified a partial accomplishment in regard to the recognition of lethal antitrans violence. "Justice is (in part) a matter of emotion," and we might even approach criminal law as an institutionalization of certain emotions.[6] Law has the power to collectively satisfy and express certain emotions, such as vengeance, rage, anger, and even hatred, thus serving justice in part. For the LGBTI+ activists, the verdict at İrem's trial restored a partial sense of emotional justice, leading to some sense of relief and satisfaction.

But how should trans people approach these prison sentences beyond their relation to emotional justice? Should they see them as merely numerical accounts of court decisions, or as calculations that are the product of complex contestations over what justice should look like in the murder trials of trans women? To be more precise, I am more concerned with the question of how such calculations are made possible and how justice is presented in mathematical terms. For instance, how would the judge calculate just punishment if İrem's sexual relationship with her murderer had been deemed a same-sex one?

Just Futures, Legal Presents

"What does it mean to establish the truth of justice?"[7] In his speech "Force of Law," Jacques Derrida poses this question to discuss the tension between law and justice. According to popular understandings of justice, people usually base their justice claims on the inscription, interpretation, and utilization of specific laws, thus deriving a definition of justice from calculable grounds. As Derrida reminds us, however, justice always exceeds law and calculation: "Law (*droit*) is not justice. Law is the element of calculation, and it is just that there be law, but justice is incalculable, it requires us to calculate with the incalculable."[8] The chief question for Derrida then becomes how to approach and understand justice in the face of calculation because "the act of justice that must always concern singularity, individuals, irreplaceable groups and lives, the other or myself *as* other, in a unique situation," poses a conflict with justice as law, which always supposes the generality of a rule, a norm, and a universal imperative.[9] With each legal decision of judgment, justice is deferred.

With reference to this definition of justice as a moment of deferral, Sara Ahmed underscores a salient point about the temporal element in Derrida's understanding of justice. She declares that justice "is also an opening toward an unlivable future, in which one lives 'with' the need to re-justify to and for others who are always yet to come."[10] This remark is crucial because justice is never only about the present but rather also about the past, which is sedimented within the present, as much as it is about the future. This future is inhabited by yet-to-come subjects who will be affected by the decisions and judgments made in the present, about the past.

The deferral of justice, however, does not mean that people should stop investing their energies in lawmaking processes or legal struggles because there is always the threat of the worst legal calculation. For example, fascism can be listed as one of the worst calculations. But, at the same time, Derrida warns us that the law itself should not be assumed as a ground for securing or achieving justice. No matter how radically progressive the legal decisions or judgments might be, they will always escape justice, or justice escapes them.

This seemingly unbridgeable gap between law and justice shapes one form of political struggle. Some of our political struggles for justice emanate in tandem with legal formulations because law itself might be unjust when it comes to specific lives, bodies, histories, and sociocultural worlds. Also, law is the language of the state that is the signatory of both acts of injustice (to activists) and justice (through the courts). That is to say, law is also the space of closure—it is a limit zone of life, desire and embodiment.

In her discussion of Derrida's article, Ahmed states that Derrida does not provide us a positive model of justice by pronouncing "what is justice" or "what are the proper criteria for deciding the case in a way which is just."[11] Justice, for him, is always and already negated in the present even as it secures the possibility of futurity due to its deferred nature. Hence, with Derrida, it is more useful to think about injustice than justice because "an injustice occurs when a (deconstructable) constitution is used to found a judgment in the name of justice."[12]

I want to return to the trial for İrem's murder to analyze the role of law in creating injustice under the guise of justice. Remember the discussion on İrem's sex/gender and the culprit's claims regarding the sexual affair between them. The sentence he received reflected the victim's sex, which also shaped what types of sexual acts or desires were regarded as legal, while others were foreclosed and seen as precipitating the construction of criminal subjects. Therefore, through the judge's court decisions, desires or sexual acts that fall outside of the heterosexual domain are inscribed as improper, and hence perpetrators who punish these desires or sexual acts deserve lesser penalties. Consequently, the state failed to uphold the right of nondiscrimination on the grounds of sexual orientation and gender identity.

It should be underscored that İrem's case presents us with the production and stipulation of a specific model of justice, which concerns İrem's lost life as well as her mother's and friends' mechanisms for coping with this loss. Heteronormativity becomes the model of both life and justice that the court advances. When İrem's medical results reached the court, the judge no longer regarded the sexual acts as same-sex intercourse. As soon as the sexual intercourse was medically proved to be non-same-sex intercourse, unjust provocation was nullified. In this way, unjust provocation served as a legal medium that distributed the values of heteronormativity accordingly over matters of queer and sex/gender-transgressive lives and deaths.

Contextualizing Unjust Provocation

Unjust provocation is defined in Article 29 of the Turkish Penal Code as a mitigating factor in the punishment of culprits who experience temporary psychological malfunction due to victims' unjust acts or behaviors just prior to their death. Certain conditions are required for a crime to be regarded as caused by unjust provocation. First, there should be an adequate provoking act prior to the incident. Second, the mentioned act should be *haksız* (unjust). Third, the defendant must have acted in the heat of rage or violent grief. Fourth, there should be a causal link among the provocation, the rage or violent grief, and the homicide. Fifth, the homicide must be a reaction triggered by this rage, anger, or violent grief; and, last, the criminal act should be directed toward the subject who provoked the act.[13] Upon satisfying these conditions, culprits can receive reduced punishments.

Before moving on to the details of unjust provocation, it is salient to mention another piece of legislation, Article 438 of the Turkish Penal Code, which allowed reduced punishments based on sexual morals until 1990. Article 438 reduced the punishment of a rapist by one-third if the victim was proved to be a sex worker. The logic behind this regulation had strong ties to a culture of honor that differentially valued non-sex-worker women over sex workers and categorized them as chaste and unchaste (*iffetli* and *iffetsiz*), respectively. Feminists organized a series of campaigns under the banner of "No to 438!," which included publicizing the issue through feminist journals, newspapers, and leaflets; delivering press statements in different parts of Istanbul (including the famous red-light district of the Beyoğlu area, Zürafa Street); and organizing a protest march from Üsküdar to Bağlarbaşı in 1990. A prominent trans feminist sex worker, Demet Demir, also took part in this campaign and read a collective press statement that defied the state's legal separation of women into chaste and unchaste through Article 438. Later in 1990, Article 438 was annulled due to the pressure created by the ongoing feminist protests.[14] Bringing trans and *natrans* women and sex workers together, this was a major achievement in the history of feminism in Turkey.

Since the annulment of Article 438, "unjust provocation" has become another crucial political platform for trans/*natrans* and queer feminists organizing against femicides in Turkey. Until recently, unjust provocation was mainly associated with "honor killings." Sentences for killing women would be reduced by one-third if it was done in the name of honor.[15] Fathers, husbands, brothers, or boyfriends who killed their daughters, wives, sisters, and girlfriends to protect their honor would benefit from reduced punishments due to unjust provocation.[16] In strong opposition to this legislation, feminist organizations organized several campaigns to have "honor killings" categorized as first-degree murders. Eventually, the Turkish state responded by introducing legal amendments to the penal code in 2005. The category of "honor crimes" was replaced with "crimes of tradition," and femicide in the name of tradition was regarded as a first-degree murder with a sentence of life imprisonment. This new terminology established strong links between femicides and specific traditions attributed to Kurdish people in Turkey—a legal inscription that reflected the Turkish state's long-existing racialization of Kurds. The legislation around crimes of tradition allowed the Turkish people to imagine themselves as modern subjects in favor of greater gender equality between men and women, as opposed to the Kurdish people, who were stereotyped as victimizing their women through "honor killings."[17] In this way, the inscription and implementation of legislation around femicides have further solidified the hegemonically imagined racial boundaries between those identified as Turkish (as developed, Westernized, and educated) and those identified as Kurdish (as backward, Eastern, and undereducated).

The replacement of "honor crimes" with "crimes of tradition" has opened a passage to sentence crimes where the entire community or family consent to the killing, and then the killing is carried out by a chosen member. But this amendment is still not effective in punishing homicides that are committed by men not as a result of communal or family decisions but out of jealousy, anger, or hatred. In these homicide court cases, a defense of unjust provocation is still frequently used to reduce the punishment. The most prominent victims of this legislation are women, gays, and trans people. For example, some court cases from 2008 and 2009 show that even trivial issues were judicially approved as adequate reasons for men to kill their wives based on unjust provocation: "I offered her some fruit juice, but she didn't take it," "She flirtatiously asked a man the time," "She wore jeans and tights," and "She didn't want to have sex with me and pushed me out of the bed."[18] These testimonies were accepted as provoking acts by the judges, confirming the perpetuation of a culture of honor by the modern state institutions themselves.[19]

In 2009, the distinction between honor crimes and crimes of tradition was nullified by the Supreme Court in a ruling related to murder. Two brothers from Kayseri, a central Anatolian city in Turkey, killed a man whom they suspected of having a love affair with their widowed mother, an affair that stained their family honor. The court of first instance treated the mother's moral turpitude as a mitigating factor when sentencing her sons for killing her lover. Because of "unjust provocation," the two brothers were sentenced to only six and ten years of imprisonment. When the Supreme Court of Turkey heard the appeal of this case in 2010, they reversed the local court's judgment because the motivating factors for the murder (i.e., to protect their mother's and the family's honor, as stated by the defendants) were the same as those for crimes of tradition—which were illegal. On the grounds of this similarity, the Supreme Court overruled the initial court decision and declared that the mother's behavior did not represent an adequately provoking act; consequently, it sentenced the culprits to life imprisonment.[20] It is difficult to guess how the Supreme Court would have ruled if the mother had happened to still be married. Nevertheless, this case became a precedent for decisions related to honor crimes. From 2009 on, the courts have had to evaluate honor crimes and crimes of tradition as one and the same and therefore have had to deliver the same sentence, that is, life imprisonment. In short, the merger of two different penal categories put an end to reduced sentences due to unjust provocation.

Despite this ruling on family or community initiated homicides, the use of unjust provocation as a mitigating factor is still effective in reducing sentences for those individuals who kill women, queer and trans people. When LGBTI+ people are concerned, there is not in fact much legal restoration at all. Now let me turn to the ways that circumstances and testimonies are constructed as unjust provocation in relation to queer and trans settings.

Wanton Proposals

A majority of court decisions concerning murders of queer and trans people show that a proposal of same-sex relations is often considered unjust provocation by judges.[21] In some of these cases, the culprits confessed that they were offered money in return for same-sex intercourse. They claimed they were humiliated, insulted, and driven crazy by such "unjust" words or acts. Many court cases demonstrate that these accounts were widely accepted by the judges as valid mitigating factors because the culprits might easily have become furious or lost their self-control. Some judges even evaluated a proposal for same-sex sexual intercourse as molestation and/or sexual assault. What is striking in these trials is the role that emotions played in shaping legal decisions. Through the use of unjust provocation, judges and culprits met at a point where disgust and repulsion were legitimated and used to attribute lesser value to queer and trans lives.[22] Disgust and repulsion embodied what was socially and morally unacceptable, beyond sexual/gender norms.

Under the Turkish Penal Code, acts that can be considered unjust provocation include extorting money, insulting someone, breaking and entering or otherwise violating the private residence, wounding someone by stabbing, limiting someone's freedom, or threatening someone, and raping or beating someone. Proposing same-sex intercourse is placed in the same legal category as these behaviors. This categorization imbues the sex/gender-transgressive person and queer sexual practice—which otherwise have no voice or visibility in the sphere of law—with a violating and repulsive character. Therefore, it can be argued that unjust provocation also constitutes the very terms under which queer possibilities appear within the law, yet in a criminal form. Queer forms of intimacy or sexual acts find no "safe habitation" within the space of law.[23]

Another instance of queer appearance within the terms of criminal law can be traced via the following incident. During the trial for a woman's murder by her husband, the Supreme Court based its judgment on striking circumstances. The woman victim and her husband were separated, and the woman was staying with a trans woman friend of hers. The following phrases can be found in the transcript of the trial: "a woman who lives with a person called *travesti*, who would hang out with random men in bars and clubs" and "according to objective criteria, the victim's choice of lifestyle might rightly cause the husband to think that he would be cheated on by his wife."[24] As a result, the victim's housing situation (i.e., being a trans woman's housemate) was legally considered an adequate provoking act for the husband to kill his wife.

Criminal law becomes a space of "hypervisibility" for queer subjects, while they do not even count as subjects in civil law.[25] Unjust provocation in Turkey is just one example of this queer visibility. Queer and sex/gender-transgressive lives—invisible in civil law—emerge as legal matters and thus gain judicial definitions via the terms of criminal law. However, not all visibility is a guarantee of empowerment or freedom.[26] Hence, part of the struggle for queer and trans justice in Turkey is to open up myriad spaces of legal visibility and to extend the already existing ones, whether it be through hate crime legislation or access to human rights. This was also the case at the trial for İrem's murder: there was a strong LGBTI+ activist presence inside and outside the court, unlike at some other trials for trans murders. Inside the court, the political struggle was over the unfair use of unjust provocation. Outside the court, a political campaign for hate crimes legislation coalesced. In an attempt to pressure the Turkish judiciary to define İrem's and many other trans women's murders as hate crimes, LGBTI+ activists problematized the understanding of such murders as sporadic crimes and linked them to larger political issues concerning trans lives and deaths.

However, this legal struggle also has its own problems because the mechanisms of closure and the exclusion of a multiplicity of voices are inherent to the constitution and inscription of laws. While laws might satisfy certain emotions, they might also cause more emotional distress, disappointment, and injustice. The rest of this chapter discusses this issue. A detailed account of LGBTI+ legal struggles in Turkey demonstrates how queer and trans people shaped definitions of, and struggled for, justice and how these definitions and this fight for queer and trans justice were contested in a complex circle of politics that involved state actors, different LGBTI+ groups, and trans people themselves.

LGBTI+ Politics of Rights and the State

Today's LGBTI+ people in Turkey increasingly emphasize making their way into the domain of law, achieving legal recognition and inclusion in the nation's body politic, and being treated as full citizens with a complete set of rights. In this sociopolitical context, the transnational discourses of human rights and hate crimes have become prevalent in the organization and circulation of LGBTI+ discourses and claims. With the intertwinement of local, regional, and global LGBTI+ worlds, LGBTI+ communities in Turkey have utilized the category of hate crimes and human rights discourses to occupy the legal gray zone, to seek to establish legal protections and to push for social justice. I approach this political language as a justice-serving mechanism and problematize the kinds of closure it constructs and the other forms of calculation it makes possible, potentially opening a larger realm of injustice. In other words, I explore how a legal struggle for justice might have unjust consequences. But first I want to elucidate the wider political context in which hate crime discourse has become a strong currency within the LGBTI+ movement.

Trans femicides are part of a broader pattern of violence against LGBTI+ people in Turkey, and the state plays a major part in it. Over the course of my research, the speeches of state actors contributed widely to the dissemination of hatred against LGBTI+ people and strengthened already existing public prejudices. What you will read in the following pages is actually the starting point of the 2022 AKP government's current official warfare against LGBTI+ lives, a situation that formally commenced in 2010 and has been accelerating and consolidating especially since 2015 (see the preface and coda).

In 2010 a speech by Selma Aliye Kavaf, minister of state for women and family issues, provoked reactions among the LGBTI+ community in Turkey due to her controversial comments on morals and values. Her opinions on same-sex sexuality and gay marriage in particular mobilized many LGBTI+ people to draw attention to "homophobic" features of the Turkish state for months succeeding Kavaf's speech. "I believe *eşcinsellik* is a biological disorder, a disease," said Kavaf in an interview with a popular newspaper. She added, "I believe [*eşcinsellik*] is something that needs to be treated. Therefore, I do not have a positive opinion of gay marriage."[27] Months later, the resonances of Kavaf's speech continued, and she became the most addressed target of LGBTI+ press conferences and declarations about hate crimes in Turkey (figure 5.1). Different LGBTI+ organizations gathered together to call on her to apologize because the words that she uttered as a state representative would contribute to increasing hate crimes against LGBTI+ people rather than preventing LGBTI+ people from being killed. Throughout my fieldwork I participated in approximately eight rallies organized by Istanbul LGBTT against hate crimes and trans femicides. As each of them took place, Kavaf gradually began to be addressed as the embodied form of official homophobia and transphobia that existed at the state level. By hailing Kavaf and her institution-affiliated position of power, people would curse or blame the state for hate crimes and call on the state to apologize to LGBTI+ people. In these rallies the state and its justice system were blamed for defending hate and not protecting the lives of LGBTI+ citizens.

On a wider political note, Kavaf's declaration served as a litmus test to draw boundaries between different political camps and organizations as being either for or against LGBTI+ rights in Turkey.[28] As LGBTI+ activists organized demonstrations to condemn Kavaf for her words, the discussion about whether to understand same-sex sexuality as a disease or not gradually evolved into a more complicated phase by inciting conservative people

5.1 Protest on March 11, 2010. The slogan on the banner reads "Latest spokesperson of the diseased system: Selma Aliye Kavaf, resign!" Photo by the author.

to articulate the matter at stake, namely, same-sex sexuality, by deploying different terminology than used in the West. Hilal Kaplan, a young religious Muslim female journalist (and currently a powerful spokesperson for the AKP government) who became popular among Islamist and liberal intellectuals, especially since 2009, spearheaded the discussion on how to talk about same-sex sexuality in appropriate Islamic terminology. In her column she described her astonishment at Muslim thinkers' and politicians' uncritical appropriation of medical language in speaking about same-sex sexuality, a language that orients itself to Western norms and values of scientific positivism. These Muslim thinkers and politicians had claimed the articulation of same-sex sexuality as a disorder. But according to Kaplan, same-sex sexuality was a sin, not a disorder. Kaplan, through her column, reminded them of the correct discursive strategy, that is, to use the language of Islam rather than resorting to Western terminology.[29] Kaplan's article outraged LGBTI+ people. Her name began to appear in demonstrations, press conferences, and protest letters for disseminating and, in a way, justifying hate against LGBTI+ people.

At almost the same time as Kavaf's speech and Kaplan's article, an essay was published by *Yürüyüş*, a journal known as the medium of an orthodox socialist front, Haklar ve Özgürlükler Cephesi (HÖC; Front for Rights and Freedom). That organization was part of the vanguard organizing a political campaign calling on the state to release inmates with cancer. As part of this campaign, many radical, progressive, and leftist organizations convened to form a platform and join their voices to convince the state to set the ill prisoners free. In addition, LGBTI+ organizations showed solidarity and participated in the rallies. There was no problem with their involvement until a vote took place to decide on certain political strategies. Some organizations objected to including LGBTI+ organizations as decision-makers about more "serious" political issues than matters of sexuality, and the platform started a days-long discussion about whether LGBTI+ organizations should be allowed to vote or not. As this discussion continued, Yürüyüş's article came out; it intensified the tensions even further by labeling LGBTI+ people as perverse and sick.[30] The article sparked a backlash against the platform, resulting in many organizations' withdrawal from the platform. This incident, similar to that in conservative Muslim circles, caused the formation of cliques in leftist circles and, in a way, revealed a set of antitrans and antiqueer leftist organizations that had previously been assumed to support LGBTI+ rights due to their own political history of oppression by the state. In this political environment, the discourse of hate crimes gained a more authoritative voice and became the most notable discursive currency in communicating about violence directed toward LGBTI+ people and about their demands of the state. Slogans such as "Hate crimes are political" (Nefret cinayetleri politiktir), "Hate kills but the state ignores it" (Nefret öldürüyor, devlet bunu görmüyor), and "Don't hate, apologize!" (Nefret etme, özür dile) became popular at rallies and demonstrations.

The deployment of hate crimes discourse by LGBTI+ people draws, however, from a larger political context in Turkey. It is a legal political strategy that emerged in Turkey after two homicides in 2006 and 2007. Baki Koşar, a queer journalist, was found stabbed to death in his house, with at least twenty knife wounds. A police investigation revealed his murderer to be a man he had met via the internet for the sake of sexual intercourse. The second incident was the assassination of an Armenian newspaper editor, Hrant Dink, who had published widely seeking recognition of the Armenian genocide and the cultivation of peace between the Turkish and Armenian people. Prior to his murder, Dink had been the target of many by Turkish nationalists. On January 19, 2007, Ogün Samast, a teenage nationalist shot Dink to death in the street. Samast was part of a wider anti-Armenian deep state network which had assigned him the task of assassinating Dink. Despite several years-long political campaign around the Dink case, the real culprits have not been sentenced to this day. Dink's murder was legally announced not as an organized crime but an individual crime, leaving thousands of people in Turkey once again in disappointment, despair, and frustration about the state's justice system.

Especially since Dink's murder, the issue of hate crimes has emerged in political circles as a legal strategy to protect minoritized communities in Turkey. Within this context, LGBTI+ organizations from different cities also launched a common platform in 2007 to gather evidence of violence inflicted on LGBTI+ people and frame this violence as human rights violations. Since then, reports have been released every year. This platform set the stage for LGBTI+ activists to gain political awareness and educate each other about hate crimes, and to strategize about how to articulate their political demands to the state. Yet an attempt to achieve such legal visibility and status inevitably triggers other notable questions: What is the cost of this element of legal visibility in queer and trans people's lives? What political contours emerge in a politics of sex/gender nonconformity? What kind of openings and closures does this legal definition engender pertaining to queer and trans understandings of justice? An examination of both the short history of hate crime legislation and potent critiques of its underlying logic exposes the possible dangers and foreclosures that are intrinsic to mobilizing hate crime discourse as a political strategy.

Hate Crimes: A Legal Tool for Justice?

In Turkey LGBTI+ activists not only draw from a broader political context in the country but also work within a transnational framework that embeds minoritized rights within human rights discourse. It is part of an ongoing transnational conversation about LGBTI+ lives and deaths, as well as political responses to regimes of queer and trans death across North America, Europe, the Middle East and beyond. In Turkey political activists against hate crimes accept the definition provided by the Organization for Security and Co-operation in Europe. This definition states that "hate crimes are criminal acts motivated by bias or prejudice toward particular groups of people. Hate crimes comprise two elements: a criminal offence and a bias motivation. A hate crime has taken place when a perpetrator has intentionally targeted an individual or property because of one or more identity traits or expressed hostility toward these identity traits during the crime."[31] In other words, hate crime laws aim at increasing the punishment for crimes propelled by certain hate motives related to religion, sex, gender, and race.

Several international reports have criticized hate speech and hate crimes in Turkey.[32] However, the state response to these criticisms has been quite defensive; the Turkish authorities have argued that legal regulations already exist to fight hate speech and hate crimes in Turkey. Although they do not use the phrase *hate crime*, these laws do exist. For example, Article 312 of the former Turkish Penal Code, which was amended in 2002, defined provoking animosity and hostility in people as a crime. Article 216 of the current Turkish Penal Code criminalizes the same act. However, research based on official statistics shows that these legal regulations, rather than protecting disadvantaged groups, function as a punitive mechanism for them.[33]

Various critics of hate crime laws, whether intellectuals or activists, have voiced similar concerns around hate crime legislation across borders. For instance, the New York–based Sylvia Rivera Law Project is a collective organization that works to increase the political voice and visibility of low-income groups and people of color who are trans, intersex, or gender nonconforming. They have written many articles and letters to demonstrate their opposition to hate crime legislation because of the way the penal code is enforced in general. The penal code always targets marginalized groups in society (i.e., primarily people of color and Black people), and the implementation of hate crime laws is no different from the general operation of the penal system in the US context.[34] Hence, hate crime laws might restigmatize and remarginalize certain minority groups rather than bettering their unequal position in society. In a similar vein, widespread references to hate crime laws might end up stigmatizing certain identity groups as occupying a victim position. With hate crime laws, "to be a victim or potential victim [might become] a defining marker of identity."[35] As a social-legal category, a hate crime should be understood as a category resulting from identity politics and would only increase intergroup tensions instead of diminishing them. Moreover, hate crime laws extend the reach of the state by creating a new criminal category, legitimizing state sanctions.[36]

Another problem associated with hate crime discourse is the risk of ignoring the power differentials among different identity groups before the law. Specific categories such as race, religion, and sexual orientation that are legally mobilized via hate crime laws might end up amalgamating all races, religions, and people with different sexual orientations by ignoring the existing power differentials among them. So far this has, in fact, been the case in US hate crime laws, through which "specific categories of persons (e.g., blacks, Jews, gays and lesbians, Mexicans, etc.) [are translated] into all-encompassing and seemingly neutral categories (e.g., race, religion, sexual orientation, national origin)."[37] Hence, the norm of sameness is put into play, and minority and majority groups are treated the same—that is, as equally at risk of being the target of hate-motivated actions. There is no differentiation between marginalized and oppressed groups and groups with social and institutional power before the law.

Last but not least, hate crime laws define the problem predominantly as an individual one without necessarily drawing on wider social and cultural forms of oppression that underlie individuals' actions.[38] Hate crime legislation mainly motivates the state's justice system to punish the perpetrator rather than improve the legal means to help the survivor and the community to which they belong to recover from this violence. As activist and critical scholar of law Dean Spade notably argues, this understanding hinders us from approaching trans killings as part of a broader gender violence issue and obscures systemic and structural transphobia.[39] Hence, there is no real effort to prevent similar incidents from happening again. We are left with one of the above-mentioned closures in the sphere of the social via legal means.

Accordingly, if the category and discourse of hate crimes functions as a justice-serving mechanism in the eyes of activists, then we should be vigilant in watching how new forms of injustice take place through the workings of this modality. Furthermore, as we have seen, hate crime legislation is a product of various legal calculations that prioritize the individual over the community, punishment over recovery, uniformity over singularity, and homogeneity over heterogeneity. It cannot translate a wider set of social relations of violence, oppression, and inequality into legal language without foreclosing or diminishing many other possible definitions of justice.

Conclusion

The LGBTI+ movement in Turkey is far from homogeneous. The activism I examine in this chapter is in close conversation with liberal understandings of politics, which rely on a specific cultural capital in accessing and evoking certain political discourses that prioritize public space as the site of action.[40] Evidently, this form of political performance does not include all

LGBTI+ people in Turkey. Differences in racial, class, and spatial (urban vs. rural) backgrounds produce tensions and disagreements within the movement over political demands and imaginations.[41]

Trans people appeal to the state through calculated legal demands. The provision of basic human rights and the introduction of the category of hate crimes into criminal law reflect these legal demands. Of course, legal inclusion is a minimum condition, necessary rather than sufficient, and not something that can in any way guarantee a more secure life. But, in fact, as political theorist Nivedita Menon argues, this constant resort to legal calculations and means often ends up increasing state control over people's lives via new legislation.[42] Moreover, the state produces "the deserving subjects of human rights" by marking certain groups, such as women and children, as innocent victims in need of care and protection by the state.[43] Hence, the state projects of legal inclusion and human rights usually aim at depoliticizing certain groups and demands.

That said, in the political campaigns and rallies of trans people, there is more than legal calculation and demand. They know better than others that the space of justice is not merely the court space or that of hate crime legislation. On the contrary, it lies somewhere beyond the court, in the social field, in the distribution of resources and life chances, and in trans people's everyday relations with institutional and noninstitutional actors, including legal authorities, medical actors, police officers, landowners, blood family members, neighbors, friends, clients, partners, total strangers, and so on. Instead of merely seeking recognition, inclusion, and incorporation, most trans people and their allies also stress transforming the current logics of the state and social equality by vocalizing the discriminatory and exclusionary conditions they faced in the trans everyday.

These two political struggles do not necessarily exclude one another: as we pay attention to legal reforms such as removing the defense of unjust provocation and treating trans killings as hate crimes, we could also be vigilant about the operation of legal systems that promote certain forms of life and ways of being over others. Dean Spade warns us to "look more at what legal regimes do rather than what they say about what they do."[44] While pondering the implications of legal reforms for queer and trans justice, their limits in addressing structural and systemic problems should always be in our minds. For instance, even if unjust provocation is removed as a defense in trials for murders of queer and trans people, and even if hate crime legislation enters the domain of criminal law, these legal changes may only increase the penalty for queer and trans deaths. A more urgent question concerns the transformation of the social order to secure an equal distribution of life chances for queer and trans people like İrem.[45] In that sense, no matter how many legal calculations are made, queer and trans justice can never be captured within these legal formulations. Rather, it falls into the material, emotional, and symbolic production and organization of the everyday, which contains but also exceeds the domain of law.

So what do trans people actually do to materialize their just claims to an ordinary life? In addition to taking to the streets and calling on the state to respond to their human rights, how else do they survive and maintain their lives and relations with one another? Violence and death should not prevent us from seeing their constructive force, their role in making new worlds, creating new lives, and transforming subjectivities. Everyday violence also creates conditions for the formation of intimacies in trans people's lives. The LGBTI+ community in general and trans people in particular develop their own ethics of caring, belonging, and bonding that are constantly being shaped, contested, and negotiated in the face of everyday forms of violence. These ethics of caring is rooted in speeches and actions in the trans everyday, within the domain of the "ordinary."[46] The next chapter details stories of trans/queer kin making not only as an intimate survival strategy and a mechanism for coping with violence in the trans everyday but also as, in Naisargi Dave's words, an "affective exercise of creative practice in order to live differently" in a world saturated with violence.[47] It is a chapter on trans world-making.

Chapter Six

Funerals & Experiments with Trans Kin

SHOES IN VARIOUS COLORS WERE LINED UP next to one another on the floor: red, blue, brown, black, and yellow. There were approximately ten pairs. Some of them were worn out; some were in good shape. All were high-heeled, either sandals or dress shoes. When Esra poked me in the arm, I was abruptly roused from staring at them. She humorously said, "Which one do you like the most? Just take it!" I smiled and made a face, showing a lack of interest in any of them. While I was gazing at these shoes, left behind by Sibel, I was not trying to decide on the best pair for myself but ruminating on someone who had recently passed away and how those shoes carried her life in them. I was caught up in thinking of Sibel, whose funeral story appeared at the beginning of this book. Shoes that once belonged to her were now sitting on the floor of Istanbul LGBTT and waiting to embrace new feet and walk with different bodies. This was the traditional practice: when a trans woman died, her *lubunya* friends would collect objects and belongings from her house and exhibit them for people to choose from according to their need. This redistribution of resources—or the intimate gift economy of the dead—frequently took place within *lubunya* networks of friendship.

The day before, we had attended Sibel's funeral with Ceyda, Sibel's close friend and a trans woman herself. As we walked toward the mosque gate, we saw Sibel's blood mother and sister accepting people's condolences. It was a pleasant surprise to see them because, as mentioned previously, many blood families reject their trans children, kick them out of house, and refuse them financial and emotional support. Some families denied their trans children funeral ceremonies and burial rituals.

During my research, death and funerals were a constant point of reference and a sore spot that LGBTI+ people loudly spoke about regarding their blood family relations. They frequently communicated their desire to be buried by their queer/trans family and kin—their *real* families (*gerçek ailesi*). Some *lubunyalar* even wrote wills to give their friends the rights normally held by families. After other trans deaths, the queer/trans community and friends often tried to reclaim the body and organize the funeral, thereby taking the place of the blood family as the real family. At trans funerals we see the intimate work of care, love, and protection and the claims that LGBTI+ activists and friends of the deceased generate after a sex/gender-transgressive death.[1] They consistently invest in their friendships and comradeships and contest the primacy given to blood families. In the following pages, I continue with Sibel's funeral story from the introduction and detail the entire process. Then I discuss how trans people learn to care for one another in the aftermath of refusal and abandonment, a praxis of love that trans studies scholar Hil Malatino defines as "trans care."[2] Trans women's intimate experiments with the kinship repertoire of home and motherhood are powerful examples of this trans care.

As discussed in the previous chapters, urban displacement, social discrimination and exclusion, sexual violence, medicolegal regulation, and police surveillance constantly shape the trans everyday in multiple spaces of life, including institutions, streets, neighborhoods, and homes. These relations of violence also constitute a social field of creative living within which trans people recast, shape, and invent forms of intimacy to dwell in the world. Experimenting with family and kinship is an important currency of intimacy that relies on a discursive as well as a practical repertoire of care, *lubunya* belonging, and bonding. Intimacy allows trans people to creatively, productively, and resolutely remake the violent conditions of the quotidian. Family and kinship become a continuous process of renewal, an intimate survival strategy to cope with everyday violence, an imaginative practice that pushes the boundaries of belonging, and a claim to a place in life and death through queer/trans belonging and bonding.

One of the many ways to define kinship is through substances that consolidate ties between persons; in Turkey blood constitutes the predominant substance of kinship. Blood ties are crucial in giving value and definition to the dominant understanding of the family. They are inscribed in social, legal, and religious frameworks. One notable example is the legal regulation of in vitro fertilization, which strictly prohibits egg, sperm, and embryo donation and surrogacy.[3] It allows married couples only to use their own eggs and sperm. Semen, womb, and breast milk are also significant substances of the body that form kin relations, but none of them approaches the prevalence of blood ties as a metaphor in everyday relations and conversations.

Anthropologist Janet Carsten suggests that we can think of the substance of kinship as "the flow of objects or bodily parts between persons, as well as the capacity to stand for the relations between those persons."[4] Elaborating on anthropologist Roy Wagner's conceptualization of "analogical kinship" in the context of non-Western societies, Carsten stresses how objects like shells, or foods like meat, can do the analogical work of the flow of substances between people in order to make kin.[5] Here I would like to push this discussion further and ask, What if we approach this substance as violence? How can we theorize violence as the mediator, the creative substance, of family and kin work among trans people? What does kin and family making look like when its substance becomes the routinized condition of exclusion, abandonment, displacement, and police abuse? How does the quotidian experience of violence shape crossings and entanglements among the family, kinship, and other forms of relatedness, belonging, and caring? I argue that the trans everyday offers us a creative way to negotiate and contest, as well as to blur, the intimate boundaries among family, kinship, and friendship and hence theorize the constitutive relationship between violence and intimacy through an embodied process of family and kin work.

Before moving on to my discussion, I want to emphasize that I avoid producing two contrasting forms of family: straight versus queer/trans families. Beyond doubt, not all cisheteronormative families are coherent or uniform within themselves. Feminist and anthropological work has long discussed the family as a product of social, cultural, and economic circumstances crosscut by class, gender, ethnicity, and race within a particular historical context.[6] Along with these social and cultural axes, as anthropologist Kate Weston emphasizes, there can be "differences in household organization, as well as differences in notions of family and what it means to call someone kin."[7] Similar dynamics are also relevant to the formation of queer/trans families. Like straight families, queer families vary to a great extent depending on cultural and social factors such as class, ethnicity, and race. It is important to read the following pages with these differences in mind.

Inheriting the Affective Debt

Popular understandings of family associate it with emotional ties and the work of love, affection, care, and interconnectedness. However, feminist and queer scholarship contests the assumed naturalness of these familial emotions.[8] For many people, the family might be a source of coercion, tension, and domestic violence as well. Family, as an institution, might also structure quarrels, exclusions, and disavowals of its own members, as has been the case for some queer and trans people around the world. Hence, the production of intimacy between family members is frequently coupled with strict rules producing, ordering, and regulating lives, bodies, and desires. The family, with all its emotional, material, and symbolic work, includes and excludes through drawing borders between different bodies and desires, inscribing its sovereignty over family members.

Sara Ahmed argues that to be a family member demands that one follow the family line, that is, the naturalization of heterosexuality as a line that directs bodies to desire the body of the opposite sex. She further conceptualizes heterosexuality as a gift given to children by their families, a gift that becomes an inheritance: "Heterosexuality is imagined as the future of the child insofar as heterosexuality is idealized as a social gift and even as the gift of life itself. . . . Heterosexuality becomes a social as well as familial inheritance through the endless requirement that the child repay the debt of life with its life. The child who refuses the gift thus becomes seen as a bad debt, as being ungrateful, as the origin of bad feeling."[9]

Inheritance of this family line is also the condition of family love. Hence, when children fail to inherit a desire for and orientation toward a heteroreproductive future, they risk the material, social, and affective capital provided by the family.[10] Family love is conditional on not only sexual orientation but also cisgender identification. In other words, most families require their children to inherit and integrate not only heterosexual desire but also cisnormativity or cisgenderism in order to be recognized as respected, loved, and cared-for members of the family. The following stories of trans people with their blood families will further exemplify these points.

"My name doesn't matter at all. We buried our names that were given by our families together with our parents. We make men call us whatever name we desire. Sometimes when we get drunk, we even forget those names." These sentences passed the lips of Bilge, a thirty-five-year-old sex worker. Bilge was one of the many other *lubunyalar* who had difficulty claiming a space for herself within her blood family. She could not and did not pay her "intimate debts" to her family, and eventually she had to leave the house. But not all trans people were completely detached from their blood families. Blood family and kin relations held an ambivalent position for those who had been able to maintain or repair their relations with blood family to a certain degree. Melis was one of them.

One day, when Melis and I were chatting about her family, she told me her family had accepted her after years of contempt. She repeated her family's words to me: "We know what you are. We know that you are *homosexual*. We accept you as you are, but Iskenderun [her hometown, a southern city] would never welcome you. You would bring disgrace on us. Our society, our social environment, wouldn't accept you." Melis visited her family for the first time only after they moved to Antakya, the neighboring city to her hometown. Nobody in Antakya knew that Melis was a trans woman. Whenever she went to visit them in Antakya, her family immediately picked her up from the terminal and quickly put her in the car so that nobody would see her. After she told me this, a sad expression appeared on her face for a few seconds, and then she told me that her mother had had to move to a different city three times because of her. In the end, they bought a house by the sea, mainly with Melis's savings from sex work. They started to meet there. Her family introduced her to their neighbors and friends as their former neighbor from Istanbul who was paying a visit. Or at other times, she was introduced as a relative from Germany. She said, "My family says, 'This is my brother's daughter,'" and added happily, "They never address me as a son but a daughter."

Despite all this hardship, she was proud of gaining partial recognition from her blood family. Later, she admitted that her reconnection with the family was enabled by her financial gains. Once she disclosed the amount of money she made through sex work, her family forgot about past tensions and disputes. She also alleged that her brothers had gone on a pilgrimage to Mecca—and thus fulfilled one of the five pillars of Islam—with her financial support. Her family decided to continue their relationship on the condition that she would not visit them frequently and would buy a house distant from their former neighbors' gaze. Melis was expected to occupy a marginal space in her hometown and family by disguising herself, intimately distancing herself, or strictly scheduling her visits—a story that resonated with other violent intimacies in this book.

I was told of similar instances in which trans people who had been disowned by their blood families sent money to their blood kin with the hope that money would resolve their conflicts sometime in the future. Some blood families assented to remittances as long as their *lubunya* children avoided visiting them in their hometowns. With other blood families, money lost its importance, and trans women invented new strategies to maintain the emotional bond, particularly with their mothers. Yelda, for instance, was a very good-looking forty-seven-year-old trans woman. She was highly invested in a hyperfeminine look, wearing high heels, miniskirts, and heavy makeup. She could retain her ties with her blood family only by replicating her previous manly appearance every time she visited her mother. She would cross-dress as a man, wear a cap to hide her hair, remove her makeup, and draw thicker eyebrows and a mustache on her face. She told me that this was the only way to sustain her bond with her mother.

I met other trans people who were afraid of familial rejection and hence tried to hide their transition as long as they could, leading both a straight and a queer/trans family life. Even among those who had completed their transition and received new IDs, some (especially trans men) had inherited the family line and preferred a heteronormative familial life through marriage. I tried to reach them through other trans friends, but they avoided me due to their reluctance to speak about their trans experience. After their GCS, they had completely incorporated themselves into a heteronormative lifestyle, detached themselves from their trans friends, and kept their trans experience a secret. Therefore, it is crucial to keep in mind that relations to blood family diverged among trans people. Some people invested in both blood and queer/trans families to varying degrees at various times.

This set of tactics, maneuvers, or experiments speaks to the contradictory and ambivalent attachments that one can have in both worlds of kinship—normative and queer/trans—by inhabiting both without fully incorporating oneself into either of them. A few anthropologists note the contested, unpredictable, and volatile nature of human intimacy, which is shaped by contradictory feelings of friendship and enmity, inclusion and exclusion, care and violence, love and hate.[11] It is crucial to understand these multiple and conflicting desires related to blood kinship and recognition by blood family as part of a larger endeavor to craft a sense of place; a place that is a product of a constant play between violence and intimacy. By insisting on inhabiting this conflicting space of intimacy, trans people contested, challenged, and pushed the boundaries of cisnormative frameworks of family and kinship. It was an everyday struggle to constantly invent oneself.

That said, although some trans women succeeded in maintaining their relations with their blood family, the majority of trans women I knew had severed their connections to their blood families. Then what happened in this everyday zone of familial abandonment and disowning? How did trans people navigate and inhabit this space? Trans deaths and funerals provided some acute answers to these questions. Before I take you back to Sibel's funeral to discuss these issues, it is helpful to provide some context about the social, legal, and religious regulation of death and burials in the country. Trans people, in life or death, have to negotiate entanglements among familial order, gender and sexuality regimes, Islamic notions of embodiment, and legal regulations around death that mediate and authorize particular forms of intimacy for them.

The Afterlife of Gender

The intimate rights to the deceased body are strongly shaped by the intersection of legal regulations, institutional practices, religious interpretations, and norms regarding the Turkish family. For instance, blood families hold a set of legal rights that allow them to make certain decisions regarding the body of the deceased, including choosing the burial practice, selecting a burial plot, and deciding whether to have an autopsy or donate organs. Blood families and spouses have de facto sovereignty over these decisions unless a will exists that specifies particular death rights and practices. Yet even with a will, blood families and/or spouses are allowed to contest the decisions of the deceased. Under these conditions, judges must interpret the situation according to existing "customs and traditions" and decide who has rights to the deceased body, a process that allows and/or forecloses intimacies for a varied group of claimants to the deceased body.[12] Further, religious actors and Islamic notions of embodiment also play a central role in shaping intimate alliances over the deceased.

In Turkey's social and cultural life, Sunni Islam, the hegemonic religious doctrine, often authorizes claims on sexed/gendered embodiment. The mainstream interpretation of Islam considers that people's bodies—both body surfaces and internal organs—come from and belong to Allah. The body is Allah's *emanet* (entrustment) to humans—Allah entrusts the body to humans, and hence an individual is responsible for taking good care of their body until they return it to Allah upon death. Therefore, not surprisingly, Sunni Islam requires a meticulous set of body-related rituals after death. A significant dimension of this religious bodywork is cleaning the body by washing away things that are considered polluting, such as blood, urine, feces, and semen. Ritual washing is essential to returning the body to Allah as clean as it was when gifted by Allah at birth. In that sense, one can never possess, or own, the body. Allah's ultimate sovereignty over both life and death is mediated through a claim on the body. Ensuring that the body is returned to Allah as clean and pure as possible reflects how it is held in trust by the deceased. This washing ritual also pays one's final respects to the deceased and prepares the body for the afterlife.

The treatment of the dead body is intimately related to the formation of communal boundaries and forms of (un)belonging within communities.[13] As explained earlier, the deceased's blood family members are the de facto agents of this bodily treatment, a designation that allows them to decide the deceased's sex and gender during washing and funeral practices. A strict gender regime at Islamic funeral practices not only reaffirms the deceased's belonging in the family but also establishes the dead body's belonging in a given sex/gender category. The coffin design, the prayers at the mosque, the washing ritual prior to burial, and the rites of inhumation differ according to the state's determination of the sex of Turkish citizens. For example, only officially trained ritual specialists and family members of the same sex as the deceased (the sex that is written on the ID) can enter the special washing place, *gasilhane* (figure 6.1) and perform the washing ritual. But it is also possible for the family to supersede the state definition of sex in the case of a trans burial. During the ritual washing, the body is covered between the belly and the knees. The genitals should not be exposed while cleaning the body. The ritual washing is repeated three times. After the washing, cotton plugs are placed in the body openings. The body is then shrouded in a simple white cloth, the *kefen*, which symbolizes the equality of all before Allah. The face should not be exposed after the shrouding (figure 6.2).

The *kefen* is made of three pieces of cloth for men and five pieces for women. The two additional pieces are used to cover women's breasts and hair, parts that most observant Muslim women prefer to cover also in life, thus marking gender/sex difference. Prior to burial, the white-shrouded

6.1   The *gasilhane* at Zincirlikuyu Cemetery. A *gasilhane* is a
place where the deceased are washed and prepared for Muslim
burials. Photo by the author, July 8, 2016.

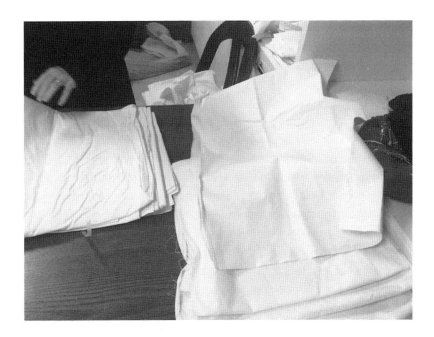

6.2 *Kefen*, a white shroud to wrap the deceased body prior to the burial. Photo by the author, July 8, 2016.

6.3 Green cloth used to cover the coffin. Photo by the author, July 8, 2016.

body is placed in a coffin that is covered with a green cloth on which verses about death from the Qur'an are printed (figure 6.3). If the deceased is a female, a headscarf is placed on the side of the coffin over the location of the head. A name tag, colored blue or pink depending on the sex/gender of the deceased, is placed on one side of the coffin. Before the dead body is transferred from the mosque to the grave, male attendees at the funeral engage in prayers under the guidance of an imam, and they assemble around the coffin. In Turkey it is usually men who perform the funeral prayer in the mosque, while women wait for its completion in the family home of the deceased. When women do attend funeral prayers at a mosque, they are required to stand at the back or outside the mosque.

The imam's prayers—in both Turkish and Arabic—address the deceased as *merhume* or *merhum* (the female and male deceased, respectively), or as *hatun kişi* or *er kişi* (female and male person, respectively), gendered terms that announce the deceased as male or female. These gendered prayers are exceptional in the Turkish language, which is, as noted earlier, gender neutral and has no distinct gendered pronouns for women and men. Upon the completion of the prayers, the dead body is carried to the graveyard, taken out of the coffin by men, and buried in the white shroud. Only men are allowed to be present in the graveyard during the burial, regardless of the gender of the deceased. Again, women are usually expected to either stand in the background or stay at home.

Given the gender dichotomy embedded within Sunni Islamic funeral practices, it is no surprise that gender-nonconforming bodies, including Sibel's, might evoke questions. Remember that Sibel's body had evoked a chaos of illegibility at her funeral ceremony and burial ritual, opening gender and sexual difference to debates and negotiations by a variety of social actors, including her blood family members, medicolegal actors from the Mezarlıklar ve Cenaze Hizmetleri Şube Müdürlüğü (the Department of Cemeteries and Funeral Services), and the religious authorities, especially the imams. The initial struggle was to find a mosque willing to hold the funeral and prayers for Sibel since most imams refused to organize a ceremony once they were told that the deceased was a trans woman (see figure 6.4 for another instance).[14] Some imams had even refused to do the funeral prayers and thus denied final religious rights to Sibel.[15] A few imams had consented to perform the prayers and burial rites as long as she was referred to as a *male*. They recognized the blue ID, the state's inscription of sex, as Sibel's true sex, dismissing Sibel's life as a woman and her identity as such. Sibel's friends rejected this option and kept looking for an imam who would agree to

6.4   An imam and a few other men conducting the burial prayers for a trans woman who died of AIDS in Antalya, a southern city in Turkey, in 2013. Her body was kept in the morgue for two days, but none of her family members claimed the body. After two days her trans friends took her body from the morgue and organized the funeral. In his prayers the imam addressed her as a man, not a woman. The newspaper headline states "No One Claimed Travesty Esra's Funeral." *Milliyet*, April 4, 2013. Courtesy of the *Milliyet* newspaper archive.

conduct *her* funeral ceremony—to recognize in death that she had lived, and died, as a woman.

People who follow Sunni interpretations of Islam might view the sex/gender-transgressive body as a challenge to Islamic notions of embodiment, that is, to Allah's ascription of sex to each body. Imams usually have recourse to and make use of state authorities and medicolegal regulations on sex and gender when they deliberate over the transgressive body. For example, the Diyanet İşleri Başkanlığı (the Directorate of Religious Affairs) dictates that the organization of funeral rituals be based on a reading of the material surface of the body—meaning that the funeral ceremonies of trans women who have not undergone GCS reflect the sex that was assigned to them at birth and marked on their state identification card. Although they lived as women during their lives, the funeral and burial rituals for their bodies are expected to be performed by men. If they had GCS and had their IDs reissued to reflect their reassigned gender/sex, then state and religious authorities require women to perform the rituals of washing, cleaning, and wrapping the corpse. In a nutshell, the state and Sunni Islam, which derive their authority from two different scripts—civil law and centuries of interpretation of and argumentation about the Qur'an, hadith, and sunna, respectively—work in tandem to reinscribe the gender/sex of the dead body.

This effort points to fissures in the alliance between state and religious authorities. These fissures are produced by communal action—in this case, the actions of a community of trans women—and a growing body of Islamic jurisprudence on sex/gender nonconformity in various Muslim contexts that reads sex/gender embodiment as open to practice, negotiation, and interpretation.[16] Alongside ongoing debates and interpretations within Islamic traditions, people themselves seek their right to religious practice. The families or friends of the deceased may succeed in persuading religious authorities to perform funeral practices according to the lived gender and sexual identity of the deceased.

Moreover, the dead trans body is not alone in causing a rupture in prescribed religious traditions relating to death. For example, anthropologist Aslıhan Sanal discusses this issue in the context of organ donation in Turkey.[17] Another example is committing suicide, one of the greatest sins in Islam, viewed as a sin greater than homicide. Since the body is an *emanet*, a thing borrowed from Allah, a human should not violate its right to live. The performance and conferral of a traditional religious funeral ceremony and burial for a person who committed suicide thus also produces an ambiguous space for imams, a space within which to practice Islamic authority. Some imams refuse to organize a religious ceremony, while others may find an excuse for the deceased's suicide, gaining and practicing some flexibility. They may, for example, justify the conferral of a religious funeral ceremony for a suicide on the grounds of a momentary loss of sanity or short-lived hysteria. The dead bodies of *hunsa*, or intersex people, also produce ambiguities and modulations in death practices. Traditionally, neither women nor men perform the full washing ritual for intersex people. Instead, the washer wraps their hand with a piece of cloth and performs a cleaning ritual on the face and arms only, using purified sand or dust. While the state-recognized sex/gender identity is seen as the principal criterion determining the gendered practices of the funeral ritual, in the case of an intersex person, an imam might try to learn how the person identified in their lifetime. If this information is impossible to acquire, then the imam could act according to the testimonies of those who knew the deceased in life.

More often than not, it is families and loved ones who locate and press sympathetic imams to confer appropriate death rites for trans people, intersex people, and people who have committed suicide in Turkey. These spaces of religious ambiguity and interpretation allow individual imams to practice their authority. They also demonstrate that alliances can be formed between imams and vulnerable communities and individuals. Sibel's friends, for example, eventually found an imam who agreed to perform her funeral and burial rituals according to her self-identified gender.

At the funeral I was nervous about how Sibel's sex/gender would be addressed in the prayers. However, I did not need to wait for the imam's prayers to figure this out: I saw the coffin, which was covered in a green cloth with a headscarf placed on the side where the person's head would rest. The imam of this mosque had recognized Sibel as a female, even though her state ID still (mis)recognized her as male. His interpretation was grounded in his authority as an imam and, more crucially, his long-term residence in Ülker Street where trans women also lived. His familiarity with *lubunya* lives and communities led him to take a different interpretive approach.

The imam concluded his gender-appropriate prayers for Sibel and asked for people's *helal*, blessings to the dead person and a last chance to forgive the deceased for misdeeds before the burial. When sending someone off to the graveyard (that is, in Islam, a passage to the other world), it is rare for someone to deny their blessings to the deceased. Under the imam's guidance, we all gave our blessings to Sibel.

Sibel's funeral, however, also presented the "problem" of the washing ritual for the deceased and the placement of her grave in the cemetery. Who would—and who should—organize the funeral rituals and material resources for the burial? As Ceyda (Sibel's close friend) and I walked toward the mosque gate, we saw Sibel's mother sitting in a chair in front of the mosque, accepting people's condolences. Sibel's mother and sister were present at the funeral but had chosen not to participate in the washing ritual—a particularly intimate familial obligation. They maintained a distance from Sibel's dead body through withholding this most intimate of death rites and the affective, social, and kinship effects these rites are meant to produce. Instead of Sibel's blood family members, Ceyda had done the ritual washing of Sibel's body. As we were leaving the mosque, Ceyda remarked on the many times she had had to wash, clean, and wrap the dead bodies of her trans friends because so many blood families had so completely abandoned their trans children that they refused to touch their bodies, even in death.[18]

The stigmatization of sex work is also at play in the distance that blood families produce by not performing death rite obligations. The majority of trans women in Turkey have difficulty finding jobs in sectors other than sex work, and the stigmatization of sex work and transphobia work in tandem to sever intimate relations with blood families over the course of trans people's lives. Despite this, throughout my research I did not come across a single story of a blood family denying burial and funeral rites to a *natrans* woman sex worker, whereas stories of funeral denials to trans women were commonplace.

After the burial we decided to meet at Istanbul LGBTT for Sibel's mourning ritual. Someone had made *helva*, another ritual for the dead. Traditionally, *ölü helvası* (*helva* of the dead) is a dessert prepared with semolina or flour, sugar, and butter and cooked and served by the deceased person's family for the participants of the funeral following the interment. As people eat *helva*, they also talk about the departed and remember them. For Sibel's funeral ceremony, one *lubunya* was assigned to cook enough *helva* and bring it to the center. I had never seen the center so jam-packed before, but Sibel's blood family was absent—as they had been absent at the cemetery. They had departed from the mosque as soon as Sibel's body did and returned to their home. Furthermore, Sibel's mother and sister asked Ceyda to tell other *lubunyalar* not to come visit them in their homes to give their condolences. They would not welcome them inside the house. Sibel's burial plot was bought with money donated by trans women. Sibel's blood family had contributed nothing. This was not the first time trans women had pooled their resources for a deceased friend, nor would it be the last. When Ceyda saw that I was impressed, she turned to me and said, "When I die, they're gonna do the same thing. After all, we are each other's family! We are the real family!"

Following Sibel's funeral, I spent the entire day with Ceyda. She recounted another story, one where their efforts to reclaim the deceased body of a trans friend, Ayşe, failed and the blood family did not let them organize a funeral. This other family had disavowed their trans daughter both in her life and in her death and had requested that the state bury Ayşe in a cemetery for the anonymous, for the unknown, for the unclaimed (*kimsesizler mezarlığı*), that is, a cemetery for the *kimsesiz*.[19] Turning into a necroviolent actor, the family denied an afterlife to Ayşe, rendered her anonymous, and cast her body out from socially recognizable scripts of mourning.

Becoming Unknown/Anonymous/Unclaimed (*Kimsesiz*)

Judith Butler has long drawn our attention to those unequal and differential economies of mourning that proclaim some deaths as grievable while denying bereavement to others.[20] One can describe the cemetery for the *kimsesiz* as one of the chief architectures in this economy of mourning. As I discussed elsewhere, the Turkish cemeteries for the anonymous manifest a spatial ordering of death and afterlives at the thresholds of social and political life in Turkey (see figures 6.5, 6.6, and 6.7).[21] These graveyards constitute a spatial marker where the state buries the bodies of those people who remain unidentified or unclaimed after a certain period of time. In practice, they are a burial site for social outcasts: homeless people, victims of femicides, disowned members of blood families, premature babies, and, more recently, unaccompanied refugees. These cemeteries also contain the bodies of political detainees who were disappeared under police interrogations and state violence.[22] Historically, the state has deemed many radical leftists and Kurdish guerrillas unidentified, denied families and communities these bodies, and buried them as anonymous corpses.

Ceyda was terrified by the cemeteries for the *kimsesiz*. Long removed from her blood family, she had already decided to donate her corpse as a cadaver to be used in anatomy courses at medical schools, in part to avoid being buried as anonymous or unclaimed.

Aslıhan Sanal's ethnography includes a detailed discussion of this arrangement between the Adli Tıp Kurumu (the Council of Forensic Medicine) and the medical schools.[23] Sanal, for instance, explores how mentally ill people were denied full personhood and rights over their own bodies from the early years of the republic because they were dependent on others. When they died, they were deemed homeless unless a relative claimed them or the anatomy lab demanded them.[24] If deemed homeless, they were buried in the cemetery for the *kimsesiz*. With the release of a circular by the Supreme Board of Judges and Prosecutors in October 2011, the Council of Forensic Medicine linked the bodies in the category of homeless to cadaver regulations even more stringently. Following this procedural change,

6.5 Old section of the cemetery for the *kimsesiz*, Kilyos Cemetery, Istanbul. Photo by the author, August 10, 2019.

6.6
A grave site where around twenty anonymous deceased people are buried; they were assigned numbers. Old section of the cemetery for the *kimsesiz*, Kilyos Cemetery, Istanbul. Photo by the author, August 10, 2019.

6.7
New section of the cemetery for the *kimsesiz*, Kilyos Cemetery, Istanbul. Photo by the author, August 10, 2019.

the Council of Forensic Medicine delivers to medical schools bodies not claimed by family members within fifteen days of death, placing these corpses in the category of the *kimsesiz*.[25] While people can request that upon death their bodies be donated to medical schools, most of the time the donor's family members are reluctant to fulfill the donor's will on their death, and the state complies with the family's wishes. Some medical schools have had to return corpses to families who insist on organizing a burial for the deceased.

Such moments further mark the body of the dead as a social body that has been (re)produced and shaped within the relations of kinship and family. The burial rituals represent not only the last obligations to the deceased but also a social obligation for the blood family to publicly perform and reproduce itself as the family. Ceyda did not think anyone in her blood family would contest her decision to donate her body to science, precisely because she did not believe that anyone in her blood family would claim her body or organize a funeral.

When talking to her about her yet-to-die body, Ceyda was drawing out the regulatory apparatus behind the making of the "known" and "unknown" cadaver: unless she donated her body to science, there was a chance she would be regarded as anonymous. Furthermore, if she donated her body, there would be no "legitimate" intimate actor to contest her will and take back her body. Ceyda was afraid that the state might not recognize the years-long relations—gelled into queer family and kin making—between her and her trans friends. If the state did not recognize these relationships, it would claim the body as its own and decline to return the body to Ceyda's trans friends for a funeral.

Moreover, she was unsure whether her trans friends could mobilize enough people and capital to buy a grave plot in a regular cemetery because such plots were extremely expensive. Ceyda was comforted by the idea of donating her body as a cadaver to medical students. She said, "At least my body could contribute to something scientific." In this way Ceyda was also proclaiming the afterlife of her deceased body. It was a claim shaped by her experiences living with deaths of her trans kin, particularly that of Ayşe— whose blood family had insisted on burying her in a cemetery for the *kimsesiz*, even though her *lubunya* family had raised funds and bought a burial plot for Ayşe in a regular cemetery. The blood family exercised their state-given right to Ayşe's dead body and refused the claims of Ayşe's *lubunya* family, even though they, and not her blood family, had cared for her for years. Ceyda and the rest of Ayşe's *lubunya* family could do nothing. Ayşe's blood family insisted on their state-given rights to her dead body to bury her in a cemetery for the *kimsesiz*.

In the absence of a will or a marriage, the blood family is the only actor to inherit the property left behind by the deceased. So trans women told stories about some blood families who did not hesitate to deny funeral rights to their trans children but at the same time claimed their wealth. The family's refusal of the obligation of intimacy in Ayşe's case was not just an act that broke ties between the blood family and the trans child; by not allowing Ayşe a burial ceremony organized by her trans friends, they also sought to destroy trans intimacies, relations, and care practices. As Ayşe's funeral story demonstrates, the blood family, as it is recognized and constructed by the state, is capable of killing a person even beyond their physical death. Queer and trans studies scholar Eric Stanley defines this act of killing as "overkill," a form of "surplus violence" that pushes a body beyond death.[26] The blood family can be one of the most violent sovereign models of intimacy, a deadly one, in fact. Sibel's funeral demonstrates how her trans friends' claims on her deceased body were mediated through the cisheteronormative family, the state, and Islam. In Ayşe's case, however, her friends' claims on her body were denied due to the state's legal inscription of blood family sovereignty over the dead body as it relates to funeral rites.

The work of queer/trans kin and family was most evident in violent moments of everyday life—when trans people faced exclusion, displacement, and abandonment. Hence, one should not take trans kin and care labor as a constant point of reference in the trans everyday. Trans kin making in Turkey is both analogous and dissimilar to Kath Weston's work on "chosen families" among gay men and lesbians in the San Francisco Bay Area.[27] Although Weston's chosen families form a sort of network in their interaction with one another by crossing household lines, they still maintain affective attachments to and through their sense of a nuclear home, which becomes central to couples' relations, and which other gays and lesbians might enter and exit as lovers, friends, and/or solidarity partners. Households based on the model of a nuclear-family home are maintained as nodes, bases, or continuities within a larger network of queer kinship. In that sense, links between a sense of home, a domestic household, and affective family retain their significance among Weston's queer families. This was not necessarily the case among trans people in Istanbul. They still created and worked with a queer/trans notion of home, but it diverged significantly from Weston's formulation.

Home

The concept of home had various meanings for trans women. For example, one dimension of home was associated with Istanbul, a city that recognizes and embraces various marginalized groups of people and integrates them hierarchically into its urban texture. In one of our conversations, Melis described Istanbul as a home for trans people: "We got used to here. This place has become our home. Istanbul has become our home. Now I am at peace with my family, and I go to Antakya from time to time. I cannot stay with them longer than a week. I get worried about here. I meet with my friends and acquaintances here in Istanbul. They understand me. I understand them. We don't see a single 'homosexual' in Antakya. You cannot meet with anyone over there."

As is clear from Melis's words, home was a place actively produced through social relations made possible by the creation of a sense of collectivity, intimacy, care, and mutual recognition. Istanbul, as a global city, allowed for a diversity of subcultures and marginalized groups, including trans people. However, this spatial recognition could not be generalized to the entire city but was specific to particular neighborhoods. The margins of the city became a site for a spatial struggle for homemaking, where trans people actively produced a sense of place, a right to the city, and a claim to existence through their collective work of care, organizing, struggle, resilience, and imagination. This story resonates with earlier discussions of the exclusions and expulsions from Ülker Street, which was home to trans women in the wider area of Beyoğlu. Similar to Ülker Street, different neighborhoods would become both a home and a space of constant violence, of expanding violent intimacies of the city.

Another dimension of home related to the places of political organizing. Queer and trans people in Istanbul were invested less in maintaining nuclear family structures in relation to the space of home than in making the family a form that brought many trans people together through LGBTI+ organizations. That is why Sibel's shoes were displayed, and her *helva* was cooked and served at Istanbul LGBTT instead of at a house. In other words, a network of trans people, emerging through political struggle and the spaces that were created by different LGBTI+ organizations, defined itself as the queer/trans family. Many members of these organizations spoke of organizing and community spaces as their home, as opposed to their individual dwellings, where they either lived alone or with roommates or partners.

References to queer/trans notions of home coincided with the energies invested, and time spent, in those organizations. These efforts prompt Malatino's emphasis on "the intricately interconnected spaces and places where trans and queer care labor occurs: the street, the club, the bar, the clinic, the community center, the classroom, the nonprofit, and sometimes, yes, the home—but a home that is often a site of rejection, shunning, abuse and discomfort."[28] However, the meanings attached to trans homes and trans family and their definitions have changed historically. For example, Sedef, an elderly trans woman activist, mentioned that in the 1990s, when state violence against the trans community was more acute, trans people would more commonly live together. Trans women were not scattered around specific neighborhoods as individuals, as they are now (see chapter 2). Sedef said the feeling of community as well as of trans kin and family was essential, empowering trans people's resilience and resistance in the face of state violence. Collective living was crucial in order to not be alone while struggling against the police and antitrans members of the public. More precisely, both state and social violence were generative of a communal intimacy that brought trans women together, who in turn carved out a place of survival for themselves through shared neighborhoods and homes. The sense of community and solidarity among trans people was more pronounced at that time. Acting as a grand family most of the time, they knew each other more intimately. However, according to Sedef, this had changed.

Sedef believed that younger trans women had inherited a relatively freer sexual and gender environment, which Sedef's generation had struggled to create.[29] According to her, the younger generations had no respect for the older ones. They might be aggressive, emotionally unstable, and eager to fight. Age differences and intergenerational tensions shaped relations among trans people, particularly for trans women older than forty, who had had vastly different experiences of violence from the police. History as a shared collective experience drew boundaries and produced tensions between different age groups among trans women. Yet, paradoxically, the narration and sharing of this history with younger generations transformed violence into a shared substance among trans people, suturing ties of queer/trans kin making.[30]

Trans kin making was never devoid of tensions, contestations, and even violence. Like any other intimate relationship, it involved fights, conflicts, avoidance, and even the severance of ties.[31] For some trans people, the meaning of queer/trans family and kin—or even trans friendships—sometimes did not go beyond strategic moves or decisions that could bring material gains (i.e., shelter, money, food, clothes, or more customers). At times, it also functioned to confirm particular notions of familial normativity. Hence, rather than romanticizing it, it is crucial to remember that queer/ trans kin work was also constrained by structural inequalities and by the state of being human, with all its complex and conflicting desires, attachments, expectations, actions, and thoughts. These complexities and conflicts manifested themselves overtly in yet another contested practice and discourse of the kinship repertoire, trans motherhood.

Trans Motherhood

Kath Weston argues that "queer sorts of families configure relationships, however creatively, from historically available materials."[32] In a similar vein, trans women in Turkey deployed a normative kinship form, motherhood, reconfiguring it to consolidate ties with one another. Though trans motherhood was more prevalent in the 1990s, thanks to widespread collective living and sharing of space, it still shapes relations among trans women.

When a new and inexperienced young trans woman in her transition period entered the urban trans world in Istanbul, an older or more experienced trans woman would take care of the new member. She would teach her the ins and outs of dressing up, wearing proper makeup, doing sex work, and coping with everyday violence in the streets, especially that of the police and her clients. New members would usually stay with their trans mothers in the same house until they proved to themselves that they had learned enough and could survive on their own. Until then, they were expected to obey the rules set by the mother. Depending on who the mother was, the rules might be strict or loose. The relationship between mothers and daughters could also become exploitative if the mother forced the daughter to pay extra money for household expenses, including rent or groceries. Mothers could even ask their daughters to share the money they made from sex work. Hence, money could play a significant role in the formation of this kinship.

Some of these mother-daughter relations were based on consent. For example, a trans woman could convey her intention to stay with an older trans woman of her choice and request to become her daughter. On those occasions, it could be regarded as the consensual formation of kinship between two trans women. However, in other situations, trans women could lack the option of choosing their mothers. Sometimes the new member would have limited opportunities to meet other trans women and might agree to an older trans woman's offer to adopt her as a daughter. Yet such an adoptive relationship was not obligatory; whereas some trans women had mothers, others did not need or refused to have one. For example, despite Sedef having been a mother to approximately thirty trans women, she herself had had no trans mother. One could also change one's mother or have multiple mothers, if needed. Mothering was usually meant for those in need, or for those who did not have any social or economic capital to survive in this world.

For those who consented to motherhood, it was temporary. Trans women did not remain the daughters of those mothers for the rest of their lives. For example, Sedef was a mother to Sevda when Sevda first stepped into this "world," as she framed it. Whenever she spoke of Sedef's mothering, it was always in the past tense. So motherhood also fulfilled a functional role for a limited time. Once the young trans woman was ready to stand on her own feet, the mother had completed her mission. While the mother-daughter relation might be over, respect for the mother often became a long-lasting emotion that was mentioned continuously among trans people. In other words, the obligation to reciprocate the gift of mothering might take an affective form. But still these relations might not be taken for granted as stable, as was apparent in the case of Sevda and Sedef. Soon after my departure from Istanbul in the summer of 2011, they had a big fight and stopped seeing each other.

For sure, the relations among trans people did not depend only on the formation of supportive intimate bonds. Negative emotions and actions such as jealousy, enmity, rivalry, revenge, fights, tensions, and quarrels also shaped those relations. And this is no surprise because people fight in all relationships and, more importantly, because these feelings and interactions took place in and were shaped by an urban margin that was a product of multiple forms of violence. People's individual and collective capacities were linked to and limited by the availability of wider social, cultural and political, and economic resources that made certain acts possible, while blocking others. As Malatino puts it powerfully, "Any act of caring is simultaneously an act of maintaining those minimal networks of support that sustain you," and this "rotating, interchangeable, reciprocal and voluntary labor" can easily cause exhaustion, burnout, rifts, and tension.[33] This limitation finds powerful expression in the words of

Gamze, a trans woman of forty-two who worked as a journalist prior to her gender transition:

> When you become a *travesti*, you start seeing only trans people. You are isolated from the society. Your *natrans* friends stop calling you. They even stop walking with you on the street. You get surprised. You look at yourself and say, "I actually look better; at least I became a woman. Then why does this person [her *natrans* friend] avoid me?" Because society thinks that you are a sex worker by default. When a friend walks with you, he is mistaken for a pimp or someone who has something to do with sex work . . . but I also understand them. Long back, trans people had told me, "The more you become a woman, the lonelier you get." I didn't believe them. But now I see they were right in saying that.

Gamze's words stress that not all trans people aspired to be surrounded mostly by trans people or to invest fully in trans friendships as kin or family making. Some trans women, like Gamze, described this situation as one of necessity rather than a personal choice. It was a question of survival. Trans women's introduction to Istanbul's urban *lubunya* world, and their survival as well as their respected and recognizable life and death, were made possible through their intimate work of blurring the boundaries between family, kinship, and friendship.

Conclusion

As Elizabeth Freeman argues, "Kinship is resolutely corporeal"; it "marks out a certain terrain of corporeal dependency," and "it is about the proximities between bodies."[34] Freeman describes queer kin work as "an embodied but not procreative model of kinship."[35] Trans people did have attachments to the normative repertoire of kinship, but through their creative practice, they appropriated and transformed the terminology of heteroprocreative kinship. Hence, kinship was both normative and creative. Trans people's emphasis on the flexibility and inventiveness of kin work pushes the limits of normative kinship that regulates human behavior toward procreation and shows us "non-procreative contributions of the body."[36] This corporeal work is intimately linked to the question of belonging. Kin work becomes the labor as well as the longing to belong by creating a sense of place for the self in a world of connections, exchanges, dependencies, and hence vulnerabilities. It gives legitimacy to one's sense of self, one's desire to belong in a relational and social world.

Queer/trans family and kin making was often more about breaks and discontinuities than about stabilities and continuities. Borrowing from critical theorist David Eng's discussion of "the feeling of kinship that threaten[s] . . . 'to disappear irretrievably' if we do not recognize and seize hold of them," I suggest that the *lubunya* community also developed a feeling of kinship that derived from a social archive of shared experience of violence and trans deaths and funerals.[37] In her work, anthropologist Dilara Çalışkan tackles this relationship among trans deaths, memory, and temporality by examining how the LGBTI+ community socialized this archive into practices of intimacy, including care, bonds, connections, protection, and division of labor in the moment of and in the aftermath of death.[38] I would like to push this insight further and claim that, both in its material and affective documentation and in its archival collection of past, present, and future intimacies in the LGBTI+ community, each deceased trans body became a tangible and intangible temporary home—as well as a space for homemaking—for trans people while dwelling in violence. Regardless of jealousy, contempt, and anger, trans lives unfolded and thrived on intimacies that they created, invented, and experimented with in violence, through violence, and even sometimes thanks to violence. Violence was the shared substance among the bodies of trans people and became a medium to suture queer/trans ties of family and kin, which in turn, was a world-making practice of the trans everyday.

Before ending this chapter, I want to challenge the "evil" blood family image a bit, as Turkey has also witnessed the opening of promising spaces to improve the troubled relationships between blood families and their LGBTI+ children. For example, Lezbiyen, Gay, Biseksüel, Trans, İnterseks Artı Aileleri ve Yakınları Derneği (LISTAG; Organization for Families and Friends of Lesbian, Gay, Bisexual, Trans, Intersex Plus People) has been an active solidarity and support group organized by blood family members of LGBTI+ people in Istanbul since 2008.[39] For many of these families, LISTAG states on its website, it was at first shocking to discover their children were queer or trans, but it has also been an educational process to discover and combat their own prejudices.[40] Their fight against anti-LGBTI+ stance has centered on raising consciousness about the discrimination, exclusion, and violence that queer and trans people experience, informing society and state actors about queer and trans people's problems, and calling other families to support them and their children in this struggle. To do this, they have organized regular monthly dinners with family members and their queer and trans children at the home of a group member; informative debates with the help of volunteer psychiatrists; private meetings with parents who wanted to share their experiences, questions, and problems; and discussion panels at universities and NGOs across Turkey. Can Candan's 2013 documentary *Benim Çocuğum* (My child) successfully depicts their process of organizing through interviews and footage from protests and marches.

Though they currently still occupy a marginal role within Turkish politics, LISTAG members, along with the growing number of other LGBTI+ family support groups across the country, have been working very hard in the midst of increasing stigmatization and targeting of their LGBTI+ children. In some cases, they themselves blur the boundaries between blood and fictive kin ties. For instance, one of the founders of LISTAG, Sema Yakar, lost her gay activist son, Boysan Yakar, in 2015. Boysan and his close friends Zeliş Deniz and Mert Serçe, who were also prominent members of the Istanbul LGBTI+ activist scene, had a car accident while traveling together, and they all died on the spot. It was a huge loss for all of us in the *lubunya* world of Istanbul. In the aftermath of their premature death, Boysan's family turned their son's house into an alternative space for queer events and solidarity activities and named it Boysan'ın Evi (Boysan's House).[41] Elif Irem Az's moving article on Boysan's House shows how Sema used her motherhood for queer organizing and how members of Boysan's House embraced Sema as their fictive mother, referring to her as "Mother Sema."[42] Mother Sema's story is fascinating in elucidating the porosity of the boundaries between blood and fictive kin ties: a blood mother to a gay man could also become a fictive mother to other LGBTI+ activists, a queer possibility of kinship that sutured new forms of relatedness.

Mother Sema and other members of the LGBTI+ support groups that are part of LGBTI+ Family Groups demonstrated great effort and political energy because they also had to bear accusations born out of dominant discourses about the hegemonic definition of the "proper" Turkish family. Fellow citizens sometimes blamed these parents for their children's "perverted" character. Members of LISTAG struggled to erase this stigmatizing image of "pervert" from their children and from themselves. Of course, the majority of trans people were not lucky enough to have such familial support and instead kept investing more in queer/trans family and kin making and friendships as an intimate survival strategy.

Coda

IN ISTANBUL IN THE SUMMER OF 2019, I went to see *#DirenAyol*, a documentary about queer and trans narratives of the Gezi uprising in 2013.[1] The documentary was screened as part of the Friday meetings organized by Feminist Mekan (Feminist Space), a rented flat in Beyoğlu for feminist meetings, screenings, and panels. A prominent trans activist, Şevval, who is the main protagonist in the documentary, moderated and took questions during the Q&A following the screening. The documentary ended, the lights came on, and we found ourselves in a sea of mixed feelings: nostalgia, despair, disappointment, longing, and a sense of loss. The film had returned to a time when "we" actually believed that a social and political revolution was possible and about to happen. The documentary included footage from the summer of 2013, when I, together with many others in the room, had been in the midst of occupied parks, barricaded streets, newly made friends, open-air forums, exciting political discussions, and the lure of collective imagination. While living through this exciting political moment, we were, at the same time, also being tear-gassed, attacked with water cannons, violated by the police, and stigmatized and marginalized by the state on national TV channels every single day.

During Gezi, trans and queer people engraved their presence in the spaces of the uprising by building barricades, holding front lines, and clashing with police (see figures C.1 and C.2). They painted seized bulldozers pink, waved the rainbow flag on top of barricades, pitched the "LGBT Blok" tent at the center of the park, and organized frequent drag-queen dances and small-group parades with slogans and songs. By painting over offensive graffiti and modifying the letters of some swear words with the female symbol, protesters disputed the humiliation of women, queers, trans people, and sex workers Together with feminists, they challenged the misogynist, homophobic, and transphobic language of the leftist political groups in the resistance. I was part of these efforts and organized "Feminist Küfür Atölyesi" (Feminist Swear-Word Workshop) to collectively imagine an alternative vocabulary for queer/trans/feminist slang.[2] In the intermixing of bodies, signs, objects, voices, stories, and emotions, the Gezi uprising renewed existing ties and spawned new intimacies and affections, giving its participants a "belonging in becoming."[3] Soccer superfans, for example, who had liberally used the abovementioned offensive language, apologized and responded by translating their political rage and passion into new and more captious chants and rallying cries. And when members of the so-called apolitical 1990s generation were injured and took shelter from police violence in the houses of trans women sex workers, existing relations of transphobia were altered. Care, intimacy, and trust were coupled with realizations and confessions of homophobia/transphobia in the moments and spaces of the uprising. The intimate and affective ties that emerged and grew between *lubunya* groups and other protesters translated into approximately forty thousand people at the Pride March on June 30, 2013. This was the largest Pride March ever, and it illustrated the support of non-LGBTI+ people in helping carry *lubunya* lives/words beyond the barricades. Like innumerable people from feminist, queer, and trans circles, I was very excited and full of hope and described Gezi in an article as "an affective and intimate economy of encounters, touches, and dialogues that have opened bodies and lives to new, unpredictable becomings."[4] I was convinced that the entire society was on the brink of radical and transformative potentials. Reflecting on these thoughts and feelings now, I find them naive and quixotic, although they still preserve an archival record of an affective political moment in the recent history of Turkey, a moment that has been extensively documented in scholarship.[5] A great deal has changed in Turkey since then. Thus, a depressive mood came over Feminist Mekan during the Q&A in 2019.

A few weeks before Gezi, the Kurdish-Turkish peace process began after decades of war between the Turkish state and the Kurdish guerrilla group PKK. The peace process broke down in just two years and led to devastating consequences, especially for Kurdish people, in 2015. State security forces imposed curfews on several Kurdish cities, including Cizre, Şırnak, Yüksekova, and Nusaybin, among others, and conducted joint police and

C.1 Abdullah Cömert Barricade, named after a twenty-two-year-old man who was killed by a tear gas canister shot by a police officer during the Gezi protests. The barricade is on the road to Taksim Square. Photo by the author, June 7, 2013.

military operations that trapped civilians in the basements of buildings, eventually killing them. In addition to unlawful killings of civilians, security forces destroyed property, incarcerated people, and temporarily displaced civilians at a massive level.[6] The majority of Turks either remained silent or took a nationalist stance regarding all the Kurds killed under the state curfew law as terrorists. Turkish ignorance, indifference, and racial hostility against Kurds revealed the fragile nature of the above-mentioned intimacies established between the Turkish and Kurdish protesters of Gezi. The decades-long racial tensions once again came to light, sharply polarizing the country around the Turkish-Kurdish racial conflict.

The AKP government's ending of the peace process paralleled further reactionary measures in other domains of political struggle. In 2015, the governorship of Istanbul released an official statement banning the Pride March, this first ban since the march's inception in 2001. Because the Muslim holy month of Ramadan coincided with Pride 2015, the governorship declared that the march would hurt public sensitivities, causing potential provocations. Yet the previous year's Pride March had also taken place during Ramadan, and everything had been fine.

C.2 Metin Göktepe Barricade, named after a photojournalist who was tortured and killed in police custody in Istanbul on January 8, 1996. The barricade is on the road to Taksim Square. Photo by the author, June 7, 2013.

The following year, the story was similar. This time, Turkey was facing vital security problems. Approximately ten bombings had shaken the country over the previous year, causing hundreds of casualties. The heightened security concerns were coupled with the Orlando massacre that claimed forty-nine lives at a gay nightclub in the United States, which had happened only ten days before the scheduled Istanbul Pride March. The perpetrator of the attack had claimed to be a member of ISIS, which also had a growing underground presence in Turkey. Consequently, LGBTI+ activists in Turkey were worried: What if ISIS planned a similar attack at the Pride March in Istanbul?

In the meantime, ultranationalist and radical Islamist groups in Turkey started to publicly threaten and harass the march organizers and potential attendees on social media platforms. Amid these popular threats and explosive violence in several cities, the governorship of Istanbul once again banned the march. Yet, this time, exceptional security concerns were given as the main reason, along with the holy month of Ramadan. The governorship declared that they would not be able to provide protection for the marchers and needed to prioritize public security and order. A few weeks after this ban, the 2016 attempted coup happened.

Immediately after the coup attempt in July 2016, the AKP government declared a state of emergency across the country, a politically regressive situation that led to increased restrictions on civil rights, especially the rights to public assembly for protests, free speech, and legal action. This state of emergency, with its attendant statutory decrees, has fundamentally changed the sociopolitical climate for different social groups, including queer and trans people in Turkey. As one member of the Pride Week organization committee noted, under the post-coup-attempt regulations and restrictions, the possibilities for *lubunya* lives and mobilities in the city dramatically diminished. In addition to a heightened pressure on the organization of Pride Week, several LGBTI+ organizations and activities began to face prohibitions of other kinds. For example, the governor of Ankara placed an indefinite ban on any LGBTI+ activities, including movie screenings, plays, exhibitions, panels, and the like. The motives were listed as "protection of public health and morals," "public sensitivities," "public security," and "rights and freedoms of others." The Directorship of Religious Affairs released several statements vilifying LGBTI+ people, which have escalated since 2019. In 2020, for the first time in their history, LGBTI+ people found themselves the subjects of countrywide religious sermons at Friday prayers, being slandered and labeled as "perverts."

The political regime also changed in 2018, during the post-coup-attempt period. The parliamentary system was replaced with a presidential one that consolidated all political power in the presidency. Under this increasing authoritarianism, cases of torture, violence, exile, displacement, and violation of rights increased sharply. The judiciary unlawfully imprisoned internationally renowned philanthropists and human rights activists like Osman Kavala without proper criminal charges. Academics (including myself) who signed a petition to stop the war between the Turkish state and the PKK faced dire penalties to varying degrees, ranging from exile to incarceration, from loss of employment to confiscation of passports, from social death to actual death in the form of suicide. Journalists, human rights NGO workers, feminist activists, students, political party members, and parliamentarians from opposition parties (mainly the Halkların Demokratik Partisi [HDP; People's Democratic Party], the pro-Kurdish party) were arrested in late-night and early morning house raids. As a consequence of this increasing authoritarianism, the country became even more polarized, transforming social and political life to a great extent.

In this sociopolitical environment, where the boundary between legal and illegal, and freedom and prohibition was constantly shifting, the lives of queers, trans people, and women were redefined within a spatial economy of violence. Visibility for LGBTI+ people and women started garnering greater scrutiny, increased vulnerability, and surveillance by state institutions and social actors. Queer, trans, and gender-nonconforming bodies were particularly considered out of place in public. For a number of LGBTI+ individuals, the stakes of visibility changed. Dispossession and violence increased in direct proportion to the shrinking of the street as a public good.

The lives of the people in this book and my relationship to them were greatly influenced by these changes. As mentioned in the introduction, Istanbul LGBTT does not exist anymore. It has not been replaced in Istanbul. The transformation of Beyoğlu into an apolitical and highly commercial center made it more difficult to find a permanent place for trans people. The same goes for the Trans*Evi (Trans*Home) project, which collapsed in late 2019 due to the difficulties of finding a new space. Trans people could not find anyone in the Taksim area willing to rent an apartment that would be used as a shelter for trans women. Most of the project's residents became homeless. Some of its furniture was put in storage, and the rest was distributed to those who were in need.

Throughout these tumultuous ten years, queer and trans people in Turkey are still doing what they have to do or want to do. Some have disappeared from the *lubunya* urban world of Istanbul due to displacement or migration. And some unfortunately died or were killed. The main characters in this book—Sedef, Esra, Ceyda, Meryem, and Sevda—are thankfully still alive at the time of this book's completion in 2022. They all quit Istanbul LGBTT at different times and handed it over to new members before its shutdown. Sedef has been relatively fortunate, as she was able to keep her house in Ülker Street. She has completely dissociated herself from the others but continues her political activity in a communist party and occasionally participates in social events organized by other groups.

Esra moved to Germany in 2014 and immediately married her girlfriend, Maria, a *natrans* woman human rights activist and director from Germany. They had fallen in love with each other on meeting for the first time in 2007 and had been in a long-distance relationship since then. Later, in 2011–12, they started to work together on a documentary about the discrimination and violence against trans people in Turkey, mainly through the lenses of Esra's life. This documentary, *Trans X Istanbul*, was first released in Istanbul in 2014 and received much attention from the LGBTI+ community.

Sevda has remained strongly connected to the broader LGBTI+ community in Istanbul and continues to work for human rights projects on temporary contracts; but she mainly works as a DJ in several queer clubs and bars. One of these bars, Şahika Teras in Beyoğlu, has been around for almost two decades but had fallen out of popularity due to the changing night scene in Beyoğlu. Üzüm, a lesbian trans woman, took over the management of this bar in 2018 and turned it into an attractive music/dance spot for LGBTI+ people in Istanbul. Sevda was a regular DJ in this bar. She has also been one of the most wanted DJs for queer parties, especially during Pride Week. Regardless of the ban on the parade, Pride Week continued to take place in the last week of June in Istanbul with various panels, meetings, and parties, and Sevda succeeded in moving crowds from all generations each time she took the stage.

The last time I saw Ceyda, in 2014, she had finished nursing school and was looking for a job in a hospital or clinic. She was enthusiastic about this new chapter in her life. She was also still active in a communist party. Then I lost touch with her. Some friends said she had moved to a distant part of town and withdrew from everything.

Meryem, whose voice mainly appeared in communal conversations in this book, has been a reclusive, quiet, poetic, and imaginative woman since I met her in 2009. She has always been an independent soul. When most of the LGBTI+ people started leaving Beyoğlu in the mid-2010s and searching for other neighborhoods to live in, she preferred to move to a historical neighborhood in the Anatolian (Asian) side of Istanbul and established a more secluded life. She works as a translator of English and French.

Ilker and Adem moved out of Istanbul. Ilker lived with her girlfriend, taught children music (including how to play oud), and later was involved in organic farming and gardening. Adem was married to a *natrans* woman and continued to work as a nurse in a hospital. Unluckily, I lost contact with Melis, Gizem, Gamze, Narin, and others.

Violent intimacies in trans lives keep changing and gaining new forms and meanings in the ongoing sociopolitical transformations in the country. People in Turkey, both trans and *natrans*, have sequestered themselves in homes or limited themselves to small, close circles and networks. The entrance of COVID-19 into the scene in 2020 only deepened the isolation from communal activities and political mobilization, aggravating feelings of political depression. Political depression actually came up as a commentary during the Q&A at Feminist Mekan. A young woman in the audience told Şevval, "Our lives are shattered, and we are losing our ground. We don't know what to do! We are feeling so depressed!" Şevval, with her usual witty and vivacious style, responded, "Ohooo! You have a long way to go, *bacım* (my sista)! This is nothing new! We spent years dealing with this violence. Indeed, we saw a worse kind. In the '90s, you would not be able to walk on this street [pointing to the street we were at]. The police would show their face from every corner and attack us. If we had gotten depressed back then and given up, I would not be alive and talking to you right now. Nor would you have been able to sit and watch this documentary." Then she laughed. Most people in the room nodded and smiled.

As critical theorist Ann Cvetkovich notes, the affects of political depression "retain its associations with inertia and despair, if not apathy and indifference, but these affects become sites of publicity and community formation."[7] Although political depression has been hovering over the country, especially since 2015, *lubunyalar*, alongside many others, continue to imagine the world otherwise and produce alternative life projects that emerge out of everyday conditions under growing authoritarianism. Certainly, people can no longer occupy the parks or the streets of Beyoğlu, bring huge portable speakers, and throw pirate street parties in the middle of the street, dancing, drinking, and smoking all night as we did back in the early 2010s. Instead, people have faced frequent arrests, violation, and displacement every time they step into the street to organize a political protest. But affects of political depression find new venues to leak out, linger in, occupy, haunt, and navigate. While the streets shrink, people grow new solidarity and survival networks through building digital publics as well as intimate places such as homes and coffeeshops. New social media campaigns and internet blogs and journals have emerged. Social media platforms, such as Facebook, Twitter, Instagram, and TikTok, have increased the visibility and popularity of feminist, queer, and trans issues by spreading the word across multiple localities and national borders. These digital platforms provide room for anonymity by using pseudonyms as well as immediate connection to different campaigns taking place in other parts of the country.[8] People continue to experiment with alternative socialities; to struggle for communal spaces of living otherwise; to form collectives of dissent, love, and care; and to build microworlds of pleasure, joy, satisfaction, and transformation. A shared sense of hope and despair, joy and pain, laughter and tears, collectivity and isolation, finds expression in old and new ways, which means that the story of violent intimacies remains incomplete. As long as creative power and imaginative struggles continue and thrive in the *lubunya* lives and beyond, there will always be more stories to tell.

Appendix

On Method & Methodology

MY METHODOLOGICAL PONDERINGS AND QUERIES, which I mentioned in the preface, resulted in research that spanned more than ten years. In the years before and after the main thirteen months of fieldwork (in 2009–10), I also spent six summers doing preliminary and follow-up fieldwork (in 2007, 2011, 2012, 2013, 2016, and 2019). Istanbul LGBTT played a central role in my research. During 2009–10, Istanbul LGBTT was still a nascent organization, trying to raise funds to survive while working to prioritize trans people's problems, their needs and concerns, while publicizing and increasing awareness about the different forms of violence trans people face. A friend, Alp Biricik, a Turkish PhD student in Sweden, introduced me to Istanbul LGBTT. Alp was helping trans women at Istanbul LGBTT write a proposal to obtain funds from a European NGO to organize the first Trans Pride in Turkey in June 2010. As he was about to return to Sweden, he asked me to replace him and write the proposal. Thanks to Alp, I entered Istanbul LGBTT as someone offering practical help and was met with trust and positivity. I started visiting the organization every day.

As an association, Istanbul LGBTT survived on informal donations collected from its members, most of whom were trans women, and tried to attract all trans people from different parts of the city. During the time I spent at Istanbul LGBTT, apart from a small number of gay and trans men, it was older, working-class trans women who most frequented the organization. Most of the trans women I worked with either were former sex workers or were still doing sex work. None of the trans women in my research worked in state-regulated brothels; they worked instead in the unregistered sex work economy. Since most of the *gacılar* worked as sex workers, they would go to bed early in the morning and not wake up until the late hours in the afternoon. In other words, their everyday life flowed in a different temporality from much of society. Hence, one of the main concerns for the center was the difficulty of attracting trans people there.

Esra, Sedef, Sevda, Ceyda, and Meryem, who had been trans activists for more than two decades by 2010, formed the core group of the organization. Esra and Sedef were the main founders of Istanbul LGBTT. Trans femicides and police violence were the two major issues they concentrated on, organizing demonstrations, protests, and legal work. Before Istanbul LGBTT, they had worked in several political organizations, including leftist political parties and Lambdaistanbul. Their separation from Lambdaistanbul and the discussions that followed had been tense and confrontational, leaving the groups somewhat estranged for a long time afterward. As soon as I stepped into the *lubunya* social world in Istanbul in 2009, I found myself trying to untangle the history and dynamics of these long-lasting dissensions and discords that immediately plunged me into an intricate social world of gossip, not to say internecine conflict. Negotiating these conflicts or those with other LGBTI+ groups, or the tensions internal to Istanbul LGBTT, I tried my best not to pick sides, which sometimes worked, sometimes did not.

I spent most of my fieldwork at this association, chatting with people, helping organize their events and protests, communicating with other political organizations via phone calls and emails, translating English materials and conversations, witnessing quarrels and breakups with other individuals and groups and among themselves, listening to and participating in gossip. I shared lots of moments of *gullüm*, solidarity, love, friendship, care, and compassion as well as of jealousy, enmity, struggle, aggression, and dislike, which were all part of the everyday life.

I also spent several months at the center for sex workers Kadın Kapısı (Women's Gate), set up by the IKGV in 1995. Thanks to my previous research on sex work as a master's student at Boğaziçi University back in 2005–7, I still had connections with Kadın Kapısı. The initial purpose of Kadın Kapısı was to prevent the spread of sexually transmitted diseases, particularly HIV/AIDS, among sex workers. Later, in 2005, Kadın Kapısı made some organizational changes and became a sex-worker support/advocacy NGO. In addition to providing sex workers with health services and educational programs about sexually transmitted diseases and HIV/AIDS, it also provided legal consultation and engaged in activism for sex workers' rights and working conditions. It was, at the same time, a safe place for sex workers to socialize; therefore, unregistered sex workers, including women, men, trans, queer, and nonbinary sex workers, frequented the center.

Besides Istanbul LGBTT and Kadın Kapısı, I also spent time with other LGBTI+ organizations and feminist associations and was part of the queer, trans, and feminist life that unfolded at dance parties, public parks, cafés, sex-worker venues and in local streets and squares and private homes. I conducted in-depth interviews with fourteen trans women, four trans men, and seven service providers (individual professionals, including social workers, doctors, lawyers, and therapists and counselors). Most of the trans people were financially marginalized. Of the four trans men I worked with, three were trans activists. I met them through common friends at Lambdaistanbul. I learned a lot from members of the larger political queer and trans scene in Istanbul, both those associated with either of the two LGBTI+ organizations and also independent activists. I also conducted interviews with lawyers, consultants, doctors, and social workers and NGO workers; gathered legal codes and documents on GCS, the issuance of new ID cards, and trans femicides; and collected official and historical documents, newspapers, blog articles, and novels about sex/gender-transgressive people in Turkey.

When crafting all this richness of the trans everyday into a book, I deliberately decided to leave out most of the stories of violence, discrimination, and exclusion among trans people. My ethnography might be read as "incomplete" without these accounts; however, there is no such thing as a "complete" ethnography. There are just subjective decisions about curating content. A great amount of arduous labor that goes into the production of a book. In my own writing process, I took Audra Simpson's reconceptualization of "ethnographic refusal" very seriously and chose not to relate certain stories and information about the people I worked with, as they already experienced varying degrees of vulnerability and dispossession in life.[1] Instead, I wanted to draw attention to more organized and institutionalized forms of cisheteronormative violence through my focus on the workings of the police, the judiciary system, the family, medicine, urban transformation, and religion, which to a great extent also structured and/or shaped the forms of violence that queer and trans people did to each other.

Notes

Preface

1 Directorate of Communications, "Statement regarding Türkiye's Withdrawal."

Introduction: Violence and Intimacy

1 Despite its various interpretations, wearing a headscarf at a funeral ceremony is a dominant religious practice among Muslim women. Even women who do not wear headscarves in their everyday lives usually do so at funerals.

2 My preference for the acronym LGBTI+ is consistent with common usage in Turkey in 2022, at the time this book was revised. During my main fieldwork in 2009–10, however, the common abbreviation was LGBTT, with the last two Ts standing for transsexuals and transgenders.

3 From 1976 to 2017, Turkish citizens were assigned different-colored ID cards based on sex. With the passage of a new ID bill in 2016, civil registry offices started to replace the blue/pink IDs with white smart IDs beginning in January 2017. The new IDs now have digitized personal finger, vein, and palm prints and are still being issued in 2022, at the time of my book revisions. They still display gender categories but in verbal form. Time will show whether this shift will create new possibilities for challenging gender binarism in institutional life.

4 See Amin, "We Are All Nonbinary." Rather than offering a radical critique of gender, some scholars argue that the cis/trans gender binary may reflect "an ethnocentric deployment of the nature/culture binary." See Hegarty, *The Made-Up State*, 10.

5 See Gill-Peterson, "Cis State"; and Gill-Peterson, "Cis State II." Cisness, more and more, is utilized as a political ideology that mandates an ontological compulsion based on the cis/trans binary; however, as Marquis Bey crucially notes, "the distinction between cis and trans is a nebulous one invested with uncertain and competing political registers and sociocultural understandings." Bey, *Cistem Failure*, 30.

6 Foucault, *Birth of Biopolitics*; and Mbembe, "Necropolitics."

7 Taussig, "Terror as Usual"; and Scheper-Hughes and Bourgois, "Introduction," 19.

8   I use *natrans* instead of *cis* because of my personal preference for a local term that the trans movement in Turkey has produced to center trans epistemology and ontology in individual accounts of those gendered selves without trans experience.

9   *Meyhane* refers to a traditional restaurant with its own unique sets of customs that involve drinking of *rakı*, an anise-flavored traditional spirit, accompanied with a rich variety of food and side dishes, *mezes*. It mainly hosts conversing groups all night with a genre of traditional music in the background.

10 Stryker and Aizura, "Introduction," 7.

11 Stryker, *Transgender History*, 1.

12 Particularly, both Riley Snorton's *Black on Both Sides* and Jules Gill-Peterson's *Histories of the Transgender Child* demonstrate how the category of transgender is actually a racial narrative that condenses transness into merely gendered confines. But from a Black historical perspective, as Hortense Spillers's "Mama's Baby, Papa's Maybe" remarkably shows, not everyone was gendered, nor had access to gender. Chattel slavery constructed gender as a definitive element of the human, a category that was reserved for white people only, a discussion that Sylvia Wynter eloquently details in "Unsettling the Coloniality of Being/Power/Truth/Freedom." Hence, having the gender difference or a place in the gender hierarchy was an anti-Black racialized location that structurally defined Black people as genderless and hence nonhuman. The denial of gender or gender difference to Black people left them without any place of departure when it came to understanding transness from their experience. Both Snorton and Gill-Peterson tackle this question and argue that both Blackness and transness animate and find articulation within each other. Similar to Stryker's definition, transness has no point of arrival; but different from hers, it does not have a clear origin either. Snorton defines transness as transitive (characterized by transition), transitory (not persistent or permanent), and transversal (acting, extending, or being across) in relation to both Blackness and gender.

13 On race and racialization, see Snorton, *Black on Both Sides*; Gill-Peterson, *Histories of the Transgender Child*; Bey, *Black Trans Feminism*; Gossett, "We Will Not Rest"; Hayward and Gossett, "Impossibility of *That*"; Tudor, "Im/possibilities"; Tudor, "Decolonizing Trans/Gender Studies?"; and Galarte, *Brown Trans Figurations*. On diaspora and migration, see Bhanji, "TRANS/SCRIPTIONS"; Luibhéid and Chávez, *Queer and Trans Migrations*; Shakhsari, "Queer Time of Death"; Snorton and Haritaworn, "Trans Necropolitics"; and Haritaworn, "Colorful Bodies in the *Multikilti* Metropolis." On surveillance and securitization, see Currah and Mulqueen, "Securitizing Gender"; and Beauchamp, *Going Stealth*. On political economy and labor, see Namaste, "Undoing Theory"; David, "Purple-Collar Labor"; and Irving,

"Trans* Political Economy Deconstructed." On disability, see Irving, "Normalized Transgressions"; Clare, "Body Shame, Body Pride"; and Puar, "Disability." On indigeneity, see Rifkin, *When Did Indians Become Straight?*; Miranda, "Extermination of the Joyas"; Cruz and Driskill, "Puo'Winue'L Prayers"; Driskill, *Asegi Stories*; Morgensen, *Spaces between Us*; Day, "Indigenist Origins"; and Leo, "Colonial/Modern [Cis]gender System."

14   Chiang, *Transtopia*, 6.

15   Feldman, *Formations of Violence*.

16   Robben and Nordstrom, "Violence and Sociopolitical Conflict," 2. See also Scheper-Hughes and Bourgois, "Introduction."

17   Das, *Life and Words*, 1.

18   Das, *Life and Words*, 8.

19   For instance, for a nuanced eloquent discussion on plural meanings of intimacy from a saintly perspective, see Kasmani, *Queer Companions*.

20   Oswin and Olund, "Governing Intimacy," 60–61.

21   Zengin and Sehlikoğlu, "Everyday Intimacies."

22   Stoler, "Intimidations of Empire," 15.

23   More explicitly, consider the microlevel connection between the self and the other. The uniqueness and singularity of the self is always conditioned by its relationality with the other(s). The self is a constant place of opening to relations of recognition and belonging; complexities of love, fantasy, and desire; and, hence, processes of subjectification, identification, imagination, and attachments. The same place of opening can also be shaped by processes of correction, detachment, estrangement, and even exclusion and abandonment. The formation of the self, in other words, has strong ties to vulnerability that might bring violence. In this respect, actual or potential violence is always already constitutive of intimacy.

24   Berlant, "Intimacy"; Lowe, *Intimacies of Four Continents*; Shah, *Stranger Intimacy*; and Wilson, "Infrastructure of Intimacy."

25   Hartman, *Wayward Lives, Beautiful Experiments*.

26   Hartman, *Wayward Lives, Beautiful Experiments*, 56.

27   Haley, "Intimate Historical Practice."

28   Berlant and Warner, "Sex in Public"; and Sehlikoğlu, *Working Out Desire*.

29   Pratt and Rosner, "Introduction," 17.

30   Price, "Race and Ethnicity II."

31   Ahmed, "Affective Economies," 117.

32   Ahmed, "Affective Economies," 117.

33   Antwi et al., "Postcolonial Intimacies," 4.

34   The Istanbul Trans Pride was different from the Istanbul LGBTI+ Pride. The latter usually took place approximately ten days after the former. Both Pride events were supported and attended by almost the same group of people. But a separate Trans Pride Week was necessary for raising awareness regarding problems specific to being trans in Turkey. The first

Trans Pride was organized when I did my fieldwork in 2010. I also actively participated in its organization. In 2013 both the Trans and the LGBTI+ Pride Marches were the most well attended compared to previous marches, swelled by the ranks of Gezi protesters. However, starting in 2015, there has been a stark and rapid transition from a march that attracted thousands of attendees to a march that is now forbidden. Yet Trans Pride activities continued until 2017 in spite of strict police pressure and surveillance.

35 Butler, "Rethinking Vulnerability and Resistance."

36 Butler, "Rethinking Vulnerability and Resistance."

37 Aretxaga, "Maddening States," 395.

38 Das and Poole, *Anthropology in the Margins*; Sharma and Gupta, *Anthropology of the State*; and Aretxaga, "Maddening States."

39 Krupa, "State by Proxy," 321.

40 Critical theories of the state problematize its conceptualization as something distinct from society and as a reified, empirical object. See Abrams, "Difficulty of Studying the State"; Gramsci, *Prison Notebooks*; Foucault, *Madness and Civilization*; Foucault, "Governmentality"; and Foucault, *Discipline and Punish*. As much as it is strictly tied to the production and distribution of specific ideologies and material resources and to the operation of transnational processes, state formation is, at the same time, a cultural process. See Sharma and Gupta, "Introduction." What people understand by the state, what kinds of meanings and values they attach to it, and how they speak about it are shaped by cultural processes, as much as by the state's active production of cultures. State formation incorporates moral and ethical norms and values (see Muehlebach, *Moral Neoliberal*), affective and psychic dynamics (see Taussig, *Magic of the State*; Rose, *States of Fantasy*; Navaro, *Faces of the State*; Aretxaga, "Sexual Games"; and Aretxaga, "Maddening States"), sensual and emotional dimensions (see Berlant, *Queen of America*; and Stoler, *Carnal Knowledge*), and even sexual and pornographic elements (see Zengin, *İktidarın Mahremiyeti*; Üstündağ, "Pornographic State"; and Puri, *Sexual States*).

41 Stoler, *Carnal Knowledge*; Aretxaga, *Shattering Silence*; Povinelli, *Empire of Love*; Hasso, *Consuming Desires*; Zengin, *İktidarın Mahremiyeti*; Zengin, "Violent Intimacies"; Zengin, "Afterlife of Gender"; and Mikdashi, *Sextarianism*.

42 Cott, afterword, 470.

43 Yuval-Davis and Anthias, *Woman-Nation-State*; Kandiyoti, "Gendering the Modern"; Berlant, *Queen of America*; Al-Ali, *Secularism, Gender and the State*; and Hasso, *Consuming Desires*.

44 Aretxaga, "Maddening States," 404.

45 As a corrective to the general linkage of the formation of the nuclear family to the establishment of the Turkish Republic, in late nineteenth-century Istanbul households, according to Alan Duben and Cem Behar, the nuclear

family was prevalent, and extended families were concentrated mainly among people with means (and there was also a high ratio of single-woman households). Today extended family units are still quite common in the countryside (home to a fifth of the nation's population), as are extended family living arrangements (such as multiple households in the same apartment block) in urban areas. These considerations mitigate rather than challenge the dominance of the nuclear family model in contemporary Turkey. See Duben and Behar, *Istanbul Households*.

46 Demirci and Somel, "Women's Bodies"; and Dursun, "Procreation, Family and 'Progress.'"

47 Sirman, "Making of Familial Citizenship."

48 Esra Özyürek's *Nostalgia for the Modern* is based on two photographic exhibitions: first, *Family Albums*, organized by the History Foundation in 1998, featuring a display of official wedding ceremony photos since the foundation of the republic; and, second, *To Create a Citizen*, organized by a private bank also in 1998, showing photos of "modern" Turkish people in their domestic lives.

49 Pateman, *Sexual Contract*; Yuval-Davis and Anthias, *Woman-Nation-State*; and Anderson, *Imagined Communities*.

50 Shryock, "Other Conscious/Self Aware."

51 Schick, "Representation of Gender and Sexuality"; Schick, *Erotic Margin*; Ze'evi, *Producing Desire*; El-Rouayheb, *Before Homosexuality*; Andrews and Kalpaklı, *Age of Beloveds*; Delice, "Janissaries and Their Bedfellows"; Avcı, "Shifts in Sexual Desire"; and Sarıtaş, *Cinsel Normalliğin Kuruluşu*.

52 Kandiyoti, "Gendering the Modern"; Kandiyoti, "Some Awkward Questions"; Arvas, "Queers In-Between"; and Sarıtaş, *Cinsel Normalliğin Kuruluşu*.

53 Arvas, "Queers In-Between."

54 Recent scholarship on the politics of intimacy in Turkey delineates the mundane as well as the extraordinary, institutional practices and discourses through which state power operates, establishing intimate and sexual links to the lives and bodies of its individual citizens. See Acar and Altunok, "Politics of Intimate"; Korkman, "Politics of Intimacy in Turkey"; Sehlikoğlu and Zengin, "Introduction: Why Revisit Intimacy?"; Yazıcı, "The Return to the Family"; and Zengin, "Violent Intimacies."

55 Canpolat and Çelik, "Roles of Women and Men"; and Akınerdem, *Marriage Safe and Sound*.

56 Sancar, *Erkeklik*; Selek, *Sürüne Sürüne Erkek Olmak*; Başaran, "'You Are like a Virus'"; Sünbüloğlu, "Nationalist Reactions and Masculinity"; Biricik, "Kamusal Alanda Mahrem Taktikler"; Gökarıksel and Secor, "Devout Muslim Masculinities"; Nuhrat, "Contesting Love through Commodification"; and Açıksöz, *Sacrificial Limbs*. Circumcision is celebrated, and the boy feted with a circumcision ceremony (*sünnet töreni*). Circumcisions are ritualized

family gatherings that rival weddings in family/social importance, with the boy, dressed in a cape, crown, and scepter, showered in displays of love and affection, along with presents. For a detailed ethnographic work on circumcision in Turkey, see Başaran, *Circumcision and Medicine.*

57 The strong and exclusive role of the military-nation formula in shaping modern Turkish hegemonic masculinity finds expression in the saying "All Turks are born soldiers" (Her Türk asker doğar), thus naturalizing the convention of conscription. See A. Altınay and Bora, "Ordu, Militarizm ve Milliyetcilik," 142. Military service also functioned in the state's "civilizing mission" to make citizens of its rural (male) masses by detaching them from their villages for two years and teaching them how to read and write. For further discussion, see A. Altınay, *Myth of the Military-Nation*; and Ewing, *Stolen Honor.*

58 None of these titles is official, yet they are popularly used in public to refer to one's ineligibility for the draft.

59 For further information, see Türk Silahlı Kuvvetleri Sağlık Yeteneği Yönetmeliği (Health Regulation for Turkish Armed Force), issued by the Council of Ministers, passed October 8, 1986, https://www.mevzuat.gov.tr /MevzuatMetin/3.5.20158136.pdf.

60 Başaran, "'You Are like a Virus.'"

61 Tapınç, "Masculinity, Femininity," 4.

62 Bereket and Adam, "Navigating Islam."

63 This orientalist tendency is particularly rampant in the international (mostly Western) circulation of the discourse of "honor crimes" wielded against Muslims in the Middle East, as well as against Muslim groups in the North American–European diaspora, a framework that has been widely criticized by feminist anthropologists working on the Middle East. Most notably, see Abu-Lughod, *Veiled Sentiments*; and Abu-Lughod, *Do Muslim Women Need Saving?*

64 See Koğacıoğlu, "Tradition Effect."

65 See Sirman, "Kinship, Politics and Love"; Parla, "'Honor' of the State"; and Koğacıoğlu, "Tradition Effect."

66 Parla, "Revisiting 'Honor.'" In a similar vein, Sarıoğlu's recent work on gendered vigilante violence demonstrates how the AKP government has re-tooled shame-honor as a masculinist populist force to fuel hostile emotions and male aggression against working-class women in Turkey. See Sarıoğlu, *Unburdened Body.*

67 Sirman, "Crossing Boundaries"; and Abu-Lughod, *Veiled Sentiments.*

68 Essentially escapist melodramas, the Yeşilçam movies tended to be grounded in social realism.

69 Married couples without children expect to face social pressure to give birth not only from their extended family members but also from friends, neighbors, and other social actors. The lives of both singles (divorced or

bachelor) and married couples without children tend to be stigmatized, or regarded as lives that are not quite lives in terms of their sexual legibility. For working women, there is a reasonably robust system of state benefits (maternity leave) to support the new mother, but this does not extend to men (as paternity leave). Furthermore, a significant part of family making is tied to women's care work. Caregiving, as a feminized form of labor, may concern not only the nuclear family members but also, especially in the context of a little-developed social welfare system, the elderly members of the extended family, such as grandparents and grandaunts and -uncles. Women are also expected to organize the domestic space and take care of everyday domestic chores, unless the family is upper or upper middle class, in which case domestic service providers are paid to cope with the everyday domestic work. See Özyeğin, *Untidy Gender*, for a detailed account on domestic workers.

70 Also see Zengin, "Devletin Cinsel Kıyıları."

71 Öktem, "Another Struggle"; and Savcı, *Queer in Translation*.

72 Zengin, "Mortal Life of Trans/Feminism." For example, annual figures recorded at least 328 women as having been killed by men in 2019. See Kepenek, "Erkek Şiddeti 2019."

73 See Kocamaner, "Regulating the Family"; and Tahaoğlu, "Kadınlar Sokağa Çıkıyor."

74 The Ministry of Environment and Urban Planning declared that bachelor apartments would be prohibited in certain districts in Istanbul. See Süzgeçyapı, "1 Ekim'de '1 + 0' Tipi Stüdyo." On the removal of two kissing passengers, see Hürriyet, "İETT Otobüsünde Öpüşme Eylemi."

75 Sandal-Wilson, "Social Justice, Conflict"; and Özbay, "State Homophobia, Sexual Politics."

76 Grewal and Caplan, "Global Identities"; Nagar and Swarr, *Critical Transnational Feminist Praxis*; Povinelli and Chauncey, "Thinking Sexuality Transnationally"; Anzaldúa, *Borderlands*; Manalansan, *Global Divas*; Decena, *Tacit Subjects*; Puar, *Terrorist Assemblages*; Moallem, *Warrior Brother*; El-Tayeb, *European Others*; Tudor, "Dimensions of Transnationalism"; and Savcı, *Queer in Translation*.

77 On transnational understandings of sex, gender, and sexuality from queer and trans perspectives in the region, see Alqaisiya, *Decolonial Queering in Palestine*; Atshan, *Queer Palestine*; Merabet, *Queer Beirut*; Mikdashi, "Queering Citizenship"; Mikdashi, "Gay Rights"; Moussawi, *Disruptive Situations*; and Khan, "Institutionalizing an Ambiguous Category."

78 Blackwood and Wieringa, "Globalization, Sexuality, and Silences."

79 Blackwood and Wieringa, "Globalization, Sexuality, and Silences," 8.

80 Turkey has different categorizations for different refugee groups. Syrians, for instance, were categorized as "guests" until they were designated with the special category of "temporary protection beneficiaries." Others from

non-European countries, including Iraq, Palestine, Afghanistan, Pakistan, Somalia, and Iran, are classified as "conditional refugees," whose time in Turkey is considered temporary, lasting only until their resettlement in another country. For further information, see Biehl, "Governing through Uncertainty"; Dağtaş "Whose *Misafirs?*"; Kuschminder, "Afghan Refugee Journeys"; S. Can, *Refugee Encounters*; and Sert and Danış, "Framing Syrians in Turkey."

81 As refugees wait for the evaluation of their resettlement claims, which can take as long as a decade in the context of the Global North's border closures, the Turkish Ministry of the Interior assigns most of them to live in one of the predetermined "satellite cities," where their lives are put under strict state surveillance. Most of these cities are located in Turkey's interior and represent relatively more conservative contexts that are distant from more cosmopolitan urban environments, such as Istanbul, Ankara, and Izmir. That said, there is a growing number of LGBTI+ refugees in Istanbul as well. In both satellite cities and metropoles like Istanbul, LGBTI+ refugees, mainly from other South West Asian and North African countries, enrich the urban life by interacting with the local queer and trans activists and other refugee groups, as well as by developing their own communal networks and survival mechanisms in the city. Even though these issues beg meticulous attention and further research, they are beyond the scope of this book. A number of inspiring scholars closely engage with these matters by examining how macro regimes of national sovereignty, universal human rights, international humanitarian aid, and national and local sociocultural contexts shape, transform, and interact with micro domains of queer and trans refugee lives in Turkey. See Shakhsari, "Killing Me Softly"; Shakhsari, "Queer Time of Death"; Sarı, "Lesbian Refugees in Transit"; Sarı, "Unsafe Present, Uncertain Future"; Saleh, "Transgender"; and Koçak, "Who Is 'Queerer.'"

82 Tsing, *Friction*, 4.

83 Gürbilek, *Vitrinde Yaşamak*; Keyder and Öncü, "Globalization"; Özbay et al., *Making of Neoliberal Turkey*; and Öniş, "State and Economic Development."

84 In 1993, Club Prive was one of those places used regularly for three months until police pressure caused them to leave for various other spots in town, where, as Lambdaistanbul, they held weekly meetings.

85 Alphan, "Onur Haftası'nın desteğinize ihtiyacı var."

86 The IKGV's website can be found at http://www.ikgv.org

87 Bursa is Turkey's fourth-biggest city.

88 For Ankara, see Kaos GL, "Kaos GL ve Pembe Hayat LGBTT Dayanışma Dernekleri." For Istanbul, see Lambdaistanbul's history on their website.

89 Hikayeci's blog can still be found at http://hikayeci.livejournal.com/.

90 Hikayeci, "Farklılıkları Yok Eden."

91 Pembe Hayat is named after Alain Berliner's movie *Ma vie en rose* which translates as "my pink life" (*pembe hayat* means pink life) and focuses on a trans girl's life story. Pembe Hayat is still a powerful actor in trans activism in Turkey with a political agenda, mainly including the provision of legal, medical, and educational support for trans people; the organization of "trans camps"; the coordination of fundraising and donation campaigns for trans prisoners; and the organization of KuirFest, the first LGBTI+ film festival in Turkey.

92 Rubin, "Of Catamites and Kings," 479.

93 Stryker, "(De)subjugated Knowledges," 3.

94 Spade, *Normal Life*.

95 This occurs most obviously at the level of nomenclature: thus the terms *lezbiyen, gey, biseksüel, transseksüel, travesti, trans*, and, very recently, *kuir* or *queer*. The term "dubs" is from Boellstorff, *Gay Archipelago*.

96 Boellstorff, *Gay Archipelago*, 84.

97 Boellstorff, "New Frontiers," 173.

98 Hirsch, Wardlow, and Phiney, "'None Saw Us,'" 94.

99 For a critical work on translation and its methodological application to understand the workings of neoliberal Islam through queer lenses in Turkey, see Evren Savcı's *Queer in Translation*.

100 Baer, *Dönme. Dönme* is derived from the root *dön*, meaning "turn."

101 *Travesti*, a highly derogatory term until recently, has been widely used by *na-trans* people to refer to mainly trans women in Turkey. It has been overused and tremendously exploited. Gaining common currency in the 1990s and early 2000s to epitomize trans people as perverts, spreaders of HIV/AIDS, thieves, and terrorizers of society, the term *travesti* was used especially by the mainstream media to degrade and trigger violence against trans people. Since its usage had transphobic connotations, and it was thus employed as a pejorative/derogatory term, trans people avoided it for a long while until recently. Currently, there is a growing effort to reclaim the term *travesti*, rescuing it from its stigmatizing force and recognizing it as part of the larger socioculturally specific history and present of transness in Turkey.

There are also specific local terms for gays in social life, including *eşcinsel* and *ibne*, the latter popularly used for pejorative purposes, yet again reclaimed by gay people to address one another. Whereas *ibne* is widely used for gay men (and occasionally for trans women), *eşcinsel* is more of an umbrella term, standing for both gay men and lesbian women (although the *gay* meaning predominates, making it rather similar to *homosexual*). When it comes to lesbians, the historically employed local terms, such as *kadın sevici* (woman lover) and *zürafa* (giraffe), no longer circulate and have largely been replaced by *lezbiyen* and its colloquial derivation, *lezzo*. Mainly straight people used the older, outdated terms to refer to lesbians.

102 Zengin, "Mortal Life of Trans/Feminism."

103 For the book version, see Özdemir and Bayraktar, *İstanbul Amargi Feminizm Tartışmaları*.

104 For a more comprehensive discussion of these disputes, see Tar, "Toplumun Dışına İtilenlerin Bilgisi Nasıl Üretilir?"; Eralp, "Background of TERF Dispute"; Yardımcı, "Trans.Candır"; and Özlen, "'No TERFS on Our TURF.'"

105 Brown et al., "Sexualities in/of the Global South," 1570.

Chapter 1: Displacement as Emplacement

1 Queer history in Turkey is far from unique in conflating gay men and trans women. Afsaneh Najmabadi presents an eloquent description of a similar dynamic in Iran in 1970–79. For further discussion on how the global flow of medicolegal discourses interacts with local state discourses and religious dynamics to shape the specific categories of gay and transgender in Iran, see Najmabadi, "Transing and Transpassing"; Najmabadi, "Verdicts of Science"; and Najmabadi, "Reading Transsexuality."

2 *Gacılar* is the plural version of *gacı*, a colloquial term for trans women in LGBTI+ circles in Istanbul (see the introduction); *-ler* and *-lar* are the Turkish plural suffixes.

3 Wardlow, *Wayward Women*.

4 Thiranagama, *In My Mother's House*, 5.

5 Lefebvre, *Production of Space*.

6 Lefebvre, "Right to the City"; and Massey, *Space, Place, and Gender*.

7 Brown, Browne, and Lim, "Introduction."

8 McKittrick, *Demonic Grounds*, 7.

9 McKittrick, *Demonic Grounds*, x.

10 A *simit* is a popular circular pastry with sesame seeds.

11 Zengin, "What Is Queer about Gezi?" Here it would also be helpful to note some of the prominent people's resistance movements in the history of modern Turkey since 1923: the Kurdish uprising of Sheikh Said in 1925; the Alevi Kurdish uprising of Dersim in 1938–39; the protest of leftist students and trade unionists against the American Sixth Fleet in 1969 (also known as Bloody Sunday); the Great Worker Resistance on June 15–16, 1970; the International Workers' Day protest on May 1, 1977 (also known as the Taksim Square Massacre); and the protest against the assassination of the Armenian journalist Hrant Dink on January 19, 2007.

12 Tamar Nalcı and Emre Can Dağlıoğlu documented the Gezi area as an ex-Armenian cemetery in *Agos*, a newspaper published by the Armenian community in Istanbul. See Nalcı and Dağlıoğlu, "'Bir Gasp Hikâyesi.'" During the Gezi uprisings of 2013, their essay, along with others, disrupted popular assumptions about Gezi Park. Also see Bieberstein and Tataryan, "What of Occupation"; and Parla and Özgül, "Property, Dispossession, and Citizenship."

13 E. Yıldız, "Cruising Politics."

14 For a comprehensive study on rent boys in Istanbul, see Özbay, *Queering Sexualities in Turkey.*

15 On queer people and Gezi Park, see Kayalı and Yaka, "Spirit of Gezi"; and Özbay and Savcı, "Queering Commons in Turkey." On challenges to neoliberal and heteronormative geographies, see Erol, "Queer Contestation."

16 Over 300,000 villages in Kurdistan were emptied and partially destroyed by the military as a strategy in its guerrilla war with the Partiya Karkerên Kurdistan (PKK; Kurdistan Workers' Party) (mostly in the late 1990s), making over a million people homeless, a sizable number of whom migrated to Istanbul. See Jongerden, *Settlement Issue in Turkey.*

17 Grande Rue de Péra, the original name for Istiklal before it was changed in 1927, is not used nowadays.

18 Büyükünal, *Bir Zaman Tüneli*, 16.

19 See Rasim, *Fuhş-i Atik*; and Mithat Efendi, *Henüz Onyedi Yaşında.*

20 Scognamillo, *Bir Levantenin Beyoğlu Anıları*, 72.

21 Ubicini, *1855'te Türkiye*, 444, as quoted in Akın, *19. Yüzyılın İkinci Yarısında*, 33.

22 Akın, *19. Yüzyılın İkinci Yarısında Galata ve Pera*; and Büyükünal, *Bir Zaman Tüneli.*

23 Scognamillo, "Beyoğlu Eğlenirken"; Bali, *Jews and Prostitution*; Zarinebaf, *Crime and Punishment*; and Wyers, *"Wicked" Istanbul.*

24 These Muslim private brothels or Muslim prostitutes' houses were documented in the districts of Aksaray, Kadıköy, and Üsküdar on the Asian side of Istanbul, but prostitution in this area was run by intermediary actors who controlled and operated these houses secretly; these houses were thus few and under strict surveillance. See Zarinebaf, *Crime and Punishment*, 87–90; and Sevengil, *İstanbul Nasıl Eğleniyordu*, 145.

25 Karpat, *Ottoman Population*; Özbek, "Regulation of Prostitution"; Yetkin, "II. Meşrutiyet Döneminde"; Wyers, *"Wicked" Istanbul*; and Belli, *Osmanlı'da Fuhuş.*

26 This regulatory mechanism was part of a wider medical effort to improve public health in the empire. Focusing on syphilis in the late Ottoman Empire, Seçil Yılmaz's work shows how prostitution was a particularly significant site for the emergence of a novel public health discourse and medical science to educate not only prostitutes but also their male clients around sexual hygiene and the prevention of sexually transmitted diseases. S. Yılmaz, "Threats to Public Order."

27 Karakışla, "Yoksulluktan Fuhuş Yapanların Islahı"; and Toprak, "İstanbul'da Fuhuş ve Zührevi Hastalıklar."

28 Toprak, "İstanbul'da Fuhuş ve Zührevi Hastalıklar," 32.

29 Deleon, *Bir Beyoğlu Gezisi*, 29.

30 On the population exchange, see Iğsız, *Humanism in Ruins.*

31 Döşemeciyan, Özuzun, and Bebiroğlu, *Müslüman Olmayan Azınlıklar Raporu.*

32 Güven, *Cumhuriyet Dönemi Azınlık Politikaları*.

33 Özlü, preface, 10.

34 *Arabesk*, an Arab-influenced style of popular music, and *lahmacun*, a flat-bread topped with minced meat, spices, and the like, are both associated with the consumption habits of poorly educated urban migrants, considered low-brow and nonmodern by the committed national subjects of the Turkish state's modernization (read also: Westernization) project. Martin Stokes argues that *arabesk* discloses the inner Orient, a representation of traditional elements and the "Arabic" influence on culture that had been systematically repressed. Stokes, *Republic of Love*, 74.

35 Kaptan, *Beyoğlu ve Kısa Geçmişi*.

36 Scognamillo, "Beyoğlu Eğlenirken," 110.

37 For further information on Büyük Ziba and Abanoz Streets, see Ersöz, "Elli Yıl Öncesinin Ünlü Evleri"; and Celep, "1940'lı Yıllarda İstanbul'da Fuhuş Problemi."

38 At least, that was the earliest date I was able to ascertain from my interviews with trans women over fifty. If there was another place of concentrated trans existence in the area before Abanoz Street, it has, to my knowledge, gone unremarked.

39 Siyah Pembe Üçgen, *80'lerde Lubunya Olmak*, 60–70.

40 Cancan is a colloquial name given to the Istanbul Deri ve Tenasül Hastalıkları Hastanesi (the Istanbul Dermal and Venereal Diseases Hospital) previously located in Cankurtaran. This hospital has a long history: It was first founded as the Emraz-ı Zührevi (Sexually Transmitted Diseases) in Kuledibi, Beyoğlu in 1908, as an emergency response to the increasing public health concerns caused by syphilis. It operated under the control of the Istanbul Police Department. In 1918, it was relocated to Hasköy, and later, to Cankurtaran. In 1982, it was delegated to the Ministry of Health. In 2009, the hospital building was vacated for a gentrification project that planned its reconstruction as a museum of design; however, it has still not reopened. Meanwhile, the hospital has become a part of the Bakırköy Psychiatric Hospital, and it operates now as a branch hospital under the name of the Istanbul Lepra Dermal and Venereal Diseases Hospital. Both registered and unregistered sex workers visit this hospital for their regular medical examinations. During my research on the regulation of sex work in Turkey in 2005–6, the hospital was still located in Cankurtaran, where I tried to enter and conduct research, but I was not allowed in due to the strict state control there. For further discussion on Cancan, see Zengin, "Devletin Cinsel Kıyıları"; and Zengin, *İktidarın Mahremiyeti*.

41 Biricik, "Kamusal Alanda Mahrem Taktikler"; D. Yıldız, "Türkiye Tarihinde Eşcinselliğin Izinde"; Zengin, "Trans-Beyoğlu"; and Savcı, *Queer in Translation*.

42 Siyah Pembe Üçgen, *80'lerde Lubunya Olmak*, 81–82.

43 The history of deportation dates back to the late Ottoman Empire, when promiscuous women or prostitutes would be exiled from their neighborhoods and cities for long periods of time. On some occasions, they were able to return to their homes conditional on the sponsorship and testimony of trusted and respected family members. For further discussion, see Belli, *Osmanlı'da Fuhuş*.

44 Bali, *6-7 Eylül 1955 Olayları*; Kuyucu, "Ethno-Religious 'Unmixing' of 'Turkey'"; Güven, *Cumhuriyet Dönemi Azınlık Politikaları*; and Arıcan, "Behind the Scaffolding."

45 Öniş, "Turgut Özal"; and Önder, "Integrating."

46 Keyder, *Istanbul*.

47 Öncü, "Myth of the Ideal Home."

48 Ünsal and Kuyucu, "Challenging the Neoliberal Urban Regime," 57.

49 Stonewall refers to the protests, mainly spearheaded by trans women of color, against the police raid on the Stonewall Inn in Greenwich Village, New York City, on June 28, 1969. Stonewall is generally recognized as pivotal in the development of the gay liberation movement and the emergence of LGBTI+ politics in the United States.

50 Kandiyoti, "Pink Card Blues."

51 Islam, "Current Urban Discourse."

52 The E5 is a well-known highway in Istanbul and a significant symbol as an everyday space for unlicensed sex work, especially for trans women.

53 Hortum was the nickname for the chief police officer Süleyman Ulusoy, known for his unprecedented violence against trans women, whom he tortured with a hose (*hortum*) (see chapter 3 below).

54 Ilkucan, "Gentrification, Community and Consumption," 68–69.

55 Selek, *Maskeler, Süvariler, Gacılar*; Siyah Pembe Üçgen, *90'larda Lubunya Olmak*; Zengin, "Trans-Beyoğlu"; and Atalay and Doan, "Reading the LGBT Movement."

56 Ingram, "Marginality," 36.

57 Adler and Brenner, "Gender and Space," 26.

58 Myslik, "Social/Sexual Identities of Places."

59 Knopp, "Ontologies of Place," 130.

60 Ingram, "'Open' Space," 100.

61 Bartu Candan and Kolluoğlu, "Emerging Spaces of Neoliberalism"; and Islam, "Current Urban Discourse."

62 *Gecekondu* literally means "settled overnight," referring to the original practice of building small houses, without permits, on state land claimed as (if) a common. This was done at night because people were free after work, because this avoided unwanted attention, and because the days are hot during the summer.

63 Dinçer, "Impact of Neoliberal Policies."

64 Sönmez, "Turkey's Second Privatization Agency."

65 Dinçer, "Impact of Neoliberal Policies." The opportunities and incentives for speculative development that this provided were a cause of the Gezi Park protest and, in 2013, were related to the corruption controversy that engulfed the national government and also the Istanbul municipality (especially in the Fatih district).

66 Ergun, "Gentrification in Istanbul."

67 Uysal, "Urban Social Movement"; Robins, "How Tell What Remains"; Karaman and Islam, "Intra-urban Borders"; Bartu Candan and Kolluoğlu, "Emerging Spaces of Neoliberalism"; and Kuyucu, "Ethno-Religious 'Unmixing' of 'Turkey.'"

68 Islam, "Current Urban Discourse," 60.

69 Smith, *New Urban Frontier*, xviii.

70 Istanbul's housing market prices have been increasing tremendously as of 2021, which has resulted in a huge housing crisis for the current residents in these neighborhoods. Rental units have become unaffordable for many, including trans people. Hence, trans people, along with others, are gradually facing the threat of eviction or the obligation to move to cheaper neighborhoods that are mostly located on the outskirts of the city.

71 Trans*Evi's website can be found at http://www.transevi.org/english.php.

72 For further information, see Tar, "Bayram Sokak'ta Trans Kadınlar."

Chapter 2: Extralegality, Surveillance, & Police Violence

1   The sixty-nine-lira fine was equivalent to around fifty dollars at that time, but the value of this in terms of the cost of living could be doubled or trebled for a better estimate of its impact in terms of US dollars.

2   Selek, *Maskeler, Süvariler, Gacılar*; Berghan, *Lubunya*; and Şeker *Başkaldıran Bedenler*.

3   Babül, "Morality"; Gönen, *Politics of Crime*; and Akarsu, "'Proportioning Violence.'"

4   Gönen, *Politics of Crime*, 5.

5   Heyman, *States and Illegal Practices*; and Smart and Zerilli, "Extralegality."

6   Nordstrom, *Global Outlaws*, xviii.

7   Beauchamp, *Going Stealth*.

8   Beauchamp, *Going Stealth*, 2.

9   Emerging research on racialized queer lives from the Kurdish region in Turkey offers novel perspectives to analyze the relationship among surveillance, securitization, and intimacy. See E. Karakuş, "Chameleons of Kurdish Turkey."

10 Robben and Nordstrom, "Violence and Sociopolitical Conflict."

11 Gönen, *Politics of Crime*.

12 Palestinian hanging, also known as reverse hanging, is a form of torture where the victim is lifted and hanged from their wrists for a prolonged period of time while their hands are tied at their back. Bastinadoing, or foot whipping, is a method of torture that involves beating the soles of someone's bare feet. For further work on torture in Turkey, see Akçam, *Siyasi Kültürümüzde Zulüm ve İşkence*; Pişkinsüt, *Filistin Askısından Fezlekeye*; Göregenli and Özer, "Medya ve İnsan Hakları Örgütlerinin"; B. Can, "Human Rights"; and Üstündağ, "Pornographic State."

13 Gönen, *Politics of Crime*, 82.

14 Bozarslan, "Human Rights"; Özsoy, "Introduction"; and Okçuoğlu, "Rethinking Democracy and Autonomy." The Truth Justice Memory Center in Istanbul published one of the most comprehensive reports on the enforced disappearances of Kurdish people in Turkey in the 1990s. This report thoroughly exposes the social, legal, and political mechanisms that led to the systematic policy of enforced disappearances, a form of "state terrorism." For further details, see Göral, Işık, and Kaya, *Unspoken Truth*.

15 Ralph, "Alibi."

16. Benjamin, *One-Way Street*.

17 Babül, "Morality."

18 Akarsu, "'Proportioning Violence.'"

19 Akarsu, "Force Experts."

20 Akarsu, "Force Experts."

21 Savcı, *Queer in Translation*, 86.

22 Turkish Law on Police Duties and Power (Law no.: 2559), publication date in official *Gazette*, July 14, 1934 (passed July 4, 1934), https://www.mevzuat .gov.tr/mevzuatmetin/1.3.2559.pdf.

23 Quoted in Sofer, "Dawn of a Gay Movement," 78.

24 Sofer, "Dawn of a Gay Movement."

25 Süleyman was formerly accused of ill-treating nine trans women in 1996–97. However, the court case was suspended before a final verdict could be reached, in accordance with the Law on Release on Probation and the Suspension of Cases and Sentences for Offences Committed before April 23, 1999. See Amnesty International, *"Not an Illness,"* 12.

26 Aretxaga, "Maddening States," 406.

27 Feldman, "Ethnographic States of Emergency," 230.

28 Feldman, "Ethnographic States of Emergency," 230–31.

29 In my previous work on registered and unregistered sex work in Turkey, I discussed the political, social, and cultural impacts of the organization of this hospital into a sex worker–only space. See Zengin, *İktidarın Mahremiyeti*.

30 Wolf, *Envisioning Power*, 4.

31 Althusser, *Lenin and Philosophy, and Other Essays*.

32 Žižek, *Sublime Object of Ideology*, 43.

33 Recent developments, first crystallized by Gezi but traceable back to the AKP's electoral victory in 2009 and the subsequent weakening of the military, appear to have severely undermined this sovereignty of law. Against that, however, one might argue that the major concerns have revolved around control of the legal-judicial apparatus rather than its abandonment.

34 To a certain extent, this situation is reminiscent of Joseph Massad's critique of the Gay International, in which he argues that Western LGBTI+ organizations have a special missionary role in the Arab and Muslim world through their universalizing discourse and advocacy of gay rights. According to Massad, local LGBTI+ groups' adoption of this epistemology of gay rights would be best characterized as incitement to a discourse of sociopolitical identification of locally existing same-sex sexual practices with the Western identity of gayness and publicity. See Massad, *Desiring Arabs*. Of course, the situation on the ground is much more complicated, plural, dynamic, and messy than its reduction to binaries of East-West and practice-identity. Massad has been widely criticized for being traditionalist and nativist through his dismissal of the postcolonial condition of the Arab world, in which colonial entanglements between the East and the West had already shaped histories of sexual relations and identities. See Georgis, "Thinking Past Pride." For further critique of Massad's work, see Makarem, "Story of HELEM"; Mikdashi, "Archive of Perversion"; and Amar and El Shakry, "Introduction."

35 Ahmed, *Queer Phenomenology*, 139–40.

36 Aizura, *Mobile Subjects*; Beauchamp, *Going Stealth*; Amar, *Security Archipelago*; and Shakhsari, *Politics of Rightful Killing*.

37 Amar, *Security Archipelago*, 232.

38 Literally translated as "known lady," *bilinen bayan* carries the connotations of "lady of ill repute." This category in particular was the subject of intense discussions, especially among women, for its vagueness (what is known about the woman in question, how it is known, etc.).

39 Similar performance criteria were introduced into different bureaucratic mechanisms to increase efficiency in service provision around the same time. One of the most prominent environments was the healthcare sector. See Erten, "At Least Three Children"; and Saluk, "Monitored Reproduction."

40 Kelly, "Documented Lives," 90.

41 Riles, *Documents*; Hull, "Documents and Bureaucracy"; Bubandt, "Enemy's Point of View"; and Navaro, *Make-Believe Space*.

42 Navaro, *Make-Believe Space*, 114; and Hull, "Documents and Bureaucracy."

43 Puri, *Sexual States*, 35.

44 That is, she was working *for* a pimp. Later on during our interview, Gizem told me that the police use the category pimp on purpose to prevent girls

from finding official positions if they ever decided to quit as unregistered sex workers. Once someone has a record as a pimp in their file, they are no longer eligible for state employment. Nor are registered sex workers.

45 Gayrettepe 155 is the main police station to which the police who ticket women are attached.

46 Certeau, *Practice of Everyday Life*, xix.

47 Certeau, *Practice of Everyday Life*, xiv–v.

48 For example, some of the fines reached 5,000 to 6,000 liras in 2010 (on the order of $4,000 according to simple exchange rates, but much more in terms of the local, real value).

49 Gray, *Out in the Country*.

50 Bianet, "Kimmiş Bu 'Bilinen Bayan'?"

51 Zengin, *İktidarın Mahremiyeti*.

52 Das, *Life and Words*.

Chapter 3: Psychiatric Demarcations of Sex/Gender

1 Facial surgery involves chin surgery, eyelid surgery, rhinoplasty (a nose job), forehead reshaping, and hair restoration. For detailed information on transgender surgery, see K. Yılmaz and Narter, "Transgender Surgery."

2 Valentine, *Imagining Transgender*, 14.

3 Until 1976 the ID document was a thirty-two-page notebook. In 2006 the personal information on ID cards was modified in two ways. First, declaring one's religion on the ID card has become optional. Second, individuals were given the right to declare themselves to be "single" or "married," which means the former can also stand for "divorced" and "widow" categories depending on the citizen's situation. For further discussion, see Bozbeyoğlu, "Citizenship Rights."

4 *Milliyet*, "İstanbul Üniversitesi Mındıkoğlu için Soruşturma Komisyonu Kurdu," October 29, 1981.

5 *Milliyet*, "Uğur Dündar Kadın Olan Erkeklerin," October 25, 1981.

6 Bozoğlu, "MülgaTCK. Madde 471," Türk Hukuk Sitesi, November 4, 2009. http://www.turkhukuksitesi.com/mevzuat.php?mid=8634.

7 *Milliyet*, "Mındıkoğlu için 1-6 Ay," February 13, 1982; and *Milliyet*, "Cerrahpaşa Tıp Mındıkoğlu için 1-6 Ay," February 26, 1982.

8 This is a highly debatable claim. The emerging archival work on the history of transness and gender nonconformity in Turkey demonstrates that there was a strong medical interest in sex/gender nonconformity and "sex change" operations in the nineteenth century Ottoman Empire and the early republican era. This area of research still remains heavily understudied. For a couple of important archival work, see Aykut, "Herculine Barbin 'Hüviyet'"; and Soydan, *Manşetlerden Gaipliğe*.

9 *Milliyet*, "İstanbul Üniversitesi Mındıkoğlu için Soruşturma Komisyonu Kurdu," October 29, 1981.

10 Öztürel, "Transseksualizm ile Hermafrodizmde Yasal"; and Atamer, "Legal Status of Transsexuals."

11 Najmabadi, *Professing Selves*, 120.

12 *Milliyet*, "Mete Akyol Bülent Ersoy'la Konuştu," August 31, 1980.

13 The state is less fragmented when it comes to trans prisoners in contemporary Turkey. The Pembe Hayat LGBTI+ association in Ankara conducted research with trans prisoners from eighteen prisons in fourteen different cities through multiple letter exchanges between 2008 and 2016. Later they released a report based on their years-long correspondence with sixty-seven trans women. According to this report, only one trans woman had had GCS and hence was incarcerated in the women's section, while the rest were in the men's section. See Berghan, *Türkiye'de Trans Kadın Mahpuslar*.

14 Ertür and Lebow, "Şöhretin Sonu"; and R. Altınay, "Reconstructing the Transgendered Self."

15 *Milliyet*, "Mete Akyol Bülent Ersoy'la Konuştu," August 31, 1980.

16 R. Altınay, "Reconstructing the Transgendered Self," 215.

17 *Milliyet*, "Mahkeme Karar Verdi,Bülent Ersoy Artık Kadın," June 6, 1988.

18 Although she was issued the pink ID, Bülent Ersoy has never changed her name. During my research I have not come across any explanation for this. I can only speculate that because of the reputation she had gained under the name Bülent, she avoided changing her name to a new one.

19 Bubandt, "Enemy's Point of View," 559; and Das, "Signature of the State," 250–51.

20 Das, *Life and Words*, 163.

21 Amendment to the Twenty-Ninth Clause of Law no. 743, Turkish Civil Code, May 12, 1988. (The English translation of the code is taken from Kandiyoti, "Transsexuals.")

22 Zevkliler, "Medeni Kanun ve Cinsiyet."

23 Zevkliler, "Medeni Kanun ve Cinsiyet"; and Sağlam, "Türk Medeni Kanunu Madde 40."

24 Zevkliler, "Medeni Kanun ve Cinsiyet," 267–70.

25 Zevkliler, "Medeni Kanun ve Cinsiyet," 286.

26 Sağlam, "Türk Medeni Kanunu Madde 40."

27 The English translation of the code is taken from Yeşim Atamer's "The Legal Status of Transsexuals in Turkey."

28 For a detailed discussion of the denial of trans people's biological reproductive rights and its role in the imagination of sexual citizenship in Turkey, see Kurtoğlu, "Sex Reassignment."

29 Some lawyers I talked to during my fieldwork interpreted this modification as a positive development helping to prevent random and arbitrary

GCSS. For them, the previous ruling bound the court to legally approve the operation and the issuing of new IDs, a limitation that prevented it from functioning as an additional layer of control. For trans people themselves, however, this is an additional bureaucratic layer that creates further challenges and exhaustion in their lives.

30 Butler, *Bodies That Matter*, xi.
31 Dole, "House That Saddam Built," 294.
32 Foucault, *History of Sexuality*.
33 Butler, *Bodies That Matter*, 1.
34 Yüksel et al., "Group Psychotherapy."
35 On this latest Version 8, see Coleman et al., "Standards of Care."
36 At the time of my research, these hospitals were few in number, for example, merely two in Istanbul, and all were public hospitals.
37 In Turkey these hospitals were legally permitted to provide a *heyet raporu*, but in practice the majority of trans people had their reports issued by public teaching and research hospitals. The reasons were threefold. First, trans people's financial constraints influenced their choice of hospitals; public teaching and research hospitals were more financially accessible due to insurance coverage. Second, private education and research hospitals had been established recently, meaning hospital personnel were usually unfamiliar with the transition process, and in any case they were also few in number. Third, many hospital personnel were prejudiced against preparing a GCS-related *heyet raporu*. During my research I did not hear of any trans person who received a *heyet raporu* from a private education and research hospital. The two public hospitals in Istanbul, Çapa and Cerrahpaşa, remained the most popular among trans people seeking GCS.
38 Irving, "Normalized Transgressions"; and Valentine, *Imagining Transgender*.
39 Dole, "House That Saddam Built."
40 Yüksel et al., "Group Psychotherapy."
41 Polat, Yüksel, and Dişçigil, "Family Attitudes," 390.
42 Najmabadi, "Transing and Transpassing"; and Najmabadi, "Verdicts of Science."
43 Najmabadi, "Transing and Transpassing," 32.
44 Najmabadi, "Transing and Transpassing."
45 Foucault, *Abnormal*, 22.
46 Freeman, "Introduction," 161.
47 Dinshaw, Edelman, and Roderick, "Theorizing Queer Temporalities," 190.
48 Since the mid-2010s, hormone use has gained significant attention especially in relation to trans childhood and adolescence. With the partial normalization of trans adulthood in a liberal social model, trans children are now presented as a new generation and, as Jules Gill-Peterson notes, a new frontier in medical science. For further critical insights into trans childhood studies in Canada and the United States, see Meadow, *Trans*

Kids; Gill-Peterson, "Growing Up Trans"; Gill-Peterson, *Histories of the Transgender Child*; Sadjadi, "Deep in the Brain"; and Sadjadi, "Vulnerable Child Protection Act."

49 The difficulties around taking hormones have intensified with the dire economic crisis in Turkey, especially since 2021. Hyperdevaluation of the Turkish lira has led to a scarcity of various medical supplies, including hormones, which were mostly imported from European countries. Trans people are one of the groups most affected by this economic downfall. Even when a specific hormone became available in the market, its skyrocketing price would make it extremely difficult to afford for working-class or underclass trans people. In addition, incarcerated trans people have serious problems in accessing hormones. According to Pembe Hayat's report on trans women prisoners in Turkey, permission to take hormones is strictly tied to an arbitrary decision-making mechanism in each individual prison. See Berghan, *Türkiye'de Trans Kadın Mahpuslar*, 19.

50 Butler, *Bodies That Matter*, 2.

51 Stone, "Empire Strikes Back."

52 Foucault, *Abnormal*, 21.

53 Salamon, *Assuming a Body*.

54 Plemons, *Look of a Woman*.

55 Salamon, *Assuming a Body*, 178.

56 Kessler and McKenna, "Theory of Gender," 173.

Chapter 4: Touch, Gaze, & the Heteropenetrative State

1 Foucault, *Madness and Civilization*; Foucault, "Governmentality"; and Foucault, *Discipline and Punish*.

2 Rodaway, *Sensuous Geographies*, 41.

3 Montagu, *Touching*.

4 Segal, *Consensuality*, 6.

5 Here I would like to stress the context within which these forms of touch happen. For sure, there are people, including those in queer and trans worlds of desire, sex, and eroticism, who derive pleasure from some of these acts when they engage in them in a consensual way. I am referring mainly to those negative and harmful touches that take place in a nonconsensual manner.

6 Nancy, *Sense of the World*.

7 Ahmed, *Strange Encounters*, 47.

8 Merleau-Ponty, *Visible and the Invisible*.

9 For instance, recent critical work on the body analyzes it as a racial assemblage rather than assuming it to be an already existing universal. See Weheliye, *Habeas Viscus*; Chen, *Animacies*; Puar, *Terrorist Assemblages*; and Schuller, *Biopolitics of Feeling*.

10 Ahmed, *Strange Encounters*, 48.

11 For specific examples, see Stallybrass and White, *Politics and Poetics*; Davis, *Planet of Slums*; and Harvey, *Rebel Cities*.

12 Cooper, *Everyday Utopias*, 52–54.

13 Cooper, *Everyday Utopias*, 51.

14 Foucault, *Discipline and Punish*; and Foucault, *Abnormal*.

15 I thank Beren Azizi for drawing my attention to this point.

16 Foucault, *History of Sexuality*; and De Lauretis, *Technologies of Gender*.

17 Sharpe, "From Functionality to Aesthetics."

18 Mikdashi, *Sextarianism*, 180.

19 Some lawyers argued for the marital status criterion as an efficient mechanism for maintaining the family structure. According to these people, the family represents the fundamental building block of society and should not be allowed to be undermined by people of "ambiguous" sex/gender identity. They believe that people choosing to transition while in a marriage would cause emotional, psychological, and moral disturbance for the spouse and children.

20 Tar, "Cinsiyet geçişinde "'Kısırlaştırma.'"

21 Trans women are also eligible to receive a disability report, at their request, once they complete the GCS process. I would like to thank Beren Azizi for stressing this point.

22 Schilder, *Image and Appearance*, as quoted in Salamon, *Assuming a Body*, 30.

23 Since pronouns in Turkish are gender neutral, sometimes it is difficult to figure out whether "he" or "she" would be the appropriate translation, as was the case in this account. Hence I use the gender-neutral pronoun *they* for this account.

24 Merleau-Ponty, *Phenomenology of Perception*.

25 Merleau-Ponty, *Visible and the Invisible*, 255.

26 See Mauss, "Techniques of the Body"; Merleau-Ponty, *Phenomenology of Perception*; and Grosz, *Volatile Bodies*.

27 Despite the relative progress that has been made in GCS, trans people still complain that doctors are not trained in medical school for these operations at all. Rather, it is something that they need to learn and improve on their own. For that reason, it is very difficult to find a talented doctor who will do the surgery at moderate or low rates.

28 Cindoğlu, "Virginity Tests."

29 Özyeğin, *New Desires, New Selves*.

30 Özyeğin, *New Desires, New Selves*, 54.

31 Ahmadi, "Recreating Virginity in Iran"; Güzel, "Pain as Performance"; Kaivanara, "Virginity Dilemma"; Mahadeen, "Hymen Reconstruction Surgery"; and Wynn, "'Like a Virgin.'"

32 Turkish in this account conflates certain distinctions that English makes between sex and gender. So I tried to choose the words *man, manhood,*

or *male* according to the meanings that were emphasized during the conversation.

33 Fausto-Sterling, *Sexing the Body*.

34 Laqueur, *Making Sex*, 88.

35 Fausto-Sterling, *Sexing the Body*, 3–4.

36 Fanon, *Black Skin, White Masks*, 83–85.

37 Bhabha, "Interrogating Identity," 60; and Yancy, *Black Bodies, White Gazes*, 60.

38 Alloula, *Colonial Harem*; Kabbani, *Europe's Myths of Orient*; Said, *Orientalism*; Schick, *Erotic Margin*; and Yeğenoğlu, *Colonial Fantasies*.

39 Alloula, *Colonial Harem*, 7.

40 Sehlikoğlu, "Exercising in Comfort," 147.

41 When I moved to Toronto from Istanbul, one of the first cultural differences I noticed was the absence of this particular sexual gaze in public life. Even when people find themselves looking at each other on the street, they often smile at each other to convey, as several of my non-Western (and non-Turkish) friends in Toronto have suggested, the message "I am not a threat to you."

42 For further discussion on this significant issue, see Razack, *Looking White People*.

43 Butler, *Undoing Gender*, 4.

Chapter 5: Justice, Criminal Law, & Trans Femicides

1 Data on trans women's murders are scattered across different websites and time periods. I brought together several sources to approximate the official number of deaths. Kaos GL has been publishing annual reports on homophobic and transphobic hate crimes in Turkey since 2007. All of these reports are accessible on their website through the subsection of their e-library. See https://kaosgldernegi.org/e-kutuphane. Bianet also has a special webpage that has brought together several reports and news sources on hate crimes targeting trans people in Turkey since 2008. See http://bianet.org/konu/nefret-cinayetleri. See also Transgender Europe, "TMM Murders." However, note that these data are based on media coverage, and the actual number is expected to be much higher due to unreported or silenced murder cases.

2 In translating the culprit's accounts from Turkish, I use the pronoun *they* for İrem, as Turkish has only one gender pronoun, *o*, for the third person, animals, and objects, in place of English *she*, *he*, and *it*. This is important because it is not clear whether (or when) the plaintiff refers to İrem as a female or a male during the trial.

3 Mynet, "İrem'in katil sanığını yakacak rapor."

4 In Turkey there is also a growing scholarship on the role of sexual acts in constituting gender identity. For further inquiries, see Bereket and Adam,

"Navigating Islam"; Başaran, "'You Are like a Virus'"; Biricik, "'Rotten Report'"; and Zengin, "Violent Intimacies."

5 The logic that informed the judge's decision here is vague. It is physiologically possible for men to have erections without testicles, and hence penetrate each other, but perhaps the judge did not know this. Hence, it is not clear whether the judge assumed that the lack of testicles would cause a lack of erection and penetration, or, alternatively, whether male reproductive functionality (rather than erectile functionality) was at the heart of the judge's construction of male gender.

6 Solomon, "Justice vs. Vengeance," 124–25.

7 Derrida, "Force of Law," 12.

8 Derrida, "Force of Law," 16.

9 Derrida, "Force of Law," 17.

10 Ahmed, "Impossible Global Justice?," 55.

11 Ahmed, "Impossible Global Justice?," 56.

12 Ahmed, "Impossible Global Justice?," 56.

13 Yıldırım, "Haksız Tahrik İndirimi."

14 Bianet, "İlk Yasal Kazanım."

15 Abdo-Zubi and Mojab, *Violence*.

16 Demirler and Gümüş, "ᴛᴄᴋ Değişirken . . ."

17 Koğacıoğlu, "Tradition Effect"; and Sirman, "Kinship, Politics and Love."

18 Çakır, "Mahkeme Haksız Tahrik."

19 Koğacıoğlu, "Tradition Effect"; Parla, "'Honor' of the State"; and Parla, "Revisiting 'Honor.'"

20 Göktaş, "Yargıtay'dan Namus Cinayeti Devrimi."

21 Doğanoğlu, *Adaletin "ʟɢʙᴛ" Hali*.

22 Nussbaum, "'Secret Sewers of Vice.'"

23 Narrain, "New Language of Morality," 260.

24 Doğanoğlu, *Adaletin "ʟɢʙᴛ" Hali*, 23.

25 Narrain and Gupta, introduction, xxvi.

26 Spade, *Normal Life*; Dave, "Indian and Lesbian"; Dave, *Queer Activism in India*; and Govindan and Vasudevan, "Razor's Edge of Oppositionality."

27 Bildirici, "Eşcinsellik Hastalık, Tedavi Edilmeli."

28 Avramopoulou, "Crossing Distances."

29 Kaplan, "İslâm ve eşcinsellik meselesi."

30 Bolat, "Zorunlu Heteroseksüellik."

31 Organization for Security and Co-operation in Europe, "What Is Hate Crime?"

32 Amnesty International, *"Not an Illness"*; ᴇᴄʀɪ, *First Report on Turkey*; ᴇᴄʀɪ, *Second Report on Turkey*; ᴇᴄʀɪ, *Third Report on Turkey*; and Human Rights Watch, *"We Need a Law."*

33 Karan, "Nefret Suçları."

34 Sylvia Rivera Law Project, "ꜱʀʟᴘ on Hate Crime Laws."

35 Ray and Smith, "Racist Offenders," 214.

36 Jenness, "Hate Crime Canon," 288.

37 Jenness, "Hate Crime Canon," 293.

38 Kohn, "Greasing the Wheel"; and Spade, *Normal Life*.

39 Spade, *Normal Life*.

40 Savcı, "Who Speaks the Language."

41 Savcı, "Who Speaks the Language"; and Zengin, "Mortal Life of Trans/ Feminism."

42 Menon, *Recovering Subversion*.

43 Babül, *Bureaucratic Intimacies*, 117.

44 Spade, *Normal Life*, 30.

45 Spade, *Normal Life*.

46 Lambek, introduction, 2.

47 Dave, *Queer Activism in India*, 8.

Chapter 6: Funerals & Experiments with Trans Kin

1 Avramopoulou, "Claims of Existence"; Çalışkan, "'Nobody Is Going to Let You'"; and Zengin, "Afterlife of Gender."

2 Malatino, *Trans Care*.

3 Mutlu, "Transnational Biopolitics."

4 Carsten, *After Kinship*, 133.

5 Wagner, "Analogic Kinship"; and Carsten, "Substantivism, Antisubstantivism, and Anti-antisubstantivism," 39.

6 Chodorow, *Reproduction of Mothering*; Fineman, *Neutered Mother*; Collier and Yanagisako, "Unified Analysis of Gender"; Joseph, *Intimate Selving*; Spillers, "Mama's Baby, Papa's Maybe"; and Hartman, *Lose Your Mother*.

7 Weston, *Families We Choose*, 27.

8 Ahmed, *Queer Phenomenology*; Berlant, *Queen of America*; and Scheper-Hughes, *Death without Weeping*.

9 Ahmed, *Queer Phenomenology*, 86.

10 Weston, *Families We Choose*.

11 Horton, "What's So 'Queer'"; and Shirinian, "Nation-Family."

12 Özel, "Medeni Hukuk Açısından Ölüm."

13 Balkan, "Charlie Hebdo"; Gill, "Sense Experiences"; and Arıcan, "1237, or Dying Elsewhere."

14 Some Sunni imams have also refused to hold death rituals for Alevis, "terrorists," and HIV/AIDS patients. See Zirh, "Following the Dead"; Özsoy, "Between Gift and Taboo"; and Bayramoğlu, "Border Panic."

15 It is significant to highlight a recent development regarding Muslim LGBTI+ funerals in Turkey. On May 13, 2022, during a symposium organized by Alevi organizations in Izmir, the prominent Alevi leaders stated that they

would offer their houses of worship, *cemevi*, for LGBTI+ people who had been rejected by their own religious leaders and sectarian groups. See Hurtas, "Turkey's Alevis to Open." Prior to the symposium, my Alevi friends Saime Topçu and Ali Yıldırım had made similar remarks in our personal conversations and pointed out an emerging practice of Alevi solidarity with LGBTI+ funerals and burials.

16 Alipour, "Transgender Identity"; Almarri, "'You Have Made Her'"; Hamzić, "Resistance from an Alterspace"; Najmabadi, *Professing Selves*; Ragab, "One, Two, or Many Sexes"; and Zainuddin and Mahdy, "Islamic Perspectives."

17 Sanal, *New Organs within Us.*

18 I want to note that these stories of abandonment, in fact, extend across the boundaries of Turkey, encompassing multiple geographies of racial, ethnic, religious, and gender difference. To give one example, some queer and transgender people were disowned by their families during the HIV/AIDS crisis of the 1980s in the United States. Recently, the American drama television series *Pose* (2018–22) portrayed such stories and struggles through a fictive lens. For a more detailed discussion on the role of touch in practices of mourning, grief, and death rituals, see Zengin, "Caring for the Dead."

19 The cemetery for the *kimsesiz* could be rendered in English as the Victorian "paupers' grave" or biblical "potter's field" or else the more prosaic "common grave," but these all fall short in expressing the loaded meanings associated with the term *kimsesiz* in the Turkish sociocultural context, where the bonds of familial and communal connection are traditionally so fundamental to identity, personhood, and status in life. Elsewhere I discuss the state's complicated relationship with the category of *kimsesiz* and the limits of social legibility and belonging in Turkey through the lenses of death and burials. See Zengin, "Cemetery for the *Kimsesiz.*"

20 Butler, *Precarious Life.*

21 Zengin, "Cemetery for the *Kimsesiz.*"

22 Göral, Işık, and Kaya, *Unspoken Truth*; and Göral, "Memory as Experience."

23 Sanal, *New Organs within Us.*

24 Sanal, *New Organs within Us*, 121.

25 *Habertürk*, "Kadavra Dağıtımı Başlıyor."

26 Stanley, *Atmospheres of Violence.*

27 Weston, *Families We Choose.*

28 Malatino, *Trans Care*, 42.

29 Sedef would presumably revise some of these strong opinions about the younger generation now, especially after the increased state warfare against LGBTI+ people in Turkey and the growing resistance of the queer/trans Generation Z in response.

30 For an alternative discussion on trans kin making in Turkey through the lenses of memory and time, see Çalışkan, "World Making."

31 Hicks, *Lesbian, Gay and Queer Parenting*.

32 Weston, "Families in Queer States," 132.

33 Malatino, *Trans Care*, 24.

34 Freeman, "Queer Belongings," 298.

35 Freeman, "Queer Belongings," 303.

36 Freeman, "Queer Belongings," 298.

37 Eng, *Feeling of Kinship*, 15.

38 Çalışkan, "'Nobody Is Going to Let You.'"

39 The first support and solidarity group established by blood families of queer and trans children was LISTAG, but as I finalized this book in 2022, other family support groups existed across the country, including Gökkuşağı Aileleri Derneği (Association for Families of Rainbow) in Ankara; Akdeniz Antalya Aile Grubu (Akdeniz Family Group) in Antalya; and LGBTI+ Aileleri Grubu (LGBTI+ Family Group) in Denizli and Izmir.

40 See LISTAG's home page, https://listag.org/english/ (accessed July 11, 2020).

41 For further information on this initiative, see the Boysan'ın Evi website, http://boysaninevi.com/ (accessed October 8, 2022).

42 Az, "Little Prayer."

Coda

1 Buşki, *#DirenAyol*.

2 I had designed the first workshop back in 2010 as part of the first Bağyan Feministival (Lady fest), a feminist festival that we had collaboratively organized with feminist, queer, and trans women in Istanbul. See Zengin, "Feminist Argo ve Küfür Atölyesi Üzerine."

3 Massumi, *Parables for the Virtual*, 79.

4 Zengin, "What Is Queer about Gezi?"

5 Here is a limited list of notable literature on Gezi: Tuğal, "'Resistance Everywhere'"; Özdüzen, "Cinema-Going during the Gezi Protests"; Dağtaş, "'Down with Some Things!'"; İnceoğlu, "Encountering Difference"; Gürcan and Peker, *Challenging Neoliberalism*; Potuoğlu-Cook, "Hope with Qualms"; Alessandrini, Üstündağ, and Yıldız, *"Resistance Everywhere"*; Yıldırım and Navaro, "Impromptu Uprising"; and Yörük, "Long Summer of Turkey."

6 Darıcı and Hakyemez, "Neither Civilian nor Combatant"; and Üstündağ, *The Mother, the Politician, and the Guerilla*.

7 Cvetkovich, *Depression*, 2.

8 Some of the most popular online magazines and platforms are Erktolia (http://erktolia.org/), *Beşharfliler* (http://www.5harfliler.com/), *Çatlak Zemin* (https://catlakzemin.com/), *Reçel Blog* (http://recel-blog.com

/), *Kaos GL* (https://www.kaosgl.org/), Istanbul LGBTT (http://www.istanbullgbti.org/lgbtt/), and the website of the Sosyal Politika, Cinsiyet Kimliği ve Cinsel Yönelim Çalışmaları Derneği (SPoD; Organization for Social Policy, Gender Identity and Sexual Orientation Studies) (http:// www.spod.org.tr/).

Appendix

1   Simpson, *Mohawk Interruptus.*

Bibliography

Abdo-Zubi, Nahla, and Shahrzad Mojab. *Violence in the Name of Honour: Theoretical and Political Challenges.* Istanbul: İstanbul Bilgi Üniversitesi Yayınları, 2004.

Abrams, Philip. "Notes on the Difficulty of Studying the State" (1977). *Journal of Historical Sociology* 1, no. 1 (1988): 58–89.

Abu-Lughod, Lila. *Do Muslim Women Need Saving?* Cambridge, MA: Harvard University Press, 2013.

Abu-Lughod, Lila. *Veiled Sentiments: Honor and Poetry in a Bedouin Society.* Berkeley: University of California Press, 1986.

Acar, Feride, and Gülbanu Altınok. "The 'Politics of Intimate' at the Intersection of Neo-liberalism and Neo-conservatism in Contemporary Turkey." *Women's Studies International Forum* 41, no. 1 (2013): 14–23.

Açıksöz, Salih Can. *Sacrificial Limbs: Masculinity, Disability, and Political Violence in Turkey.* Oakland: University of California Press, 2020.

Adler, Sy, and Johanna Brenner. "Gender and Space: Lesbians and Gay Men in the City." *International Journal of Urban and Regional Research* 16, no. 1 (1992): 24–34.

Ahmadi, Azal. "Recreating Virginity in Iran: Hymenoplasty as a Form of Resistance." *Medical Anthropology Quarterly* 30, no. 2 (2016): 222–37.

Ahmed, Sara. "Affective Economies." *Social Text* 22, no. 2 (2004): 117–39.

Ahmed, Sara. "An Impossible Global Justice? Deconstruction and Transnational Feminism." In *Feminist Perspectives on Law and Theory*, edited by Janice Richardson and Ralph Sandland, 53–70. London: Cavendish, 2000.

Ahmed, Sara. *Queer Phenomenology: Orientations, Objects, Others.* Durham, NC: Duke University Press, 2006.

Ahmed, Sara. *Strange Encounters: Embodied Others in Post-coloniality.* London: Routledge, 2000.

Aizura, Aren. *Mobile Subjects: Transnational Imaginaries of Gender Reassignment.* Durham, NC: Duke University Press, 2018.

Akarsu, Hayal. "Force Experts and the Violence of Standardization: Politicizing Effects of Police Reforms in Turkey." *American Anthropologist*, forthcoming.

Akarsu, Hayal. "'Proportioning Violence': Ethnographic Notes on the Contingencies of Police Reform in Turkey." *Anthropology Today* 34, no. 1 (2018): 11–14.

Akçam, Taner. *Siyasi Kültürümüzde Zulüm ve İşkence.* Istanbul: İletişim, 1992.

Akın, Nur. *19. Yüzyılın İkinci Yarısında Galata ve Pera.* Istanbul: Literatür, 2002.

Akınerdem, Feyza. "Marriage Safe and Sound: Subjectivity, Embodiment and Movement in the Production Space of Television in Turkey." Phd diss., City University London, 2015.

Al-Ali, Nadje. *Secularism, Gender and the State in the Middle East: The Egyptian Women's Movement*. Cambridge: Cambridge University Press, 2000.

Alessandrini, Anthony, Nazan Üstündağ, and Emrah Yıldız, eds. *"Resistance Everywhere": The Gezi Protests and Dissident Visions of Turkey*. Washington, DC: Tadween, 2014.

Alipour, M. "Transgender Identity, the Sex-Reassignment Surgery Fatwās and Islāmic Theology of a Third Gender." *Religion and Gender* 7, no. 2 (2017): 164–79.

Alloula, Malek. *The Colonial Harem*. Translated by Myrna Godzich and Wlad Godzich. Minneapolis: University of Minnesota Press, 1986.

Almarri, Saqer A. "'You Have Made Her a Man among Men': Translating the Khunta's Anatomy in Fatimid Jurisprudence." *TSQ: Transgender Studies Quarterly* 3, nos. 3–4 (2016): 578–86.

Alqaisiya, Walaa. *Decolonial Queering in Palestine*. New York: Routledge, 2023.

Alphan, Melis. "Onur Haftası'nın Desteğinize Ihtiyacı Var." *Hürriyet*, May 29, 2014. https://www.hurriyet.com.tr/yazarlar/melis-alphan/onur-haftasi-nin -desteginize-ihtiyaci-var-26504327.

Althusser, Louis. *Lenin and Philosophy, and Other Essays*. New York: Monthly Review Press, 1972.

Altınay, Ayşe Gül. *The Myth of the Military-Nation: Militarism, Gender, and Education in Turkey*. New York: Palgrave Macmillan, 2004.

Altınay, Ayşe Gül, and Tanıl Bora. "Ordu, Militarizm ve Milliyetcilik." In *Modern Türkiye'de Siyasi Düşünce: Milliyetçilik*, edited by Tanıl Bora, 140–54. Istanbul: İletişim, 2002.

Altınay, Rustem Ertug. "Reconstructing the Transgendered Self as a Muslim, Nationalist, Upper-Class Woman: The Case of Bulent Ersoy." *WSQ: Women's Studies Quarterly* 36, no. 3 (2008): 210–29.

Amar, Paul. *The Security Archipelago: Human-Security States, Sexuality Politics, and the End of Neoliberalism*. Durham, NC: Duke University Press, 2013.

Amar, Paul, and Omnia El Shakry. "Introduction: Curiosities of Middle East Studies in Queer Times." *International Journal of Middle East Studies* 45, no. 2 (2013): 331–35.

Amin, Kadji. "We Are All Nonbinary: A Brief History of Accidents." *Representations* 158, no. 1 (2022): 106–19.

Amnesty International. *"Not an Illness nor a Crime": Lesbian, Gay, Bisexual and Transgender People in Turkey Demand Equality*. London: Amnesty International, 2011.

Anderson, Benedict Richard O'Gorman. *Imagined Communities: Reflections on the Origin and Spread of Nationalism*. London: Verso, 1991.

Andrews, Walter G., and Mehmet Kalpaklı. *The Age of Beloveds: Love and the Beloved in Early Modern Ottoman and European Culture and Society*. Durham, NC: Duke University Press, 2005.

Antwi, Phanuel, Sarah Brophy, Helene Strauss, and Y-Dang Troeung. "Postcolonial Intimacies: Gatherings, Disruptions, Departures." *Interventions* 15, no. 1 (2013): 1–9.

Anzaldúa, Gloria. *Borderlands*. San Francisco: Aunt Lute Books, 1987.

Aretxaga, Begoña. "Maddening States." *Annual Review of Anthropology* 32 (2003): 393–410.

Aretxaga, Begoña. "The Sexual Games of the Body Politic: Fantasy and State Violence in Northern Ireland." *Culture, Medicine and Psychiatry* 25, no. 1 (2001): 1–27.

Aretxaga, Begoña. *Shattering Silence: Women, Nationalism, and Political Subjectivity in Northern Ireland*. Princeton, NJ: Princeton University Press, 1997.

Arıcan, Alize. "1237, or Dying Elsewhere." *Current Anthropology* 62, no. 1 (2021): 110–16.

Arıcan, Alize. "Behind the Scaffolding: Manipulations of Time, Delays, and Power in Tarlabaşı, Istanbul." *City and Society* 32, no. 3 (2020): 482–507.

Arvas, Abdulhamit. "Queers In-Between: Globalizing Sexualities, Local Resistances." In *The Postcolonial World*, edited by Jyotsna G. Singh and David D. Kim, 97–116. London: Routledge, 2016.

Atalay, Ozlem, and Petra L. Doan. "Reading the LGBT Movement through Its Spatiality in Istanbul, Turkey." *Geography Research Forum* 39 (2019): 106–26.

Atamer, Yeşim. "The Legal Status of Transsexuals in Turkey." *International Journal of Transgenderism* 8, no. 1 (2005): 65–71.

Atshan, Sa'ed. *Queer Palestine and the Empire of Critique*. Stanford, CA: Stanford University Press, 2020.

Avcı, Mustafa. "Shifts in Sexual Desire: Bans on Dancing Boys (Köçeks) throughout Ottoman Modernity (1800s–1920s)." *Middle Eastern Studies* 53, no. 5 (2017): 762–81.

Avramopoulou, Eirini. "Claims of Existence between Biopolitics and Thanatopolitics." In *De/Constituting Wholes: Towards Partiality without Parts*, edited by Manuele Gragnolati and Christoph F. E. Holzhey, 67–84. Vienna: Turia+Kant, 2017.

Avramopoulou, Eirini. "Crossing Distances to Meet Allies: On Women's Signatures, the Politics of Performativity and Dissensus." In *Politics of Coalition: Thinking Collective Action with Judith Butler*, edited by Delphine Gardey and Cynthia Kraus, 78–103. Zurich: Seismo, 2016.

Aykut, Ebru. "Herculine Barbin 'Hüviyet' ve Osmanlı'nın Tardiue'sü Doktor İbrahim Şevki." In *Michel Foucault Sunar: Herculine Barbin, Namı Diğer Alexina B.*, 229–52. Istanbul: Sel Yayıncılık, 2019.

Az, Elif Irem. "Little Prayer: Ambiguous Grief in the LGBTQIA+ Movement in Turkey." *European Journal of Women's Studies* 29, no. 4 (2022): 523–41.

Babül, Elif. *Bureaucratic Intimacies: Translating Human Rights in Turkey*. Stanford, CA: Stanford University Press, 2017.

Babül, Elif. "Morality: Understanding Police Training on Human Rights (Turkey)." In *Writing the World of Policing: The Difference Ethnography Makes*, edited by Didier Fassin, 139–61. Chicago: University of Chicago Press, 2017.

Baer, Marc David. *The Dönme: Jewish Converts, Muslim Revolutionaries, and Secular Turks*. Stanford, CA: Stanford University Press, 2010.

Bali, Rıfat. *The Jews and Prostitution in Constantinople, 1854–1922*. Istanbul: Isis, 2008.

Bali, Rıfat. *6–7 Eylül 1955 Olayları ve Tanıklar-Hatıralar*. Istanbul: Libra, 2012.

Balkan, Osman. "Charlie Hebdo and the Politics of Mourning." *Contemporary French Civilization* 41, no. 2 (2016): 253–71.

Bartu Candan, Ayfer, and Biray Kolluoğlu. "Emerging Spaces of Neoliberalism: A Gated Town and a Public Housing Project in Istanbul." *New Perspectives on Turkey* 39 (2008): 5–46. https://www.cambridge.org/core/journals/new-perspectives-on-turkey/article/abs/emerging-spaces-of-neoliberalism-a-gated-town-and-a-public-housing-project-in-istanbul/19076661DE830AB3ADF07DC3588404D8.

Başaran, Oyman. *Circumcision and Medicine in Modern Turkey*. Austin: University of Texas Press, 2023.

Başaran, Oyman. "'You Are like a Virus': Dangerous Bodies and Military Medical Authority in Turkey." *Gender and Society* 28, no. 4 (2014): 562–82.

Bayramoğlu, Yener. "Border Panic over the Pandemic: Mediated Anxieties about Migrant Sex Workers and Queers during the AIDS Crises in Turkey." *Ethnic and Racial Studies* 44, no. 9 (2021): 1589–606.

Beauchamp, Toby. *Going Stealth: Transgender Politics and U.S. Surveillance Practices*. Durham, NC: Duke University Press, 2019.

Belli, Burcu. *Osmanlı'da Fuhuş: II. Abdülhamid Dönemi'nde Kayıtlı Fuhuş, Devlet ve Modernlik (1876–1909)*. Istanbul: Tarih Vakfı Yurt Yayınları, 2021.

Benjamin, Walter. *One-Way Street and Other Writings*. Translated by Edmund Jephcott and Kingsley Shorter. London: Harcourt Brace Jovanovich, 1978.

Bereket, Tarık, and Barry Adam. "Navigating Islam and Same-Sex Liaisons among Men in Turkey." *Journal of Homosexuality* 55, no. 2 (2008): 204–22.

Berghan, Selin. *Lubunya: Transseksüel Kimlik ve Beden*. Istanbul: Metis, 2007.

Berghan, Selin. *Türkiye'de Trans Kadın Mahpuslar*. Ankara: Pembe Hayat, 2017. https://www.pembehayat.org/yayinlar/detay/1437/turkiyede-trans-kadin-mahpuslar.

Berlant, Lauren. "Intimacy: A Special Issue." *Critical Inquiry* 24, no. 2 (1998): 281–88.

Berlant, Lauren. *The Queen of America Goes to Washington City: Essays on Sex and Citizenship*. Durham, NC: Duke University Press, 1997.

Berlant, Lauren, and Michael Warner. "Sex in Public." *Critical Inquiry* 24, no. 2 (1998): 547–66.

Berliner, Alain. *Ma Vie en Rose = My Life in Pink*. Culver City, CA: Columbia Tristar Home Video, 1997. DVD.

Bey, Marquis. *Black Trans Feminism*. Durham, NC: Duke University Press, 2021.

Bey, Marquis. *Cistem Failure: Essays on Blackness and Cisgender*. Durham, NC: Duke University Press, 2022.

Bhabha, Homi K. "Interrogating Identity: Frantz Fanon and the Postcolonial Prerogative." In *The Location of Culture*, 57–93. London: Routledge, 1994.

Bhanji, Nael. "TRANS/SCRIPTIONS: Homing Desires, (Trans)sexual Citizenship and Racialized Bodies." In *Transgender Migrations: The Bodies, Borders and Politics of Transition*, edited by Trystan T. Cotten, 157–74. Abingdon, UK: Routledge, 2011.

Bianet. "İlk Yasal Kazanım." April 9, 2003. https://bianet.org/kadin/siyaset/66-ilk -yasal-kazanim.

Bianet. "Kimmiş Bu 'Bilinen Bayan'?" May 10, 2012. https://bianet.org/biamag /lgbti/138234-kimmis-bu-bilinen-bayan.

Bieberstein, Alice von, and Nora Tataryan. "The What of Occupation: 'You Took Our Cemetery, You Won't Have Our Park!'" Fieldsights, *Society for Cultural Anthropology*, October 31, 2013. https://culanth.org/fieldsights/the-what-of -occupation-you-took-our-cemetery-you-wont-have-our-park.

Biehl, Kristen Sarah. "Governing through Uncertainty: Experiences of Being a Refugee in Turkey as a Country for Temporary Asylum." *Social Analysis* 59, no. 1 (2015): 57–75.

Bildirici, Faruk. "Eşcinsellik Hastalık, Tedavi Edilmeli." *Hürriyet*, March 7, 2010. https://www.hurriyet.com.tr/kelebek/escinsellik-hastalik-tedavi-edilmeli -14031207.

Binder, Maria, dir. *Trans X Istanbul*. Istanbul: İKGV-İnsan Kaynağını Geliştirme Vakfı, 2014.

Biricik, Alp. "Kamusal Alanda Mahrem Taktikler." In *Başkaldıran Bedenler— Türkiye'de Transgender, Aktivizm ve Altkültürel Pratikler*, edited by Berfu Şeker, 187–200. Istanbul: Metis, 2013.

Biricik, Alp. "The 'Rotten Report' and the Reproduction of Masculinity, Nation, and Security in Turkey." In *Making Gender, Making War: Violence, Military, and Peacekeeping Practices*, edited by Annica Kronsell and Erika Svedber, 76–89. New York: Routledge, 2011.

Blackwood, Evelyn, and Saskia E. Wieringa. "Globalization, Sexuality, and Silences: Women's Sexualities and Masculinities in an Asian Context." In *Women's Sexualities and Masculinities in a Globalizing Asia*, edited by Saskia E. Wieringa, Evelyn Blackwood, and Abha Bhaiya, 1–22. New York: Palgrave Macmillan, 2007.

Boellstorff, Tom. *The Gay Archipelago: Sexuality and Nation in Indonesia*. Princeton, NJ: Princeton University Press, 2005.

Boellstorff, Tom. "Some Notes on New Frontiers of Sexuality and Globalisation." In *Understanding Global Sexualities: New Frontiers*, edited by Peter Aggleton, Paul Boyce, Henrietta L. Moore, and Richard Parker, 171–85. London: Routledge, 2013.

Bolat, Demet. "Zorunlu Heteroseksüellik ve Türkiye Muhalefet Alanına Dair Bir Tartışma." *Ankara Üniversitesi SBF Dergisi* 71, no. 4 (2016): 1091–117.

Bozarslan, Hamit. "Human Rights and the Kurdish Issue in Turkey: 1984–1999." *Human Rights Review* 3, no. 1 (2001): 45–54.

Bozbeyoğlu, Alanur Cavlin. "Citizenship Rights in a Surveillance Society: The Case of the Electronic ID Card in Turkey." *Surveillance and Society* 9, nos. 1–2 (2011): 64–79.

Brown, Gavin, Kath Browne, Rebecca Elmhirst, and Simon Hutta. "Sexualities in/ of the Global South." *Geography Compass* 4, no. 10 (2010): 1567–79.

Brown, Gavin, Kath Browne, and Jason Lim. "Introduction, or Why Have a Book on Geographies of Sexualities?" In *Geographies of Sexualities: Theory, Practices, and Politics*, edited by Kath Browne, Jason Lim, and Gavin Brown, 1–20. Aldershot, UK: Ashgate, 2007.

Bubandt, Nils. "From the Enemy's Point of View: Violence, Empathy, and the Ethnography of Fakes." *Cultural Anthropology* 24, no. 3 (2009): 553–88.

Buşki, Rüzgar, dir. *#DirenAyol*. Kanka Productions, 2016.

Butler, Judith. *Bodies That Matter: On the Discursive Limits of Sex*. New York: Routledge, 1993.

Butler, Judith. *Gender Trouble: Feminism and the Subversion of Identity*. New York: Routledge, 1990.

Butler, Judith. *Precarious Life: The Powers of Mourning and Violence*. London: Verso, 2004.

Butler, Judith. "Rethinking Vulnerability and Resistance." In *Vulnerability in Resistance*, edited by Judith Butler, Zeynep Gambetti, and Leticia Sabsay, 12–27. Durham, NC: Duke University Press, 2016.

Butler, Judith. *Undoing Gender*. London: Routledge, 2004.

Büyükünal, Feriha. *Bir Zaman Tüneli: Beyoğlu*. Istanbul: Doğan Kitap, 2006.

Çalışkan, Dilara. "'Nobody Is Going to Let You Attend Your Own Funeral': A Funeral for a Trans Woman and Naming the Unnamed." In *Women Mobilizing Memory*, edited by Ayşe Gül Altınay, María José Contreras, Marianne Hirsch, Jean Howard, Banu Karaca, and Alisa Solomon, 206–18. New York: Columbia University Press, 2019.

Çalışkan, Dilara. "World Making: Family, Time, and Memory among Trans Mothers and Daughters in Istanbul." In *Queer Kinship: Race, Sex, Belonging, Form*, edited by Tyler Bradway and Elizabeth Freeman, 71–94. Durham, NC: Duke University Press, 2022.

Can, Başak. "Human Rights, Humanitarianism, and State Violence: Medical Documentation of Torture in Turkey." *Medical Anthropology Quarterly* 30, no. 3 (2016): 342–58.

Can, Şule. *Refugee Encounters at the Turkish-Syrian Border: Antakya at the Crossroads*. London: Routledge, 2019.

Candan, Can, dir. *Benim Çocuğum* (My Child). Istanbul: Surela Film, 2013.

Canpolat, Nesrin, and Nuriye Çelik. "Roles of Women and Men Produced on TV Series: The Sample of Ece (The Turkish Soap Opera Series)." *OPUS International Journal of Society Researches* 14, no. 20 (2019): 905–28.

Carsten, Janet. *After Kinship*. New York: Cambridge University Press, 2004.

Carsten, Janet. "Substantivism, Antisubstantivism, and Anti-antisubstantivism." In *Relative Values: Configuring Kinship Studies*, edited by Sarah Franklin and Susan McKinnon, 29–53. Durham, NC: Duke University Press, 2001.

Celep, Barış. "1940'lı Yıllarda İstanbul'da Fuhuş Problemi." *Sosyal Bilimler Enstitüsü Dergisi* 12, no. 3 (2022): 1579–98.

Certeau, Michel de. *The Practice of Everyday Life*. Translated by Steven Rendall. Berkeley: University of California Press, 1984.

Chen, Mel Y. *Animacies: Biopolitics, Racial Mattering, and Queer Affect*. Durham, NC: Duke University Press, 2012.

Chiang, Howard. *Transtopia in the Sinophone Pacific*. New York: Columbia University Press, 2021.

Chodorow, Nancy. *The Reproduction of Mothering: Psychoanalysis and the Sociology of Gender*. Berkeley: University of California Press, 1978.

Cindoğlu, Dilek. "Virginity Tests and Artificial Virginity in Modern Turkish Medicine." *Women's Studies International Forum* 20, no. 2 (1997): 253–61.

Clare, Eli. "Body Shame, Body Pride: Lessons from the Disability Rights Movement." In *The Transgender Studies Reader 2*, edited by Susan Stryker and Aren Z. Aizura, 261–65. New York: Routledge, 2013.

Coleman, Eli, Asa E. Radix, Walter P. Bouman, A. L. C. de Vries, M. B. Deutsch, R. Ettner, L. Fraser, et al. "Standards of Care for the Health of Transgender and Gender Diverse People, Version 8." *International Journal of Transgender Health* 23, no. 1 (2022): 1–259.

Collier, Jane Fishburne, and Sylvia Junko Yanagisako. "Toward a Unified Analysis of Gender and Kinship." In *Gender and Kinship: Essays toward a Unified Analysis*, edited by Jane Fishburne Collier and Sylvia Junko Yanagisako, 14–51. Stanford, CA: Stanford University Press, 1987.

Cooper, Davina. *Everyday Utopias: The Conceptual Life of Promising Spaces*. Durham, NC: Duke University Press, 2013.

Cott, Nancy F. Afterword to *Haunted by Empire: Geographies of Intimacy in North American History*, edited by Ann Laura Stoler and Willy Brandt, 469–72. Durham, NC: Duke University Press, 2006.

Cruz, Louis Esme, and Qwo-Li Driskill. "Puo'Winue'L Prayers: Readings from North America's First Transtextual Script." *GLQ: A Journal of Lesbian and Gay Studies* 16, nos. 1–2 (2010): 243–52.

Currah, Paisley, and Tara Mulqueen. "Securitizing Gender: Identity, Biometrics, and Transgender Bodies at the Airport." *Social Research* 78, no. 2 (2011): 557–82.

Cvetkovich, Ann. *Depression: A Public Feeling*. Durham, NC: Duke University Press, 2012.

Çakır, Bawer. "Mahkeme Haksız Tahrik İndirimiyle Erkeğin Bahanesini Kabul Ediyor." *Kaos GL*, November 11, 2009. https://kaosgl.org/haber/mahkeme -haksiz-tahrik-indirimiyle-erkegin-bahanesini-kabul-ediyor.

Dağtaş, Mahiye Seçil. "'Down with Some Things!' The Politics of Humour and Humour as Politics in Turkey's Gezi Protests." *Etnofoor* 28, no. 1 (2016): 11–34.

Dağtaş, Mahiye Seçil. "Whose *Misafirs*? Negotiating Difference along the Turkish-Syrian Border." *International Journal of Middle East Studies* 49, no. 4 (2017): 661–79.

Darıcı, Haydar, and Serra Hakyemez. "Neither Civilian nor Combatant: Weaponised Spaces and Spatialised Bodies in Cizre." In *Turkey's Necropolitical Laboratory: Democracy, Violence and Resistance*, edited by Banu Bargu, 71–94. Edinburgh: Edinburgh University Press, 2020.

Das, Veena. *Life and Words: Violence and the Descent into the Ordinary*. Berkeley: University of California Press, 2007.

Das, Veena. "The Signature of the State: The Paradox of Illegibility." In *Anthropology in the Margins of the State*, edited by Veena Das and Deborah Poole, 225–52. Santa Fe, NM: School of American Research Press; Oxford: James Currey, 2004.

Das, Veena, and Deborah Poole, eds. *Anthropology in the Margins of the State*. Santa Fe, NM: School of American Research Press; Oxford: James Currey, 2004.

Dave, Naisargi. "Indian and Lesbian and What Came Next: Affect, Commensuration, and Queer Emergences." *American Ethnologist* 38, no. 4 (2011): 650–65.

Dave, Naisargi. *Queer Activism in India: A Story in the Anthropology of Ethics*. Durham, NC: Duke University Press, 2012.

David, Emmanuel. "Purple-Collar Labor: Transgender Workers and Queer Value at Global Call Centers in the Philippines." *Gender and Society* 29, no. 2 (2015): 169–94.

Davis, Mike. *Planet of Slums*. London: Verso, 2007.

Day, Madi. "Indigenist Origins: Institutionalizing Indigenous Queer and Trans Studies in Australia." *TSQ: Transgender Studies Quarterly* 7, no. 3 (2020): 367–73.

Decena, Carlos Ulises. *Tacit Subjects: Belonging and Same-Sex Desire among Dominican Immigrant Men*. Durham, NC: Duke University Press, 2011.

De Lauretis, Teresa. *Technologies of Gender: Essays on Theory, Film, and Fiction*. Bloomington: Indiana University Press, 1987.

Deleon, Jak. *Bir Beyoğlu Gezisi*. Istanbul: Remzi Kitabevi, 2002.

Delice, Serkan. "'The Janissaries and Their Bedfellows: Masculinity and Male Friendship in Eighteenth-Century Ottoman Istanbul." In *Gender and Sexuality in Muslim Cultures*, edited by Gül Özyeğin, 115–38. London: Ashgate, 2015.

Demirci, Tuba, and Selçuk Akşin Somel. "Women's Bodies, Demography, and Public Health: Abortion Policy and Perspectives in the Ottoman Empire of the Nineteenth Century." *Journal of the History of Sexuality* 17, no. 3 (2008): 377–420.

Demirler, Derya, and Pınar Gümüş. "TCK Değişirken." *Bü'de Kadın Gündemi* 7, November 2004. http://www.feminisite.net (accessed December 5, 2011).

Derrida, Jacques. "Force of Law: The 'Mystical Foundation of Authority.'" In *Deconstruction and the Possibility of Justice*, edited by Drucilla Cornell, Michel Rosenfeld, and David Gray, 1–67. New York: Routledge, 1992.

Dinçer, İclal. "The Impact of Neoliberal Policies on Historic Urban Space: Areas of Urban Renewal in Istanbul." *International Planning Studies* 16, no. 1 (2011): 43–60.

Dinshaw, Carolyn, Lee Edelman, and Ferguson Roderick. "Theorizing Queer Temporalities: A Roundtable Discussion." *GLQ: A Journal of Lesbian and Gay Studies* 13, no. 2 (2007): 177–95.

Directorate of Communications. "Statement regarding Türkiye's Withdrawal from the Istanbul Convention." Presidency of the Republic of Türkiye, March 21, 2021. https://www.iletisim.gov.tr/english/haberler/detay/statement-regarding-turkeys-withdrawal-from-the-istanbul-convention.

Doğanoğlu, Senem. *Adaletin "LGBT" Hali*. Ankara: LGBT Haklari Platformu, 2009.

Dole, Christopher. "The House That Saddam Built: Protest and Psychiatry in Post-disaster Turkey." *Journal of the Ottoman and Turkish Studies Association* 2, no. 2 (2015): 281–305.

Döşemeciyan, Kirkor, Yervant Özuzun, and Murat Bebiroğlu. *Müslüman Olmayan Azınlıklar Raporu*. Istanbul, 2011. https://hyetert.blogspot.com/2011/02/musluman-olmayan-azinliklar-raporu-2011.html.

Driskill, Qwo-Li. *Asegi Stories: Cherokee Queer and Two-Spirit Memory*. Tucson: University of Arizona Press, 2016.

Duben, Alan, and Cem Behar. *Istanbul Households: Marriage, Family, and Fertility, 1880–1940*. Cambridge: Cambridge University Press, 1991.

Dursun, Selçuk. "Procreation, Family and 'Progress': Administrative and Economic Aspects of Ottoman Population Policies in the 19th Century." *History of the Family* 16, no. 2 (2011): 160–71.

ECRI (European Commission against Racism and Intolerance). *First Report on Turkey*. Strasbourg: Council of Europe, 1999. https://rm.coe.int/first-report-on-turkey/16808b5c75.

ECRI (European Commission against Racism and Intolerance). *Second Report on Turkey*. Strasbourg: Council of Europe, 2001. https://rm.coe.int/second-report-on-turkey/16808b5c78.

ECRI (European Commission against Racism and Intolerance). *Third Report on Turkey*. Strasbourg: Council of Europe, 2005. https://rm.coe.int/third-report-on-turkey/16808b5c7b.

El-Rouayheb, Khaled. *Before Homosexuality in the Arab-Islamic World, 1500–1800*. Chicago: University of Chicago Press, 2009.

El-Tayeb, Fatima. *European Others: Queering Ethnicity in Postnational Europe.* Minneapolis: University of Minnesota Press, 2011.

Eng, David L. *The Feeling of Kinship: Queer Liberalism and the Racialization of Intimacy.* Durham, NC: Duke University Press, 2010.

Eralp, Feride. "Background of TERF Dispute: How Did It All Come Down to the Locker Rooms?" *Çatlak Zemin,* October 30, 2020. https://en.catlakzemin.com/background-of-terf-dispute-how-did-it-all-come-down-to-the-locker-rooms/.

Ergun, Nilgun. "Gentrification in Istanbul." *Cities* 21, no. 5 (2004): 391–405.

Erol, Ali E. "Queer Contestation of Neoliberal and Heteronormative Moral Geographies during #OccupyGezi." *Sexualities* 21, no. 3 (2018): 428–45.

Ersöz, Cezmi. "Elli Yıl Öncesinin Ünlü Evleri ve Kadınlarıyla Abanoz Sokağının İffeti." *Cumhuriyet* 82 (1987): 10–11.

Erten, H. Nilay. "At Least Three Children: Politics of Reproduction, Health and Care in Pronatalist Turkey." PhD diss., Yale University, 2020.

Ertür, Başak, and Alisa Lebow. "Şöhretin Sonu: Bülent Ersoy'un Kanunla İmtihanı." In *Cinsellik Muamması: Türkiye'de Kültür ve Muhalefet,* edited by Cüneyt Çakırlar and Serkan Delice, 391–426. Istanbul: Metis, 2012.

Ewing, Katherine Pratt. *Stolen Honor: Stigmatizing Muslim Men in Berlin.* Stanford, CA: Stanford University Press, 2008.

Fanon, Frantz. *Black Skin, White Masks.* Translated by Richard Philcox. 2nd ed. London: Pluto, 2008.

Fausto-Sterling, Anne. *Sexing the Body: Gender Politics and the Construction of Sexuality.* New York: Basic Books, 2000.

Feldman, Allen. "Ethnographic States of Emergency." In *Fieldwork under Fire: Contemporary Studies of Violence and Culture,* edited by Carolyn Nordstrom and Antonius C. G. M. Robben, 224–52. Berkeley: University of California Press, 1995.

Feldman, Allen. *Formations of Violence: The Narrative of the Body and Political Terror in Northern Ireland.* Chicago: University of Chicago Press, 1991.

Fineman, Martha. *The Neutered Mother, the Sexual Family, and Other Twentieth Century Tragedies.* New York: Routledge, 1995.

Foucault, Michel. *Abnormal: Lectures at the Collège de France, 1974–1975.* Translated by Graham Burchell. New York: Picador, 2004.

Foucault, Michel. *The Birth of Biopolitics: Lectures at the Collège de France, 1978–1979.* Translated by Graham Burchell. New York: Palgrave Macmillan, 2010.

Foucault, Michel. *Discipline and Punish: The Birth of the Prison.* Translated by Alan Sheridan. New York: Vintage, 1995.

Foucault, Michel. "Governmentality." In *The Foucault Effect: Studies in Governmentality,* edited by Graham Burchell, Colin Gordon, and Peter Miller, translated by Colin Gordon, 87–104. Chicago: University of Chicago Press, 1991.

Foucault, Michel. *The History of Sexuality.* Vol. 1, *An Introduction.* Translated by Robert Hurley. New York: Vintage, 1980.

Foucault, Michel. *Madness and Civilization: A History of Insanity in the Age of Reason*. Translated by Richard Howard. New York: Vintage, 1988.

Freeman, Elizabeth. "Introduction." *GLQ: A Journal of Lesbian and Gay Studies* 13, nos. 2–3 (2007): 159–76.

Freeman, Elizabeth. "Queer Belongings: Kinship Theory and Queer Theory." In *A Companion to Lesbian, Gay, Bisexual, Transgender, and Queer Studies*, edited by George E. Haggerty and Molly McGarry, 293–314. Malden, MA: Blackwell, 2008.

Galarte, Francisco J. *Brown Trans Figurations: Rethinking Race, Gender, and Sexuality in Chicanx/Latinx Studies*. Austin: University of Texas Press, 2021.

Georgis, Dina. "Thinking Past Pride: Queer Arab Shame in *Bareed Mista3jil*." *International Journal of Middle East Studies* 45, no. 2 (2013): 233–51.

Gill, Denise. "Sense Experiences: Religious Affairs and the Palpability of State Power." *Public Culture* 33, no. 3 (2021): 393–415.

Gill-Peterson, Jules. "The Cis State." *Sad Brown Girl* (Substack), April 14, 2021. https://sadbrowngirl.substack.com/p/the-cis-state.

Gill-Peterson, Jules. "The Cis State II." *Sad Brown Girl* (Substack), June 3, 2022. https://sadbrowngirl.substack.com/p/the-cis-state-ii.

Gill-Peterson, Jules. "Growing Up Trans in the 1960s and the 2010s." In *Misfit Children: An Inquiry into Childhood Belongings*, edited by Markus P. J. Bohlman, 213–29. Lanham, MD: Lexington Books, 2016.

Gill-Peterson, Jules. *Histories of the Transgender Child*. Minneapolis: University of Minnesota Press, 2018.

Gökarıksel, Banu, and Anna J. Secor. "Devout Muslim Masculinities: The Moral Geographies and Everyday Practices of Being Men in Turkey." *Gender, Place and Culture* 24, no. 3 (2017): 381–402.

Göktaş, Kemal. "Yargıtay'dan Namus Cinayeti Devrimi."*Vatan*, May 18, 2010. https://www.memurlar.net/haber/167306/yargitay-dan-namus-cinayeti -devrimi.html

Gönen, Zeynep. *The Politics of Crime in Turkey: Neoliberalism, Police and the Urban Poor*. London: I. B. Tauris, 2017.

Göral, Özgür Sevgi. "Memory as Experience in Times of Perpetual Violence: The Challenge of Saturday Mothers vis-à-vis Cultural Aphasia." *Kurdish Studies* 9, no. 1 (2021): 77–95.

Göral, Özgür Sevgi, Ayhan Işık, and Özlem Kaya. *The Unspoken Truth: Enforced Disappearances*. Istanbul: Truth Justice Memory Center, 2016. https:// hakikatadalethafiza.org/wp-content/uploads/2015/02/Konusulmayan -Gercek_ENG.pdf.

Göregenli, Melek, and Evren Özer. 2010. *Medya ve İnsan Hakları Örgütlerinin Verilerinden Hareketle 1980'lerden Günümüze Türkiye'de İşkence: Epidemiyolojik Bir Başlangıç Çalışması*. Ankara: Türkiye İnsan Hakları Vakfı. http:// istanbulprotokolu.com/download.php?f=8ed57222e834994c8bacdd549ac 99ef2.

Gossett, Che. "We Will Not Rest in Peace: AIDS Activism, Black Radicalism, Queer and/or Trans Resistance." In *Queer Necropolitics*, edited by Jin Haritaworn, Adi Kuntsman, and Silvia Posocco, 31–50. Abingdon, UK: Routledge, 2014.

Govindan, Padma, and Aniruddhan Vasudevan. "The Razor's Edge of Oppositionality: Exploring the Politics of Rights-Based Activism by Transgender Women in Tamil Nadu." In *Law like Love: Queer Perspectives on Law*, edited by Arvind Narrain and Alok Gupta, 84–112. New Delhi: Yoda, 2011.

Gramsci, Antonio. *Selections from the Prison Notebooks of Antonio Gramsci.* Edited by Quintin Hoare and Geoffrey Nowell Smith. New York: International Publishers, 1971.

Gray, Mary L. *Out in the Country: Youth, Media, and Queer Visibility in Rural America.* New York: New York University Press, 2009.

Grewal, Inderpal, and Karen Caplan. "Global Identities: Theorizing Transnational Studies of Sexuality." *GLQ: A Journal of Lesbian and Gay Studies* 7, no. 4 (2001): 663–79.

Grosz, Elizabeth. *Volatile Bodies: Toward a Corporeal Feminism.* Bloomington: Indiana University Press, 1994.

Gürbilek, Nurdan. *Vitrinde Yaşamak: 1980'lerin Kültürel İklimi.* Istanbul: Metis, 1992.

Gürcan, Efe Can, and Efe Peker. *Challenging Neoliberalism at Turkey's Gezi Park: From Private Discontent to Collective Class Action.* New York: Palgrave Macmillan, 2015.

Güven, Dilek. *Cumhuriyet Dönemi Azınlık Politikaları Bağlamında 6/7 Eylül Olayları.* Istanbul: Tarih Vakfı, 2005.

Güzel, Hande. "Pain as Performance: Re-virginisation in Turkey." *Medical Humanities* 44, no. 2 (2018): 89–95.

Habertürk. "Kadavra Dağıtımı Başlıyor." March 30, 2012. http://www.haberturk .com/saglik/haber/729564-kadavra-dagitimi-basliyor.

Haley, Sarah. "Intimate Historical Practice." *Black Perspectives* (blog), May 18, 2020. https://www.aaihs.org/intimate-historical-practice/.

Hamzić, Vanja. "The Resistance from an Alterspace: Pakistani and Indonesian Muslims beyond the Dominant Sexual and Gender Norms." In *Religion, Gender and Sexuality in Everyday Life*, edited by Peter Nynäs and Andrew Kam-Tuck Yip, 17–35. Burlington, VT: Ashgate, 2016.

Haritaworn, Jin. "Colorful Bodies in the Multikulti Metropolis: On the Neoliberal and Punitive Bases of Trans Vitality and Victimology in the Berlin Hate Crime Debate." In *Transgender Migrations: The Bodies, Borders, and Politics of Transition*, edited by Trystan Cotten, 11–31. New York: Routledge, 2012.

Hartman, Saidiya. *Lose Your Mother: A Journey along the Atlantic Slave Route.* New York: Farrar, Straus and Giroux, 2008.

Hartman, Saidiya. *Wayward Lives, Beautiful Experiments: Intimate Histories of Social Upheaval.* New York: W. W. Norton, 2019.

Harvey, David. *Rebel Cities: From the Right to the City to the Urban Revolution.* New York: Verso, 2012.

Hasso, Frances. *Consuming Desires: Family Crisis and the State in the Middle East.* Stanford, CA: Stanford University Press, 2011.

Hayward, Eva, and Che Gossett. "Impossibility of *That*." *Angelaki* 22, no. 2 (2017): 15–24.

Hegarty, Benjamin. *The Made-Up State: Technology, Trans Femininity, and Citizenship in Indonesia.* Ithaca, NY: Cornell University Press, 2022.

Heyman, Josiah McC., ed. *States and Illegal Practices.* Oxford: Berg, 1999.

Hicks, Stephen. *Lesbian, Gay and Queer Parenting: Families, Intimacies, Genealogies.* London: Palgrave Macmillan, 2011.

Hikayeci. "Farklılıkları Yok Eden İkili Cinsiyet (Kadın/Erkek) Sistemine HAYIR." October 17, 2009. http://hikayeci.livejournal.com/2009/10/17/.

Hirsch, Jennifer S., Holly Wardlow, and Harriet Phiney. "'No One Saw Us': Reputation as an Axis of Sexual Identity." In *Understanding Global Sexualities: New Frontiers*, edited by Peter Aggleton, Paul Boyce, Henrietta L. Moore, and Richard Parker, 91–107. London: Routledge, 2013.

Horton, Brian A. "What's So 'Queer' about Coming Out? Silent Queers and Theorizing Kinship Agonistically in Mumbai." *Sexualities* 21, no. 7 (2018): 1059–74.

Hull, Matthews S. "Documents and Bureaucracy." *Annual Review of Anthropology* 41 (2012): 251–67.

Human Rights Watch. *"We Need a Law for Liberation": Gender, Sexuality, and Human Rights in a Changing Turkey.* New York: Human Rights Watch, 2008. https://www.hrw.org/reports/2008/turkey0508/.

Hurtas, Sibel. "Turkey's Alevis to Open Their Houses of Worship to LGBTQ Funerals." *Al-Monitor*, May 20, 2022. https://www.al-monitor.com/originals/2022/05/turkeys-alevis-open-their-houses-worship-lgbtq-funerals.

Hürriyet. "IETT Otobüsünde Öpüşme Eylemi." April 24, 2011. https://www.hurriyet.com.tr/gundem/iett-otobusunde-opusme-eylemi-17624593.

Iğsız, Aslı. *Humanism in Ruins: Entangled Legacies of the Greek-Turkish Population Exchange.* Stanford, CA: Stanford University Press, 2018.

Ilkucan, Altan. "Gentrification, Community and Consumption: Constructing, Conquering and Contesting 'The Republic of Cihangir.'" Master's thesis, Bilkent University, Ankara, 2004.

İnceoğlu, Irem. "Encountering Difference and Radical Democratic Trajectory." *City* 19, no. 4 (2015): 534–44.

Ingram, Gordon Brent. "Marginality and the Landscapes of Erotic Alien(n)ations." In *Queers in Space: Communities, Public Places, Sites of Resistance*, edited by Gordon Brent Ingram, Anne-Marie Bouthillette, and Yolanda Retter, 27–52. Seattle, WA: Bay, 1997.

Ingram, Gordon Brent. "'Open' Space as Strategic Queer Sites." In *Queers in Space: Communities, Public Places, Sites of Resistance*, edited by Gordon Brent Ingram, Anne-Marie Bouthillette, and Yolanda Retter, 95–125. Seattle, WA: Bay, 1997.

Irving, Dan. "Normalized Transgressions: Legitimizing the Transgender Body as Productive." *Radical History*, no. 100 (2008): 38–59.

Irving, Dan, Vek Lewis, Nael Bhanji, Raewyn Connell, Qwo-Li Driskill, and Viviane Namaste. "Trans* Political Economy Deconstructed: A Roundtable Discussion." *TSQ: Transgender Studies Quarterly* 4, no. 1 (2017): 16–27.

Islam, Tolga. "Current Urban Discourse, Urban Transformation and Gentrification in Istanbul." *Architectural Design* 80, no. 1 (2010): 58–63.

Jenness, Valerie. "The Hate Crime Canon and Beyond: A Critical Assessment." *Law and Critique* 12, no. 3 (2001): 279–308.

Jongerden, Joost. *The Settlement Issue in Turkey and the Kurds: An Analysis of Spatial Policies, Modernity and War*. Leiden: Brill, 2007.

Joseph, Suad. *Intimate Selving in Arab Families: Gender, Self, and Identity*. Syracuse, NY: Syracuse University Press, 1999.

Kabbani, Rana. *Europe's Myths of Orient: Devise and Rule*. London: Macmillan, 1986.

Kaivanara, Marzieh. "Virginity Dilemma: Re-creating Virginity through Hymenoplasty in Iran." *Culture, Health and Sexuality* 18, no. 1 (2015): 71–83.

Kandiyoti, Deniz. "Gendering the Modern: On Missing Dimensions in the Study of Turkish Modernity." In *Rethinking Modernity and National Identity in Turkey*, edited by Sibel Bozdoğan and Reşat Kasaba, 133–56. Seattle: University of Washington Press, 1997.

Kandiyoti, Deniz. "Pink Card Blues: Trouble and Strife at the Crossroads of Gender." In *Fragments of Culture: The Everyday of Modern Turkey*, edited by Deniz Kandiyoti and Ayşe Saktanber, 277–93. London: I. B. Tauris, 2002.

Kandiyoti, Deniz. "Some Awkward Questions on Women and Modernity in Turkey." In *Remaking Women: Feminism and Modernity in the Middle East*, edited by Lila Abu-Lughod, 270–87. Princeton, NJ: Princeton University Press, 1998.

Kandiyoti, Deniz. "Transsexuals and the Urban Landscape in Istanbul." *Middle East Report*, no. 206 (Spring 1998). https://merip.org/1998/06/transsexuals-and-the-urban-landscape-in-istanbul/.

Kaos GL. "Kaos GL ve Pembe Hayat LGBTT Dayanışma Dernekle." April 28, 2011. https://kaosgl.org/haber/1-mayis-meydanlarinda-10-yildir-gokkusagi-bayragi-dalgalaniyor.

Kaplan, Hilal. "İslâm ve eşcinsellik meselesi." *Taraf*, April 3, 2010. http://www.aktuelpsikoloji.com/haber.php?haber_id=7090.

Kaptan, Özdemir. *Beyoğlu ve Kısa Geçmişi*. Istanbul: Aybay Yayınları, 1988.

Karakışla, Yavuz Selim. "Yoksulluktan Fuhuş Yapanların Islahı: Askeri Dikimevlerinde İşe Alınan Fahişeler." *Toplumsal Tarih*, no. 112 (April 2003): 98–101.

Karakuş, Emrah. "Chameleons of Kurdish Turkey: Ethnographic Reflections on a Queer Counter/Insurgency." *Anthropology Today* 38, no. 1 (2022): 13–17.

Karaman, Ozan, and Tolga Islam. "On the Dual Nature of Intra-urban Borders: The Case of a Romani Neighborhood in Istanbul." *Cities* 29, no. 4 (2012): 234–43.

Karan, Ulaş. "Nefret Suçları ve Nefret Söyleminin Türkiye Yasalarında Karşılığı." In *Nefret Suçları ve Nefret Söylemi* , edited by Ayşe Çavdar and Aylin B. Yıldırım, 233–43. Istanbul: Hrant Dink Vakfı, 2010.

Karpat, Kemal. *Ottoman Population, 1830–1914: Demographic and Social Characteristics*. Madison: University of Wisconsin Press, 1985.

Kasmani, Omar. *Queer Companions: Religion, Public Intimacy, and Saintly Affects in Pakistan*. Durham, NC: Duke University Press, 2022.

Kayalı, Serhat, and Özge Yaka. "The Spirit of Gezi: The Recomposition of Political Subjectivities in Turkey." *New Formations: A Journal of Culture/Theory/Politics* 2014, no. 83 (2014): 117–38.

Kelly, Tobias. "Documented Lives: Fear and the Uncertainties of Law during the Second Palestinian Intifada." *Journal of the Royal Anthropological Institute* 12, no. 1 (2006): 89–107.

Kepenek, Evrim. "Erkek Şiddeti 2019." *Bianet*, February 14, 2020. https://bianet .org/bianet/print/219203-erkekler-2019-da-en-az-328-kadini-oldurdu.

Kessler, Suzanne J., and Wendy McKenna. "Toward a Theory of Gender." In *The Transgender Studies Reader*, edited by Susan Stryker and Stephen Whittle, 165–82. New York: Routledge, 2006.

Keyder, Çağlar. *Istanbul: Between the Global and the Local*. Lanham, MD: Rowman and Littlefield, 1999.

Keyder, Çağlar, and Ayşe Öncü. "Globalization of a Third-World Metropolis: Istanbul in the 1980s." *Review (Fernand Braudel Center)* 17, no. 3 (1994): 383–421.

Khan, Faris A. "Institutionalizing an Ambiguous Category: 'Khwaja Sira' Activism, the State, and Sex/Gender Regulation in Pakistan." *Anthropological Quarterly* 92, no. 4 (2019): 1135–71.

Knopp, Larry. "Ontologies of Place, Placelessness, and Movement: Queer Quests for Identity and Their Impacts on Contemporary Geographic Thought." *Gender, Place and Culture* 11, no. 1 (2004): 121–34.

Koçak, Mert. "Who Is 'Queerer' and Deserves Resettlement? Queer Asylum Seekers and Their Deservingness of Refugee Status in Turkey." *Middle East Critique* 29, no. 1 (2020): 29–46.

Kocamaner, Hikmet. "Regulating the Family through Religion." *American Ethnologist* 46, no. 4 (2019): 495–508.

Koğacıoğlu, Dicle. "The Tradition Effect: Framing Honor Crimes in Turkey." *Differences: A Journal of Feminist Cultural Studies* 15, no. 2 (2004): 119–51.

Kohn, Sally. "Greasing the Wheel: How the Criminal Justice System Hurts Gay, Lesbian, Bisexual and Transgendered People and Why Hate Crime Laws Won't Save Them." *New York University Review of Law and Social Change* 27, nos. 2–3 (2001): 257–80. https://socialchangenyu.com/wp-content/ uploads/2019/09/SALLY-KOHN_RLSC_27.23.pdf.

Korkman, Zeynep Kurtuluş. "Politics of Intimacy in Turkey: A Distraction from 'Real' Politics?" *Journal of Middle East Women's Studies* 12, no. 1 (2016): 112–21.

Krupa, Christopher. "State by Proxy: Privatized Government in the Andes." *Comparative Studies in Society and History* 52, no. 2 (2010): 319–50.

Kurtoğlu, Ayca. "Sex Reassignment, Biological Reproduction and Sexual Citizenship in Turkey." *Fe Dergi* 1, no. 2 (2009): 79–88.

Kuschminder, Katie. "Afghan Refugee Journeys: Onwards Migration Decision-Making in Greece and Turkey." *Journal of Refugee Studies* 31, no. 4 (2018): 566–87.

Kuyucu, Tuna. "Ethno-Religious 'Unmixing' of 'Turkey': 6–7 September Riots as a Case in Turkish Nationalism." *Nations and Nationalism* 11, no. 3 (2005): 361–80.

Lambdaistanbul. June 10, 2022. https://lambdaistanbul.org/tarihce/.

Lambek, Michael. Introduction to *Ordinary Ethics: Anthropology, Language, and Action*, 1–38. New York: Fordham University Press, 2010.

Laqueur, Thomas. *Making Sex: Body and Gender from the Greeks to Freud*. Cambridge, MA: Harvard University Press, 1990.

Lefebvre, Henri. *The Production of Space*. Oxford: Blackwell, 1991.

Lefebvre, Henri. "The Right to the City." In *Writings on Cities*, by Henri Lefebvre, edited and translated by Eleonore Kofman and Elizabeth Lebas, 147–59. Oxford: Blackwell, 1996.

Leo, Brooklyn. "The Colonial/Modern [Cis]gender System and Trans World Traveling." *Hypatia* 35, no. 3 (2020): 454–74.

Lowe, Lisa. *The Intimacies of Four Continents*. Durham, NC: Duke University Press, 2015.

Luibhéid, Eithne, and Karma R. Chávez, eds. *Queer and Trans Migrations: Dynamics of Illegalization, Detention, Deportation*. Urbana: University of Illinois Press, 2020.

Mahadeen, Ebtihal. "Hymen Reconstruction Surgery in Jordan: Sexual Politics and the Economy of Virginity." In *Body, Migration, Re/constructive Surgeries: Making the Gendered Body in a Globalized World*, edited by Gabriele Griffin and Malin Jordal, 159–72. London: Routledge, 2018.

Makarem, Ghassan. "The Story of HELEM." *Journal of Middle East Women's Studies* 7, no. 3 (2011): 98–112.

Malatino, Hil. *Trans Care*. Minneapolis: University of Minnesota Press, 2020.

Manalansan, Martin F. *Global Divas: Filipino Gay Men in the Diaspora*. Durham, NC: Duke University Press, 2003.

Massad, Joseph A. *Desiring Arabs*. Chicago: University of Chicago Press, 2008.

Massey, Doreen B. *Space, Place, and Gender*. Minneapolis: University of Minnesota Press, 1994.

Massumi, Brian. *Parables for the Virtual: Movement, Affect, Sensation*. Durham, NC: Duke University Press, 2002.

Mauss, Marcel. "Techniques of the Body." *Economy and Society* 2, no. 1 (1973): 70–88.

Mbembe, Achille. "Necropolitics." *Public Culture* 15, no. 1 (2003): 11–40.

McKittrick, Katherine. *Demonic Grounds: Black Women and the Cartographies of Struggle*. Minneapolis: University of Minnesota Press, 2006.

Meadow, Tey. *Trans Kids: Being Gendered in the Twenty-First Century*. Oakland: University of California Press, 2018.

Menon, Nivedita. *Recovering Subversion: Feminist Politics beyond the Law*. Urbana: University of Illinois Press, 2004.

Merabet, Sofian. *Queer Beirut*. Austin: University of Texas Press, 2014.

Merleau-Ponty, Maurice. *The Phenomenology of Perception*. London: Routledge, 1962.

Merleau-Ponty, Maurice. *The Visible and the Invisible: Followed by Working Notes*. Evanston, IL: Northwestern University Press, 1968.

Mikdashi, Maya. "An Archive of Perversion: 1966 and a Desire to Criminalize." *Jadaliyya*, September 29, 2010. https://www.jadaliyya.com/Details/23524.

Mikdashi, Maya. "Gay Rights as Human Rights: Pinkwashing Homonationalism." *Jadaliyya*, December 16, 2011. https://www.jadaliyya.com/Details/24855.

Mikdashi, Maya. "Queering Citizenship, Queering Middle East Studies." *International Journal of Middle East Studies* 45, no. 2 (2013): 350–52.

Mikdashi, Maya. *Sextarianism*. Stanford, CA: Stanford University Press, 2022.

Milliyet. "Cerrahpaşa Tıp Mındıkoğlu için 1-6 üniversiteden çıkartma kararı aldı." February 26, 1982.

Milliyet. "İstanbul Üniversitesi Mındıkoğlu için Soruşturma Komisyonu Kurdu." October 29, 1981.

Milliyet. "Mahkeme Karar Verdi," Bülent Ersoy Artık Kadın." June 6, 1988.

Milliyet. "Mete Akyol Bülent Ersoy'la Konuştu." August 31, 1980.

Milliyet. "Mındıkoğlu için 1-6 ay 'üniversiteden çıkarılma' cezası istendi." February 13, 1982.

Milliyet. "Uğur Dündar Kadın Olan Erkeklerin Dramını Ekrana Getiriyor." October 25, 1981

Miranda, Deborah A. "Extermination of the Joyas: Gendercide in Spanish California." *GLQ: Journal of Lesbian and Gay Studies* 16, nos. 1–2 (2010): 253–84.

Mithat Efendi, Ahmet. *Henüz Onyedi Yaşında*. Istanbul: Bordo Siyah Yayinlari, 2019.

Moallem, Minoo. *Between Warrior Brother and Veiled Sister: Islamic Fundamentalism and the Politics of Patriarchy in Iran*. Berkeley: University of California Press, 2005.

Montagu, Ashley. *Touching: The Human Significance of the Skin*. New York: Harper and Row, 1971.

Morgensen, Scott Lauria. *Spaces between Us: Queer Settler Colonialism and Indigenous Decolonization*. Minneapolis: University of Minnesota Press, 2011.

Moussawi, Ghassan. *Disruptive Situations: Fractal Orientalism and Queer Strategies in Beirut*. Philadelphia: Temple University Press, 2020.

Muehlebach, Andrea. *The Moral Neoliberal: Welfare and Citizenship in Italy*. Chicago: University of Chicago Press, 2012.

Mutlu, Burcu. "Transnational Biopolitics and Family-Making in Secrecy: An Ethnography of Reproductive Travel from Turkey to Northern Cyprus." PhD diss., Massachusetts Institute of Technology, 2019.

Mynet. "İrem'in katil sanığını yakacak rapor." January 26, 2011. http://haber.mynet.com/iremin-katil-sanigini-yakacak-rapor-552989-yasam/.

Myslik, Wayne. "Renegotiating the Social/Sexual Identities of Places: Gay Communities as Safe Havens or Sites of Resistance?" In *BodySpace: Destabilizing Geographies of Gender and Sexuality*, edited by Nancy Duncan, 155–68. London: Routledge, 1996.

Nagar, Richa, and Lock Swarr. *Critical Transnational Feminist Praxis*. New York: State University of New York Press, 2010.

Najmabadi, Afsaneh. *Professing Selves: Transsexuality and Same-Sex Desire in Contemporary Iran*. Durham, NC: Duke University Press, 2013.

Najmabadi, Afsaneh. "Reading Transsexuality in 'Gay' Tehran (around 1979)." In *The Transgender Studies Reader 2*, edited by Susan Stryker and Aren Z. Aizura, 380–400. New York: Routledge, 2013.

Najmabadi, Afsaneh. "Transing and Transpassing across Sex-Gender Walls in Iran." *wsq: Women's Studies Quarterly* 36, no. 3 (2008): 23–42.

Najmabadi, Afsaneh. "Verdicts of Science, Rulings of Faith: Transgender/Sexuality in Contemporary Iran." *Social Research: An International Quarterly* 78, no. 2 (2011): 533–56.

Nalcı, Tamar, and Emre Can Dağlıoğlu. "'Bir Gasp Hikâyesi." *Agos*, August 27, 2011.

Namaste, Viviane. "Undoing Theory: The 'Transgender Question' and the Epistemic Violence of Anglo-American Feminist Theory." *Hypatia* 24, no. 3 (2009): 11–32.

Nancy, Jean-Luc. *The Sense of the World*. Minneapolis: University of Minnesota Press, 1997.

Narrain, Arvind. "A New Language of Morality: From the Trial of Nowshirwan to the Judgment in Naz Foundation." In *Law like Love: Queer Perspectives on Law*, edited by Arvind Narrain and Alok Gupta, 253–77. New Delhi: Yoda, 2011.

Narrain, Arvind, and Alok Gupta. Introduction to *Law like Love: Queer Perspectives on Law*, edited by Arvind Narrain and Alok Gupta, xi–lvi. New Delhi: Yoda, 2011.

Navaro, Yael. *Faces of the State: Secularism and Public Life in Turkey*. Princeton, NJ: Princeton University Press, 2002.

Navaro, Yael. *The Make-Believe Space: Affective Geography in a Postwar Polity*. Durham, NC: Duke University Press, 2012.

Nordstrom, Carolyn. *Global Outlaws*. Berkeley: University of California Press, 2007.

Nuhrat, Yağmur. "Contesting Love through Commodification." *American Ethnologist* 45, no. 3 (2018): 392–404.

Nussbaum, Martha. "'Secret Sewers of Vice': Disgust, Bodies, and the Law." In *The Passions of Law*, edited by Susan A. Bandes, 17–62. New York: New York University Press, 1999.

Okçuoğlu, Dilan. "Rethinking Democracy and Autonomy through the Case of Kurdish Movement." In *Democratic Representation in Plurinational States: The Kurds in Turkey*, edited by Ephraim Nimni and Elcin Aktoprak, 211–27. Cham, Switzerland: Palgrave Macmillan, 2018.

Öktem, Kerem. "Another Struggle: Sexual Identity Politics in Unsettled Turkey." *Middle East Report Online*, September 15, 2008. https://merip.org/2008/09/another-struggle/.

Öncü, Ayşe. "The Myth of the Ideal Home Travels across Cultural Borders to Istanbul." In *Space, Culture and Power: New Identities in Globalizing Cities*, edited by Ayşe Öncü and Petra Weland, 56–72. London: Zed Books, 1997.

Önder, Nilgün. "Integrating with the Global Market: The State and the Crisis of Political Representation: Turkey in the 1980s and 1990s." *International Journal of Political Economy* 28, no. 2 (1998): 44–84.

Öniş, Ziya. "The State and Economic Development in Contemporary Turkey: Etatism to Neoliberalism and Beyond." In *Turkey between East and West: New Challenges for a Rising Regional Power*, edited by Vojtech Mastny and R. Craig Nation, 155–78. London: Routledge, 2019.

Öniş, Ziya. "Turgut Özal and His Economic Legacy: Turkish Neo-liberalism in Critical Perspective." *Middle Eastern Studies* 40, no. 4 (2004): 113–34.

Organization for Security and Co-operation in Europe. "What Is Hate Crime?" 2022. https://hatecrime.osce.org/.

Oswin, Natalie, and Eric Olund. "Governing Intimacy." *Environment and Planning D: Society and Space* 28, no. 1 (2010): 60–67.

Özbay, Cenk. "State Homophobia, Sexual Politics, and Queering the Boğaziçi Resistance." *South Atlantic Quarterly* 121, no. 1 (2022): 199–209.

Özbay, Cenk. *Queering Sexualities in Turkey: Gay Men, Male Prostitutes and the City*. London: I. B. Tauris, 2017.

Özbay, Cenk, Maral Erol, Umut Türem, and Ayşecan Terzioğlu. *The Making of Neoliberal Turkey*. London: Routledge, 2016.

Özbay, Cenk, and Evren Savcı. "Queering Commons in Turkey." *GLQ: A Journal of Lesbian and Gay Studies* 24, no. 4 (2018): 516–21.

Özbek, Meral. "The Regulation of Prostitution in Beyoğlu (1875–1915)." *Middle Eastern Studies* 46, no. 4 (2010): 555–68.

Özdemir, Esen, and Sevi Bayraktar. *İstanbul Amargi Feminizm Tartışmaları*. Istanbul: Amargi Yayinevi, 2012.

Özdüzen, Özge. "Cinema-Going during the Gezi Protests: Claiming the Right to the Emek Movie Theatre and Gezi Park." *Social and Cultural Geography* 19, no. 8 (2018): 1028–52.

Özel, Çağlar. "Medeni Hukuk Açısından Ölüm Anının Belirlenmesi ve Ceset Üzerindeki Hakka İlişkin Bazı Düşünceler." *Ankara Üniversitesi Hukuk Fakültesi Dergisi* 51, no. 1 (2002): 43–77.

Özlen, Lara. "'No TERFs on Our TURF': Building Alliances through Fractions on Social Media in İstanbul." *Kohl: A Journal for Body and Gender Research* 6, no. 3 (2020). https://kohljournal.press/no-terfs-our-turf.

Özlü, Demir. Preface to *Beyoğlu in the 30s: Through the Lens of Selahattin Giz,* edited by Ali Özdamar, 1–12. Istanbul: Çağdaş Yayıncılık, 1991.

Özsoy, Hişyar. "Between Gift and Taboo: Death and the Negotiation of National Identity and Sovereignty in the Kurdish Conflict in Turkey." PhD diss., University of Texas at Austin, 2010.

Özsoy, Hişyar. "Introduction: The Kurds' Ordeal with Turkey in a Transforming Middle East." *Dialectical Anthropology* 37, no. 1 (2013): 103–11.

Öztürel, Adnan. "Transseksualizm Ile Hermafrodizmde Yasal, Tipsal ve Adli Tip Problemleri (Kadınlaşan Erkekler, Erkekleşen Kadınlar, İki Cinsliler)." *Ankara Üniversitesi Hukuk Fakültesi Dergisi* 38, nos. 1–4 (1981): 253–92.

Özyeğin, Gül. *New Desires, New Selves: Sex, Love, and Piety among Turkish Youth.* New York: New York University Press, 2015.

Özyeğin, Gül. *Untidy Gender: Domestic Service in Turkey.* Philadelphia: Temple University Press, 2010.

Özyürek, Esra. *Nostalgia for the Modern: State Secularism and Everyday Politics in Turkey.* Durham, NC: Duke University Press, 2006.

Parla, Ayşe. "The 'Honor' of the State: Virginity Examinations in Turkey." *Feminist Studies* 27, no. 1 (2001): 65–88.

Parla, Ayşe. "Revisiting 'Honor' through Migrant Vulnerabilities in Turkey." *History and Anthropology* 31, no. 1 (2020): 84–104.

Parla, Ayşe, and Ceren Özgül. "Property, Dispossession, and Citizenship in Turkey; Or, the History of the Gezi Uprising Starts in the Surp Hagop Armenian Cemetery." *Public Culture* 28, no. 3 (80) (2016): 617–53.

Pateman, Carole. *The Sexual Contract.* Stanford, CA: Stanford University Press, 1988.

Pişkinsüt, Sema. *Filistin Askısından Fezlekeye: İşkencenin Kitabı.* Ankara: Bilgi Yayınevi, 2001.

Plemons, Eric. *The Look of a Woman: Facial Feminization Surgery and the Aims of Trans-Medicine.* Durham, NC: Duke University Press, 2017.

Polat, Aslıhan, Şahika Yüksel, and Aysun Genç Dişçigil. "Family Attitudes toward Transgendered People in Turkey: Experience from a Secular Islamic Country." *International Journal of Psychiatry Medicine* 35, no. 4 (2005): 383–93.

Potuoğlu-Cook, Öykü. "Hope with Qualms: A Feminist Analysis of the 2013 Gezi Protests." *Feminist Review* 109, no. 1 (2015): 96–123.

Povinelli, Elizabeth A. *The Empire of Love: Toward a Theory of Intimacy, Genealogy, and Carnality.* Durham, NC: Duke University Press, 2006.

Povinelli, Elizabeth A., and George Chauncey. "Thinking Sexuality Transnationally: An Introduction." *GLQ: A Journal of Lesbian and Gay Studies* 5, no. 4 (1999): 439–50.

Pratt, Geraldine, and Victoria Rosner. "Introduction: The Global and the Intimate." *Women's Studies Quarterly* 34, no. 1/2 (2006): 13–24.

Price, Patricia L. "Race and Ethnicity II: Skin and Other Intimacies." *Progress in Human Geography* 37, no. 4 (2013): 578–86.

Puar, Jasbir K. "Disability." *TSQ: Transgender Studies Quarterly* 1, nos. 1–2 (2014): 77–81.

Puar, Jasbir K. *Terrorist Assemblages: Homonationalism in Queer Times.* Durham, NC: Duke University Press, 2007.

Puri, Jyoti. *Sexual States: Governance and the Struggle over the Antisodomy Law in India.* Durham, NC: Duke University Press, 2016.

Ragab, Ahmed. "One, Two, or Many Sexes: Sex Differentiation in Medieval Islamicate Medical Thought." *Journal of the History of Sexuality* 24, no. 3 (2015): 428–54.

Ralph, Laurence. "Alibi: The Extralegal Force Embedded in the Law (United States)." In *Writing the World of Policing: The Difference Ethnography Makes,* edited by Didier Fassin, 267–88. Chicago: University of Chicago Press, 2017.

Rasim, Ahmed. *Fuhş-i Atik.* Istanbul: Üç Harf Yayınları, 2005.

Ray, Larry, and David Smith. "Racist Offenders and the Politics of 'Hate Crime.'" *Law and Critique* 12, no. 3 (2001): 203–21.

Razack, Sherene. *Looking White People in the Eye: Gender, Race, and Culture in Courtrooms and Classrooms.* Toronto: University of Toronto Press, 1998.

Rifkin, Mark. *When Did Indians Become Straight? Kinship, the History of Sexuality, and Native Sovereignty.* New York: Oxford University Press, 2011.

Riles, Annelise, ed. *Documents: Artifacts of Modern Knowledge.* Ann Arbor: University of Michigan Press, 2006.

Robben, Antonius C. G. M., and Carolyn Nordstrom. "The Anthropology and Ethnography of Violence and Sociopolitical Conflict." In *Fieldwork under Fire: Contemporary Studies of Violence and Culture,* edited by Carolyn Nordstrom and Antonius C. G. M. Robben, 1–23. Berkeley: University of California Press, 1995.

Robins, Kevin. "How Tell What Remains: Sulukule Nevermore." *Cultural Politics* 7, no. 1 (2011): 5–40.

Rodaway, Paul. *Sensuous Geographies: Body, Sense, and Place.* London: Routledge, 1994.

Rose, Jacqueline. *States of Fantasy.* Oxford: Clarendon, 1998.

Rubin, Gayle. "Of Catamites and Kings: Reflections on Butch, Gender, and Boundaries." In *The Transgender Studies Reader,* edited by Susan Stryker and Stephen Whittle, 471–81. London: Routledge, 2006.

Sadjadi, Sahar. "Deep in the Brain: Identity and Authenticity in Pediatric Gender Transition." *Cultural Anthropology* 34, no. 1 (2019): 103–29.

Sadjadi, Sahar. "The Vulnerable Child Protection Act and Transgender Children's Health." *TSQ: Transgender Studies Quarterly* 7, no. 3 (2020): 508–16.

Sağlam, İpek. "Türk Medeni Kanunu Madde 40 Üzerine Bir Değerlendirme." *Ankara Üniversitesi Hukuk Fakültesi Dergisi* 8, nos. 3–4 (2004): 455–69.

Said, Edward. *Orientalism.* New York: Pantheon Books, 1978.

Salamon, Gayle. *Assuming a Body: Transgender and Rhetorics of Materiality.* New York: Columbia University Press, 2010.

Saleh, Fadi. "Transgender as a Humanitarian Category: The Case of Syrian Queer and Gender-Variant Refugees in Turkey." *TSQ: Transgender Studies Quarterly* 7, no. 1 (2020): 37–55.

Saluk, Seda. "Monitored Reproduction: Surveillance, Labor, and Care in Pronatalist Turkey." PhD diss., University of Massachusetts Amherst, 2020.

Sanal, Aslıhan. *New Organs within Us: Transplants and the Moral Economy.* Durham, NC: Duke University Press, 2011.

Sancar, Serpil. *Erkeklik: İmkânsız İktidar, Ailede, Piyasada ve Sokakta Erkekler.* Istanbul: Metis, 2009.

Sandal-Wilson, Hakan. "Social Justice, Conflict, and Protest in Turkey: The Kurdish Issue and LGBTI+ Activism." *Social Research: An International Quarterly* 88, no. 2 (2021): 561–86.

Sarı, Elif. "Lesbian Refugees in Transit: The Making of Authenticity and Legitimacy in Turkey." *Journal of Lesbian Studies* 24, no. 2 (2020): 140–58.

Sarı, Elif. "Unsafe Present, Uncertain Future: LGBTI Asylum in Turkey." In *Queer and Trans Migrations: Dynamics of Illegalization, Detention, Deportation,* edited by Eithne Luibhéid and Karma R. Chávez, 90–105. Urbana: University of Illinois Press, 2020.

Sarıoğlu, Esra. *The Unburdened Body: Violence, Emotions, and the New Woman in Turkey.* New York: Oxford University Press, 2023.

Sarıtaş, Ezgi. *Cinsel Normalliğin Kuruluşu: Osmanlı'dan Cumhuriyet'e Heteronormatiflik ve İstikrarsızlıkları.* Istanbul: Metis, 2020.

Savcı, Evren. *Queer in Translation: Sexual Politics under Neoliberal Islam.* Durham, NC: Duke University Press, 2021.

Savcı, Evren. "Who Speaks the Language of Queer Politics? Western Knowledge, Politico-Cultural Capital and Belonging among Urban Queers in Turkey." *Sexualities* 19, no. 3 (2016): 369–87.

Scheper-Hughes, Nancy. *Death without Weeping: The Violence of Everyday Life in Brazil.* Berkeley: University of California Press, 1992.

Scheper-Hughes, Nancy, and Philippe Bourgois. "Introduction: Making Sense of Violence." In *Violence in War and Peace: An Anthology,* edited by Philippe Bourgois and Nancy Scheper-Hughes, 1–31. Malden, MA: Blackwell, 2004.

Schick, Irvin Cemil. *The Erotic Margin: Sexuality and Spatiality in Alteritist Discourse.* New York: Verso, 2012.

Schick, Irvin Cemil. "Representation of Gender and Sexuality in Ottoman and Turkish Erotic Literature." *Turkish Studies Association Journal* 28, nos. 1–2 (2007): 81–103.

Schilder, Paul. *The Image and Appearance of the Human Body: Studies in the Constructive Energies of the Psyche.* United States: Wiley, 1964.

Schuller, Kyla. *The Biopolitics of Feeling: Race, Sex, and Science in the Nineteenth Century.* Durham, NC: Duke University Press, 2018.

Scognamillo, Giovanni. "Beyoğlu Eğlenirken." *Istanbul* 8 (1994): 107–10.

Scognamillo, Giovanni. *Bir Levantenin Beyoğlu Anıları.* Istanbul: Metis, 1990.

Segal, Naomi. *Consensuality: Didier Anzieu, Gender, and the Sense of Touch*. Amsterdam: Rodopi, 2009.

Sehlikoğlu, Sertaç. "Exercising in Comfort: Islamicate Culture of Mahremiyet in Everyday Istanbul." *Journal of Middle East Women's Studies* 12, no. 2 (2016): 143–65.

Sehlikoğlu, Sertaç. *Working Out Desire: Women, Sport, and Self-Making in Istanbul*. Syracuse, NY: Syracuse University Press, 2020.

Sehlikoğlu, Sertaç, and Aslı Zengin. "Introduction: Why Revisit Intimacy." *Cambridge Journal of Anthropology* 32, no. 2 (2015): 20–25.

Şeker, Berfu, ed. *Başkaldıran Bedenler: Türkiye'de Transgender, Aktivizm ve Altkültürel Pratikler*. Istanbul: Metis, 2013.

Selek, Pınar. *Maskeler, Süvariler, Gacılar*. Istanbul: Aykırı Yayıncılık, 2001.

Selek, Pınar. *Sürüne Sürüne Erkek Olmak*. Istanbul: İletişim, 2008.

Sert, Deniz Ş., and Didem Danış. "Framing Syrians in Turkey: State Control and No Crisis Discourse." *International Migration* 59, no. 1 (2021): 197–214.

Sevengil, Refik Ahmet. *İstanbul Nasıl Eğleniyordu (1453'den 1927'ye Kadar)*. Edited by Sami Önal. Istanbul: Iletisim Yayinlari, 1993.

Shah, Nayan. *Stranger Intimacy: Contesting Race, Sexuality and the Law in the North American West*. Berkeley: University of California Press, 2011.

Shakhsari, Sima. "Killing Me Softly with Your Rights: Queer Death and the Politics of Rightful Killing." In *Queer Necropolitics*, edited by Jin Haritaworn, Adi Kuntsman, and Silvia Posocco, 93–108. New York: Routledge, 2014.

Shakhsari, Sima. *Politics of Rightful Killing: Civil Society, Gender, and Sexuality in Weblogistan*. Durham, NC: Duke University Press, 2020.

Shakhsari, Sima. "The Queer Time of Death: Temporality, Geopolitics, and Refugee Rights." *Sexualities* 17, no. 8 (2014): 998–1015.

Sharma, Aradhana, and Akhil Gupta, eds. *The Anthropology of the State*. Malden, MA: Blackwell, 2006.

Sharma, Aradhana, and Akhil Gupta. "Introduction: Rethinking Theories of the State in an Age of Globalization." In *The Anthropology of the State*, edited by Aradhana Sharma and Akhil Gupta, 1–42. Malden, MA: Blackwell, 2006.

Sharpe, Andrew. "From Functionality to Aesthetics: The Architecture of Transgender Jurisprudence." In *The Transgender Studies Reader*, edited by Susan Stryker and Stephen Whittle, 621–32. London: Routledge, 2006.

Shirinian, Tamar. "The Nation-Family: Intimate Encounters and Genealogical Perversion in Armenia." *American Ethnologist* 45, no. 1 (2018): 48–59.

Shryock, Andrew. "Other Conscious/Self Aware: First Thoughts on Cultural Intimacy and Mass Mediation." In *Off Stage/On Display: Intimacy, Ethnography in the Age of Public Culture*, edited by Andrew Shryock, 3–28. Stanford, CA: Stanford University Press, 2004.

Simpson, Audra. *Mohawk Interruptus: Political Life across the Borders of Settler States*. Durham, NC: Duke University Press, 2014.

Sirman, Nükhet. "Crossing Boundaries in the Study of Southern Europe." In *Tradition in Modernity: Southern Europe in Question; Proceedings of the ISA Regional Conference for Southern Europe, Istanbul, Turkey, June, 20-21, 1997*, edited by Çağlar Keyder, 45–54. Madrid: International Sociological Association, 1998.

Sirman, Nükhet. "Kinship, Politics and Love: Honor in Post-colonial Contexts—the Case of Turkey." In *Violence in the Name of Honor*, edited by Shahrzad Mojab and Nahla Abdo, 39–57. Istanbul: Bilgi Üniversitesi Yayınları, 2004.

Sirman, Nükhet. "The Making of Familial Citizenship in Turkey." In *Citizenship in a Global World: European Questions and Turkish Experiences*, edited by Fuat Keyman and Ahmet Icduygu, 147–72. London: Routledge, 2013.

Siyah Pembe Üçgen. *80'lerde Lubunya Olmak*. Izmir: Siyah Pembe Üçgen, 2012.

Siyah Pembe Üçgen. *90'larda Lubunya Olmak*. Izmir: Siyah Pembe Üçgen, 2013.

Smart, Alan, and Filippo M. Zerilli. "Extralegality." In *A Companion to Urban Anthropology*, edited by Donald M. Nonini, 221–38. Malden, MA: Wiley Blackwell, 2014.

Smith, Neil. *The New Urban Frontier: Gentrification and the Revanchist City*. London: Routledge, 2005.

Snorton, C. Riley. *Black on Both Sides: A Racial History of Trans Identity*. Minneapolis: University of Minnesota Press, 2017.

Snorton, C. Riley, and Jin Haritaworn. "Trans Necropolitics: A Transnational Reflection on Violence, Death and the Trans of Color Afterlife." In *The Transgender Studies Reader 2*, edited by Susan Stryker and Aren Z. Aizura, 66–76. New York: Routledge, 2013.

Sofer, Jehoeda. "The Dawn of a Gay Movement in Turkey." In *Sexuality and Eroticism among Males in Moslem Societies*, edited by Arno Schmitt and Jehoeda Sofer, 77–82. New York: Haworth, 1992.

Solomon, Robert. "Justice vs. Vengeance: On Law and the Satisfaction of Emotion." In *The Passions of Law*, edited by Susan Bandes, 123–48. New York: New York University Press, 1999.

Sönmez, Mustafa. "Turkey's Second Privatization Agency: TOKI." Reflections Turkey, May 29, 2012. http://www.reflectionsturkey.com/2012/05/turkeys-second-privatization-agency-toki/.

Soydan, Serdar. *Manşetlerden Gaipliğe: Bay-Bayan Kenan Çinili'nin Evrak-ı Metrukesi*. Istanbul: Sel Yayınları, 2021.

Spade, Dean. *Normal Life: Administrative Violence, Critical Trans Politics and the Limits of Law*. New York: South End, 2011.

Spillers, Hortense. "Mama's Baby, Papa's Maybe: An American Grammar Book." *Diacritics* 17, no. 2 (1987): 65–81.

Stallybrass, Peter, and Allon White. *The Politics and Poetics of Transgression*. Ithaca, NY: Cornell University Press, 1986.

Stanley, Eric A. *Atmospheres of Violence: Structuring Antagonism and the Trans/Queer Ungovernable*. Durham, NC: Duke University Press, 2021.

Stokes, Martin. *The Republic of Love: Cultural Intimacy in Turkish Popular Music.* Chicago: University of Chicago Press, 2010.

Stoler, Ann Laura. *Carnal Knowledge and Imperial Power: Race and the Intimate in Colonial Rule.* Berkeley: University of California Press, 2002.

Stoler, Ann Laura. "Intimidations of Empire: Predicaments of the Tactile and Unseen." In *Haunted by Empire: Geographies of Intimacy in North American History,* edited by Ann Laura Stoler, 1–22. Durham, NC: Duke University Press, 2006.

Stone, Sandy. "The Empire Strikes Back: A Posttranssexual Manifesto." In *The Transgender Studies Reader,* edited by Susan Stryker and Stephen Whittle, 221–35. New York: Routledge, 2006.

Stryker, Susan. "(De)subjugated Knowledges: An Introduction to Transgender Studies." In *The Transgender Studies Reader,* edited by Susan Stryker and Stephen Whittle, 1–17. New York: Routledge, 2006.

Stryker, Susan. *Transgender History: The Roots of Today's Revolution.* Berkeley, CA: Seal, 2017.

Stryker, Susan, and Aren Z. Aizura. "Introduction: Transgender Studies 2.0." In *The Transgender Studies Reader 2,* edited by Susan Stryker and Aren Z. Aizura, 1–12. New York: Routledge, 2013.

Sünbüloğlu, Nurseli Yeşim. "Nationalist Reactions and Masculinity following Hrant Dink's Assassination." In *Rethinking Transnational Men: Beyond, between and within Nations,* edited by Jeff Hearn, Marına Blagojevıc, and Katherine Harrison, 204–18. New York: Routledge, 2013.

Süzgeçyapı. "1 Ekim'de '1 + 0' Tipi Stüdyo Dairelerin Yapımına Yasak Başlıyor." August 17, 2017. https://suzgecyapi.com/1-ekimde-10-tipi-studyo -dairelerin-yapimina-yasak-basliyor/.

Sylvia Rivera Law Project. "SRLP on Hate Crime Laws." Accessed February 11, 2022. https://srlp.org/action/hate-crimes/.

Tahaoğlu, Çiçek. "Kadınlar Sokağa Çıkıyor." *Bianet,* February 8, 2013. http:// bianet.org/bianet/toplumsal-cinsiyet/144197-tek-mesru-yasam-aile-degil.

Tapınç, Hüseyin. "Masculinity, Femininity, and Turkish Male Homosexuality." In *Modern Homosexualities: Fragments of Lesbian and Gay Experiences,* edited by Ken Plummer, 39–49. London: Routledge, 1992.

Tar, Yıldız. "Bayram Sokak'ta Trans Kadınlar Bir Kez Daha Gözaltına Alındı, Polis Sokağı Kapattı!" *Kaos GL,* December 2, 2020. https://kaosgl.org/haber /bayram-sokak-ta-trans-kadinlar-bir-kez-daha-gozaltina-alindi-polis -sokagi-kapatti.

Tar, Yıldız. "Cinsiyet Geçişinde 'Kısırlaştırma' Karar Kalktı, Ameliyat Duruyor." *Kaos GL,* March 20, 2018. https://kaosgl.org/haber/cinsiyet-gecisinde -kisirlastirma-sarti-kalkti-ameliyat-duruyor.

Tar, Yıldız. "Toplumun Dışına İtilenlerin Bilgisi Nasıl Üretilir?" *Kaos GL,* August 11, 2019. https://kaosgl.org/gokkusagi-forumu-kose-yazisi/toplumun-disina -itilenlerin-bilgisi-nasil-uretilir.

Taussig, Michael T. *The Magic of the State.* New York: Routledge, 1997.

Taussig, Michael T. "Terror as Usual: Walter Benjamin's Theory of History as a State of Siege." *Social Text*, no. 23 (1989): 3–20.

Thiranagama, Sharika. *In My Mother's House: Civil War in Sri Lanka*. Philadelphia: University of Pennsylvania Press, 2011.

Toprak, Zafer. "İstanbul'da Fuhuş ve Zührevi Hastalıklar 1914–1933." *Tarih ve Toplum* no. 39 (March 1987): 31–40.

Transgender Europe. "TMM Murders." Transrespect vs. Transphobia, last updated September 2022. https://transrespect.org/en/map/trans-murder-monitoring/#.

Tsing, Anna Lowenhaupt. *Friction: An Ethnography of Global Connection*. Princeton, NJ: Princeton University Press, 2005.

Tudor, Alyosxa. "Decolonizing Trans/Gender Studies? Teaching Gender, Race, and Sexuality in Times of the Rise of the Global Right." *TSQ: Transgender Studies Quarterly* 8, no. 2 (2021): 238–56.

Tudor, Alyosxa. "Dimensions of Transnationalism." *Feminist Review* 117, no. 1 (2017): 20–40.

Tudor, Alyosxa. "Im/possibilities of Refusing and Choosing Gender." *Feminist Theory* 20, no. 4 (2019): 361–80.

Tuğal, Cihan. "'Resistance Everywhere': The Gezi Revolt in Global Perspective." *New Perspectives on Turkey* 49 (2013): 157–72.

Ubicini, J. H. A. *1855'te Türkiye*. Translated by Ayda Düz. Istanbul: Tercüman 1001 Temel Eser, 1977.

Ünsal, Özlem, and Tuna Kuyucu. "Challenging the Neoliberal Urban Regime: Regeneration and Resistance in Başıbüyük and Tarlabaşı." In *Orienting Istanbul: Cultural Capital of Europe?*, edited by Deniz Göktürk, Levent Soysal, and İpek Türeli, 51–70. London: Routledge, 2010.

Üstündağ, Nazan. *The Mother, the Politician, and the Guerrilla*. New York: Fordham University Press, 2023.

Üstündağ, Nazan. "Pornographic State and Erotic Resistance." *South Atlantic Quarterly* 118, no. 1 (2019): 95–110.

Uysal, Ülke Evrim. "An Urban Social Movement Challenging Urban Regeneration: The Case of Sulukule, Istanbul." *Cities* 29, no. 1 (2012): 12–22.

Valentine, David. *Imagining Transgender: An Ethnography of a Category*. Durham, NC: Duke University Press, 2007.

Wagner, Roy. "Analogic Kinship: A Daribi Example." *American Ethnologist* 4, no. 4 (1977): 623–42.

Wardlow, Holly. *Wayward Women: Sexuality and Agency in a New Guinea Society*. Berkeley: University of California Press, 2006.

Weheliye, Alexander G. *Habeas Viscus: Racializing Assemblages, Biopolitics, and Black Feminist Theories of the Human*. Durham, NC: Duke University Press, 2014.

Weston, Kath. "Families in Queer States: The Rule of Law and the Politics of Recognition." *Radical History Review* 2005, no. 93 (2005): 122–41.

Weston, Kath. *Families We Choose: Lesbians, Gays, Kinship*. New York: Columbia University Press, 1991.

Wilson, Ara. "The Infrastructure of Intimacy." *Signs: Journal of Women in Culture and Society* 41, no. 2 (2016): 247–80.

Wolf, Eric R. *Envisioning Power: Ideologies of Dominance and Crisis*. Berkeley: University of California Press, 1999.

Wyers, Mark David. *"Wicked" Istanbul: The Regulation of Prostitution in the Early Turkish Republic*. Istanbul: Libra, 2012.

Wynn, L. L. "'Like a Virgin': Hymenoplasty and Secret Marriage in Egypt." *Medical Anthropology* 35, no. 6 (2016): 547–59.

Wynter, Sylvia. "Unsettling the Coloniality of Being/Power/Truth/Freedom: Towards the Human, after Man, Its Overrepresentation—an Argument." *CR: The New Centennial Review* 3, no. 3 (2003): 257–337.

Yancy, George. *Black Bodies, White Gazes: The Continuing Significance of Race in America*. 2nd ed. Lanham, MD: Rowman and Littlefield, 2017.

Yardımcı, Sibel. "Trans.Candır." *Skopbülten*. August 13, 2019. http://bit.ly/2yUJOrK.

Yazıcı, Berna. "The Return to the Family: Welfare, State, and Politics of the Family in Turkey." *Anthropological Quarterly* 85, no. 1 (2012): 103–40.

Yeğenoğlu, Meyda. *Colonial Fantasies: Towards a Feminist Reading of Orientalism*. Cambridge: Cambridge University Press, 1998.

Yetkin, Aydın. "II. Meşrutiyet Döneminde Toplumsal Ahlak Bunalımı: Fuhuş Meselesi." *Tarihin Peşinde: Uluslararası Tarih ve Sosyal Araştırmalar Dergisi* 6 (2011): 21–54.

Yıldırım, Umur. "Haksız Tahrik İndirimi-TCK 29. Madde." *Kadim Hukuk ve Danışmanlık*, 2022. https://kadimhukuk.com.tr/makale/haksiz-tahrik-indirimi-tck-29-madde/.

Yıldırım, Umut, and Yael Navaro. "An Impromptu Uprising: Ethnographic Reflections on the Gezi Park Protests in Turkey." Fieldsights, *Society for Cultural Anthropology*, October 31, 2013. https://culanth.org/fieldsights/series/an-impromptu-uprising-ethnographic-reflections-on-the-gezi-park-protests-in-turkey.

Yıldız, Deniz. "Türkiye Tarihinde Eşcinselliğin Izinde Escinsel-Lik Hareketinin Tarihinden Satır Başları-1: 80'ler." *Kaos GL* 92 (2006): 48–51.

Yıldız, Emrah. "Cruising Politics: Sexuality, Solidarity and Modularity after Gezi." In *The Making of a Protest Movement in Turkey: #occupygezi*, edited by Umut Özkırımlı, 103–20. London: Palgrave Pivot, 2014.

Yılmaz, Kahraman Berkhan, and Kamil Fehmi Narter. "Transgender Surgery: A Review Article." *Journal of Urological Surgery* 8, no. 4 (2021): 227–33.

Yılmaz, Seçil. "Threats to Public Order and Health: Mobile Men as Syphilis Vectors in Late Ottoman Medical Discourse and Practice." *Journal of Middle East Women's Studies* 13, no. 2 (2017): 222–43.

Yörük, Erdem. "The Long Summer of Turkey: The Gezi Uprising and Its Historical Roots." *South Atlantic Quarterly* 113, no. 2 (2014): 419–26.

Yüksel, Şahika, Işin Baral Kulaksizoğlu, Nuray Türksoy, and Doğan Şahin. "Group Psychotherapy with Female-to-Male Transsexuals in Turkey." *Archives of Sexual Behavior* 29, no. 3 (2000): 279–90.

Yüzgün, Arslan. *Mavi Hüviyetli Kadınlar.* Istanbul: Hüryüz Yayıncılık, 1987.

Yüzgün, Arslan. *Türkiye'de Eşcinsellik.* Istanbul: Hüryüz Yayıncılık, 1986.

Yuval-Davis, Nira, and Floya Anthias, eds. *Woman-Nation-State.* Basingstoke, UK: Macmillan, 1989.

Zainuddin, Ani Amelia, and Zaleha Abdullah Mahdy. "The Islamic Perspectives of Gender-Related Issues in the Management of Patients with Disorders of Sex Development." *Archives of Sexual Behavior* 46, no. 2 (2017): 353–60.

Zarinebaf, Fariba. *Crime and Punishment in Istanbul: 1700–1800.* Berkeley: University of California Press, 2010.

Ze'evi, Dror. *Producing Desire: Changing Sexual Discourse in the Ottoman Middle East, 1500–1900.* Berkeley: University of California Press, 2006.

Zengin, Aslı. "The Afterlife of Gender: Sovereignty, Intimacy, and Muslim Funerals of Transgender People in Turkey." *Cultural Anthropology* 34, no. 1 (2019): 78–102.

Zengin, Aslı. "Caring for the Dead: Corpse Washers, Touch, and Mourning in Contemporary Turkey." *Meridians: Feminism, Race, Transnationalism* 21, no. 2 (2022): 349–69.

Zengin, Aslı. "The Cemetery for the *Kimsesiz*: Unclaimed and Anonymous Death in Turkey." *Comparative Studies of South Asia, Africa and the Middle East* 42, no. 1 (2022): 163–81.

Zengin, Aslı. "Devletin Cinsel Kıyıları: İstanbul'da Fuhşun Mekanları." In *Cins Cins Mekan*, edited by Ayten Alkan, 264–83. Istanbul: Varlık, 2009.

Zengin, Aslı. "Feminist Argo ve Küfür Atölyesi Üzerine." Bianet, April 17, 2010. https://m.bianet.org/bianet/toplumsal-cinsiyet/121389-feminist-argo-ve -kufur-atolyesi-uzerine.

Zengin, Aslı. *İktidarın Mahremiyeti: İstanbul'da Hayat Kadınları, Seks İşçiliği ve Şiddet.* Istanbul: Metis Yayınevi, 2011.

Zengin, Aslı. "Mortal Life of Trans/Feminism: Notes on 'Gender Killings' in Turkey." *TSQ: Transgender Studies Quarterly* 3, nos. 1–2 (2016): 266–71.

Zengin, Aslı. "Trans-Beyoğlu: Kentsel Dönüşüm, Şehir Hakkı ve Trans Kadınlar." In *Yeni Istanbul Çalışmaları: Sınırlar, Mücadeleler, Açılımlar*, edited by Ayfer Bartu Candan and Cenk Özbay, 360–75. Istanbul: Metis Yayınevi, 2014.

Zengin, Aslı. "Violent Intimacies: Tactile State Power, Sex/Gender Transgression, and the Politics of Touch in Contemporary Turkey." *Journal of Middle East Women's Studies* 12, no. 2 (2016): 225–45.

Zengin, Aslı. "What Is Queer about Gezi?" Fieldsights, *Society for Cultural Anthropology*, October 31, 2013. https://culanth.org/fieldsights/what-is-queer-about-gezi.

Zengin, Aslı, and Sertaç Sehlikoglu. "Everyday Intimacies of the Middle East." *Journal of Middle East Women's Studies* 12, no. 2 (2016): 139–42.

Zevkliler, Aydın. "Medeni Kanun ve Cinsiyet." *Türkiye Barolar Birliği Dergisi*, no. 2 (September 1988): 258–86.

Zirh, Besim Can. "Following the Dead beyond the 'Nation': A Map for Transnational Alevi Funerary Routes from Europe to Turkey." *Ethnic and Racial Studies* 35, no. 10 (2012): 1758–74.

Žižek, Slavoj. *The Sublime Object of Ideology.* London: Verso, 1989.

Index

care (continued)
relations of violence, 6; trans care, 171;
queer and trans care labor, 191; work of, 190;
World Professional Association for Transgender Health's Standards of Care, 114. *See
also* Hil Malatino

Çelik, Belgin, 51

Cerrah, Celalettin, 82. *See also* police

Cerrahpaşa Medical School, 101

Charing Cross Hospital, 104, 108

CHP (Cumhuriyet Halk Partisi; Republican
People's Party), 95

Cihangir Güzelleştirme Derneği, 9, 58. *See also*
urban

cisgenderism and cisnormativity, 173

cisheteronormative: family, 138, 172, 189;
frameworks of intimacy and embodiment,
24; legal regulations, 2; order, 96; and patriarchal logic, 83; public life, 70; powers of the
state, 2; sexuality, 23; society, 22; standards of
Turkish society, 122; structures of everyday
life, 23; violence, 2–4, 207

cisheteronormativity: as a form of communal and spatial intimacy, 11; as a political
ideology, 3; forces of, 11; social and cultural
network of, 127; violent framework of, 2

cisheteroreproductive, 16–18, 21–24, 136

cisness, 3, 209

civil law, 26, 96, 111, 160, 182

coalitions, 15, 4, 7

cohabitation, 8, 11, 35

common morals, 21. *See* public decency

Constitutional Court, 138

corporeal: corporeal life of sex/gender, 132;
corporeality of everyday life, 14–15, 132,
145, 148, 194; dependency, 194; forms of
touch and corporeal proximities, 15; space,
148; work, 194; workings of everyday state
power, 14

counterspectacle, 80

crimes of tradition, 20, 158, 159

criminal type, 87, 95

criminalization, 12, 16, 70, 93, 97

cultural genital, 129

çürük raporu (rotten report), 19

Dalan, Bedrettin, 53

Das, Veena, 7

death: aftermath of, 195; bureaucracies of,
14; differential values over life and death,
4; intimacy with violence and death, 9;
premature death, 3, 196; punishment of,
22; recognizable life and, 194; rites, 83,
184; rituals, 232n14, 233n18; sex/gender-
transgressive, 171; social, 201; spatial
ordering of death and afterlives, 185.
See also femicides

debt: accumulated, 69; affective, 173; debt to
the state, 93; of life, 173

deceased, 1- 2, 171, 176–84, 187–89, 195

Dink, Hrant, 164, 218n11

disability, 5, 139, 211, 229

Diyanet İşleri Başkanlığı (the Directorate of
Religious Affairs), 181

Dolapdere, 41–43, 50, 54, 64

domestic: abuse, 134; household, 189; intimacy,
17; lives, 213n48; space, 8, 17, 215n69; work,
215n69; violence, 8, 12, 173

domesticity, 7, 8, 14, 21

Dündar, Uğur, 101, 225, 253

embodiment: cartography of, 133; cisheteronormative frameworks of intimacy and,
24; experiences of trans embodiment, 141;
of female family members, 21; force of,
132; imaginative forms of, 141; intimate
spatialities of, 10; Islamic notions of, 176,
181; materializing our sense of, 149; sex/
gender, 4, 176, 182; temporalities of trans
embodiment, 129; trans women's senses of
their embodiment, 142

Ersoy, Bülent, 15, 102–10, 226, 246, 253

Europe, 13, 33, 104, 147, 165, 230–31, 245–64

European Parliament Subcommittee on
Human Rights, 27

Evren, Kenan, 51

extralegal: force, 72; means of surveillance and
securitization, 35; police force, 93; police
station, 80; police violence, 11; practices of
police surveillance and securitization, 70;
punitive practice, 94; site for the state, 70;

strategies, 70, 96–97; tactics of securitization, 6; technics, 71; violence, 67, 72–73, 81, 92, 97

family: Boysan's family, 196; cisheteronormative, 138; cisheteroreproductive, 16, 23; creative substance family and kin work, 6; domain of family and kinship, 2; dominant Turkish family structure, 16; extended, 16, 213n45, 214n69; family line, 173, 175; "Great Family Gathering," xv; honor, 159; LGBTI+ Family Groups, 196, 234n39; maintaining nuclear family structures, 190; Ministry of Women and Family, 85, 162; nuclear, 18, 24, 212n45, 215n69; protecting family life, 11; queer family and kin making, 188; queer/trans kin and, 171–72, 175, 189, 191, 195–96; "real" family, 1, 171; reputation, 22

Feldman, Allen, 79

forensic: Adli Tıp Kurumu (the Council of Forensic Medicine), 185, 188; authorities, 136; forensics, 135; medicine, 15; report, 109; scientists, 16, 141; state forensic office, 149

Foucault, Michel, 112, 131, 239

Freeman, Elizabeth, 122, 194, 227n46, 234nnn34–36

friendship, 8, 36, 170–75, 194, 206

Galata, 42–47, 57, 64, 219, 237

gasilhane, 177–78

gecekondu (squatter housing), 63, 221n62

gender transition, 99, 119, 124

General Directory of Security, 72

gentrification, 12, 42, 44, 55, 56, 63–64, 133, 220

Gezi: park, 40, 42, 75; protests, 12, 36, 42, 69, 73, 86; uprising, 41, 197–98

ghetto, 59, 61

gift, 17, 57, 139, 170, 173, 193

Gill-Peterson, Jules, 3, 209n5, 210nn12–13, 227n48

governmental techniques, 14, 81

governorship of Istanbul, 27, 199, 200

group psychotherapy, 114–20

güllüm, 9, 25, 80, 143, 144, 206

gynecology, gynecologist, 113, 123, 138

haptic, 131–33, 145

Hartman, Saidiya, 8

hate crimes, 6, 13–14, 25, 35, 61, 84, 150, 152, 161–68, 230

Hayat, Pembre, 29, 216–17, 226–28, 240, 250

Haydarpaşa Numune Hospital, 102

hegemonic masculinity, 18–19, 22, 139, 214

hermaphrodites, 111

heteroreproductive future, 173

heteroreproductivity, 138

heyet raporu (comprehensive health report), 113–14, 227n37

Hijazi, Sarah, xiii

HÖC (Haklar ve Özgürlükler Cephesi; Front for Rights and Freedom), 163

home: community's, 55; family, 180, 189; homeless, 11, 66, 133, 185, 202, 219; home to various marginalized populations, 44; home village, 140; Istanbul as a home, 190; kinship repertoire of home and motherhood, 171; making and unmaking of a home for trans women, 54; political home for trans people, 28; queer/trans notion of home, 189; "real" home, 65; *See also* Trans*Evi; Ülker Street

homosexuality, 13, 19, 74–75, 84–85, 103, 119

honor: crimes, 158, 159, 214; culture of honor, 157, 158; family honor, 159; killings, 20, 157, 158. *See* Ayşe Parla

hormone: intake, 99, 115, 124–25, 227n48; prescription, 125; replacement therapy, 33; test, 114; treatment, 33, 99, 114–15, 123–25, 227–28

human rights: abuse of, 83; activists/NGO workers, 201–2; deserving subjects of, 168; framework of, 152; hate crimes and, 25, 84, 161; international discourses on, 28; political claims on 86; transnational discourses of, 161; violation of, 138. *See also* transnational

humor, 9, 80, 143

Malatino, Hil, 171, 193

Manukyan, Matild, 56

marginalization: everyday social marginalization, 2; financially marginalized, 207; marginalized bodies, 146; marginalized groups, 3–4, 10, 44, 53, 64, 133, 149, 166–67, 190; marginalized by the state, 197; marginalized sexuality/sexual identity, 27, 39; 10, 35, 64, 70; spatial, 53, 64

masculinist, 15, 22, 150, 214n66

Massad, Joseph, 224

materialization of sex/gender, 149

medical certification, 99

Mezarlıklar ve Cenaze Hizmetleri Şube Müdürlüğü (the Department of Cemeteries and Funeral Services), 2, 180

migrant, 16, 18, 47, 108, 137

Mikdashi, Maya, 19, 21, 137

military: AKP's weakening of the military, 224n33; military government, 50, 103–4, 214, 238, 240, 241; military-nation formula, 214n56; military regime, 51; operations, 199; rule, 50, 109; service, 18–19, 103, 139, 214n57

Mındıkoğlu, Ali Nihat, 101–4

Ministry of State for Women and Family Issues, 23, 162

Misdemeanor Law, 90

modernization, 17, 26, 96, 133, 220

motherhood: trans motherhood, 24, 171, 192–93, 196

mourning, 13, 184–85, 233

Najmabadi, Afsaneh, 20, 103, 218n1

Navaro, Yael, 88, 212n40, 224nn41–42, 234n5

neoliberalism, 26, 240

neoliberal governmentality, 3

normalization, 112, 141, 227

North America, 19, 21, 33, 243

Özal, Turgut, 53, 221, 255

Pangaltı, 43, 61, 64

Parla, Ayşe, 20. See culture of honor

Partiya Karkerên Kurdistan, 9

patriarchal, 15, 17, 20, 83, 136, 143, 144

pembe tezkere (pink discharge paper), 19

Penal Code, 74, 158, 166

penetration, 14, 20, 131, 136, 137, 231

Pera, 42, 45, 47, 219, 237

Plemons, Eric, 128

police: custody, 15, 72, 74, 200; raids, 48, 51, 58, 59; surveillance, 4, 70, 82, 171; terror, 80; torture, 74; violence, 4–6, 11–14, 24–27, 54–60, 70–74, 81–97, 198, 206

Polis Vazife ve Selahiyet Kanunu (the Law on Police Duties and Power), 74

polygamous, 18

population exchange, 47, 219

Pride March, 15, 24, 43, 103, 151, 198–200

Pride Week, 201, 203, 211

prostitution: Turkish code on, 46–48, 80, 92–96, 219; history of prostitution in Istanbul, 45–48, 219n24; public health, 219n26. *See also* brothels

protest, 12, 27, 75, 157, 163, 218n11, 222n65

psychiatric observation, 99, 131

Psychiatry Department of the Istanbul School of Medicine, 114

public decency, 12, 21, 90. *See* common morals

racial discrimination, 3, 26

racialization, 146, 158, 210

Radikal Demokrat Yeşil Parti (the Turkish Green Radical Democratic Party), 75

rainbow flag, 13–15, 28, 197

Ramadan, 103, 199, 200

rape, 12, 130–31

refugees, 3, 26, 46, 66, 133, 137, 185, 216

resistance, 6, 7, 9, 10, 11, 41, 54, 72, 73, 80, 97, 191, 198, 218, 233

right to the city, 190. *See* Henri Lefebvre

ritual washing, 177, 184

Roma (people), 44, 53, 64

rumor, 79, 80

Rums (Greeks), 45, 46

Salamon, Gayle, 128, 139

Sansaryan Inn, 52